Islamic Liberation Theology

Are we today witness to a renewed confrontation between "Islam and the West" or are the signs of an imperial domination of globalized capital versus new modes of resistance to it already evident?

This book is a radical piece of counter-intuitive rethinking on the clash of civilizations theory and global politics.

In this richly detailed criticism of contemporary politics, Hamid Dabashi argues that after 9/11 we have not seen a new phase in a long-running confrontation between Islam and the West, but that such categories have in fact collapsed and exhausted themselves. The West is no longer a unified actor and Islam is ideologically depleted in its confrontation with colonialism. Rather, we are seeing the emergence of the United States as a lone superpower, and a confrontation between a form of imperial globalized capital and the rising need for a new Islamic theodicy.

Expanding on his vast body of scholarship in reading political Islamism during the last quarter of a century, Dabashi here lays the groundwork for a progressive rethinking of the place of Islamic cosmopolitanism in navigating modes of legitimate resistance to globalized imperialism.

The combination of political salience and theoretical force makes *Islamic Liberation Theology* a cornerstone of a whole new generation of thinking about political Islamism and a compelling read for anyone interested in contemporary Islam, current affairs and US foreign policy. Dabashi drives his well-supported and thoroughly documented points steadily forward in an earnest and highly readable style.

Hamid Dabashi is Hagop Kevorkian Professor of Iranian Studies and Comparative Literature at Columbia University in New York, USA. He is the author of several books including: *Authority in Islam: From the Rise of Muhammad to the Establishment of the Umayyads* (1989/1992); *Iran: A People Interrupted* (2007); *Theology of Discontent: The Ideological Foundations of the Islamic Revolution in Iran* (1993/2005); *Dreams of a Nation: On Palestinian Cinema* (edited with an Introduction, 2006); and *Close up: Iranian Cinema, Past, Present, Future* (2001).

Islamic Liberation Theology
Resisting the empire

Hamid Dabashi

LONDON AND NEW YORK

First published 2008
by Routledge
2 Park Square, Milton Park, Abingdon, Oxon, OX14 4RN

Simultaneously published in the USA and Canada
by Routledge
270 Madison Ave, New York NY 10016

Routledge is an imprint of the Taylor & Francis Group, an informa business

Transferred to Digital Printing 2010

© 2008 Hamid Dabashi

Typeset in Times New Roman by
Taylor & Francis Ltd

All rights reserved. No part of this book may be reprinted
or reproduced or utilised in any form or by any electronic,
mechanical, or other means, now known or hereafter invented,
including photocopying and recording, or in any information
storage or retrieval system, without permission in writing
from the publishers.

British Library Cataloguing in Publication Data
A catalogue record for this book is available from the British Library

Library of Congress Cataloging in Publication Data
Dabashi, Hamid, 1951-
Islamic liberation theology : resisting the empire / Hamid Dabashi.
p. cm.
Includes bibliographical references and index.
[etc.]
1. Religious awakening–Islam. 2. Islam and world politics. 3. Islamic
countries–Politics and government. 4. Islamic renewal–Islamic countries.
5. Globalization–Religious aspects–Islam. 6. Islam–21st century. I. Title.
BP163.D3 2008
297.2'72–dc22
2007042488

ISBN13: 978-0-415-77154-2 (hbk)
ISBN13: 978-0-415-77155-9 (pbk)
ISBN13: 978-0-203-92838-7 (ebk)

For my children
Kaveh, Pardis and Chelgis
My signs of hope for their America

'The revolutionary situation which prevails today, especially in the Third World, is an expression of this growing radicalization. To support the social revolution means to abolish the present status quo and to attempt to replace it with a qualitatively different one; ... it means to attempt to put an end to the domination of some countries by others ...'
Gustavo Gutiérrez, Roman Catholic theologian and Peruvian Dominican Priest

'Power never takes a back step – only in the face of more power.'
Malcolm X, American Muslim Revolutionary

Contents

	Introduction	1
1	Resisting the empire	25
2	The end of Islamic ideology	59
3	Blindness and insight	99
4	Islam and globalization	143
5	The Shi'i passion play	171
6	Liberation theodicy	196
7	Malcolm X as a Muslim revolutionary	234
	Conclusion: Prolegomena to a future liberation theodicy	254
	Notes	267
	Index	295

Introduction

> There's a friend of mine who lives in New Orleans, is black, and I wrote down exactly, word for word, what she said, because I think it bears repeating. She said, "After 9/11, I was American. Now [after Hurricane Katrina in August 2005] I'm back to being black." And I think among the feathers in George Bush's resume is that I think he has lost a whole generation of black people who might have felt that way after 9/11, and now are like, "You know what? I can't believe I started to buy into that bullshit."'
>
> Bill Maher, *Real Time with Bill Maher*
> (HBO, 15 September 2005)

A global rise in terrorist attacks and the terrorizing US military campaigns during the first decade of the twenty-first century have once again raised the specter of Islam as the principal nemesis of "the Western civilization." The daily headlines across the world report of deadly terrorist attacks and even more devastating carnage caused by the US-led military invasions and colonial occupations of sovereign nation-states. In the midst of this violent spiral of fear and fury, "Islam and the West" are once again posited as the principal coded categories of this global confrontation between two irreconcilable adversaries.

While sharing the fear of millions of others from this frightening predicament around the world, I differ in my reading of its causes and consequences. My primary point of departure in this book is that contrary to the assumptions of a clash of civilization between "Islam and the West," we have in fact concluded the period of civilizational conflict. The period of civilizational thinking had a very short but crucial role in the course of the colonial encounter of Muslims with European modernity. That mode of civilizational thinking has now effectively exhausted its uses and abuses in facilitating the operation of the globalized capital. In this book I wish to propose, in direct opposition to Samuel Huntington's thesis of "the clash of civilizations," that in fact we have already entered a post-civilizational period in global conflict – one in which we need a fresh understanding of the nature of globalizing power and the emerging revolutionary manners of resisting it.

Predicated on this argument, my principal purpose in this book is to investigate the emerging modes of Islamic revolutionary mobilization in the aftermath of the collapse of "Islam and the West" as the most potent dialectical binary that was generated and sustained in the course of the Muslim colonial encounter with European modernity. My argument in this book is predicated on the counter-intuitive suggestion that with the collapse of the Twin Towers of the World Trade Center in New York on September 11 2001 also imploded the twin towers of "Islam and the West" as the most potent binary oppositions crafted and constructed in the course of colonial modernity. At once postcolonial and postmodern, the emerging global reconfiguration of power has no use for that outdated binary, but plenty of room for the globalized empire and manners of revolutionary resistance to it. This is not a war between "Islam and the West" any more. We are at the threshold of a whole new reconfiguration of power and politics, empire-building, and moral and normative resistances to it.

In this book, I wish to investigate the specifically "Islamic" manners of opposing this imperial upsurge in the aftermath of the "Islam and the West" binary opposition. The signs of this resistance are all over the globe – but difficult to read because the dying ashes of the old dialectic and the emerging fire of the new confrontation are still mixed and too early to decipher. Released from the binary nexus of "Islam and the West," Islam as the faith of a globalized community, and the imperial proclivities innate to the operation of capital continue to be evident and operative. What precisely is the nature and function of that globalized imperial power and what an Islamic (or any other) mode of resistance to it would be is still too early to tell. A few facts are evident and articulating them in some detail will clear the air for further urgent reflections. If, as I suggest, the supposition of an eternal conflict between "Islam and the West" is no longer a legitimate category, and if, as I will demonstrate, "the West" has lost all its categorical legitimacy to be an antagonistic interlocutor for Islam – what then? Today Muslims, as millions of other people around the globe who do not confess their faith but share their fate, face an incessantly globalized empire whose amorphous shape has not yet allowed for an articulated response. The purpose of this book is to articulate and historicize the contours of that response.

What I propose in this book is radically different from the current wisdom of looking into political Islamism in order to understand the nature and function of spectacular acts of violence that militant Muslims commit. The prevalent understanding of contemporary militant Islamism, whether generated by the US propaganda machinery or otherwise, continues to operate on an outdated epistemic assumption that we have inherited from the colonial phase of Muslim encounter with European modernity. In this book, I will propose the end of that form of Islamic ideology, and begin to articulate the terms of its emerging geopolitics, and, more importantly, the liberation theology that is contingent on the changing parameters of a whole new social history for a globalized Islam.

In short, and quite simply, this book is about the end of Islamic ideology as the organizing principal of political resistance to colonial modernity. My thesis, simply put, is this: militant Islamism emerged from the early nineteenth century in response to European colonialism, gradually mutating a medieval faith into a solitary site of ideological resistance to colonial modernity. These almost 200 years of incessant transformation of Islam into Islamic ideology came to an end with the success and subsequent failure of the Islamic revolution in Iran. My purpose in this book is to bring an analytical attention to the following critical developments in the aftermath of the Islamic revolution in Iran: (1) the creation of the Wahabi-inspired Taliban in Afghanistan both to expel the Soviets and to prevent the spread of the Shi'i-inspired Islamic revolution of Iran into Central Asia; (2) the US support for Saddam Hussein to invade Iran, engage in an eight-year mutually destructive war, and thus to prevent the spread of the Islamic revolution westward into the rest of the Islamic and the Arab world; (3) the cataclysmic collapse of the Soviet Union and the Eastern European extensions of its empire; (4) the rise of an amorphous blowback in the aftermath of the Soviet departure form Afghanistan, when the US-sponsored, Saudi-financed, and Pakistani-administered creation of the Taliban came back to bite its own creators; (5) Saddam Hussein's taking advantage of the same amorphous blowback condition and invading Kuwait; (6) the collapse of the Soviet Union and the subsequent US invasion of Iraq; and ultimately (7) the rise of the USA as the single surviving superpower, the historic rift between the USA and Europe over the Second Gulf War, the rapid unification of Europe into a major global power quite independent and in fact in competition with the USA – and thus the end of "the West" as a legitimate category with any enduring credence left to its economic or political consequences. With "the West" thus dismantled as an organizing principle of Euro–North American modernity, I propose that "Islam" too has lost its principal interlocutor over the last 200 years. The result, a simultaneous dismantling of both "Islam" and "the West" as the mirror image of each other and the evident emergence of a new mode of imperial domination and revolutionary resistance to it. My task in this book is to begin to understand what the parameters of these new revolutionary agenda might be – while arguing emphatically that we have passed through a major turning point in the global manners of both imperial power and revolutionary resistances to it.

On Tuesday September 11 2001, four passenger airliners were hijacked and crashed into the World Trade Center in New York, the Pentagon in Washington DC, and into a field in Pennsylvania. Upwards of 3,000 people were reported killed in these attacks. All the assailants were killed along with their victims. No militant organization immediately assumed responsibility for the operation. The US officials, however, immediately blamed a shadowy organization called al-Qaeda, its leader Osama bin Laden, his supporters among the Taliban leadership in Afghanistan. The Taliban (literally "Students"), formerly known as "Mujahedin" (or "Freedom Fighters"), were mostly recruited from Afghan refugees in Pakistan, financed by the Saudis, and trained by Pakistani intelligence, all with the direct involvement of the USA, to fight against the Soviets in Afghanistan while preventing the eastward spread of the Islamic revolution in Iran – to prevent its westward spread, the selfsame alliance plus Europeans had massively aided Saddam Hussein in his invasion of Iran. In less than a month, on October 7 2001, the USA led a massive military campaign against Afghanistan in order to topple the Taliban regime and hunt for Osama Bin Laden, who was reported to have masterminded the September 11 attacks. The Taliban regime – brought to power by a US–Saudi–Pakistani alliance – soon collapsed, Osama bin Laden remained at large, and tens of thousands of Afghans were killed, a conservative estimate of almost ten Afghans for every single American killed on 9/11. "Operation Enduring Freedom," as the US invasion of Afghanistan was termed in the emerging Orwellian Newspeak of Washington, commenced the US "War on Terror" – itself the master Newspeak term packaging the commencement of a renewed and improved US imperial design for the globe.

In the very same month of October 2001, the US Senate approved the US Patriot Act, giving unprecedented and sweeping power to the federal government to abrogate US and international law in its "War on Terror." In the following year, in his January 2002 State of the Union address, President George Bush included Iraq, Iran, and North Korea in what he now termed an "Axis of Evil." There was, this speech suggested, a grand design linking two Muslim and one non-Muslim countries to conspire with runaway terrorists and maim and murder Americans at random and with no provocation. President Bush, now standing obviously for the polar opposite of an "Axis of Evil," or a singular source of "Good," would not stand for that and would initiate what he called "pre-emptive strikes" against those he suspected of wishing to harm America and Americans. By November of that year, President Bush signed into law a bill creating a Department of Homeland Security, believed to be the widest and most far-reaching reorganization of the federal government in half a century, thus promoting a vast atmosphere of fear and intimidation, in which unprecedented measures were taken to "protect" Americans against future terrorist attacks, while systematically dismantling their time-honored civil and human rights. Domestic abuse of power and military adventurism abroad were now squarely predicated on a deliberate campaign of fear that the US neocons, the ideological arm of the Bush administration, generated and sustained in order to justify their megalomaniac design for a planetary control of the earth (along with a militarized space program that extended the domain of that control into extra-terrestrial realms). As "The Project for a New American Century," the ideological blueprint of the US neocons outlined it, this delusional urge to command and control went far beyond the planet earth or the universe around it and broke through the narrative of spatial control and sought to claim exclusive ownership of the very concept of *time*, the very idea of *history*. The planet earth was not enough, its course of rotation into the solar system and in perpetuity was the object of desire.

The Afghan campaign still very much under way and causing havoc on the civilian population, the US President commenced yet another war on March 20 2003 against the sovereign nation-state of Iraq – this time around on the pretense that the Iraqi President Saddam Hussein was involved with the events of 9/11 and that he was in fact amassing weapons of mass destruction (WMD). Every single member of the Bush administration, beginning with the President himself, down to his Secretary of State Colin Powel and Secretary of Defense Donald Rumsfeld, and of course aided, abetted, and endorsed by the CNN, *The New York Times*, Fox News and the rest of the US propaganda machinery, systematically lied and deceived Americans, and with them the rest of the world, into believing that Saddam Hussein was indeed developing weapons of mass destruction. He was not. Months and years into the carnage that the USA unleashed in Iraq, the Bush administration finally admitted publicly that they found no evidence of WMD in Iraq, or any indication that Saddam Hussein and Osama bin Laden had any link whatsoever, or that Iraq in any shape or form was involved in the events of 9/11. These were all lies – lies deliberately manufactured by the Bush administration and through the willing agency of CNN and *The New York Times* sold to the gullible or sport utility vehicle (SUV)-infested segments of the American public. No one was fired, no one resigned, no one was impeached. *The New York Times*, CNN, Fox News and the industry of disinformation and deceit they collectively represent proceeded to do business as usual. "Operation Iraqi Freedom," as the lexicon of the US Newspeak continued to by conjugated in ever more obscene terms, expanded the US imperial design and military operations both in the region and around the globe. The principal allies of the USA in the region were Pakistan, Saudi Arabia, and Israel – a military dictatorship, a medieval potentate, and an appartheit Jewish state.

A few weeks after the commencement of the US invasion of Iraq, on May 1 2003, President Bush declared victory and in a public ceremony on the US aircraft carrier Abraham Lincoln announced that his mission was accomplished. Months and years after that declaration, Iraq continued to be the scene of the most savage warfare and insurrectionary resistance, and soon after that civil war – all generated, sustained, instigated, and prolonged by the US-led invasion and occupation of Iraq. A Johns Hopkins University study estimated that some 655,000 Iraqis had been killed since the commencement of the illegal and immoral US-led invasion. Thousands of US soldiers were also killed in scenes reminiscent of the carnage the US military had caused in Vietnam. The ratio of casualties now went well beyond ten Iraqis per one American. In two years under American military occupation, more innocent Iraqi civilians were raped, maimed, and murdered than in the entire preceding quarter of a century under President Saddam Hussein – and President Saddam Hussein was by far the most brutal mass murderer in the entire Arab and Muslim world. Meanwhile in Afghanistan, the carnage continued apace and regular reports of war and insurrection were coming out apace. A puppet regime installed by the USA and headed by an incompetent bureaucrat beholden to the US support, Hamid Karzai, stood idly by as the nefarious Taliban regrouped and came back to haunt the central administration, all under the watchful eyes of General Pervez Musharraf, the head of the military junta running Pakistan – the military subcontractor of the USA and Saudi Arabia.

The combined effects of operations "Enduring Freedom" and "Iraqi Freedom" caused the uncounted murder of innocent Afghans and Iraqis, massive destruction of civil and industrial infrastructures of two nation-states and the astronomical profits that it generated for major US and EU corporations, a rapid and furious rise in terrorism and lawlessness around the world (first and foremost by the USA and its European allies themselves), the systematic corrosion of civil liberties and human rights at the home front, all aided and abetted by a US propaganda industry (headed by CNN, *The New York Times*, and Fox News) that with leaps and bounds surpassed the legendary operation of master propagandists like Joseph Goebbels in the heyday of the Nazi Germany. Never in human history was a nation so besieged and flooded as Americans were at the threshold of the twenty-first century with not just deceit and disinformation but with charlatan propagandists effectively determining the terms of even dissent against the status quo. This was no ordinary empire with its politicians, journalists, and even literary figures partaking in its imperial vernacular. This was a brute and naked lust for power with a systematic mendacity written over all its pathological attempts at publicly justifying it. Ahmad Chalabi, an Iraqi businessman seeking his fortune in a post-Saddam era, conspired with an even more opportunity journalist named Judith Miller of the *New York Times* in manufacturing a belief that Saddam Hussein had weapons of mass destruction. Ahmad Chalabi and Judith Miller in turn persuaded an even more than willing partner, *The New York Times*, and they collectively deceived an entire nation, and with them the world, into believing that was indeed the case – and they thus treacherously manufactured a consent to an illegal and immoral war costing hundreds of thousands of innocent and poor lives – Afghan, Iraqi, and American. No one was held accountable. No one committed hara-kiri. There are cultures that have a noble sense of guilt, shame, and honor – and there are those that don't.

In May 2004, almost a year after President Bush had declared victory in Iraq, the revelations about the US torture chambers in Abu Ghraib prison became the first public evidence as to what sort of "victory" the President of the USA had exactly in mind. Similar torture chambers by the US military were reported in the Bagram Air Base in Afghanistan as well as in the US military base in Guantanamo Bay, and in a network of subterranean dungeons on various European sites. Snapshots and video recording of US military personnel suddenly circulated in the world media, showing them – in some of the obscenest gestures humanity has ever witnessed – sexually abusing and physically torturing their Iraqi prisoners. The holy book of Muslims, the Qur'an, was reported to have been regularly flushed down toilets by way of adding psychological to physical torture, while hooded inmates were shot in the image of the crucifix.

Such atrocities were not limited to Iraqi inmates and extended well into the civilian population, repeatedly subject to mass murder by American soldiers – sent there to liberate them from tyranny and despotism. In one particularly gruesome case of rape and murder of Iraqi civilians by the liberating US army, a criminal investigation unearthed the killing of a family of four Iraqis in their home in Mahmudiya, south of Baghdad, in March 2006. The US soldiers were all charged with planning, carrying out, and covering up the rape and murder. All four soldiers – Specialist James Barker, Pte Jesse Spielman, Sgt Paul Cortez, and Pte Bryan Howard – belonged to the 2nd Brigade of the elite 101st Airborne Division. They were all charged with conspiring to rape the girl in the attack after shooting dead her parents and her five-year-old sister. In subsequent investigations, the Iraqi medics reported that when they arrived on the scene they found in the living room of the family's home the body of the 14-year-old victim – she had been raped and then burnt from the waist up. The rest of her family were also found murdered in the same house, her mother shot in the chest, her father in the head, and her little sister with a bullet in her face. Instead of outrage, the leading US legal and human rights activists and intellectuals – Alan Dershowitz and Michael Ignatieff chief among them – openly, publicly, eloquently, and with detailed analysis supported, endorsed, rationalized, theorized and sought to legalize the systematic torturing of people – "the lesser evil," they called it. Their civilization, they argued, was in danger, and they had to defend it against barbarians.

Meanwhile, the carnage caused by the US invasion of Iraq and the legitimate resistance of a people against the colonial occupation of their homeland raged through a ravaged nation with fury and fire. Every single day since the commencement of the US occupation of Iraq in 20 March 2003, an entire nation was subjected to what the then US Secretary of State Donald Rumsfeld dubbed a "campaign of shock and awe," to which Iraqis responded with widespread insurrectionary uprising, causing more death and destruction, in turn leading to massive massacres in cities like Falluja, Najaf, or Talafar. No one was counting the Iraqi casualties – men, women, and children maimed, murdered, and savagely raped as if no one was watching. CNN was counting – one by one – the number of US military personnel killed while illegally and immorally occupying Iraq. After a while one could not tell whether Paul Wolfowitz worked for CNN and Wolf Blitzer for the Pentagon, or whether it was the other way around. What remained constant was the common denominator of a wolf – a wolfish, predatory, savagery that defined the age, and with it the contours of a bestial empire that carried the American flag on its mast.

In November 2004, Americans elected George W. Bush once again as their president – democratically, openly, and with a clear and decisive victory for their incumbent president. This was all *after* the carnage in Afghanistan and in Iraq, after the reports of torture and rape of Afghans and Iraqis. There were millions of Americans who opposed George W. Bush and voted against him. But President Bush came to power not through a military coup or any other kind of hostile take over. He was elected officially, openly, democratically, and legally, on the basis of the venerable democratic institutions of the USA – voted into office by Americans themselves, the descendents of Thomas Jefferson, Abraham Lincoln, and John F. Kennedy. No Martian or Afghan or Iraqi or a citizen of the Axis of Evil was allowed to vote in the US Presidential election 2004. Only Americans – born and bred in the USA could vote for or against President Bush. The majority of them voted for President Bush. "I have gained political capital," the US President George W. Bush clearly and correctly declared soon after his victory, "and I intend to spend it" – and when the leader of the world capitalist economy says he intends to "spend" rather than "invest" his capital, people at the four corners of the globalized world have plenty of reasons to fear their very livelihood.

In August 2005, the deadly Hurricane Katrina hit southern USA, swept through the gulf coast states, and buried the city of New Orleans under water. Millions of poor, mostly black, people, systematically ignored and hidden from global sight by the combined will (not conspiracy) of CNN, *The New York Times*, Fox News and the rest of the propaganda machinery they best represent, were left to their own non-existent devices. Hurricane Katrina blew away, among poor people's very meager livelihood, the systematic cover-up of poverty and destitution in the heart of a flailing empire. The criminal negligence of the US officials in attending to the poorest, weakest, and most vulnerable among its own population was marked and underlined by the initial response of the federal government – sending in the army and the National Guard and their sharpshooters to shoot and kill defenseless citizens if they dared to go to a shopping center to find food or shelter. Maintaining law and order, they called it, defending their civilization against barbarians. The residents of New Orleans had an uncanny similarity to the citizens of Afghanistan and Iraq – poor and disenfranchised people divided into two opposing camps, both at the mercy of a merciless empire, mostly run by white people.

If hurricane Katrina in late August 2005 was the undoing of the trauma of 9/11, then how else can we read the vicious cycle of violence between the US empire and its shapeless nemesis that the events of 9/11 has inaugurated? As Chalmers Johnson has demonstrated in *The Sorrows of Empire: Militarism, Secrecy, and the End of the Republic* (2004), the aggressive militarization of the USA during the Cold War and soon after the collapse of the Soviet Union has ultimately come to a fully fledged imperial proportion in the aftermath of the events of 9/11 and the wars in Afghanistan and Iraq. As Kevin Phillips has thoroughly documented the development in his *American Theocracy: The Peril and Politics of Radical Religion, Oil, and Borrowed Money in the 21st Century* (2006), this imperial arrogance has assumed an incessantly Christian eschatological disposition. The principal ally of this Christian empire is an avowedly Jewish state called Israel. The Christian empire and the Jewish state have collectively decided to call their mutual nemesis "Islamism." There is an Islamic republic in the immediate vicinity of this Jewish state that is both its mirror image in religious fanaticism and the *locus classicus* of this apparition they call Islamism. Both the factual evidence of the Islamic republic and the delusional apparition the US and Israel call Islamism have a deep rooted origin in a legitimate, but long since outdated, mode of ideological resistance to European colonialism and American imperialism. As the last remaining apartheid outpost of European colonialism in the region, Israel is particular in pointing out the threat that Islamism poses to its illegitimate existence. Since the very inception of the state of Israel in 1948, the existence of a Jewish state has legitimized and exacerbated the increasing rise of militant Islamism in its neighborhood. Since the events of 9/11, the USA has aggressively joined the Jewish state in branding its enemy as Islamist in origin and disposition. In the immediate aftermath of 9/11, it is imperative to come out from under the shadow of the US- and Israeli-manufactured knowledge about Islamism and systematically historicize the events prior and after 9/11 and thus make a definitive distinction between the legitimate mode of Islamic revolutionary movements over the last 200 years, a perfectly rightful component of other anti-colonial movements such as nationalism and socialism, and the Islamism that is now identified with Osama bin Laden and al-Qaeda – an Islamism that is the immediate byproduct of the US imperial designs for the region at large. My principal objective in this book is to make this distinction between Islamic revolutionary movements throughout the nineteenth and twentieth century and the mode of Islamism identified with the events of 9/11, then acknowledge with appreciation and in fact give a homage to the extraordinary significance of anti-colonial Islamic revolutionary movements, while categorically differentiating them with the sort of militant adventurism and barbaric and senseless acts of violence identified with the figure of Osama bin Laden, and then, most importantly, give an outline of the emerging Islamic liberation theology that is as legitimate as its predecessor in the nineteenth and twentieth centuries, with the added advantage of not falling into the trap of an absolutist, puritanical, and totalistic disposition. That this Christian empire and that Jewish state (built on the broken back of Palestinians) ought to be opposed and ended (and free and democratic states restored in their stead) I am absolutely convinced. That classical anti-colonial Islamic movements have done their services, made their mistakes, achieved their limited ends, and are now categorically outdated, I have no doubt. That the mode of militant Islamism that Osama bin Laden and his shadowy organization al-Qaeda represent are signs of senseless and barbaric violence with no legitimate political project I know for a fact. And ultimately that a new mode of Islamic liberation theology will have to emerge to join other modes of revolutionary resistance to this predatory empire and that colonial settlement is the principal point of my concern in this book. This in short is my project in a nutshell.

I write this book in the shadow of an incompetent empire – successful in threatening, endangering, and outright torturing and murdering people around the globe, and yet incapable of providing the most basic necessities of a decent livelihood for its own citizens, an empire not only categorically devoid of anything resembling an ideological legitimacy, but in fact chiefly responsible for generating nothing but a global hatred for anything remotely connected to things called "American." Innocent and courageous Americans, valiantly and on a regular and sustained level risking their very livelihood and in an overwhelming atmosphere of fear and intimidation resisting the imperial atrocities of their government, are as much at the mercy of this global hatred of Americans as those chiefly responsible for having and holding their president in power. The main US media – defined by CNN, *The New York Times*, and Fox News and without a single exception owned and operated by corporate interests – are chiefly responsible for sustaining the imperial hubris of this country. The "war on terrorism" is itself a supreme act of terrorism, a collectively manufactured pseudonym for the US imperial designs for the globe. Detailed, articulate, and magnificent books like Chalmers Johnson's *The Sorrows of Empire: Militarism, Secrecy, and the End of the Republic* (2004) have already started giving frightening accounts of how this empire seeks to operate. Michael Mann's *Incoherent Empire* (2003) provides a wide spectrum of examples on the rampant incompetence of the US empire. V. G. Kiernan's *America: The New Imperialism* (2005) traces the rise of the US empire from white settlement to an attempted world hegemony. Meanwhile Howard Friel and Richard Falk's *The Record of the Paper: How The New York Times Misreports US Foreign Policy* (2004) has fully exposed the effective collaboration perpetrated by a news organization completely at the service of the US imperial projects. In his *Chain of Command: The Road from 9/11 to Abu Ghraib* (2004), Seymour Hersh has mapped out the route leading to the horrors of the US torture chambers in Iraq. The singular contribution of British historians to this collective acts of courageous revolt against manufacturing consent for the US empire is Niall Ferguson's *Colossus: The Price of America's Empire* (2004), unabashedly calling for the USA to take over where the British had left off plundering the world for the benefit of a few – all on the economic model best theorized by Milton Friedman (1912–2006), the Natan Sharansky of capitalism whose recent death reminded the world of the terror of predatory imperialism he best and singularly represented.

From a perspective located somewhere in between the overextended wings of that imperial hubris and the spectacular acts of senseless and vile violence identified with the fact and figure of Osama bin Laden, I wish to give an outline of the potential modes and manners of resisting that empire in a variety of mutually complementary ways, including an Islamic liberation theology that first and foremost denounces the militant adventurism of Saudi millionaires gone rebel. To make that succinct argument, I will first need to clear the air of our contemporary condition. My principal proposal in this book is entirely counterintuitive and launched against the prevalent propaganda manufactured in the USA and regurgitated globally that the current war that the USA has launched in Afghanistan and Iraq – and by extension its client state Israel carries against Palestinians and Lebanese – is the result of a height in radical Islamism and as such the manifestation of a civilizational conflict between "Islam and the West." I disagree with and oppose that reading. I believe otherwise. My argument in this book is that the events of 9/11 and all that has happened after that in Afghanistan and Iraq are in fact the signs of *the end* of radical Islamism and not its height or commencement. Acts of violence have always been definitive to all political projects. From Karl Marx to Max Weber to George Sorel to Che Guevara to Frantz Fanon to Malcolm X – all major theorists and practitioners of revolutionary movements have long since recognized the centrality of violence in all political acts – for the establishment or in search of the destruction of a state apparatus. At least since the Boston Tea Party (December 16 1773) even Americans have known that. The state for Weber was defined as the monopoly of violence. Any act of violence targeted against the state simply reciprocates that wisdom. Like all other revolutionary movements throughout the nineteenth and twentieth centuries – from nationalism to socialism – Islamism has had its share of perfectly legitimate (that is Weber's term) use of violence to project and advance its political agenda. But what we have witnessed during the events of 9/11 are acts of violence *without* any such legitimacy or project and as such entirely outside the fold of any programmatic use of violence for specific political projects. These are acts of violence for purely spectacular and instantaneous purposes, immediate visual gratification, without the slightest attention to any systematic political project. Osama bin Laden and his associates, the way they have been manufactured and projected on the world media, lack any serious or legitimate political project, or grassroots support, or identifiable constituency, for that matter. Their militant adventurism is launched with the abiding purpose of achieving spectacular attention. It is wrong to try to read Osama bin Laden's Aljazeera video appearances in search of any political project, the way for example that Bruce Lawrence has sought to do in his *Messages to the World: The Statements of Osama bin Laden* (2005). These performances are sheer visual stunts and must be viewed as "video installations" that use Aljazeera as their site of citation. Any attempt to link the spectacular acts of violence attributed to Osama bin Laden to Islamic revolutionary movements of the last 200 years is either a manufactured mode of knowledge for political purposes or else a sheer act of historical illiteracy. With the phenomenon of Osama bin Laden, the shadowy assumption of al-Qaeda, and the events of 9/11 we are all at the threshold of a whole new epistemic shift in political Islam and the yet to be identified interlocutor it will have to identify as its nemesis.

Predicated on this argument, my main thesis in this book is that "the West," as a civilizational category, has long since ended, and as a result the epistemic collapse of the sustained and lopsided dialogue between "Islam and the West" is no longer a viable proposition – first and foremost because "the West," as the iconic referent of the European Enlightenment modernity, has self-destructed in what is now code-named postmodernity, and second because the emerging geopolitics of the capital has generated a new and unprecedented geopolitics of power in which the notion and location of a fictive fabrication called "the West" has no longer any function to perform. Islamic revolutionary movements as legitimate political projects, throughout the nineteenth and twentieth centuries, were very much articulated in combatant conversation with colonial consequences of "the West" as their principal interlocutor. With "the West" now dead, Islam lacks an interlocutor and the leading Muslim intellectuals, activists, and leaders do not know to whom they are talking. Spectacular acts of violence, *à la* those attributed to Osama bin Laden, are intermediary and confused acts of visual anarchism in dire search for a post-Western interlocution, location, site, and citation. It is still too early to tell what will emerge from our current condition. But what is certain is that "Islam and the West" as one of the most potent delusional binaries of the last 200 years has in fact exhausted all its epistemic possibilities and thus ended its regenerative epistemic energy. One must not confuse the propaganda machinery of CNN and Co, manufacturing a *belligerent Islamism* and positing it against a *besieged West* for the real condition of our global whereabouts. Without understanding that emerging geopolitics, without dismantling the outdated and depleted epistemic binary historically manufactured between "Islam and the West," and without discrediting the senseless and barbaric acts of iconic violence now globally attributed to and code-named "al-Qaeda," it is impossible to see the rising contours of the US empire, the potential manners of resisting it, and the specific mode of an Islamic liberation theology that can be party (but never definitive) to that global resistance.

My argument here is that "Islam and the West," as a set of binary opposition that in its cross-essentializing force gave both its components an aura of ontological authenticity, can no longer hold because "the West" has now economically and normatively imploded and so has the "Islam" that it had engendered in a combative and prolonged dialogue, and thus such contemporary Muslim intellectuals as Abdolkarim Soroush or Tariq Ramadan have no clue to whom they are talking – or against what contestant interlocutors are articulating the particulars of their own faith. At their analytical best, I will demonstrate in this book, Muslim intellectuals are talking to an interlocutor long since dead. The entire oeuvre of Abdolkarim Soroush, as perhaps the best such example, is an eloquent, persuasive, at times exceptionally erudite conversation with a dead interlocutor, a ghost, an apparition, a goblin, a reality that no longer exists. From this premise, I will then proceed to argue that "the Islamic ideology" that has been crafted over the last 200 years has *ipso facto* ended. As a mode of liberation theology, the Islamic ideology was created over the last 200 years in combative correspondence to and critical conversation with a global colonial monstrosity code-named "the West." With "the West" and the "Islam" that it dialectically generated as a site of ideological resistance to colonialism, now ended, we have neither that "West" to demand and exact binary opposition to itself, nor indeed do we have that "Islam" that was created as one particularly potent version of that binary opposition.

As a set of commanding binary opposition, "Islam and the West" was created under specific historical conditions, with a presumed center for the operation of the capital and a designated periphery to its colonial extensions. That center and thus that periphery have now disappeared, for the rapidly and blatantly globalized capital no longer allows for such illusions. As a mode of resistance to "the West" that had dialectically generated and sustained it, Islamic ideology (a political ideology predicated on Islam, pretty much on the same model that Liberation Theology was predicated on Christianity) was equally essentialized, categorical, and monolithic. It allowed for no diversity; it in fact eliminated and destroyed its own diverse intellectual legacies under the pressure and in correspondence with the European Enlightenment Modernity, to which it was beholden, whether it resisted it in its radical versions or else embraced it in its more liberal mutations – or even in blatantly "secular" ideologies articulated and institutionalized in Muslim societies. Muslims, believing or otherwise, were beholden to the power and mystique of "the West," more a figment of their own captured imagination than a reality *sui generis*, and no matter what they did, opposed or embraced it, they ended up corroborating and further ossifying the ontological veracity of that thing they kept calling "the West."

"The West" has now withered in correspondences with the amorphous capital, which no longer has any center. A principal target of 9/11 attacks, the World Trade Center in New York, was a misnomer. The world trade has no center. The center is already in the periphery, the periphery in the center. The colonial has always been embedded in the capital, the capital in the colonial. The Third World is now squarely in the First, and the First in the Third. The amorphous capital, centerless, has now generated a globalized empire that operates without hegemony, no longer under the grand narrative of "the West," and with brute force and an ideological machinery that is more a globalized source of hatred and infamy against the US than a convincing source of engineering consent with its warmongering.

With a limited range of operation among the Washington DC neocons, the self-projection of the USA as an empire is aided and abetted by the Christian evangelical zeal in active and ideological collaboration with a US–Israel axis of neo-Zionism. Israel is now (just like the United Arab Emirates) a shopping mall extension of the US-inspired global capitalism encircling US military and strategic interests. Shopping malls are no hegemony. The US empire does not only lack the ability to generate communal consensus, acceptance, and compliance among those it seeks to dominate, it in fact (as judged by poll after poll conducted by US and European pollsters alike) generates hatred and revulsion against it. So what the world faces is a globalized empire, seeking to protect the operation of an amorphous capital, which the rise of a mere hurricane can send jitters through its spines, with a mercenary army, a phantasmagoric military machinery extended into the outer space, and an al-Qaeda blueprint for its own guerrilla operations. Al-Qaeda, I propose here, is not just a minor guerrilla operation hiding somewhere in a proverbial Afghan cave with possible extended sympathizers around the region. Al-Qaeda is also the code-name of a re-imagined US imperial military operation – projecting itself as an omnipotent, omniscient, and omnipresent military force that can strike at anytime anywhere in the world. That projected power is delusional – both in the assumption that there actually exists such a global terrorist organization and in the wish to rebuild the Pentagon on the model of its blueprint.

On the basis of this argument, I propose that resisting a US-inspired globalized empire requires a radical rethinking of the very notion of ideology – whether in its secular or theological variations. Neither anti-colonial nationalism, nor Soviet-style socialism, nor indeed nativist grassroots ideologies such as Islamic ideology of the last 200 years in Muslim countries or its Christian version the liberation theology of the last quarter of the century in Latin America is capable of mobilizing and sustaining enough revolutionary synergy to resist this predatory empire. In terms domestic to any liberation theology (Christian or Islamic), no such resistance can any longer be in terms of a singular ideology embedded in a medieval theology, or an ideologically updated version of it to resist a center-based "Western" empire, or else through spectacular acts of senseless and iconic violence. Precisely because the nature and disposition of this flailing empire, like the operation of the capital it wants to control, is amorphous, then resistance to it must be in terms of ideological guerrilla operations – light weight, regional, cross-cultural, non-essentialist, and if it be in theological terms then in terms that account for the existence of *alterity* in the world, that is to say of veritable theological incongruities – in principal a radically counter-authentic notion of ideologies, revolutions, and revolutionaries. The ethics of this theology is other-based, not self-based, Levinasian rather than Husserlian – its ethics, in Levinas' words, is "otherwise than being or beyond essence." It does not authenticate itself. It embraces its own otherwise. The worst revolutionaries of this generation would be the authentic revolutionaries – the best ones are the syncretic, those who think, in Gianni Vattimo's words, with an *"il pensiero debole"* – with weak thoughts, and always breaking through the colonially manufactured boundaries of dividing thoughts and sentiments to rule people and their destinies.

The worst aspect of "Islamic ideology," ultimately its undoing, was its consistent conversation with "Western modernity," its arch nemesis and thus its principal interlocutor. "Islamic ideology" replicated the systematic essentialism of "Western modernity" with which it was historically interlocked in a sustained and prolonged combat. "Islam and the West" thus generated, sustained, and corroborated each other in each other's metaphysical absolutism, dead certainties, cul-de-sacs. On the "Western side" of the binary, this meant a civilizational gloss over national, subnational, cross-national, and non-national universes of affinities. On the Islamic side of the self-same equation, this meant an almost inevitable adaptation of Islamic ideology of Islamic law, of the *Shari'ah* – at the very heavy price of all non-legalistic dimension of a vastly multifaceted, polyfocal, and heterodimensional world religion – the consequences of which for a free and democratic society have been simply catastrophic, for the "Islam" of "Islam and the West" mutates the potentially free and autonomous subjects of a republic into legal subjects of a medieval jurisprudence that no matter how liberally it is interpreted it remains deadly contrary to the creation of free and autonomous citizens of a republic. As much as it had a fundamental share in anti-colonial movements throughout the Muslim world, Islamic ideology, as a mode of liberation theology, ultimately failed to emancipate itself from the limited imaginary of Islamic law and replicated its nomocentric rigidity.

The only way that an (Islamic) liberation theology can be part of a global resistance to any empire (American or otherwise) is to be party to a global conversation, safeguarding its theological monotheism by placing it within a heterogeneous, multifaceted, and syncretic theodicy that instead of trying to rationalize and thus dismiss the existence of alterity, incongruity, and choice in the world, it in fact embraces its ideological rivals and theological alternatives. As specific examples of this liberation theology, towards the end of my book, I will examine the case of the American Muslim revolutionary Malcolm X, who consistently broke into newer insurrectionary grounds, while looking at the political possibilities dormant in such revolutionary movements as those of Hezbollah in Lebanon, Hamas in Palestine, and the Shi'is in Iraq. These revolutionary movements are now at a crossroads. Either following the dead end of an Islamic republic (of Iran), a Jewish state (of Israel), or a Christian empire (of the USA), or else becoming integral to a national and regional liberation movement that predicated on a theodicy accounting for and accepting their alternatives, entering into a syncretic dialogue with them, and regionally engendering a mode of revolutionary mobilization that only in its theodicy is it (or can it be) theological. In specifically Islamic theological terms, this liberation theology will relearn the wisdom of the old Mu'tazilite position – when facing a choice between "free will" (*ikhtiyar*) and "predestination" (*jabr*) – known as *"al-manzila bayn al-manzilatayn"* ("the position between the two positions"). In the midst of that emancipatory dialectic dwells the enduring significance of a liberation theology that can face and embrace its own alterities.

I write this book from the heart of an empire that writes its own imperialism in quotation marks. I wish to attend to the matter of resisting the predatory urges of this imperialism outside any quotation marks. What I am after in this book is deciphering the contours of a new liberating theology in Islam that is conducive to the predicament of Muslims around the globe and in terms specific to their moral and imaginative modes of resistance to an empire that, chasing after an amorphous capital, is as ruthless in its militant disposition as it is rootless in any enduring idea, principle, or judgment. What President Bush, Prime Minister Blair, and His Holiness Pope Benedict collectively concur to call "Islamism" is the byproduct of the US–UK war of terrorism and has absolutely nothing (nothing) to do with the fate of millions of Muslims around the globe, all at the mercy of a globalized mode of warmongering that has terrorized the lives of Muslims and non-Muslims alike. In a new planetary vision of our world, where the distorting parallels of "Islam and the West" no longer holds, Islam is freed both from any such binary opposition and from the luxurious adventurism of the Bin Laden variety – and thus Muslims are free once again to rethink their faith in terms domestic to their aspirations and global to their worldliness. This time around, this theology should no longer define itself via a combative conversation with an altered ipseity like "the West," but must instead learn the enduring wisdom of embracing its ideological alterities. What Muslims and all other human beings face are the predatory monstrosities of an imperial proclivity embedded in the logic of the capital itself. That capital is not American, but American militarism seeks to claim it. Resisting the tyrannies of both that capital and the militarism that seeks to steer it the American way are not just Muslims, but poor and disenfranchised people all over the world. Rich Muslims of the Saudi family type are not the subject of this resistance, for they are the agents of crushing it. Poor and disenfranchised Americans, of the sort whose dead bodies were floating in the streets of New Orleans, are not the agents of US imperialism. They are as much its victims as their counterparts in Afghanistan or Iraq. Alongside Muslims are thus ordinary people of all sorts of religions, cultures, ideologies, and emotive universes – universes that can no longer be reduced to religious and secular bipolarities. From amidst this cacophony of moral imaginaries (in plural), Muslims will have to learn the logic of their own inauthenticity, syncretism, pluralisms, and alterities. The more amorphous the nature of the globalized capital, and the more vile and violent the imperial design that seeks to sustain and benefit from it, the more solid and enduring must be the nature of the syncretic liberation theologies that need to join other liberation moments to resist them both.

The outline of my argument in this book, working towards an articulation of an Islamic liberation theology, will proceed as follows: throughout the nineteenth and the twentieth centuries, Muslims were dragged out of their medieval slumber and their collective faith was gradually mutated from a multifaceted religion into a singular site of ideological resistance to European colonialism. Like much of the rest of the world, Muslims received the European modernity through the birth channel of colonialism, and the paradox embedded in colonial modernity – at once purporting to engender and yet aborting agency – was the paradox at the heart of Muslim predicament in modernity. Constitutional to the project of capitalist modernity was a colonial shadow in which liberation theologies such as Christian liberation theology in Latin America or Islamic political movements in the Muslim world emerged. Muslims thus became politically instrumental in robbing themselves of their own intellectual heritage as they aggressively transformed their religion into a singular site of combatant conversation with and revolutionary uprising against colonial modernity. These are the principal issues that I will raise and address in my first chapter, "Resisting the empire." My point of departure in this chapter, however, is not a distant past, but the immediate present and the unfolding future. So I will first give an outline of the current emergence of the USA as a globalized empire, then I will give an outline of the outdated bipolarity between "Islam and the West" as a belated mode of producing legitimate resistances to this empire, and then by way of a background I will provide a history of how within the epistemic limitations of that binary, Muslim ideologues had articulated an Islamic mode of resistance to European colonialism. I will conclude this chapter by arguing that the amorphous nature of the US empire, chasing after the protection of an equally nebulous capital, requires a mode of resistance neither evident in the spectacular acts of iconic violence represented in the events of 9/11, identified with a shadowy organization called al-Qaeda, and personified in a militant adventurer named Osama bin Laden, nor indeed possible to emerge from the outdated binary opposition manufactured at the height of European colonial modernity and posited as quintessential and ahistorical opposition between "Islam and the West."

In the second chapter, "The End of Islamic Ideology," I will demonstrate in some analytical detail how after 200 years of sustained developments throughout the Muslim world, militant Islamism came to a sudden but inevitable end at the conclusion of one of its most spectacular revolutionary successes. I will argue and demonstrate that the 1979 success of the Islamic revolution in Iran was the end of militant Islamism – both the height of its ideological success and the final evidence of its institutional failure. Here, I will extend my argument far beyond the specifics of the Islamic revolution in Iran and give an account of the quintessential paradox at the heart of Islam as a religion of protest – that it morally succeeds precisely at the moment of its political failure and that it morally fails at the moment of its political success, and that it is precisely this paradox that will need to be overcome via a necessary and strategic move away from the radically ideologized Islam and worked creatively towards an Islamic theodicy – namely a mode of liberation theology that does not simply account for the existence of its moral and normative shadows but in fact embraces them.

The exhaustion of an epistemic mode of knowledge and ideology production, a theme that I borrow from the long and illustrious tradition of the sociology of knowledge, does not mean a sudden end of continued (though futile) conversation with "the West." To demonstrate this point, in the third chapter, "Blindness and Insight," I will concentrate on the writings of one of the most prolific Muslim public intellectuals alive, Abdolkarim Soroush, in pointed and analytical comparison with the globalized adventurism of neo-Wahhabi militants like Osama bin Laden, Ayman al-Zawahiri, and Abu Musab al-Zarqawi. Here, I will give a detailed outline of why and how at the most serious epistemic level Islamism of the sort that is still conversant with the European colonial modernity has hit rock bottom, a cul-de-sac, and come to a cataclysmic end – and how is it that prominent intellectuals like Abdolkarim Soroush manage at once to write with an astonishing intellectual proficiency and yet have absolutely nothing to say about the global predicament of Muslims today, ultimately ending up in an inevitable mystical quagmire. My argument in this chapter is that the intellectual vacuity of Abdolkarim Soroush and militant adventurism of Osama bin Laden and co. are in fact the two sides of the same coin – conversing with a dead interlocutor. Here, I will examine Abdolkarim Soroush as the very last Muslim ideologue – the Muslim ideologue who ends the Islamic conversation with colonial modernity, and Osama bin Laden as the very last pseudo-Saladin, fighting against imaginary crusaders (Bush and Blair are no Crusaders. They carry no cross sign – just dollar and pound signs. They are after oil, not the Holy Grail). In this respect, Abdolkarim Soroush has a rather bizarre similarity with Osama bin Laden, for he too carries, though on an intellectual plane, a futile, pointless, outdated and entirely irrelevant conversation with a "West" that simply no longer exists. In the same vein, there is also another uncanny similarity between Soroush's ideas and the neo-Wahhabi sentiments at the root of such al-Qaeda propagandists as Ayman al-Zawahiri – both the late neo-Wahhabism of al-Zawahiri and the post-Islamic revolutionary Shi'ism of Soroush represent entirely outdated modes of encounter with the emerging amorphous empire. The USA is not "the West." Not even Western Europe that initially gave rise to the notion of "the West" is "the West" anymore – for the unification of Europe (EU) in juxtaposition against the economic might of the USA has already signaled the collapse of "the West" as the civilizational umbrella of Western European–North American capitalism and points to an entirely different geopolitics of capital and its habitual cultural camouflaging of its brute intentions. "Western modernity," as a result, with which "Islam" carried a 200-year old combatant conversation, has now yielded to a postmodern imperialism, with no regard for national boundaries or civilizational divides – a condition of capital in which Bush, Blair, and Benedict have emerged as the most eloquent scholars of what Islam "is" and what Muslims ought to do. Samuel Huntington's thesis of the "clash of civilization" was neither a diagnosis nor a prognosis – it was an autopsy, though entirely unbeknown to the author himself. He was too busy thinking he was providing US imperialism with a vernacular ideology (he did not) to notice it. Samuel Huntington and Bernard Lewis, the would be ideologues of US imperialism, are wasting the US taxpayers money with their frequent flier programs to the US Pentagon – for instead of providing the US imperial proclivities with convincing ideologies and attempted justification they are in fact doing exactly the opposite: increasing the global hatred of the USA. Someone in the US Treasury ought to put a recall on these ideologues and ask for the US taxpayers' money back.

My principal argument in this chapter is that if from Jamal al-Din al-Afghani early in the nineteenth century, through such principal ideologues of Muslim Brotherhood as Sayyid Qutb, Muslim reformists like Allamah Iqbal, and all the way down to such ideologues of the Islamic revolution in Iran as Ali Shari'ati in later twentieth-century militant Islamism cultivated a healthy combination of radical theory and revolutionary praxis, at the threshold of the twenty-first century, people like Osama bin Laden (Saudi Arabia), Ayman al-Zawahiri (Egypt) and Abu Musab al-Zarqawi (Jordan) are associated with no such revolutionary project and only with a useless, senseless, and vile mode of spectacular acts of iconic violence with no theoretical articulation, intellectual backbone, or social project – while theorists like Abdolkarim Soroush (recently joined by a publicity-manufactured reformist named Tariq Ramadan) carry on a misplaced and outdated conversation with a "Western modernity" that no longer exists and is simply a figment of their own arrested imagination. In this chapter I will pay close attention to Osama bin Laden as a particularly poignant pathology. As a revolutionary project, militant Islamism is today completely eclipsed by the figure and fantasy of Osama bin Laden – the rambling practitioner of spectacular terror. There is neither a sustained revolutionary project nor a proposed political agenda to the spectacular acts of violence attributed to Osama bin Laden. As such he represents an inarticulate and iconic degeneration of Islamic revolutionary movements of the last two centuries into random acts of spectacular violence – whether he is actually behind them or not is an almost moot and entirely academic question, and as such perfectly fit to be theorized by Tony Blair or else pontificated by the Holy Father Pope Benedict. In this respect, Osama bin Laden has his functional equivalent in the USA in Bernard Lewis and Samuel Huntington (and an avalanche of neocon artists they have occasioned) who too have posited the global configuration of power in empty and equally iconic civilizational terms – executed with an even more barbaric "campaign of shock and awe" by their Secretary of defense Donald Rumsfeld. The principal point of this chapter is to demonstrate the intellectual exhaustion of "Islam and the

West" to produce any revolutionary project capable of resisting the US aspirations for a globalized empire.

In the next two chapters, I will document in detail two complementary sets of evidence, one historical and the other doctrinal, that will demonstrate the specific conditions in which the decline and demise of militant Islamism is both socially visible and doctrinally inevitable – thus setting the stage for a new liberation theology that will correspond and converse more specifically with the globalized condition of Muslims living in the shadow of a postmodern empire. In the fourth chapter, "Islam and Globalization," I will analyze the political fragmentation of the social basis of militant Islamism under the conditions called *globalization* – and then on that premise investigate the emerging modes of revolutionary resistances to any manner of globalizing empire. As a revolutionary template of such actual and potential movements, in the fifth chapter, "Ta'ziyeh as theater of protest," I will give an account of the historically most militant Islamic sect, Shi'ism, but this time through a reading of its Passion Play (Ta'ziyeh) – the symbolically most explosive repertoire of its insurrectionary disposition, its theater of protest. As the single most performative evidence of Islam as a religion of protest, a religion that can never lose its revolutionary disposition without *ipso facto* contradicting – and thus getting ready to redeem – itself, Ta'ziyeh is a theater of redemption and protest inundated with rich revolutionary potentials. I wish to explore these potentials and through an examination of its particular mode of (non-Aristotelian) mimesis investigate its renewed significance in an emerging liberation theology. My proposal in this chapter is that the asyncretic mimesis operative in Ta'ziyeh (that there is no one-to-one correspondence in its iconic acts of representation) corresponds to a manner of liberation theology in which a mode of permanent but inconclusive revolution can face the amorphous empire by remaining always on the offensive but never in power.

My concluding argument begins to trace the moral and material foundations of the rise of a new mode of liberation movement that if it were to be articulated in religious domains then it must be designated as a *theodicy* rather than a *theology* – the difference between the two being of grave political consequences. In the sixth chapter, "Liberation theodicy," I give an account of how a new strategy of resistance is needed as Islam recedes into the fabric of the societies it defines at large. While Osama bin Laden's presumed adventurism and Saddam Hussein's evident thuggery have dismantled Islamism to its last measures, Islam is yet again emerging – though this time around as the localized site of political resistance to the globalizing empire. In my final argument, I give an account of a liberation theodicy that corresponds to the geographical transmutation of Islam beyond its imaginary boundaries. The transnational globalizing geography that has now fully bloomed is no longer bound to an East–West or North–South axis – nor indeed is the doctrinal bifurcation of the world into *dar al-Islam* ("Domain of Peace") and *dar al-Harb* ("Domain of War") is any longer possible. The creative, though dangerous, liaison colonially postulated between "Islam and the West" having exhausted its historical usefulness, both the US empire and the emerging pockets of resistance to it will have to cross over presumed cultural divides and their corresponding countries. In this chapter I will navigate through such anti-imperial movements as the Hamas and Islamic Jihad in Palestine, Hezbollah in Lebanon, the Shi'i community in Iraq, and read them along with Muslim communities in Europe and see in what particular ways they can overcome the dangers of their corruption into perpetrators of senseless violence, on the model of suicidal violence and indiscriminate and mass murder of innocent people, and instead articulate a revolutionary project of national and regional liberation movements committed to resisting the predatory US empire and the dismantling of the discredited and failed Zionist state in favor of a one-state solution for all inhabitants of Palestine – Jews, Christians, Muslims, and atheists alike – which can become the exemplary model of a similar state for the entire region, so that instead of the Islamic republic of Iran being replicated in the region, the democratic republics of Iraq, Lebanon, and particularly Palestine – free, democratic, equitable, with constitutional rights for *all* its citizens – will be exported to all the backward and retarded Arab and Muslim states.

With the massive presence of Muslim migrant laborers throughout the globe, Islam is now irreversibly globalized; its very sacred language is no longer spoken just in Arabic, Persian, Turkish, or Urdu but in fact in the varieties of English spoken from Brooklyn, USA, to Bradford, UK, and now above all full of neologisms on al-Jazeera. The globalized empire has arisen from the very same material forces that have occasioned the globalization of Muslim migrant laborers and thus the emerging Islam itself. The beneficiaries of the globalized capital are no longer (if they ever were) some fictitious white Europeans or Americans; nor indeed are those disenfranchised by it all Muslims, Orientals, or colored. The Arab Sheikhs in Kuwait and the ruling clerics in Iran are as much the beneficiaries of the globalized capital as more than 35 million US citizens who live under the poverty line are disenfranchised by it. With Condoleezza Rice and Colin Powel in positions of warmongering power, shoulder-to-shoulder with George Bush and Dick Cheney, the color line is no longer the defining moment of the twenty-first century, even if it were in the twentieth. Capitalism is color blind and gender neutral. If Condoleezza Rice is willing to kill to keep capitalism rolling, she can be the next president of the USA for all capitalism cares. An Islamic liberation theology that still divides the world into East–West – or Muslim–non-Muslim, believer–non-believer, practicing–non-practicing – will mean absolutely nothing in the troubled years ahead. The only liberation movement against the terror of a globalizing empire that will be meaningful and mobilizing will have to be cross-cultural and global – precisely in the same way that the empire it must oppose and the capital it must curtail are global. That liberation movement will have to account for the existence and accommodate the inclusion of the non-Islamic – and as a result not a liberation *theology* but a liberation *theodicy* – that at once recognizes and celebrates diversity. *Theodicy* in this sense is not accounting for the existence of any "evil" in the world, but the presence of diversity, alterity, shades and shadows of truth, variations that collectively make the world wonder at its own marvel. Theodicy of liberation liberates Islam itself, before anything else, from the dogged dogmatism of its nomocentric juridicalism having brutally suppressed its own logocentric and homocentric domains in Islamic philosophy and mysticism. At the heart of Islamic political culture is a paradox – it is only in power when it is not in power, and it loses legitimacy when it is in power. The only way that this innate paradox at the heart of Islam can be put to work for a permanent good is for Islam no longer to be triumphalist but tolerant, aware of its own polyfocality, and in that awareness and tolerance not just to resist the abuse of power but also the temptation of power. The massive globalization of Islam by Muslim labor migrations throughout the world now provides for the former, its liberation theodicy for the latter.

No globally minded liberation movement will have a spec of legitimacy without categorically including the disenfranchised communities within the USA – in the very heart of the empire – and as globally exposed in the scandalous events around hurricane Katrina in August 2005. The fattened beneficiaries of the globalized capital in the USA cannot and must not be allowed to appropriate its revolutionary history. The anti-colonial history of the USA needs to be retrieved in the name and for the cause of its poor, sick, homeless, unemployed, uninsured, and massively impoverished communities. The USA is a microcosm of the world at large – there is already a Third World in the very heart of this heartless empire. These are the poor and the disinherited among the Native Americans, African Americans, Latino-Americans, Asian Americans, and then among a rainbow of new – legal and illegal – immigrants from around the globe. The revolutionary disposition of those colonies that once fought the British empire is not a distant and forgotten memory; it has in fact a glorious paragon of contemporary hope – his name is Malcolm X. In his revolutionary legacy, Malcolm X will link any global Islamic liberation movement to the heart of the most progressive uprising of the wretched of this earth against their obscene oppressors. For that hope to materialize, any understanding of Islamic liberation theology must embrace the princely memory of Malcolm X.

In my concluding (seventh) chapter, "Malcolm X as a Muslim Revolutionary," I will turn to Malcolm X and retrieve his legacy as a Muslim revolutionary in the heart of the empire and demonstrate how in his character and culture he already represents the model of a radical epistemic shift in the manufactured dialogue between "Islam and the West." Malcolm X, in my judgment, is a singularly important revolutionary character whose conversion to Islam and the massive epistemic shift that it occasioned in the course of his revolutionary career is yet to be properly understood and thoroughly theorized. In the revolutionary character of Malcolm X is gathered the most critical link necessary between the alienated colonial corners of capitalist modernity and the disenfranchised communities in its metropolitan center. By far the most pernicious achievement of Orientalism was not that it was a discourse of *domination* – but that it was a discourse of *alienation*. Through the generation of a false consciousness in the form of civilizational divides, Orientalism was instrumental in alienating the colonial corners of capitalist modernity from their integral connection to the capital. By summoning and dispatching the colonial world into a manufactured civilizational other – Islamic, African, Chinese, Indian, etc. – Orientalism was the most pernicious ideological force at the service of colonial modernity, systematically alienating the living labor of the colonials from their dead labor accumulated in metropolitan capital. A false categorical distinction was thus generated and sustained between the working class in the heart of capitalism and those in its colonial periphery, because they were assigned to two colonially fabricated civilizations – "the West" versus "the rest." It is not until the dawn of the so-called *globalization* that this fabricated distinction between metropolitan and colonial labor is *ipso facto* bridged.

The significance of Malcolm X is that he rises from the heart of the metropolitan disenfranchised poor in the USA and moves out to reach one of the most massively manufactured civilizational other of "the West" in the Islamic world. In his revolutionary character, as a result, we already have a transgressive bridge connecting the wretched of the earth otherwise treacherously separated by the pernicious project of Orientalism (squarely at the service of European colonialism) into two false civilizational camps – a project initiated and sustained to divide the world to rule it better. If Bernard Lewis has spent a long life manufacturing and perpetuating a hateful division between "Islam and the West," Malcolm X spent a short but glorious life linking that binary opposition and proving Bernard Lewis and his band of Orientalists wrong. There is no other evolutionary figure who like Malcolm X so gracefully and courageously climbs over that dilapidated wall which mercenary Orientalists have constructed between the Western part of their own perturbed imagination and the rest of the world to separate the poor and the working class into manufactured cultures and civilizations – in order to be able to dispatch poor Americans to maim and murder their own brothers and sisters around the globe. Retrieving the critical character of Malcolm X as a Muslim revolutionary is quintessential to any Islamic liberation project that must by definition include the ailing heart of this empire.

Donald Rumsfeld's campaign of "shock and awe" that announced the commencement of the US war against Iraq in spring 2003, combined with the mind-numbing theft and destruction of world cultural heritage in Mesopotamia that it occasioned, have indeed frightened the world out of a collective wit. Artifacts that were testaments to the very alphabets of our humanity and had survived from Chengiz Khan to Attila the Hun, from Tamerlane to Hitler, finally collapsed at the foot of Donald Rumsfeld and the predacious brutality of the war machine he unleashed. The whole world is indeed in a state of shock and awe at the sheer enormity of this unforgivable crime against humanity. Today more than ever, voices of reason and visions of sanity must prevail. We are no longer safe in the serenity of our professional careers and private lives. We must speak truth to power in a clear and concise language. Reading the specifics of our vanishing history is now more than ever the guiding light of our collective reason. This book is a sustained moment to pause and reflect against the grain of that speed with which our historical memory is being corroded. How and why did militant Islam begin to converse with colonial modernity? When and why did it run out of ideological energy? And ultimately what are the emerging forces of discontent that seek and must liberate Muslims from their own local tyranny in face of a predatory global empire in terms domestic to their hopes, loyal to the best in their character and culture? Posing these questions and seeking to answer them is no longer limited to Muslims or non-Muslims. We are all trapped. The cycle of violence benefits the worst amongst us and endangers the rest. We must be put on reverse gear to maneuver out of this nasty spot and then move on.

1 Resisting the empire

> I ain't got no quarrel with those Vietcong ... no Vietcong ever called me nigger.
> Muhammad Ali

Over the last 200 years, until the threshold of the twenty-first century, Muslims around the world have been engaged in a vital confrontation first with European colonialism and after the demise of that calamity with the rise of the US empire. This fateful confrontation has meant a systematic corrosion of the innate cosmopolitanism of Islamic cultures and its gradual mutation into a singular site of ideological resistance to foreign domination – in both political and cultural terms. The rise of Islamic ideologies worldwide corroborated the centrality of European capitalist modernity in which its colonial edges were categorically denigrated and denied agency – a reality against which a series of anti-colonial ideologies and movements took shape, among them both Christian and Islamic liberation theologies. In this chapter I intend to give an account of the outdated bipolarity between "Islam and the West" that for two centuries defined the terms of domination and resistance in the entire Muslim world. My intention here ultimately is to argue that the amorphous nature of capital in its current stage has generated an equally amorphous empire, and the dialectic of these two historical forces will perforce generate a succession of different and differing modes of resistance to it by people inevitably disenfranchised by its operation and devastated by its ravages. My ultimate intention in this book is to see in what particular terms might militant Islamic movements, beyond and above the current vicious cycle one can call the Bush–Bin Laden syndrome, have a share in this legitimate resistance to a predatory empire.

"People of this part of the world ought to know that Americans care." It was an unguarded moment at an apparently impromptu press conference with President Bush, and there was nothing particularly unusual about this nonsensical and blasé phrase, which I heard and watched on CNN on Friday September 2 2005 – nothing except, President Bush was not in Baghdad, Basra, Kandahar or Kabul. He was in Biloxi, Mississippi, visiting the ravaged area a few days after Hurricane Katrina had devastated New

Orleans and the tri-state region surrounding it, from Louisiana to Mississippi to Alabama. President Bush was not in "this part of the world." He was in Biloxi, Mississippi. When did Biloxi, Mississippi become "this part of the world," to the President of the USA? Strange. But true.

The mutation of Biloxi, Mississippi, into "this part of the world," when a US president is caught off guard exporting in reverse his vacuous foreign policy vernacular into a devastating domestic scene cannot and should not be dismissed as yet another indication of President Bush's by now proverbial penchant for dyslexic expressions and outlandish remarks. President Bush was never more accurate and precise, eloquent and correct, in his reference to Biloxi, Mississippi, as "this part of the world." The scenes of poor, hungry, and frightened colored people, roaming around the dead bodies of their neighbors and loved ones, while watched over by heavily armed, mostly white, military patrols in armored personnel carriers, brandishing machine guns and automatic rifles, was almost identical with similar scenes from Baghdad, Basra, Kandahar, and Mazar-e Sharif. Hurricane Katrina had blown away the carpet under which this massive poverty and destitution was systematically brushed. Was this the USA? Where is the "Third World" these days? It has always been in "this" or "that part of the world." But never presumed in Biloxi, Mississippi. When hungry and poor people, left by their presumably elected officials to their own non-existent devices, had begun entering supermarkets to find food and survive, the first thing that local and federal officials sent to the area was sharp shooters to shoot and kill the "intruders." It was straight out of the 1950s propaganda machinery of racist states that reports of rape and murder began circulating in order to justify the shoot-to-kill order issued by federal and state officials. For days after the carnage of Katrina, the local and federal government kept sending heavily armed military troops to the area instead of medical personnel, social aid workers, civil engineers, etc. *The New York Times* and CNN were competing with each other reporting on how more troops were being sent into New Orleans in order to restore "calm" in the area. Protecting the absolute and irreconcilable principle of capitalism and private property was far more sacrosanct than saving human lives, people dying in their own excrement and being eaten by rats. "New Orleans has become exactly like Baghdad," began a poem circulating on the Internet at just about this time:

> Wow, see how drowned in sadness looks New Orleans,
> Worse than Bam[1] now appears New Orleans –
> Just like Baghdad, liberated from law and order,
> Is now New Orleans, oh world is so full of wonders –
> Black Folks, their fortunes all on retreat,
> Hungry and mourning swim through their streets –
> Ready at hand were of course plenty of police officers,
> With canon balls and tanks, guarding shops, banks, offices –

All awaiting President Bush who soon came up with his orders
That voice of black folks ought to be warded –
New Orleans the city of legendary Jazz and heartwarming Blues,
Full of black folks playing the trumpet with their souls all bruised –
In their voices rings the sound of being left to their own devices,
With no connections, no protection, throwing their own dices –
They are still all in bondage and yes indeed also in slavery,
Though this time around hidden behind a veil full of embroideries –
Upon this veil is cast the shape of – are you ready? – "democracy,"
Hiding the fact that black folks are rebelling against this hypocrisy –
From the other side of the veil you can hear the sound of Blues
Linking their nights of sorrow to their days of abuse:
"I come from the backs burned by lashes,
I come from bodies covered with wounds and ashes –
I am from the Sunday slave markets of yore,
I am black, soft like cotton not anymore –
I am black, full of abandoned hopes and in desperation,
Talk to me, tell me of kindness, not of cotton plantations" –
Did the black people not have enough pains of their own,
Did they need to be in a Katrina zone? –
A Hurricane in New Orleans – call it Katrina, Larry, or Dan;
Hurried furiously looking just like a gang of Ku Klux Klan –
Killing on its way all the black people it could,
And if they survived, homeless they stood –
The news came finally from the White House:
"Beware of black folks: male, female, husband and spouse:
That according to the rule at the time of war
They will be shot and killed by the US army at supermarket door –
"These are all thieves and plunderers," said President Bush,
No hungry person and a loaf of bread, when shove came to push![2]

This was a poem not by an American poet, or even a poet from that huge and hollowed hole called "the West." The poem was by Hadi Khorsandi, an expatriate Iranian satirist, unable to return to his own homeland because of his political views. Having lived in London and then Los Angeles for a while, and now effectively living nowhere except in the no-man's-land of the Internet, where he runs a website and tells the world what he thinks of it in his mother tongue. Between President Bush referring to Biloxi, Mississippi, as "this part of the world," and Hadi Khorsandi composing a poem on the predicament of his fellow human beings in the no-man's-land of the Internet, the fate of the globalized planet, the state of defenseless and atomized individuals, the whims of the amorphous capital that reigns supreme, and then the cries and whispers of the incompetent empire that seeks to rule it, are all cast and narrated. Does this world have a shape, or is it as shapeless as the nebulous capital that spins it? Is the abysmal pit of the "war on terrorism" the hellhole from which arises a hurricane of a different sort – a senseless, shapeless, shoreless violence, with no beginning, no middle, and no end, breaking poor people's already dilapidated roofs on their head, while their richer neighbors have always already fled the scene of the crime?

This empire is amorphous, nationless, nameless, merciless. It is not American, so far as millions of anti-war activists are concerned, ordinary Americans from all walks of life who poured into streets of their cities and towns condemning Bush's warmongering and crying out loud, "Not in Our Name!" Resisting this empire has no cultural designation, no denominational domain. It is as global as the monster it seeks to face.

Among the side effects of Hurricane Katrina in 2005 was the restoration of a modicum of decency to an otherwise entirely bankrupt US media. On the fourth anniversary of 9/11, the criminal negligence at the root of exposing millions of impoverished Americans to hazardous conditions – just one collateral damage of its predatory pursuit of a whimsical empire – finally forced some observers to dub the catastrophe in New Orleans and its surrounding areas the "anti-9/11."[3] It was of course a matter of time that the corporate take over of the US media would soon start whitewashing the terror experienced by millions of people in Alabama, Louisiana, and Mississippi. But nevertheless, among homes and dreams, Hurricane Katrina had also blown away not just poor people's livelihood but also the cover of the corruption at the vilest and crudest core of the US predatory capitalism and the massive poverty that it generates and sustains not just all around the globe but in its own backyard – and thus the perfectly apt reference of President Bush to Biloxi, Mississippi, as "this part of the world," for this indeed was part of the rest of the world, akin to Baghdad, Basra, Falluja, Kandahar, Kabul, and Mazar-e Sharif all left in ruins, while between the two of them Bush and Bin Laden had found the planet earth too small for their megalomaniac egos.

By virtue of that very minor slippage, of calling Biloxi, Mississippi, "this part of the world," if indeed anyone was watching and listening, it was no longer possible to think, read, and write about Islam and Muslims without simultaneously doing the same about other sites of legitimate resistances to the predatory pursuit of power and capital by US neocons – sites of resistance that were no longer limited to Afghanistan, Iraq, or Palestine, but that had indeed gone around the globe and come to include "this part of the world," Biloxi, Mississippi, and its environs, and then beyond them from East LA to the Bronx and Harlem. "It's not just Katrina," as Cornel West put it in an essay published pointedly on the fourth anniversary of 9/11,

> it's povertina. People were quick to call them refugees because they looked as if they were from another country. They are. Exiles in America. Their humanity had been rendered invisible so they were never given high priority when the well-to-do got out and the helicopters

came for the few. Almost everyone stuck on rooftops, in the shelters, and dying by the side of the road was poor black.[4]

Cornel West was never so precise in pointedly dissecting the fate of his people. "Charlie Parker," said West of the legendary jazz musician, "would have killed somebody if he had not blown his horn. The history of black people in America is one of unbelievable resilience in the face of crushing white supremacist powers." Cornel West did not spare those who had joined the ruling elite to justify the horrors of a racist culture:

> They shot brother Martin dead like a dog in 1968 when the mobilization of the black poor was just getting started. At least one of his surviving legacies was the quadrupling in the size of the black middle class. But Oprah [Winfrey] the billionaire and the black judges and chief executives and movie stars do not mean equality, or even equality of opportunity yet. Black faces in high places do not mean racism is over. Condoleezza Rice has sold her soul.[5]

In the aftermath of Katrina, "it was a war of all against all," Cornel West concluded, "'you're on your own' – in the centre of the American empire."[6]

How do we read Islam and Muslims in the aftermath of not just "9/11" but also of "anti-9/11," of a subdued class warfare at the heart of the (flailing and incompetent) US empire? Did Persians perish in destitution when the Achamenids were ruling the world? Did Romans live in poverty when their generals went about conquering the earth? Did Dickens mean to say something about the poverty and destitution of the British when their colonial officers went around the globe colonizing people? There is no reading of any enduring and meaningful resistance to the predatory US empire (Osama bin Laden and co. are neither enduring nor meaningful) unless and until Cornel West's reading of the plight of poor people in the USA is wedded to a larger calamity that the US military is causing around the globe. There is much confusion in the USA, and by extension around the world, about what is happening in and about Islam, to and by Muslims – as they all live under the shadow of the American empire. This confusion is not accidental. It is both historically rooted and deliberately manufactured. There are professional spin doctors, without as much as a preliminary knowledge of the very languages that Muslims speak, shamelessly adding to this systematic mystification of Muslims, confounding the abysmal level of public knowledge about the world at large with their own pathological ignorance and a malignant proclivity to side with power and partake in it. As the historically illiterate US propagandists are manufacturing an Islamic threat based on a violent ideology, they are in fact propagating, *ipso facto*, a violent ideology of their own, corresponding with a predatory design to rule an unruly world. This is and will remain (as long as it lasts) an empire with no hegemony, except a hegemony by proxy – the manufacturing of a fictive enemy that like the effigy of a phantom fear they put together and burn in public squares (until of course a hurricane comes and blows away all the cover-up of the massive poverty over which presides the phantasmagoric nightmare of a global empire). The central task of these spin doctors, and the propaganda machinery they represent,[7] is to separate the fate of the poor and disenfranchised in the USA from those of the people in Iraq, Afghanistan, and the rest of the world, via the creation of an imbecilic, when not nauseatingly fake, mode of patriotism. Uniting the fate of poor people in the USA with those around the globe and then asking if Muslims have anything positive, progressive, and constructive to say about that mass of humanity in turmoil is the only way that not just Islam but any world religion can have any meaningful presence in the world.

It is imperative to combat the professional spin doctors who are in the business of manufacturing fictive enemies around the world, while whitewashing the horrors of the impoverished masses, and clear the air of this massive, deliberately manufactured confusion and come up with a clear and concise conception of the predicament of Muslims, inseparable from the rest of mankind at large, just before and then in the aftermath of 9/11, and then place it right next to the predicament of their American counterparts of the "anti-9/11." If the US media yet again does not whitewash the Katrina catastrophe, the "anti-9/11" must supersede and dismantle the massive propaganda machinery it set in motion in the aftermath of 9/11. For this time around there are no dark-skinned Arabs and Muslims categorically to blame – just dark-skinned Americans lying dead, dying, and decaying, or else left homeless and hungry while "the richest most powerful," as the joke goes, country in the world stood by and watched.

How do we clear the confusions at the heart of the global fear of the "Islam" manufactured by the US neocons – and how do we proceed from there to see what are the emerging patterns of legitimate Islamic resistances to US imperial designs? Very simply – by beginning at the ground zero and the year zero of the US imperial age – the iconic 9/11, and then work our way towards the "anti-9/11." To combat the propaganda machinery, predicated on a pathological contemporaneity, of the US neocons and their penchant for muddying the waters, we need first and foremost to denounce the horrific events of 9/11 without the slightest hesitation, equivocation, prevarication, evasion, "buts, ifs, however, nevertheless," etc. The indiscriminate acts of violence perpetrated on that horrific day are not justifiable on any scale, basis, or assumption. 9/11 was a singular act of diabolic insanity, horrific insignia of vicious violence at the service of no cause, an ignoble manifestation of deranged minds incapable of figuring out where the core of a global injustice is located and thus lashing out at the iconic signs of an imperial project, irrespective of the sanctity of innocent lives they thus desecrated and wantonly wasted. To the degree that this act of deranged violence was done in the name of Islam, Islam itself, outside any quotation mark, is accountable for the carnage of 9/11. But that degree is as tenuous as Judaism being responsible for the criminal atrocities of Baruch Goldstein in particular or Zionism even in more vicious and systematic ways piling one generation of vicious injustice upon Palestinians after another. The same holds true in the distinction we must make between the Christianity of poor people (liberation theology of Latin America) and that of the Crusaders or Christian missionary accomplices of European colonialism – or between Hinduism and the criminal thugs representing the BJP in India. Osama bin Laden has a similar claim on Islam, and he does, as Baruch Goldstein has on Judaism, Jim Jones on Christianity, or the BJP on Hinduism. None of such comparisons or contrasts should detract from the more fundamental fact that insane acts of violence, whether committed in the name of Islam, Christianity, Judaism, or Hinduism, must be categorically and consistently denounced.

Once we categorically denounce such indiscriminate acts of violence, we also need to separate the actual reality of the events of 9/11 from the nauseating propaganda machinery into which they were fed in order to justify the Bush administration's even more horrid acts of violence. If we do not make that distinction, we will inevitably end up in the rise of pathological conspiracy theories that in fact attribute the events of 9/11 to some secret design by the US government itself.[8] Instead of falling into that trap, we need to separate the sheer insanity of those acts of random violence in 9/11 from any subsequent abuses to which they were put by a neocon-inspired global warmongering. Perfectly legitimate sympathy with the victims of 9/11 and their bereaved loved ones must never be marred by the fact that they are viciously abused in a politics of mourning to justify the terrorizing war that the Bush administration has unleashed. Quite to the contrary: the memory of the innocent victims of 9/11 must be turned around and used for the cause of peace and legitimate resistance to this predatory empire.[9]

Equally important is not to allow the legitimate global anger against the US imperialism in general and against the Bush administration's criminal neocon project in particular to be translated into an illegitimate sympathy for the equally criminal atrocities of Osama bin Laden and his associates. At the mercy of both George W. Bush and Osama bin Laden are innocent people the world over, whether in New York and New Orleans or in Kandahar and Baghdad. That a band of criminally minded neocons have taken over the sacrosanct institutions of a democracy and driven it to sheer criminal madness around the globe, does not mean that equally criminal adventurers like Osama bin Laden or Abu Musab al-Zarqawi are harbingers of truth, salvation, freedom, and democracy. It is imperative for us to see that Francis Fukuyama, Samuel Huntington, and Bernard Lewis are Ayman al-Zawahiri and Abu Musab al-Zarqawi in business suits, clean-shaven, wearing colorful ties, and speaking a passable English. In a contorted worldview and moral derangement there is no difference between

Bush, Blair, Berlusconi, and Bin Laden. Anger with any one of them should not amount to sympathy for the other.

Along the same argument, we also need to place the historical amnesia subsequently loaded in the iconic sign of "9/11" (before the "anti-9/11" scandalized it) in the context of the last 200 years – when and how did Islamic Ideology as a mode of resistance to European colonialism emerge, when and how did it serve its purposes and die out, what and whence are the current globalized terrorist exchanges between the two camps of President Bush and Osama bin Laden, and ultimately what lays out into the future, signs of hope, reasons for despair, loci of critical attention to articulate the modes and manners of resisting a globalized empire – infinitely superior in its manners of inflicting pain, causing terror, wreaking havoc, and spreading fear than any presumed enemy it says it wants to fight.[10]

Once the air is thus cleared of any confusion of ideas and sentiments, we are ready for a critical encounter with the events of 9/11.

The apocalyptic events of September 11 2001 and the subsequent unleashing of the massive US military machinery in Afghanistan and Iraq that they occasioned once again brought Islam to the forefront of global attention. The US-led invasion of Afghanistan (2001) and Iraq (2003) – both predominantly Muslim countries – and the rise of the Arab and Muslim world in anger and fear have resuscitated the specter of a massively politicized Islam as the single most defiant mode of political resistance to the rising US empire. The continued Israeli occupation of Palestine and the cycle of genocidal, homicidal, and suicidal violence that it has occasioned is a deep wound in the side of Muslims the world over – unable to dismantle the last vestige of a European colonialism in their midst, unwilling to live with its extension into a military base for the US imperial operations in their midst. Under the pretext of a US–Israeli strategic alliance, Israel as a quintessentially colonial settlement now categorically functions as a military hardware integral to the operation of the US empire. While the so-called Israeli intellectuals are busy debating Zionism and post-Zionism, one- or two-state solutions, what they call their country links its European colonial heritage to its mutation into a military base for US imperialism – a fact beyond their 1948, 1967, 1973, 1982, or any other date in which Zionist barbarity has inflicted more pain on the broken (but defiant) back of Palestinians. Meanwhile the militant presence of a *Jewish state* in the region has already given rise to an *Islamic republic*, and scores of other countries located in between the Jewish state and the Islamic republic are in dire danger of collapsing into other forms of religious tribalism if their current medieval potentates fail to cultivate institutions of civil liberties, civil societies, and civil rights.

The US-led invasion of Iraq in March 2003, "shock and awing," as the US Secretary of State Defense Donald Rumsfeld put it at the time, a nation into submission, culminating in the horrific pictures of the Iraqi prisoners' abuse in the US torture chambers in Abu Ghraib prison in April and May 2004 and then paving the way for an Iraqi constitution that might in effect create yet another Islamic republic in the region, has made the entire area – from the Indian Ocean to the Arabian Sea to the Persian Gulf – exceptionally volatile. Over the spectrum of these facts on the ground is now rising the specter of a global empire with no regards for international law or for diplomacy, and confident in the pursuit of its sheer, brute, and naked material and strategic interests. In conjunction with that imperial design and execution, a global rise in terrorist attacks, now extended into European and US soils, has once again raised the fear of Islam as the principal nemesis of "the Western civilization," – leading the US neocons to demand and exact apologies from Muslims across the world, asserting categorically that there is something inherently violent about their religion and culture. The daily headlines around the globe report of deadly terrorist attacks and even more devastating carnage caused by the US-led military invasions and colonial occupations of sovereign nation-states. An estimated 655,000 Iraqis and unknown tens of thousands of Afghans have been murdered after the US-led invasion of Iraq (March 2003) and Afghanistan (October 2001). The total number of terrorist acts attributed to Muslims amounts to nothing more than 1 percent of that number. This comparison does not make Muslim terrorists any less barbaric than their American and Israeli counterparts. It makes them all identical partners in a global spiral of violence that above all has allowed the world to degenerate into medieval tribal identifications.

Under these frightful circumstances, terms and phrases have assumed iconic power of their own, with no or merely vacuous connections to reality. If a desperate teenager in Palestine blows himself and everything and everyone around him up into smithereens that is a "terrorist *attack*;" but if the IDF (Israeli Defense Force) razes an entire Palestinian village or refugee camp to the ground, or else carpet bombs from air, sea, and land from one end of Lebanon to the other, it is a "*defensive* act." If Iraqi people of varied political persuasions defend their country against a foreign invasion, they merit the term "terrorists," but if the deadliest military machinery in history is brought in to "shock and awe" them into submission it is called "liberation" through something called "Operation Iraqi Freedom." In the midst of such linguistic obscenities, foreclosing the violent spiral of fear and fury, "Islam and the West," projected as two eternal arch nemesis, are once again posited as the principal coded categories of this global confrontation between two irreconcilable adversaries – two cosmic forces of good and evil. Manichaeism seems to have finally triumphed in "the West," unbeknown to its Christianity.

Against this fabricated binary opposition, and beyond the smoke screen of a manufactured Islamic threat,[11] today more than ever we are in need of a calm and quiet reconfiguration of the initial rise of militant Islamism in the shadow of colonial modernity in the nineteenth and twentieth centuries, in contradistinction with its current demise under the shade of a postcolonial empire – as Muslims and other disenfranchised people the world over reconfigure their hopes and reassess their fears in anticipation of new liberation strategies. The fastidious take over of public discourse by embedded journalists and their counterparts among the recruited (bought and paid for) pundits have hijacked our sense of security and paralyzed our informed and responsible discourses. With academic intellectuals institutionally compromised by their privatized intellect, compromised integrity, mind-numbing specialization, and thus public irrelevance, the arena has been left vacant for lucratively paid and yet astonishingly illiterate charlatans to steal our reasoned conversations and leave us bereft of sane and sustained reflection on our global destiny. No country on planet earth has a fattier dose of these propagandist officers masquerading as journalists and columnists than the USA. The fate of Muslims and non-Muslims is today more than ever intertwined, and the forces of darkness and ignorance at the service of a global empire can no longer be allowed to divide the world into its sectarian proclivities to rule it. People in the USA, since 9/11 the eye of the storm, are as much implicated in this global condition of fear as anyone else. This has never been a question of "Islam versus the West." This binary opposition is politically manufactured and has cast the globe in a permanent condition of fear – fear of terrorist attacks from one side and fear of the US/UK predatory designs on the world on the other, no less terrorizing, and in fact infinitely more deadly, than what they brand as "terrorism." Al-Qaeda and the Pentagon are now the two sides of the same coin, when it comes to ordinary, innocent, and bewildered citizens – Americans and non-Americans, Muslims and non-Muslims – all squarely at the mercy of both.

Contrary to the prevalent assumptions of a clash of civilization between "Islam and the West," we have in fact concluded the period of civilizational conflict. One of my principal arguments in this book is that civilizational thinking had a very short but crucial role in the course of the colonial encounter of Muslims with European modernity, but that it has now effectively exhausted its uses and abuses in facilitating the operation of the globalized capital. In direct opposition to Samuel Huntington's thesis of "the clash of civilizations," we have already entered a post-civilizational period in global conflict – one in which we need a fresh understanding of the nature of globalizing power and the emerging revolutionary manners of resisting it. My reading of the global conflict, as a result, is radically opposed to the outdated binary that posits a civilizational conflict between "Islam and the West." The binary opposition between "Islam and the West" was manufactured as civilizational opposites by a mercenary band of Orientalists in the course of colonial modernity and the category has long since lost its epistemic instrumentality in creating a false consciousness alienating the colonized labor from accumulated capital. In the course of the rapid globalization of labor and capital it is no longer possible to sustain any legitimacy for that separation between the capital and the colonial, between the West and the Rest, for the capital has always been in the colonial, the colonial in the capital, and the very notion of "the West" was a coded category privileging the beneficiaries of the capital from the massive multitudes it denigrated, enslaved, and abused.

Towards the end of the last century, civilizational thinking emerged in the USA for a last gasp, principally to suppress the multicultural insurrection of disenfranchised communities and recent labor immigrants – a white supremacist move at home to manufacture a global hegemony abroad.[12] These, however, were feeble attempts, unable to fathom the treacherous logic of capital that never wears a worn out item of cultural clothing twice – that once the usefulness of the manufactured idea of "the West" and all the other civilizational categories it needed and thus engendered had done their services the meandering, expansive, and amorphous logic of the capital was off to greener pastures and more useful rhetoric to sustain the logic of its operation.

The flailing hegemonic disposition of the emerging empire and any manner of revolutionary response to it will have a dialectical relationship to each other. Because the nature of that hegemony is not yet clear, the disposition of revolutionary resistances to it is not yet quite evident. There will not be any action and reaction this time around. The globe is too much aware and very much self-conscious of itself – and al-Jazeera is a mighty competitor for CNN. The emerging logic of capital and the empire that wishes to control it will have a dialectical rhetoric to them. At this moment, we have exited the historic usefulness of "Islam and the West" as one particular mode of dialectics between empire building and revolutionary resistances to it; and yet we have not entered the next stage because the capital that the emerging empire wishes to serve is an amorphous and capricious jinni.

The phenomenon code-named *globalization*, with its deeper roots going back to the very origin of the global disposition of capital at its very inception, is now shedding the older versions of cultural formations corresponding to the centrality of capital in forming ideologies that sustain and energize it. That capital no longer has a presumed center to its operation. The colonial edges of that capital have always been central to its operation. When the labor that capital abuses in its immediate neighborhood is writ large and global it is called colonialism. When that colonialism is internal to the polity of capitalist modernity it is called abused labor. Structurally the abused laborers in London, Paris, and New York are identical in their relation of power to capital with colonized persons the world over. Civilizational categories such as "Islam and the West," "The West and the Orient," or more basically "The West and the Rest" are the principal services that mercenary Orientalists have performed to authenticate the presumed centrality of capital and its high culture in a figment of imagination called "the West." This "West" has now imploded under the pressure of globalization. The collapse of the Soviet Union, the breakdown of the Eastern European bloc, the unification of Europe, and the rise of the EU (European Union) as a major economic and potentially military rival to the USA are among the signs of a remodulation of globalized capital that no longer has any use for the outdated category of "the West."[13] With "the West" having now imploded, all its binary oppositions that mercenary Orientalists had fabricated to corroborate its existence have also lost their historical interlocutor. The "Islam" that was manufactured as a metanarrative of authenticity to corroborate "the West" has now ended and it is now left for Muslims to figure out what they mean and signify. In the face of a predatory empire that has now emerged wishing to steer the course of the unruly globalized capital, the emerging Islam will also have to be understood in terms that safeguard the hope and aspirations of millions of poor and disenfranchised Muslims around the globe in terms compatible with those of millions of non-Muslims equally at the mercy of this barbaric empire. In understanding the terms of this emerging Islam, it is imperative not to allow the propaganda machinery at the service of the empire to muddy the water and create tribal affiliations that further divide the world to rule it better – a Jewish state here, and Islamic republic there, all in the neighborhood of a Hindu fundamentalism and all in need of a superior Christian empire to make them behave. It is equally important to link the fate of millions of disenfranchised human beings at the heart of the Christian empire, the poor and racialized people that with the violent winds of just a hurricane the cover of propaganda cast over them is blown away for the whole world to see. The savageries of the empire are global, its victims as much Americans as Iraqis or Afghans, poor Christians in Latin America are equally desperate as poor Muslims in Asia and Africa – and thus the necessity of resistance to that empire in equally global terms, terms that can no longer be in puritanical Islamic juridical terms, but in emancipatory terms at once Islamic for Muslim to have a claim over it and yet in a manner Islamic that embraces all the shades and shadows of a world religion with a varied cosmopolitanism definitive to its historical character.

Between hurricanes Rumsfeld and Katrina, the globe is shrunk in size and proportion. To justify its expansive designs on the world, the US empire has manufactured a global Islamic threat, in which context its principal ideologues – Samuel Huntington and Bernard Lewis chief among them – have resuscitated the outdated cliché of "Islam versus the West." No act of responsible scholarship in opposition to this calamitous propaganda machinery can remain aloof and merely academic. It is a matter of global sanity and public safety persistently to historicize, re/contextualize, inform, and open the domain of public debate. The globalized terrorism that US imperialism at once generates, sustains, perpetrates, legitimizes, and needs in order to justify itself is squarely based on the illusion that "Islam" and "The West" are two quintessential realities and that they are at odds with each other – and that illusion will have to be publicly exposed and analytically dismantled. President Bush is not "the West," for "the West" has ended, disintegrated somewhere in the middle of the Atlantic Ocean in the aftermath of the collapse of the Soviet Union and the unification of Europe as an emerging site of military and economic power. Osama bin Laden is not "Islam," for "Islam" is the faith of multitudinous masses of people, always subject to historical changes, emotive mutations – its metaphysical certainties always at the mercy of its political vicissitudes.

The binary opposition generated and sustained for over 200 years between "Islam and the West" (as a particular version of a more global power-basing proposed between "the West and the Rest") is no longer valid or operative, the moral and material conditions that necessitated and thus articulated it are no longer extant, and we are on the verge of a new configuration of power and manners of resistances to it by the disenfranchised multitude left poor, homeless, hungry, and indignant by the predatory logic of capital. Released from that binary nexus, Islam, as the faith of a globalized community, has now entered a new phase in its long and arduous history. What the particulars of that new configuration will be is still too early to tell. But that "the West" is no longer the principal interlocutor of Islam is globally evident – for "the West" itself has (a mere 200 years after its invention) long since disintegrated.

As one of the most potent political events in colonial modernity, namely from early in the nineteenth to late in the twentieth century, Islamic political activism was a major force of contention resisting the onslaught of European colonialism. That mode of resistance to colonialism performed its task and is now over and done for – and recognizing that fact is necessary if we are to clear the confusion generated around the "Islamic terrorism" that is now codified by "9/11." Based on that premise we then need to proceed to see the emerging sites of legitimate Muslim resistances to the US empire – entirely independent of the fabricated illusion around Osama bin Laden and his cohorts. One of my principal arguments in this book is that militant Islamic ideologies of the last 200 years (before the events leading to 9/11) emerged in combatant conversation between the ancestral faith of a people and their political predicament at the wake of colonial modernity in the nineteenth and twentieth centuries. As that interlocutor has drastically changed its normative and material demeanors so has militant Islamism lost its revolutionary agenda. This proposition inevitably rests on a historical conception of Islam as the collective consciousness of a people. It posits the political history of the faith over the last 200 years not as a reality *sui generis* but in fact as the dialectical outcome of a destabilizing dialogue with the catastrophic consequences of European colonialism. That European colonial modernity has now given rise to an American postcolonial empire, and thus have militant Islamic ideologies lost their erstwhile interlocutor and with it their own historical resonances. What the shape of Islam in combative conversation with the US empire will be is yet to be seen. Osama bin Laden is a decoy, a subterfuge, a smoke screen. He is a mirage that is taken for the real thing. The real thing is yet to come. Osama bin Laden is a figment of Pentagon imagination – created, crafted, and envisioned to justify US imperial designs.

The end of *Islamic Ideology* as we have known it and as the organizing principle of political resistance to colonial modernity is a momentous historical occasion, now categorically camouflaged by a smoke screen generated between a mismatched band of militant adventurers collectively identified with Osama bin Laden, on one side, and a gang of pestiferous and bankrupt ideas identified as neo-conservatism and represented by the Bush administration (2000–2008), a period that will go down in history as the most catastrophic manifestation of the absolute worst in American political culture. My thesis, simply put, is this: militant Islamism emerged from the early nineteenth century in direct and combative response to European colonialism, gradually changing a medieval faith into a solitary site of ideological resistance to colonial modernity. These almost 200 years of incessant transformation of Islam into *Islamic Ideology* came to an end with the success and subsequent failure of the Islamic revolution in Iran. The demise of Islamic Ideology was all but evident soon after the Islamic revolution in Iran. Islamic Ideology succeeded to dismantle the Pahlavi monarchy, but the Islamic republic failed to become a model of democratic institutions for the region, as the Islamic revolution failed to expand beyond the immediate Iranian borders. The creation of the Wahabi-inspired Taliban in Afghanistan, by a combination of US, Saudi, and Pakistani forces, to expel the Soviets was equally successful in preventing the spread of the Shi'i-inspired Islamic revolution of Iran into Central Asia. The formation of the Taliban in Afghanistan thus precipitated a course of events that linked the end of a legitimate Islamic Ideology to the rise of an adventurous Islamism entirely devoid of any social or economic project. If Ayatollah Khomeini was the last Muslim ideologue of the twentieth century, Osama bin Laden is the first militant Muslim adventurer of the twenty-first century. Reading Ayatollah Khomeini or any other Muslim ideologue of the last 200 years going back to Jamal al-Din al-Afghani and Muhammad Abduh is to read a particularly revolutionary project with widespread social and political agenda. This is absolutely not the case with Osama bin Laden or anyone else among his militant entourage.

The US support for Saddam Hussein when he invaded Iran and engaged in an eight-year mutually destructive war was equally instrumental in preventing the spread of the Islamic revolution westward into the rest of the Islamic and the Arab world – as the creation of the Taliban had done the same on the Eastern borders of the Islamic republic. The Islamic revolution was thus trapped, the Islamic Republic embattled, and Islamic Ideology – some 200 years into the making – ever more discredited.

Soon after the end of Iran–Iraq war (1980–1988), the cataclysmic collapse of the Soviet Union and the Eastern Europe radically changed the global geopolitics. Following the collapse of the Soviet Union, the US-sponsored, Saudi-financed, and Pakistani-administered creation of the Taliban backfired and gave rise to an amorphous blowback in the aftermath of the Soviet departure from Afghanistan.[14] The Taliban were no longer "freedom fighters" in the US lexicon. Overnight they became "terrorists." Mirroring the same blowback, Saddam Hussein took full advantage of the same amorphous conditions and invaded and occupied Kuwait. The collapse of the Soviet Union and the subsequent US invasion of Iraq to push it back from Kuwait marked the rise of the USA as the single surviving superpower and the emergence of a historic rift between the USA and Europe – Europe that is except the United Kingdom. By the time of the Second Gulf War (the US-led invasion of Iraq in March 2003), Europe had rapidly unified into a major global power and was acting increasingly as independent and in fact in competition with the USA – and thus the end of "the West" as a legitimate category with any enduring credence left to its economic or political consequences.

The USA and Europe were now in competition with each other over how to rule the world economically and maintain it militarily. The dissolution of "the West," as an organizing principle of Euro-North American modernity, also meant that "Islam" had lost its historic interlocutor over the last 200 years – the modernity with which it was engaged in a combatant, counter-colonial, conversation. The result, a simultaneous dismantling of both "Islam" and "the West" as the mirror image of each other and the evident emergence of a new mode of US imperial domination and revolutionary resistance to it. To begin to understand what the parameters of these new revolutionary agenda might be – while noting that we have passed through a major turning point in the global manners of both imperial power and revolutionary resistances to it – is the emerging agenda of a whole new generation of reading, writing, and scholarship. "Islam," just like the fate of the world caught between a flailing (US) and an emerging (EU) superpower, is now up for grabs. Osama bin Laden is no match for this historic game. He is a false alarm.

The end of "Islamic Ideology" by virtue of forces at once internal to its own contradictions and endemic to the binary opposition posited between "Islam and the West" does not mean that in the course of its historic development it was an entirely useless project. It is a historic anachronism (and thus logically flawed) to dismiss militant Islamic thoughts and movements of the last 200 years, prior to the rise of Osama bin Laden, as completely failed political projects.[15] As it emerged out of a militant confrontation with European colonialism – and thus the origin and demise of "Islam and the West" as a binary opposition – "Islamic Ideology" was a potent political force that in ideological rivalry with nationalism and socialism helped to map out the contours of Muslim countries resisting the European colonial savageries.[16] At the conclusion of "Islamic Ideology" as a perfectly legitimate political project and the collapse of "Islam and the West" as the productive epistemic machinery that gave rise to it, it is crucial to have an accurate conception of its rise and demise, successes and failures. This assessment is not just a matter of academic interest. It is a critical foregrounding for a clear conception of what will happen next – in the course of a new generation of Islamic liberation theology that will have to face the flailing USA and the emerging EU imperialisms after the smoke screen of Osama bin Laden has evaporated and disappeared.

Two revolutionary movements in the eighteenth and the nineteenth centuries mark the passage of medieval Islamic political thought and revolutionary movements into the main course of Muslim encounter with colonial modernity. Inspired by the staunchly conservative Sunni theologian Ibn Taymiyyah (1268–1328), the puritanical ideas of Muhammad ibn Abd al-Wahab (1703–1791) initiated the Wahabi movement in Arabia, almost a century before Seyyed Ali Mohammad Shirazi "Bab" (1819–1850) led a Shi'i millenarian movement whose theological ideas and political aspirations can be traced back to the political philosophy of Sheykh Ahmad Zeyn al-Din al-Ahsa'i (1753–1826) and even further back to the transcendental philosophy of Mulla Sadra Shirazi (1571–1640), and of course ultimately back to Shi'i doctrine of *Imamate*.[17] After these two last gasps of medieval Islamic political thought, one Sunni in disposition and the other Shi'i, the remainder of Islamic political thoughts and movements in the course of the nineteenth and twentieth centuries is categorically located on the sites of Muslim encounters with European colonialism. The British and the French colonial presence in North Africa and the Levant, the Russian incursions into Central Asia and Iran, while the British were concerned about the Russian and French intrusion into "their" Indian subcontinent are the principal carriers of the colonial syndrome of an increasingly globalized capital, against which Muslims pick up their Qur'an and take up their arms opposing their European conquerors. What emerge in this process are the systematic corrosion of medieval Islamic political thought and the simultaneous rise of a succession of militant anti-colonial Islamic ideas and movements throughout the Muslim world in direct and dialogical confrontation with colonial modernity.[18]

Very much confined to Arabia since its initial success in 1811 (and subsequently in the 1820s and finally in the 1900s), Wahabism had very little effect in the rest of the Muslim world, for it was an essentially intrinsic Muslim movement and only of catalytic significance where Muslims were facing the onslaught of European colonialists. Against the background of Wahabism and Babism, ideas, ideals, and aspirations far more attractive, powerful, and moving came to fruition in direct exchange with colonial modernity.[19] From India and Afghanistan to the Ottoman domains and North Africa, the mobilizing ideas of Seyyed Jamal al-Din al-Afghani (1838–1897) were formulated and put into action in direct opposition to European imperialism in general and the British colonialism in particular. Afghani's political ideas, ranging from anti-colonial nationalism to militant pan-Islamism, were all formulated in dialogical disputation with European colonial presence in Muslim lands – forcing Islamic doctrinal disposition to flex its muscles with new historical circumstances.[20] It was in direct response to the European colonial presence that al-Afghani reawakened certain selective aspects of both Islamic and nationalist sentiments and thoughts, seeking to use them to mobilize the Muslim masses for national and regional liberation movements. Al-Afghani very much set the discourse for almost two centuries of incessant re/formulations of an "Islamic Ideology," in direct and dialectical conversation with European colonial modernity – and thus providing Muslims with a legitimate liberation theology compatible with their contemporary historical predicament.

Al-Afghani's ideas were propagated in Egypt, and through Egypt into the rest of the Arab and Muslim world by his principal disciple Sheykh Muhammad Abduh (1849–1905), and after Abduh by his student Rashid Rida (1865–1935).[21] Despite their at times radical differences with each other, the triumvirate project of al-Afghani–Abduh–Rida became increasingly important throughout the Muslim world as the very cornerstone of Islamic liberation theology in much of the nineteenth and twentieth centuries. The initial success of Muhammad Ali (1769–1849) in securing a certain degree of autonomy and power against the Ottomans and his subsequent failures in preventing the onslaught of European colonialism had left Egypt entirely exposed to political and cultural colonialism (of which European Christian missionaries were taking full advantage). Among the three responses to European colonialism, al-Afghani's was by far the most radical in revolutionary ideas and global perspective, with a clearly articulated conception of European imperialist designs around the world. Much of al-Afghani's ideas on Islamic revolutionary potentials and practices were in fact informed by this global perspective. Equally important was al-Afghani's trans-sectarian disposition, having been initially schooled in Shi'i philosophical predisposition to the rationalist (Mu'tazilite) school of theology, he did not think of himself as a Shi'i activist and freely expounded his political ideas to and through Muhammad Abduh, a staunchly Sunni (even anti-Shi'i) Egyptian. What al-Afghani took from Shi'ism, namely its philosophical proclivity to the Mu'tazilite principiality of the Oneness of God and His Everlasting Justice, he re-articulated in a universal Islamic vernacular autonomous of any sectarian coinage.[22] Equally important to al-Afghani and his disciples is the crossing of artificial (colonially manufactured) national boundaries. Of Afghan origin (Iranians claim him too and prefer to call him "Astarabadi"), al-Afghani freely associated with his fellow Muslims throughout the Islamic world and sought to formulate a pan-Islamic response to European colonialism. What is paramount in the ideas of al-Afghani-Abduh-Rida is that the collective fate of Muslims at the mercy of colonial modernity is the principal interlocutor of the ideas and aspirations they either revive from Islamic intellectual history or else initiate on their own. There is a hermeneutic cycle at work here that both generates new ideas and resuscitates older ones, but all in a dialogical conversation with the European colonial onslaught that in its Enlightenment ideas and material (military) superiority quintessentially challenged the Muslims world – in body and in spirit.[23]

The appeal of reformist movements such as those initiated by al-Afghani and followed by Abduh and Rida was far vaster in ideological domains than in actual class formations. These reformist ideas were articulated in a discursive space located somewhere in between the emerging modern bourgeoisie, in whose ideological disposition it partook freely in the globalized European Enlightenment modernity, and the urban poor, the impoverished and dislocated peasantry, and the bazaar mercantile class, and its organic links to the clerical establishment. There is no one-to-one correspondence between the ideals and aspirations of the generation of al-Afghani and his followers and any particular class formation. But as a catalytic force their ideas have been critically instrumental in generating anti-colonial and national liberation movements. Massive nineteenth-century anti-colonial movements, such as the one led by Abdel Qadir al-Jaza'iri (1808–1883) in Algeria against the French, or the Chechen leader Shaykh Shamyl (1796–1871) in the Caucasus against the Russians, or the Sansussi revolt in North Africa against Italians, and the Mahdists in Sudan against the British, were not directly influenced by these reformists' ideas.[24] But the globally articulated anti-colonial disposition of these ideas was catalytically important in occasioning such mass movements. The cumulative effects of both those ideas and these movements were identical and integral to a global Muslim response to European colonialism. Whether ideals of European Enlightenment were propagated as compatible with Islam, or else they generated a puritanical reaction, they both corroborated and ossified the generic notion of "the West" and were thus mutually integral in a systematic corrosion of pre-modern Islamic intellectual history and all its diverse discursive institutions.

For long after al-Afghani and his disciples, Egypt remained the intellectual capital of much of the Arab and Muslim world in producing pan-Islamic ideas and movements, the most significant of which was led by Hasan al-Banna (1906–1949) and organized around the activities of the Muslim Brotherhood that he had founded in 1928. With a global reach far beyond Egypt, the Muslim Brotherhood was motivated with a deeply rooted hatred of the British colonial domination of Egypt. The intellectual force of the Muslim Brotherhood was much reinvigorated when Sayyid Qutb (1906–1966) joined it in 1952. As the principal intellectual architect of the Muslim Brotherhood, Sayyid Qutb was deeply influenced by (1) the ideas and aspirations of the Indian reformist Abu al-Ala al-Mawdudi (1903–1979), whose ideas were in turn formulated in direct response to the British colonial occupation of his homeland; (2) a short visit Qutb had paid to the USA (1948–1950); and above all (3) the colonial occupation of Palestine and the subsequent establishment of the state of Israel.[25]

Much is made of the "anti-modern" or even "anti-modern civilization" attitudes and ideas of thinkers like Sayyid Qutb.[26] The minor detail that such assessments categorically fail to consider is the *colonial* context of the

Muslim reception of European modernity. European modernity came to Muslim lands through the gun barrel of colonialism. The British colonial occupation of India for Muslim ideologues like Mawdudi, the French, British, and even Italian colonial occupation of North Africa for militant activists like Sayyid Qutb, and most poignantly the European Zionist occupation of Palestine and the dispossession and expelling of millions of Palestinians from their homeland for effectively all Muslim liberation theologians were paramount in whatever they thought Muslims ought to do. Islam for such ideologues as Sayyid Qutb (as indeed for all Muslims) is the moral domain of legitimate defiance against injustice. They thus formulate a liberation theology, aka an Islamic Ideology, that opposes the quintessential injustice embedded in forcefully plundering a people of their dignity, ancestral land, and independence through the most brutal and vicious forms of colonial occupation and outright thievery of other people's natural resources. Muslims have never had access to European modernity except through colonialism – and thus their defiance against colonialism *ipso facto* means a rejection of European modernity. There was, in this particular case, no way to separate the baby from the bathwater.[27]

What people like Sivan and Werblowsky, or anyone else for that matter who dismisses and characterized Muslim ideologues of this period as anti-modern, fail to note is that such anti-colonial revolutionaries as Franz Fanon, Aimé Césaire, or Albert Memmi (who were not Muslim) were equally critical of the modernity that came through colonialism. The same is true of the entire liberation theology movement of Latin America – in fact all the way from Father Bartolomé de Las Casas (1484–1566) in the sixteenth century down to Gustavo Gutiérrez in the twentieth century. Fanon went so far as writing an essay (though flawed in its social assumptions) on the necessity and anti-colonial significance of Muslim veiling in Algeria.[28] Moreover, there is now for more than a century an exceedingly powerful moral and philosophical critique of the European modernity launched from within the European intellectual domain proper – particularly in the aftermath of the horrors of the Jewish Holocaust: from Nietzsche and Kierkegaard to Adorno and Horkheimer, to Heidegger and Derrida, Foucault and Levinas, down to Deleuze and Guattari, Baudrillard and Lyotard, and Paul de Man and Gianni Vattimo. Last time we checked none of these philosophers were militant Muslim ideologues, and yet their critique of Enlightenment modernity is infinitely more powerful and destabilizing of the project than anything suggested by any Muslim or any other anti-colonial ideologue. Whereas for much of the European critic of modernity it took the nightmare of the Holocaust to alert them to the terror (the "dialectic" as Adorno and Horkheimer preferred to call it) of their modernity, for the rest of the world that holocaust spelled out *colonialism* and was writ large around the globe. For reasons not too difficult to fathom, observers like Sivan and Werblowsky are too eager to brand Muslims barbarians incapable of grasping the splendor of European modern civilization (the way the very last vestige of European colonialism, what they call their "Israel," has been).

So the legitimate and perfectly poignant critic of a modernity that was exported throughout the world via European colonialism is neither limited to Muslims nor indeed necessarily philosophically flawed, but above all amounts to a barbaric refusal of "modern civilization." Why and how the Islamic liberation theologies of the last 200 years failed has nothing to do with its perfectly legitimate reasons to oppose a modernity that European colonialism had delivered to Muslims' doorsteps. Islamic Ideology failed – and it is a good thing that it failed for the horrors of the Islamic republic of Iran is the microcosm of the terror that it would have perpetrated upon the entirety of the Muslim world if it had succeeded. Islamic ideologies failed and their failure is good because their principal interlocutor was the grand narrative of "Western modernity," in which it paradoxically but freely partook and of which it became a carbon copy – and thus systematically mutating the multifaceted reality of Muslim intellectual history into a solitary site of ideological resistance to colonialism and as a result manufacturing a principally intolerant, short-sighted, puritanical, and outright fanatical worldview, particularly when it came down to the critical question of civil (women in particular) rights. For this calamity no one was more directly responsible than Muslim ideologues themselves. In combatant conversation with "Western modernity," implicitly partaking in its metaphysical violence, as Gianni Vattimo aptly calls it,[29] Muslim ideologues effectively took the epistemic modality of Islamic law (*Shari'ah*) and categorically mutated it into an absolutist ideology identical in its intensity, ferocity, and fanaticism to all other ideologies with which it competed – ranging from socialism to nationalism, and above all identical in its arrogance with the European modernity it engaged in a combatant conversation. What was systematically lost in the process was not just the democratic diversity of various schools of Islamic law (four canonical Sunni plus two Shi'i schools) and theology, but infinitely more important the counter-narratives of theo-erotic Sufism and polyfocal Islamic philosophical disposition – all of which had been historically underwritten by a powerful literary humanism (*Adab*). The range of Islamic political ideologies and movements were thus bound to inevitable and welcome failure. But while they lasted, and as they gave expression to the struggles of millions of Muslims the world over, they were perfectly legitimate, natural, necessary, and welcomed modes of resistance to the savageries of European colonialism. From the hindsight of the terrors of the Islamic republic of Iran we can welcome the ultimate failure of Islamic ideologies, but we cannot condemn Muslims all over the world for having rethought their faith and picked up arms to resist the creatures that had gone half-way around the globe to steal, rob, and deny them their humanity. A recognition of the moral and political failures of Islamic ideologies are thus not an occasion to blame bygone generations for what they had to do, but an opportunity to rethink their manner of moral and political resistance in a way that will make that resistance even more effective but not susceptible to political tyranny – and Muslims, as historical agents, and Islam, as a cosmopolitism world religion, are perfectly capable of that critical self-reflection.

It is the common colonial experiences of the Muslim ideologues of this period that unites them in their collective opposition to colonial modernity and deeply affects their reading of their own faith in combatant conversation with European modernity. As the principal intellectual architect of Muslim Brotherhood, Sayyid Qutb was very much attracted to the ideas of the Indian reformist Mawlana Sayyid Abu al-'A'la Mawdudi (1903–1979), who had in turn helped establish his version of the Muslim Brotherhood (he called it *Jama'at-i Islami* – Islamic Society) in Pakistan in 1941. The origin of Muslim awakening in the Indian subcontinent goes back to Sir Seyyed Ahmad Khan (1817–1898), long before al-Mawdudi, and was equally shaped by his contemporary Allamah Muhammad Iqbal (1875–1938).

Mawlana Mawdudi was one of the most significant Muslim ideologues of his generation. His version of Islam was actively reconstructed during one of the most crucial episodes in the history of Muslim encounters with colonial modernity. Born and bred in the Indian subcontinent during the heyday of British colonialism, Mawlana Mawdudi crafted his revivalist rendition of Islam in direct response to the rising needs of Indian Muslims to define their post/colonial identity and destiny.[30] Evident in the political life and ideological disposition of Mawlana Mawdudi is that dialogical mechanism through which politically viable remembrances of the medieval memories of "Islam" became possible in response to the intertwined projects of modernity and colonialism. Mawdudi's life coincided with the last vestiges of the British colonial rule in India. By tracing the life and the ideas of Mawlana Mawdudi through his formative years in colonial India up to and including his turn to Islamic revivalism, we observe one of the earliest systematizations of a political program of action, later to be institutionalized in the *Jama'at-i Islami*, Mawdudi's political party, in which distanced memories of a sacred imagination came to meet the challenges of the overpowering project of European colonial modernity. That project was brought into the Indian subcontinent by the inevitable logic of the capitalist mode of production – the creation of surplus value, the need for raw material and cheap labor, an open and expansive market, imperialist competition among the emerging capitalist economies, and ultimately the military arm of all these interrelated developments: colonialism. The mode of revivalism in which Mawdudi renarrated Islam was dictated by the political necessity of giving millions of Indian Muslims a cohesive identity, a pride of place, with which to negotiate a space for themselves against the simultaneous forces of Hindu sectarianism, on one hand, and the Indian nationalist and socialist projects, on the other – all under the overriding presence of British colonialism. Unmistakably evident in Mawlana Mawdudi's conception of an Islamic state is the totalizing narrative of modernity successfully disguised in a patently Islamic language. Equally important to Mawdudi is the radical transformation of an ideologue from a modernizing visionary into an active political pragmatist once the colonial project ended with the partition of India and the formation of Pakistan as an autonomous Muslim state.

Surrounded by the Indian subcontinent on one side and the Arab Muslim world on the other, Iran was influenced by anti-colonial ideas and movements in both these regions, more directly experiencing the pointed onslaught of European colonialism. Iran was never officially colonized as were India, Egypt and much of the rest of the Arab and Muslim world, but shared in every other aspects of a colonial experience. Among the first Muslim ideologues of anti-colonial uprising in Iran was Mulla Ahmad Naraqi (1771–1829), who early in the nineteenth century was critically important in mobilizing national Shi'i sentiments against Russian colonial incursions into Qajar territories. Perhaps his most enduring significance was his formulation of the notion of "the authority of the jurisconsult" (*Velayat-e Faqih*), which later became a central organizing idea of Ayatollah Khomeini's (1900–1989) revolutionary ideology.[31] A crucial characteristic of Mulla Ahmad Naraqi that will be repeated by many other religious revolutionaries was that he was far more socially active than scholastically trained. Biographers of Mulla Ahmad Naraqi report that he had not traveled or studied in major scholastic learning as had all the other major clerics.[32] His principal teacher was his father, Mulla Mehdi Naraqi. Instead, Mulla Ahmad was a gifted poet with an exquisite command of his craft. Naraqi gradually emerged as an exceedingly powerful cleric, dismissing and appointing governors in his home state of Kashan. The reigning monarch, Fath Ali Shah (reigned, 1797–1834) was quite attentive to Naraqi's wishes and demands, asking him to translate for him into Persian works on ethics of kingship and piety. Naraqi was instrumental in mobilizing Iranians against the successive Russian invasion of northern Qajar territories and the gradual annexation of considerable Central Asian domains following two successive treaties of Golestan (1813) and Turkamanchai (1828). Mulla Ahmad personally attended the military camp of Crown Prince Abbas Mirza (1786–1833) wearing a shroud and ready for battle and martyrdom. Mulla Ahmad Naraqi is also known for having written a polemical tract against a British missionary called Henry Martin, who had traveled to Iran, pretended to have converted to Islam, and then launched a theological disputation against Muslims.[33]

The role that Mulla Ahmad Naraqi played in mobilizing forces against the Russian incursions into Northern Qajar territories was to be repeated later in the century by Ayatollah Mirza Shirazi (1815–1895) against colonial concessions that the British had exacted from corrupt Qajar rulers. Following the grant of a major contract to a British company for a monopoly over the production and distribution of tobacco in 1889, Mirza Shirazi wrote a succession of letters to the reigning monarch, Nasir al-Din Shah (1848–1896), prohibiting him against this colonial concession. When his letters were left unanswered, Mirza Shirazi issued a famous *fatwa* (edict) prohibiting the use of tobacco, and thus instigating a major national crisis, which eventually forced the reigning monarch to cancel the contract. "The Tobacco Revolt," as it was later dubbed, effectively became a dress rehearsal for the Constitutional Revolution of 1906–1911, led by two major clerics – Seyyed Abdullah Behbahani and Seyyed Muhammad Tabataba'i. Although the support of the clerical class for the constitutional revolution was not unanimous, and such prominent clerics as Sheykh Fazlollah Nuri (1842–1909) actively and adamantly opposed it, the progressive elements within the clergy were chiefly responsible for the success of the revolution. Although Seyyed Abdullah Behbahani and Seyyed Muhammad Tabataba'i led the revolutionary uprising against absolutist monarchy, the principal theoretical tract of the period was written by Sheykh Muhammad Hossein Na'ini (1860–1936). His *Tanbih al-Ummah wa Tanzih al-Millah* (1909) is one of the most significant political texts of the early twentieth century, articulating a decidedly Shi'i anti-colonial politics. Na'ini was as much active in the course of the constitutional revolution of 1906–1911 as he was in Iraq against the British, who in 1920 had taken colonial control of that country, having installed Faysal, the son of Hussein bin Ali, the Sharif of Mecca, as their puppet king on 23 August 1921.

Na'ini's *Tanbih al-Ummah wa Tanzih al-Millah* went through many successive editions, one of which, published in 1955 had an introduction by a radical cleric named Mahmoud Taleqani (1910–1979), who later became a leading revolutionary activist in the decades leading to the 1979 Islamic revolution in Iran. Almost coterminous with Taleqani was yet another major clerical revolutionary, Ayatollah Motahhari (1920–1979), who wrote extensively on a vast spectrum of social, political, and philosophical issues. On a separate track, and equally important in their revolutionary impacts, were the writings of Jalal Al-e Ahmad and Ali Shari'ati (1933–1977). Banking on both these tracks was the single-minded determination of the revolutionary ascetic Ayatollah Khomeini (1900–1989), who ultimately succeeded in bringing down the Pahlavi monarchy.[34]

If Na'ini's political thoughts and activism in the early part of the twentieth century were articulated primarily against British colonialism in the region, their active adaptation and expansion by the generation of Ayatollah Taleqani and his fellow clerics – leading all the way to Ayatollah Khomeini – were principally charged against US imperialism in the very same region. There is thus a logical consistency and a historical continuity between the articulation of militant Islamic ideas and actions that began with active ideological and political opposition to European colonialism and ended with similar responses to American imperialism – systematically razing the polyfocality of its own medieval intellectual disposition, while transforming Islam into a singular site of ideological resistance to European colonialism and US imperialism. It is thus very easy, the way for example Olivier Roy does in *The Failure of Political Islam* (1996), to point to the constitutional failures of radical Islamic ideas and movements over the last 200 years. But in the absence of any critical attention to European colonial domination of these societies we will have no idea who and what these Muslims were arguing against. Their ideas and actions, as a result, are all put together as an indication that they simply have a constitutional (pathological) fear of modernity or an inability to come to terms with the modern world, very much what Bernard Lewis and other Zionist Islamist historians have been telling the world over the last half a century. One cannot resist the observation that while Olivier Roy's French ancestors were chiefly responsible for savagely plundering North Africa and thus generating an Islamic response (as well as anti-colonial nationalist and socialists responses), he is now here to tell North Africans and other Muslims that their politics have failed to secure institutions of civil liberty for them. He is of course right. But the principal source of the disease is in Olivier Roy's own French colonial history, now extended into a new phase of neo-Orientalism of the sort that Olivier Roy and Gilles Kepel, yet another French Islamist, best represent.

On Monday 24 March, 1980, the day that Archbishop Óscar Romero (1917–1980) was assassinated in San Salvador, a mimeographed hate sheet had appeared in the streets comparing the courageous liberation theologian to Ayatollah Khomeini.[35] The thematic, social, and revolutionary similarities and correspondences between the Christian and Islamic versions of liberation theology does not begin or end in that momentous occasion. Although there are no apparent reasons to believe that Ayatollah Khomeini and Archbishop Óscar Romero had any direct contact with each other, the fact that at the time of Archbishop Romero's assassination, Ayatollah Khomeini had been on the front page of the world media for more than a year, as he was busy toppling the Pahlavi monarch, makes the comparison quite timely and self-evident. The enemies of the archbishop had a perfect sense of what exactly moves liberation theologians – Muslim or Christian.

A principal problem with our understanding of militant Islamic ideologies and movements over the last 200 years is that they are mostly treated in isolation, and rarely along the lines of other national and regional liberation movements. The rise and demise of Islamic ideologies need to be read in the comparative context of the similar fate of all other ideologies, and the crisis (or what the distinguished American sociologist Daniel Bell has called *the end*) of ideology in general.[36] Islamic ideologies the world over emerged in responses to European colonialism and in sideways dialogical conversations with other anti-colonial (nationalist and socialist) ideologies in their immediate neighborhood. As forms of liberation theologies, moreover, Islamic ideologies of the last two centuries, must also be seen in conjunction with their Christian counterparts, the liberation theology that emerged in Latin America in particular. To be sure, there are many serious differences between Christian and Islamic liberation theologies, in both context and content, as indeed there are many similarities. But both their differences and their similarities point to an identical source in their mutual rise: the predatory power of European colonialism and American imperialism and their wanton disregard for human decency.

The history of European colonial savageries in Latin America and various revolutionary reactions to them go back to the fifteenth century, when Muslims were still ruled by three Islamic empires – the Ottomans, the Safavids, and the Mughals. The rise of Islamic liberation theologies in earnest dates back to the early nineteenth century when British, French, and Russian colonial adventures in the region ushered in a variety of ideological and political responses, including those rooted in a militant reinterpretation of Islam. In Latin America, the roots of liberation theology is rightly traced back to the heroic activism of Father Bartolomé de Las Casas (1484–1566) and to his eloquent defense of the defenseless native Americans, *A Brief Account of the Destruction of the Indies* (1552), which left behind for posterity an eyewitness account of the criminal atrocities of Spanish colonialism in the Americas, particularly in the Caribbean, in Central America, and in Mexico. From the time of Father Bartolomé de Las Casas in the sixteenth century to the rise of liberation theology across Latin America in the mid-1950s – with the establishment of the CELAM (*Conselho Episcopal Latino Americano* – Latin American Episcopal Conference) in 1955 in Rio de Janeiro (Brazil) – the history of Latin American liberation theology is interwoven with varied responses to European colonial thieveries. But it was in direct response to US imperialism and the trail of miseries that it left behind in Latin America that the new wave of liberation theology began to take shape and momentum in the 1960s. During the course of their 1968 Medellin Conference in Colombia, CELAM articulated the terms of a liberation theology which was best theorized by the Peruvian priest Gustavo Gutiérrez in his *A Theology of Liberation: History, Politics and Salvation* (1972), although some have also identified the Brazilian Friar Father Rubem Alves' doctoral dissertation (subsequently published), written at Princeton, "A Theology of Human Hope" (1968), as a precursor of Latin American liberation theology.[37] The history of Latin American liberation theology thus in effect embraces that of the Islamic, pre-dates it back to the sixteenth century, remains dormant during the heydays of Islamic liberation theologies in much of the nineteenth and early part of the twentieth century, and then rejoins it from the mid-twentieth century forward. What remains constant in both Christian and Islamic liberation theologies is first and foremost their common reactions first to the European and then American colonial and imperial savageries, and second their respective conversations with nationalist and socialist ideas in general and with Marxism in particular – so much so that the idea and aspiration of Gustavo Gutiérrez are almost identical with those of Ali Shari'ati.

Another major difference between Islamic and Christian liberation theologies is the conservative power and the normative predominance of an ecclesiastical order in Catholicism and its absence in Islam. Latin American liberation theologians, who are all Catholic, have had to deal with the Vatican systematically objecting to their social concerns and accusing them of materialism, Marxism, and even heresy with Cardinal Joseph Ratzinger (now Pope Benedict XVI) and his predecessor, Pope John Paul II, having been chiefly responsible for chastising, condemning, and doctrinally refuting liberation theology and its widespread appeal among the poor and the disenfranchised. Precisely because of this tight control of the Vatican over the ecclesiastical order, and despite its origins in the ideas and activism of Bartolomé de Las Casas, Christian liberation theology does not start in earnest until much later in the twentieth century, while the savageries of European colonialism in Latin America were no less than those in Muslim lands in Asia and Africa. European colonial adventures in Latin America throughout the nineteenth and twentieth centuries do not produce a liberation theology on par with Muslims' precisely because of the Vatican's tight control of the doctrines of the faith and *also* because of the principiality of the role of Christianity itself in colonialism. Much of the history of Christianity throughout the classical period of colonialism, from the sixteenth century forward, around the world is the history of the official European Christianity aiding and abetting the cause of European colonialism. The best case in point is Juan Ginés de Sepúlveda (1490–1573), a Spanish theologian who was the principal nemesis of Bartolomé de las Casas in justifying the Spanish colonial conquest of the Americas. The overwhelming function of Christianity after Sepúlveda in the colonial world has been to consider the non-white natives as savages and beasts and at best tell them to turn the other cheek as their fellow colonial officers slap them in the face. It was not until the 1960s, when the whole world was up in arms, and when revolutionary movements led by the generation of Che Guevara (and before him by Jose Martí) in Latin America finally put Christian theologians to shame. The execution of Che Guevara in 1967 in Bolivia and the almost simultaneous rise of Christian liberation theology in Brazil, Colombia, and the rest of Latin America cannot be totally coincidental. The Christ-like figure of the executed Che (in 1967) must have very much been on the mind of liberation theologians like Rubem Alves (in 1968) and Gustavo Gutiérrez (in 1972) when they put pen to paper to write the particulars of their faith in a manner that responded to the misery that Jose Martí and then Che Guevara's generations of Marxist revolutionaries sought to address.

Any comparative assessment of Islamic and Christian liberation theologies raises the obvious question of Judaism. What about Judaism? After a long and noble history of safeguarding the dignity and identity of a people against overwhelming atrocities and prejudices, it has been the contemporary historical fate of Judaism not to have joined Islam and Christianity in producing a militant liberation theology launched against the horrors of colonialism. Not only that, and quite paradoxically, Judaism has in fact given rise to political Zionism, itself integral and definitive first and foremost to European colonialism and then US imperialism. Theodor Herzl (1860–1904) cuts a figure far more similar to that of Juan Ginés de Sepúlveda than to Bartolomé de las Casas. It is thus quite odd and entirely paradoxical that the political equivalent but moral reverse of both Islamic and Christian liberation theologies has been Zionism – itself a European colonial project aiming at the establishment of a colonial settlement on the broken back of another people. Zionism has thus implicated Judaism in one of the most vicious and barbaric acts of colonial occupation and domination in Palestine, rather than being the voice of defiance and rebellion against global domination. Today Zionism has implicated Judaism in by far the vilest and most violent imperial machineries the world has ever seen. Israel, a Jewish state founded on Zionism, replicates, augments, and extends the imperial savageries of the USA in its region. What ever might be the future of Christian and Islamic liberation theologies, Judaism still has the horrors of Zionism to account for before it can claim the horrors of Nazi Germany and the Jewish Holocaust for an entirely different purpose than stealing another people's country and calling it "Israel."

No comparative assessment of Islamic liberation theology is complete without an awareness of the rise of a political theology from a corner that has caught much of the contemporary philosophical world by storm: Karl Schmitt's political theology, formulated right from the heart of European Nazi Germany. Karl Schmitt's *Political Theology* (1922) and *The Concept of the Political* (1932) emerged at one of the most critical moments in European self-reflection on the inner contradictions of its Enlightenment modernity, when the crisis of the Weimar Republic was about to give birth to the monstrosity of Nazism. Schmitt's argument that the defining moment of the political was not polity but enmity became, for him, the moral and normative fountainhead of generating ideals and aspirations for which people will be ready to kill and die. It is good and providential, Schmitt thought, that men go to war to kill each other for what they believe in – this is how the providence, the Catholic philosopher and legal theorist believed, has seen to it that superior ideals are generated and sustained in a culture. The constitution of an enemy is thus *ipso facto* also constitutive of what is good (and what Kant would also add) sublime and beautiful. Thus for Schmitt liberalism was the absolute last enemy of humanity, a moral atheism that allows anything to go and fights for absolutely nothing. Schmitt despised liberals because they neutralize the enemy and thus kill the political, and with the political, for Schmitt, they deny the divine the worldly domain of His Providence, the site of moral regeneration.

What the recent scholarship of Heinrich Meier has revealed is Leo Strauss's rejoinder to Schmitt, pushing the boundaries of the latter's theological disposition to specifically philosophical domains.[38] Reading Schmitt and Strauss through the groundbreaking work of Heinrich Meier, one cannot help thinking that in fact both Schmitt and Strauss, at evident odds with each other, speak identically from the absolute abstractions of faith for the former and nature for the latter – and as such addressing what cannot but culminate in political fascism of one sort for Schmitt (Nazism) or another for Strauss (American imperialism). No such abstraction, needless to say, is even possible on the colonial edges of the selfsame European modernity that at one acutely critical moment in the fragile Weimar Republic gave rise to the monstrosity of Nazism, the political theology of Schmitt, *and* the political philosophy of Leo Strauss all at the same time.

Karl Schmitt's nightmare was that liberal democracies will one day dominate and rule the world – a prognostication now aptly fulfilled in the bureaucratic declaration of the end of history by Francis Fukuyama, which amounts to yet another ping-pong game between European (German) Fascism and American imperialism categorically not just seeking to rule the world but forgetting that from the vantage point of the world at large people have absolutely no use or patience for their philosophical gesticulations. The varieties of liberation theologies launched either from the colonial edges of European modernity or else from within the ghettos of the metropolitan "West" have not been cast from the absolutist abstractions of The Political (Schmitt) or The Philosophical (Strauss) for us in turn to take our pick and choose between the two sorts of fascism that Schmitt and Strauss offer. Liberation theologies from Latin America to Muslim lands to the hearts of Harlem and ghettos of Chicago, New Orleans, Miami, Michigan, and Los Angeles have been offered from the material evidence of history, and the enemy that they constitute is no theological abstraction or philosophical proposition – it is the real enemy, it is the machinery of white European colonialism (followed by white American imperialism) that demands and exacts raw material and cheap labor with the same logic that mutates that cheap labor to nothing but that raw material – and in the dangerous delusions of its theological and philosophical abstractions produces Schmitt and Strauss and then posits them as two absolutist opposites, where they are in fact identical terrors.

Regretting too much attention that Schmitt's theology had received after the publication of his book on Schmitt and Strauss, Heinrich Meier wished that when the English translation of his book came out in the USA, Americans would compensate for this imbalance and pay more attention to Strauss and his philosophical propositions in contradistinction to Schmitt's theology. "As far as I can tell," wrote Heinrich Meier in his February 1995 Preface to "the American edition," of his book, "the reception of the book thus far in Germany, as well as in France and Japan, where translations appeared in 1990 and 1993, respectively, has concentrated almost exclusively on Schmitt and political theology. Perhaps the publication of the American edition will bring greater attention to the other side, Strauss and political philosophy."[39] This wish was uttered in 1995 when the American edition of

Meier's book appeared – precisely at the moment when the American Straussians were positioning themselves as a brand name called neoconservatism to take over the democratic institutions of the USA and hand them over to the Bush administration.[40] In the events after 9/11 professor Meier did indeed have his wishes fulfilled and an entire empire began to take Leo Strauss more seriously, and if Schmitt's predilections were coterminous with the rise of Nazi Germany as a particularly nasty manifestation of his political theology, the US empire under the Bush administration was the historical rendezvous of Leo Strauss with an even more monstrous hatred of liberal democracies.

In one critical observation, Heinrich Meier remains categorically correct, that Schmitt's anti-Semitism must be understood not despite his conception of The Political but in fact through it. "The question raised by Schmitt's decision of 1933 in favor of the Third Reich," Heinrich Meier aptly points out, "has not been appropriately asked so long as it is addressed to Schmitt the "reckless adventurer" or "opportunist." The question must be aimed directly at Schmitt the political theologian."[41] The Enemy for Schmitt in his Catholic conception of The Political was The Jew, The Gypsy, The Foreigner, and ultimately The Oriental – the mode of racist constitution of "The West" of which "Islam and the West" is but one poignant example, and it is precisely the same Schmittian proposition that in the first generation of Leo Strauss's disciples (Paul Wolfowitz studied with Joseph Cropsey, Francis Fukuyama with Harvey Mansfield)[42] mutates, in the course of George W. Bush's war of terrorism, into the constitution of The Muslim and The Arab as precisely the same philosophical Other that makes the Straussian polity possible. Schmitt and Strauss are not even the *two* sides of the same coin. They are on the identical side of the same nightmare. "After all," Strauss is reported to have pointed out at one point, "he [Schmitt] could not possibly allow himself to acknowledge his dependence on a Jew."[43] Strauss was of course correct in pinpointing Schmitt's anti-Semitism, concealing his indebtedness to Strauss's critique of his ideas. But Strauss himself, as subtextually evident in the letters that Strauss wrote to Schmitt before the latter had joined the Nazi party,[44] remains far too indebted to Schmitt than he was willing to admit.

Finally, our reconsideration of liberation theologies across the Muslim lands will have also to include similar theologies that have emerged from the heart of the metropolitan miseries of the underclass and the subaltern within the heart of the imperium where, whether from Martin Luther King's Christianity or Malcolm X's Islam, we witness a struggle almost identical with their counterparts in Latin America, Africa, or Asia. The era of the Civil Rights Movements in the USA, particularly in the ideas and activisms of Martin Luther King Jr. (1929–1968) and Malcolm X (1925–1965), provides ample opportunities to map out a larger frame of reference in any assessment of Islamic and Christian liberation theologies in a manner that is no longer limited to the colonial peripheries of Euro-American imperialism but sees a far more transnational and planetary domain for the operation of presumed divine providence in addressing the terrors perpetrated on the poor and the disenfranchised the world over.[45]

The task facing the next generation of scholarship, theory, and activism is radically different from the current practice of looking into political Islamism in order to understand the nature and function of spectacular acts of violence that militant Muslims commit.[46] I believe the common and current understanding of militant Islam continues to operate on an outdated epistemic assumption that we have inherited from the colonial phase of the Muslim encounter with European modernity. That form and manner of Islamic ideological production has now ended, and we thus need to begin to articulate the terms of an emerging geopolitics and, more importantly, the liberation theology that is contingent on the changing parameters of a whole new social history for a globalized Islam.

My counterintuitive suggestion, against all the current and dominant wisdom and propaganda alike, is that the collapse of the Twin Towers of the World Trade Center in New York City on September 11 2001 also imploded the twin towers of "Islam and the West" as the most potent binary oppositions crafted and constructed in the course of colonial modernity. At once postcolonial and postmodern, the emerging global reconfiguration of power has no use for that outdated binary, but plenty of room for the globalized empire and manners of revolutionary resistance to it. The specifically Islamic manners of opposing this empire in the aftermath of the "Islam and the West" binary opposition will engage and preoccupy a generation of a whole new pattern of thinking and activism. The signs of this resistance are all over the globe – but still too early to read because the dying ashes of the old dialectic and the emerging fire of the new are mixed. Throughout the colonial world in the course of the nineteenth and the twentieth centuries, anti-colonial nationalism, Soviet-style socialism, and liberation theologies were the rampant modes of resistance to European colonialism and American imperialism. In the course of the twenty-first century, neither anti-colonial nationalism nor Soviet-style socialism will have much ideological zest or energy to offer. People will inevitably resort to their most common denominator and most basic instincts. A new wave of liberation theologies will thus follow the current phase of iconic violence that at this moment, and as exemplified in the events of 9/11, meets the challenge of the amorphous capital and its wayward empire. Such liberation theologies will obviously emerge in the hotbed of poverty and disenfranchisement – with Latin America for Christian, and Asia and Africa for Islamic versions of it. To the extent that Zionism and the state of Israel claim it, Judaism has sided with the amorphous empire and will have no historical rendezvous with its other Abrahamic versions. But the moral authority of Judaism, as indeed the honored memory of the victims of the Jewish Holocaust in Europe, can never be exhausted by Israel, no matter how horrendous, how barbaric, its military occupation of another people's homeland. Signs of prophetic Judaism seeking to salvage the mother of all world religions from the vagaries of the Zionist colonial adventurism are already evident from the peace activists in Israel to progressive synagogues across the globe, particularly in the USA. "The prophetic tradition," in the words of Noam Chomsky, "is very much alive today. We just call it dissidence."[47] Islam too will have its official al-Azhar version in Cairo (actively supporting or tacitly condoning the medieval potentate of Husni Mubarak), as well as its nightmarish theocratic version in the Islamic republic, as will Christianity its Christian fundamentalist side in the USA, as well as a notoriously conservative Cardinal Joseph Ratzinger as Pope Benedict XVI – both joining the Judaism claimed by Zionism and Israel in siding with and in fact constituting predatory power. All religions will share the fate of Christianity and have their versions of Bartolomé de Las Casas and Juan Ginés de Sepúlveda. But from the slums of Cairo to the shantytowns in the suburbs of Casablanca, and from concrete blocks of poverty in Mexico to *campesino* cooperatives in Guatemala, all the way to the pockets of poverty and resistance in the USA itself, Islam and Christianity will have other sites and sights of hope and despair.

Islam is now on the verge of a new worldly reconfiguration in its long and languid history, a mode of historical repositioning that reflects and corresponds with the amorphous capital and its corresponding global empire. The circumstances of the demise of militant Islamism (with all the services it proffered and all the atrocities it inevitably committed – like all other ideologies) and the conditions of its current decline are all the signs of its future reconfigurations. The demise of political Islam as we have known and documented it over the last 200 years is coterminous with the collective fate of people around the globe, all of them now in the throes of an emerging global empire, generating emergent modes of anti-imperial resistances to it. If we do not fully document the end of militant Islamism as we have known it – as once a particularly potent mode of revolutionary resistance to colonial modernity – and continue to think in outdated terms, we will be dangerously delusional and thus blinded both to the imperial configuration of the emerging empire and the necessary modalities of resistance that it is beginning to engender and dialectically empower and legitimize. A historical examination of the rise and demise of militant Islamism, as a result, is a test case study of one particular mode of resistance to imperialism; and an attempt to articulate the broad outlines of what is succeeding in its stead is a necessary move to see the particulars of the empire itself – its manners of self-hegemonizing and thus inadvertently manufacturing its own antidotes, manners of resisting, and modes of puncturing it. As the empire is trying to modulate itself on the model of a guerilla organization it purports to battle (al-Qaeda), it has (unbeknown to itself) its real guard down, thus exposing the terms of its own defeat. With a bizarre combination of hubris and stupidity, the emerging empire takes its cues from old hands like Samuel Huntington and Bernard Lewis, who are still advising its generals in very old and tired terms. The military machinery and the intelligence arm of the emerging empire are light years apart (its smart bombs are guided by very stupid strategists) – and that precisely is its Achilles heel (but it does not know it). If there was ever an empire with not even a claim to hegemony, the American empire is it. This particular neoconservative empire has neither a Virgil nor even a Kipling.

Released from the binary nexus of "Islam and the West," Islam as the faith of a globalized community, and the imperial proclivities innate to the operation of capital continue to be evident and commanding the most sacrosanct pieties of millions of people around the globe. What precisely is the nature and function of that globalized imperial power and what an Islamic (or any other) mode of resistance to it would be is still too early to tell. A few facts are evident and articulating them in some detail will clear the air for further urgent reflections. If, as I suggest, the supposition of an eternal conflict between "Islam and the West" has exhausted its fabricated ferocity and is thus no longer a legitimate binary, and if, as I also propose, "the West" has lost all its categorical legitimacy to be an antagonistic interlocutor for Islam – what then? Today Muslims, as do millions of other people around the globe who do not confess their faith but share their fate, face an incessantly globalized empire whose amorphous shape has not yet allowed for an articulated response. The task ahead of us, Muslim or otherwise, is to articulate and historicize the contours of that response.

The deadly danger that this globalized empire poses is no mere theoretical proposition. Ever since 9/11, the USA and Israel are consistently perceived around the globe, poll after poll, as two lawless warmongers and a consistent danger to global peace.[48] There is plenty of justifiable reason for this anger and resentment against the USA and its colonial subsidiary Israel. An estimated 655,000 people are reported killed in Iraq alone after the US-led invasion. Not even Saddam Hussein murdered that many people in Iraq – and he was a mass murderer, executed in the US–UK occupied Iraq for the murder of 148 Shi'is. If Saddam Hussein must be hanged for the murder of 148 people in Iraq, people obviously wonder, then who is responsible for the murder of 655,000 other Iraqis since the illegal and immoral US-led invasion of that sovereign nation-state, and what court should pass a judgment on them?[49] Not a single day passes without the USA (and Israel) producing one evidence after another to justify their reputation of state-sponsored terrorism and global warmongering around the world. Egregious disregard for international law and world opinion, illegal arrests and incarcerations, a widespread networks of subterranean torture chambers, legal theorists (Allan Dershowitz) and human rights scholars (Michael Ignatieff) openly and widely circulating their ideas on how to torture people, the moral degeneracy of the very idea of preventive war, unconditional support for the vilest and most retrograde corrupt regimes around the world, equally unconditional endorsement of the Israeli criminal occupation and systematic eradication of Palestine and Palestinians, a wanton disregard for human, civil, and women's rights around the globe, an equally atrocious record of not caring what calamity befalls our environmental condition, while criminally neglecting the social and economic wellbeing of millions of poor and disenfranchised Americans, are among the hallmarks of the American empire. If even before the US-led invasion of Iraq in March 2003, hundreds of thousands of Iraqi children were killed because of a US-initiated economic embargo, the Bush administration's record of childcare within the USA is not any nobler. Massive cuts in social programs involving single mothers as well as job-training and healthcare projects, for example, have been the chief accomplishments of the Bush administration and its tax cuts that categorically benefit the rich and harm the poor. Meanwhile, if Afghanistan was not a sufficient sign of the catastrophe of neoconservative imperialism, Iraq has proved positively nerve-wracking to face and fathom the diabolic disposition of this band of criminal thugs riding on a constellation of banal and bankrupt ideas. For this gang of highway bandits, camouflaged in clean-shaven faces and wearing ugly ties and polyester business suits, war is unconditionally good and peace is unfathomably bad. These bureaucratic banalities think the world and all its inhabitants virtually within their laptop screens on which they imagine remapping the world after the image of their own tormented minds. They actively re-invoke the colonial image of Lawrence of Arabia, sadistically sewing the seeds of violence and hatred and then *they* call their critics "extremists." Bernard Lewis, one of their prophets of doom, advises them that Arabs and Muslims should fear and respect them, and should never be even considered worthy of hating the criminals that have afflicted their world. They joke and tease and cavort with the most vicious ideas ever uttered and they ascribe namesake doctrines to each other. The Bush Doctrine, the Wolfowitz Doctrine, the Ledeen Doctrine, *ad nauseum*. What is the Ledeen Doctrine? "Every ten years or so, the USA needs to pick up some small crappy little country and throw it against the wall, just to show the world we mean business."[50] The same Ledeen character, the would-be Machiavelli of this ghoulish aping of an age that at least produced a Michelangelo for proportionately childish atrocities that it committed, has written a book on Machiavelli in which he barefacedly, as if no one is watching, speaks of how war is in fact a virtue, peace a vice – war producing such qualities as "manly vigor," "virility," and "character," peace "insolence," "corruption" and "effeminate behaviour" – and then this banality hires the Hirsi Alis, Azar Nafisis, and Irshad Manjis of the Muslim world to help them go liberate Muslim women.[51] These creatures speak of "robust imperialism," of "tactical nuclear weapons," and of "campaigns of shock and awe." Such warmongering is taking place at a time when the military budget of the USA is reaching staggering heights, while the infrastructure of the society at large is crumbling without anyone, particularly at CNN or

The New York Times, making a fuss about this true terrorism that is endangering the life and dignity of the entire nation in whose name this barefaced imperialism is perpetrated. The world and its varied cultures, its hopes and aspirations, have all been mutated into a conglomerate of graceless thieveries called corporations with people like Bush, Cheney, and Rumsfeld at the head, a beneficiary minority immediately under and supporting them, and a global poverty of unfathomable proportions beneath them all. Some 870 million people go to sleep hungry every night around the globe, and this vicious barbarity allows itself the privilege of deciding what "civilization" is winning the historical game and the obscenity of declaring history ended. This empire means business, and resisting its vicious threats to the global peace cannot be limited to every once in a while picking up a Michael Ledeen here or a Bernard Lewis there, throwing their ignoble names and reputations against the wall of reason and sanity, just to show the world we too mean business. Resisting this empire requires a whole global effort to rethink the most sacrosanct, among them major world religions, which can be, as they have been, as much the source of criminal carnage as the springboard of a crescendo of enabling liberation theologies.

2 The end of Islamic ideology

Because my mouth
Is wide with laughter
And my throat
Is deep with song ...
Because my feet
Are gay with dancing
You do not know
I die?
Langston Hughes

In the previous chapter I put forward an argument that the emerging neo-conservative imperialism in the USA is the single most important danger to world peace, as evident in the blatant warmongering of its leading ideologues, rampant disregard for international law, and the trail of death and destruction that over his two terms in office President Bush has left behind in Afghanistan and Iraq. That this, or any other, mode of imperialism must be resisted by any means necessary is a self-evident fact. What is at issue here is whether or not major world religions – Judaism, Christianity, or Islam, in particular – can have a progressive role to play in resisting that predatory imperial proclivity, instead of either aiding and abetting it, as it is done in the name of Judaism and Christianity, or else launching insane acts of violence further exacerbating instead of resisting that empire, as it is done in the name of Islam. In the case of Islam in particular, over the last 200 years, roughly from the onslaught of European colonialism early in the nineteenth century in North Africa and southern and western Asia, it has had a major role in providing a combative anti-colonial ideology resisting the European and subsequently American domination of Muslim nations. Its positive role in contributing to that global resistance to brute power notwithstanding, that mode of Islamic Ideology was formed and framed in a dialogical opposition with a figment of perturbed imagination code-named "the West." As a self-raising/other-lowering category, "the West" was invented in the domain of colonial imagination but then corroborated by Muslim and other non-Westernized people around the globe, in fact getting into a combative mode of conversation against it.

That combat was of course not against an abstract category, but indeed against the factual ferocity of European colonialism first and American imperialism second. But that particular mode of planetary domination had opted to call itself "the West," and thus the anti-colonial movements inevitably called their enemy by its own name – and thus their dissident synergy was often termed "anti-Western," "anti-modern," and thus inevitably vile, violent, and barbaric. The result of this otherwise innocuous semiotics of domination was the gradual but systematic mutation of a multifaceted medieval religion (Islam) into a singular site of ideological resistance to foreign domination articulated in Islamic ideological terms. The particulars of that history of domination, encounter, and combativeness, I have argued, have now radically changed because the underlying moral and material basis of the world have started changing through a planetary phenomenon called *globalization*, a moment in contemporary history when under the pressure of an amorphous capital the power-basing cultural construction of "the West" has in fact lost all its meaning and epistemic prowess. "The West" has now ended and with it has also ended the particular conception of all the binary categories that it had once generated and sustained (via the intermediary of an army of mercenary Orientalists). In conjunction with the demise of "the West" and all its cultural and civilizational corollaries, Islam (now released from that forced conversation), as all other world religions that have had a share in resisting the planetary tendencies of global domination, will have to change if it is to remain pertinent and relevant to the earthly life of millions of people that confess it around the globe.

The phenomenon known as al-Qaeda and identified with the figure of Osama bin Laden and through the mind-bugling (but illiterate) neoconservative propaganda machinery – extended from multibillion dollar think-tanks to major news organizations – designated as the nemesis of this empire is certainly *not* that legitimate mode of resistance to this amorphous monster. Al-Qaeda is a ghostly apparition that reflects the vision of an illusory enemy that this empire seeks to fabricate and fight in order conversely to authenticate and corroborate itself. This time around neither Islam nor any other world religion having something to say or to do in resisting that empire must begin from the ground zero of historical facts and thus from a grassroots perception of reality that does not simply reciprocate the language of the conquerors in order to authenticate the terms of its resistances. This time around the language of resistance must be domestic and definitive to the people who do the resisting. If Francis Fukuyama, Samuel Huntington, and Bernard Lewis (most emphatically the last one) decide and determine the terms of a civilizational conflict, the language of resistance to the empire that these three strategists (among others) represent and seek to theorize must not be in terms that further corroborate their delusions, but that in fact dismantles and overcomes them – overcomes them by first noting their delusional dispositions, then by recognizing that these are habitual smoke screens that capital always creates in cultural and civilizational terms, and finally by articulating the terms of resisting that empire in modes and manners domestic to liberation theologies that unites the grassroots movements in Judaism, Christianity, and Islam, and thus ultimately in cross-cultural terms that in fact overcomes all such tribal affiliations and sees the common human misery they all seek to address. Because the nature of this empire is amorphous, then Islam, like all other world religions that may have a share in resisting it, must radically rethink its terms of principled opposition to global domination – and it must do so in terms that includes the most disenfranchised and forsaken at the very heart of the imperium.

Predicated on that argument, in this chapter[1] I wish to provide a historical account of the demise of Islamic Ideology in its last gasp for air, so we can move on to our current condition without any delusional hang up, thus always a prey to the campaign of disinformation and lies that targets our sanity and intelligence. Here I intend to demonstrate how after a long history of almost two centuries of battling colonialism, Islamic ideologies have finally come to a dead-end. The Islamic revolution of 1979 in Iran, I intend to argue in this chapter, amounted to the effective end of militant Islamism as we have known it – at once the zenith of its ideological legitimacy and the testimonial evidence of its institutional failure. Based on this specific historical example in our own time, and indeed on many more similar cases throughout Islamic history, I also intend to make a larger theoretical argument and provide an account of the enduring paradox at the heart of Islam as a religion of protest – that it can only morally succeed when it is politically weak and combative, and conversely it morally weakens and loses legitimacy when it is in political power. It is precisely this paradox, I intend to argue, that will need to be overcome via a necessary and strategic move away from the radically ideologized Islam and worked creatively towards an Islamic *theodicy* – a mode of liberation theology that accounts for the existence of its moral and normative shadows by in fact embracing them.

Early in the year 2000, as the world was tuned into a millenarian turn in the Christian calendar, in an Islamic republic Iranians were minding their own business – poised to cast their fateful vote in the sixth round of parliamentary elections after the success of an Islamic revolution in their homeland in 1979.

The parliamentary election for the sixth Majlis was a momentous occasion for a nation much maligned in its modern history by a debilitating combination of domestic tyranny and imperial hubris. This parliamentary election marked yet another turning point in the political maturity of a people who have inherited all the malignant ailments of a semi-colonized state and none of the institutional experiences of a fully colonized country. Iran was neither fully colonized like India so that in its post-independence history could transform its anti-colonial struggles into an institutional basis of a democracy, nor was it totally immune to Russian, the French, the

62 The end of Islamic ideology

British, and ultimately American imperialism so that it could mature politically in its own domestic terms.

By the commencement of the colonially mitigated project of modernity early in the nineteenth century, no political community in the world could any longer mature in its own domestic terms. Instead, incorporation into an increasingly global mode of economic production became the defining moment of every major and minor component of the planetary momentum. In Iran, successive generations of corrupt politicians facilitated the colonial plundering of the nation, while aborting any pregnant possibility of domestic political maturity. The success of the Islamic revolution in 1979 put an effective end to half a century of tyrannical Pahlavi monarchy and its active complacency in integrating Iran into a servile state in the global configuration of capital. But three decades into its success the Islamic republic too has catastrophically failed to rescue the nation from the full and tightening grip of the global reign of a neoliberal free-market economy which demands very little from Iran more than providing its faltering logic of production with oil and buying nothing more than consumer products.

The general contour of the economic predicament of Iran at the threshold of the twenty-first century is exactly as it was at the turn of the twentieth century: a minuscule link in the global chain of economic production. The collapse of the Qajars, the rise and demise of the Pahlavis, and the successful institutionalization of an Islamic republic have not in the slightest measures changed the predicament of Iran from a single-product economy principally contingent on the erratic logic of global capitalism. The catastrophic consequences of this predicament have been the effective formation of a capital-intensive (rather than labor-intensive) economy with very little grassroots pressure to demand and exact (rather than theorize and expect) democratic reforms. Democratic reforms, as a result, have always been promised ideologically rather than predicated on social-structural class formations. Social revolutions, military coup d'état, foreign interventions, and now for the first time parliamentary elections have been the sites and sights of the most intensive ideological contestations of material forces in Iran.

On Friday the 18 February, 2000, the Iranian electorate, the young men and women in particular, were called on to rescue the beleaguered presidency of Mohammad Khatami, whose landslide victory in May 1997 caught the entrenched vested interest of the religious right by surprise. This parliamentary election in particular revealed beyond any shadow of a doubt the cataclysmic moment when the long and arduous history of Islamic Ideology[2] (as a mode of liberation theology) had finally come to an end. The running wisdom in Iran and abroad had been that this election had a potential to have the Islamic parliament occupied by "Reformists," ousting the "Conservatives," and thus giving President Khatami yet another popular mandate to draw his nation out of its moral and material nightmares. This assessment, however, is only the tip of an iceberg far more colossal in its historical implications. The hasty collapse of the Iranian political tension between the two opposing camps of the Reformists and the Conservatives is as much insightful as blinding to the realities of a nation (and by extension an Islamic political culture) in the tightening grips of a debilitating moral and material crisis. The dominant and domineering political discourse between the Reformists (as the Liberal Left), and the Conservatives (as the Religious Right) has now assumed an almost entirely ideological disposition and the legitimate demands of Iranians for freedom of expression has successfully obscured the underlying economic forces that define and delimit the rhetorical excesses of *both* these ideological claims. Confined and limited by the *material* forces beyond the measures of their control, the Liberal Left and the Religious Right, the Reformists, and the Conservatives were nevertheless engaged in a fateful and momentous battle for the moral and material mandate of a nation.

On the side of the Reformists was an army of hopes invested in President Mohammad Khatami and his delightfully smiling face, compensating for two decades of sober and sad faces, angry and stubborn looks, stark and austere demeanors. Some 80 percent of the Iranian electorate, more than 38 million people, some 60 percent of them under the age of 25, were initially reported to have gone to voting polls with the frightful memories of two decades of a theocratic terror in their mind. They were thirsty and hungry, impatient and restless for change. Names such as Abdolkarim Soroush, Mohsen Kadivar, Abdollah Nuri, and Akbar Ganji, were emerging as the iconic invocations of a new dawning of freedom and hope. None of these names meant anything to anyone at the dawn of the Islamic revolution 20 years ago. All of these names have emerged from the very depth of the Islamic revolution itself. They are its dialectical negations. Having read and analyzed, admired and criticized, these post-revolutionary visionaries of a better future, young men and women in unprecedented numbers and with precocious political alertness flooded into streets and made their presence, their demands, and their inalienable rights, palpable, undeniable, factual. Chafing under two decades of a medieval theocracy, the young people in particular had no enduring memory of the Islamic revolution and by all accounts could not care less about that piece of historical amnesia. They were the harbingers of a new dawn in Iranian history, vanguard of a whole new visionary recital of the possible, heralding the beginning of a fresh defiance. They had successfully learnt to forget, if not forgive, their parental paralysis.

But all is not well in the state of Islamic Republic. The defining moment of its very constitution is the medieval principle of the Absolutist Rule of a Single Jurist (*Velayat-e Motlaqeh-ye Faqih*). He is the Letter of the Law personified, the vertiginous claim of his tyrannical claim to power having deafened and blinded a whole nation. Under the Sacred Canopy of that terror, the most powerful institution safeguarding a curious combination of lucrative economic interest and medieval theocratic convictions, the twelve-member (male only) Guardian Council was constitutionally poised to disqualify some 600 candidates, among them some 200 committed Reformists, who must have in one way or another posed constitutional threats to the very legitimacy of the state, or at the very least politically modulated a reformist groundswell.

The defiant voice of Abdollah Nuri, a convinced, convincing, and convicted Reformist, had to be treacherously silenced and jailed so that the most retrograde force of entrenched economic interest of the ruling elite, Ali Akbar Hashemi Rafsanjani, could once again hope to emerge as the power-broker of the religious right. The bogus charge of "weak commitment to Islam," leveled against these candidates by the Guardian Council, is the clearest ideological code of their potential threat. The resistance to the possibility of a political backlash against more than two decades of tyranny covering up an equally long period of disastrous economic mismanagement of the national resources has been quite adamant. Mohammad Reza Bahonar, spokesman for the "Coalition of Followers of the Line of Imam and the Leader" had expressed his confidence that his faction will win more than 50 percent of the 290 seats of the parliament in the February 2000 election. His sadly mistaken assurance was predicated on the fact that the supervisory Guardian Council, an unelected and undemocratic panel of senior clerics and jurists, had carefully screened the candidates for their ideological complacency with the Islamic republic and its theocratic predicates. The Supreme Leader Ayatollah Khamenei had as usual squarely sided with the most retrograde forces in the election battle and accused the Reformist camp of representing "The Enemy." Real and fictitious enemies of the Islamic republic are ritually invoked in Khamenei's speeches in order to create an atmosphere of immanent danger over which republic of fear he can then supremely preside, occupying, as he does, the most insulting office to the most common conceptions of democratic principles, that of the Supreme Jurist (*Velayat-e Faqih*). The parliamentary election of February 2000 was thus the fateful site of yet another momentous encounter in ideological battle for the moral soul of a nation, to control the material body of its evidence.

Khamenei failed, however, in giving a new lease on life to such tired and old clichés. The former Speaker of the parliament for nine years and President for eight, Ali Akbar Hashemi Rafsanjani, who was at the time the powerful chairman of the equally undemocratic Expediency Council, returned to the campaign trail to run for a seat in Tehran and continue to represent the most powerful vested interest of the theocracy. His entering the race on 15 December, 1999, was a last-minute scramble to foster the dwindling position of the political and economic beneficiaries of the ruling theocracy and an attempt to rein in the totally out of control revolt of the youthful population. He was squarely defeated and only after some massaging of the ballots was he able to be the thirtieth of the 30 members of the parliament elected from Tehran.

The fact that Rafsanjani had once again emerged as a key power-broker putting all his political and parliamentary prowess at the disposal of the reigning theocracy pointed to the desperation of the Religious Right. The "Rafsanjani factor," banking on his reputation as a wily pragmatist, was the key communicative factor trying to check and balance the potentially overwhelming victory of the Liberal Left. Rafsanjani's revolutionary credentials go back all the way to the early years of the revolution when Ayatollah Khomeini appointed him as a member of the Islamic Revolutionary Council. He was among the founding members of the ruling Islamic Republic Party. He was in the Assembly of Experts that drafted the constitution of the Islamic republic, while the smoke-screen of the American hostage crisis diverted everyone's attention. Elected to the parliament in 1980, he became its Speaker and held on to that prominent position until Khomeini's death in 1989. Khomeini's death created a vacuum in the position of the Supreme Leader, to which was promoted instantly the far less juridically qualified but far more politically correct President Ali Khamenei, who in turn bestowed his vacated post to Rafsanjani. The political faction that Rafsanjani now represented called itself *Kargozaran-e Sazandegi* or "The Executives of Reconstruction." Rafsanjani himself has been bestowed with the superlative title of *Sardar-e Sazandegi* by this group, "The Generalissimo of Reconstruction." The Persian penchant for the superlative is positively diabolic.

"The Rafsanjani factor" failed to factor much. The constitutional crisis of the Religious Right, the fact that the overwhelming majority of the legislators were thrown out of the Majlis by one of the most significant democratic events in modern history, the fact that an entirely new generation of parliamentary democracy was now poised to recast the course of Iranian political culture, all pointed to the dawn of a whole new day beyond the fateful encounter between Islam and colonial modernity.

If the presidential election of the second of Khordad (1376/Friday May 23 1997) that brought Mohammad Khatami to power was not strong enough an indication, if the student uprising in the month of Tir (1378/July 1999) was not cataclysmic enough an outburst, then the 29 of Bahman (1378/ Friday February 18 2000) that swept the Iranian parliament clean of all but a memory of the Religious Right is the incontrovertible evidence that we have witnessed the end of an era, the end of Islamic Ideology as a specific product of the fateful encounter between the ancestral faith of a people and the colonially mitigated project of modernity. The unfolding history of the Islamic Republic may indeed falter and meander, bring one faction or another to power, but the ideological exhaustion of the Islamic Republic of all political legitimacy points to more enduring phenomena. Just before the inauguration of the sixth Majlis in May 2000, in April the judiciary banned scores of reformist newspapers, and yet in the August of the same year a number of leading jurists issued a fatwa consenting to women congregation authorities leading public prayers – a clear indication of a homegrown form of feminism not entirely controlled by the Islamic Republic. In June 2001, Khatami was elected for a second term, confirming the national demand for reformist changes against the entrenched will and interest of the conservative clergy. By January 2002, the US President Bush responded to that sign of hope by placing Iran on an Axis of Evil. This open declaration of war by the choice imperial presidency of the neoconservative warmongers (Paul Wolfowitz and co.) did not dampen the courage and imagination of hundreds of thousands of students who led an anti-government protest in June 2003, a democratic spirit that was much boosted in the following October when Shirin Ebadi received the Nobel Peace Prize. But what President Bush's announcement and the subsequent tug of war over the nuclear issue did do was to drag the internal affairs of the Islamic Republic into regional politics and potentially fortified its artificial endurance. The death of some 40,000 people and the destruction of the ancient city of Bam in December 2003 gave the clerical clique ruling the Islamic republic yet another occasion to assume (a non-existent) benevolent authority and appear in position of power and control. By February 2004, the Religious Right was back in parliament, with the Council of Guardians having disqualified scores of Reformist candidates from running for election. This victory was a premonition for the even more emphatic triumph of the clerical clique during the presidential election of June 2005 when Mahmoud Ahmadinejad came to power – and thus resumed yet another cycle of reform and reaction, a circumambulatory cycle that does nothing but point to the quintessential absence of moral and normative legitimacy of the Islamic Republic.

What the factional bifurcation and political seesawing in the Islamic republic between the Liberal Left Reformists and the Religious Right Conservatives partially reveals and thus successfully conceals is a larger political fragmentation and the gradual dissipation of the whole ideological foregrounding of the Islamic revolution, some two centuries after its historical formation. Deeply rooted in the anti-colonial movements in the early parts of the nineteenth century, the Islamic Ideology gradually emerged as the dialectical outcome of a dialogical conversation between the ancestral faith of Muslims and the colonially mitigated project of a European modernity over the material and moral articulation of which they had little or no control. The seeds of the active desedimentation of the Islamic Ideology were already evident in the critical moments of its formation. Islamic Ideology emerged and was gradually articulated in successive moments of critical crisis in modern Islamic history. What has happened in Iran of the last 200 years and to Shi'ism in particular is not exclusive to either. It is symptomatic of far more universal events in the Muslim world at large and Islam in general.[3]

The collective mutation of Islam into an Islamic Ideology is a much more global development, documentable all the way back to the earliest encounters between the Islamic world and the colonially mitigated project of modernity.[4] The active production of the Islamic Ideology as a site of ideological resistance to colonialism has been a more universal event producing a religiously nativist response to colonialism. The rhetorical confrontation between "Islam and the West" is the most immediate symptomatic of this encounter.[5] The making of an Islamic Ideology, a project that begins in the earliest parts of the nineteenth century with such figures as Mulla Ahmad Naraqi (d. 1829) and concludes with Ali Shari'ati in the latter part of the twentieth (d. 1977), is the most vociferous version of a much more universal event.[6]

What we see in Shi'ism and the production of an Islamic Ideology from its critical encounter with colonialism is the microcosmic version of a far more universal mutation. In this respect, Shi'ism is not just a branch of Islam. It is Islam's disruptive dream of itself, remembering its own revolutionary bursting into history. All Muslims are, as it were, in the Shi'i state of their faith when they revolt against injustice. Shi'ism is the collective remembrance of a promise not delivered – a *conscience collective* that keeps remembering and dis-remembering itself. The active mutation of Shi'ism into an Islamic Ideology is thus a symptomatic mutation at the bone marrow of a metaphysical conviction charged to complement history. Shi'is believe that a grave injustice was perpetrated when their first charismatic leader, Ali, did not succeed the Prophet as the legitimate leader of all Muslims. They cast this inaugural injustice as a long shadow over history. They have institutionalized the charismatic authenticity of their leaders' claim to authority from Ali forward and call it *Imamah*. This institution received its most revolutionary moment in the year 680 when a band of Shi'is followed yet another of their leaders, al-Husayn (d. 680), to a revolutionary uprising against yet another usurper tyrant. From then on insurrectionary uprising has been second nature to the Shi'is, martyrdom (or *Shahada*) the very cornerstone of their faith. The Shi'is believe that their charismatic leaders are infallible (or *Ma'sum*) and thus outside the crosscurrent of materiality and history. By far the most revolutionary aspect of Shi'ism, however, is their doctrinal belief in *ghaybah*, or occultation, or simply the belief that the last of their charismatic leaders is well and alive but out of sight. He is present but absent, evident but invisible. The doctrine of *ghaybah* is constitutional to Shi'ism and its sense of insurrectionary expectation. They are always waiting for their Hidden Imam to arrive, and that expectation gives their attendance upon history a critically anticipatory disposition.[7]

In its combative mode, Shi'ism is a tempestuous template of revolutionary uprising. The gradual re-articulation of Shi'ism into an Islamic Ideology was predicated on the fertile ground of this faith as historically the most militant version of Islam. Shi'ism is Islam in its most combative claim upon the world. Shi'ism began with a negation, a denial, a usurpation. As a result, Shi'ism is *ipso facto* a religion of protest, a faith avenging itself upon the world for having done it wrong. Shi'ism is an incomplete religion, always waiting for its own final delivery, always anticipating its own fulfillment, and the world is the very site of this shortcoming, militantly translated throughout history into an agenda of insurrectionary action. Shi'ism is in a perpetual state of *expectation*, awaiting its own delivery, hoping for its own promise, anticipating to deliver itself. The active mutation of Islam in general into an Islamic Ideology is thus most immediately and iconically represented in the ideological mutation of Shi'ism, its most charismatic moment in history, a moment institutionalized into a faith.[8]

By virtue of its doctrinal disposition, Shi'ism throughout its history has fed the revolutionary aspirations of the most radical social movements. From the insurrectionary disposition of the follower of Ali (d. 661), from which Shi'ism found its very name ("The Party of, *Shi'a*, Ali") to the paradigmatic battle of Karbala (680), to the revolt of Zayd ibn Ali (d. 740), early Islamic history is inundated with revolutionary movements under the raised flag of Shi'ism. What is paramount in these movements is their inaugurating, originary power over the rest of Islamic history. Shi'ism is historically condemned to remember the trauma of its birth forever. Not a historical moment has lapsed in which Shi'ism has not transmitted itself into one form of massive social movement or another. In the Isma'ili branch of Shi'ism, from the latter part of the eighth century forward, we witness one of the most radical social movements in medieval Islamic societies, ranging from North Africa to central Asia.[9] Ruled by a pantheon of everlasting martyrs, Shi'ism has been a red flag raised high upon the entirety of the Islamic history. Martyrdom, as a result, is constitutional to the agitated memory that is Shi'ism. Whether patently identified with Shi'ism or not, insurrectionary movements that have led the cause of the oppressed against entrenched power have had a share in the inaugurating moment of Shi'ism in history. What gives Shi'ism its constitutionally revolutionary disposition is its doctrinal refusal to let go of the charismatic moment of Mohammed's prophetic mission. The Shi'is have sought to perpetuate that charismatic moment by transferring it from the Prophet to their Imams and then from the Imams into the doctrinal institution of *Imamah*, and from there personified in the present absence of the Last Imam. The result is the generation and sustaining of a perpetually charismatic moment pulsating the routinized course of any Islamic history.

But all is not emancipatory revolt in Shi'ism – and thus the paradox. Precisely the same insurrectionary disposition that inaugurates Shi'ism into history constitutes its Achilles heel. Shi'ism is predicated on a paradox. It fails upon success. Just like the myth of Sisyphus. Shi'ism is a religion of protest. It can never succeed. As soon as it succeeds politically, it negates itself metaphysically. Its material success is its moral failure. The success of the Islamic revolution in Iran over the last two decades is the most recent example marking its political predicament that when it has succeeded politically it has, *ipso facto*, reversed its own legitimacy. Shi'ism cannot be turned into an official ideology of repression without immediately negating its own very reason for being. The key operative concept constitutional to Shi'ism is that of *mazlumiyyat*, "having been wronged," or "having been tyrannized." The paradigmatic expression of this key operative concept is the third Shi'i martyred Imam, al-Husayn, whose very honorific appellation is *Husayn-e Mazlum* ("Husayn the Tyrannized"). So far as Shi'ism is on the side of the oppressed it is in its full revolutionary blossoming. The instant that it becomes fully institutionalized into an apparatus of power it *ipso facto* mutates into a most brutal theocratic tyranny. All its revolutionary zeal now comes back to haunt and turn it into a monstrous negation of itself. This is the defining moment of Shi'ism because it has never surpassed its Karbala paradox. Not now, not ever. The defeat of the third Shi'i Imam in the Battle of Karbala in 680 is constitutional to its moral and material culture. If Imam Husayn had succeeded in Karbala, Shi'ism would have had an entirely different disposition *vis-à-vis* political power – and thus the origin of the Shi'i myth that Imam Husayn was divinely ordained to be defeated in Karbala for Islam to survive. The defeat of Imam Husayn in the Battle of Karbala has made Shi'ism both a religion of protest and a moral manifesto against all successful constitutions of power. Shi'ism covets what it cannot attain, and thus it is a religion of protest. Shi'ism cannot attain what it covets, and thus it is a moral manifesto against all political power. Between those two normative opposites, Shi'ism dwells as a paradox.

The result of this paradox has been the historical formation of Shi'i dynasties that in their very institutional claim to power have lost all their charismatic claim to authority. The Islamic republic in Iran is not the first instance when the mutation of Shi'ism from revolutionary protest to dominant state ideology has robbed it of its own critical claim to legitimacy. As early as the early part of the tenth century, the Hamdanid dynasty of Mosul (904–991) and Aleppo (944–991) had claim to a Shi'i state religion. So did the Buyids in Iran and Iraq (923–1055). The Fatimid dynasty of Egypt (909–1171) extended the Isma'ili branch of Shi'ism and institutionalized its power over much of North Africa. Had these Shi'i dynasties not have their own internal sectarian and political differences they would have completely taken over the entire medieval Islamic world from the Sunnite majority. As far west as Iraq and Syria, as far north as Azarbayjan and Mazandaran, as far east as Deccan, Lucknow, and Kashmir in India, and as far south as Bahrain and other Persian Gulf regions came under the full political power of one Shi'i dynasty or another throughout the medieval world. But no dynasty ever reached the paramount power of the Safavid empire that ruled over a major segment of the Islamic world from the dusk of the medieval world in 1501 to the dawn of colonial modernity in 1722. These successive and simultaneous dynasties drained every ounce of revolutionary energy from the creative memory of Shi'ism. In the repressive measures of these imperial powers, Shi'ism became an effective state ideology and all but lost its defining doctrinal moments. In becoming the state religion of reigning tyrannies, Shi'ism does not as much passively forget as actively dis-remembers itself. In these dynastic formations, Shi'ism became a historical antithesis of itself, a contradiction in terms, an oxymoronic self-negation, a paradox. If and when it succeeds politically it fails, *ipso facto*, metaphysically. Its material victory is its moral defeat.

It was in an attempt to reach towards this paradox that Ali Shari'ati, by far the most brilliant ideologue of Islamic Ideology in recent memory, while getting Shi'ism ready for yet another revolutionary posturing, distinguished between two kinds of Shi'ism: the Safavid Shi'ism and the Alavid Shi'ism.[10] What he meant by Safavid Shi'ism was the historical metamorphosis of an aggressive mode of revolutionary resistance into an ideology of repression. And, conversely, what he meant by Alavid Shi'ism was the archetypal endurance of revolutionary resistance to tyranny, a global insurrection without frontiers in time or space. Quite intuitively, Shari'ati identified the successful institutionalization of Shi'ism into a dynastic rule with its moral failure, and its revolutionary posturing as a religion of protest with its political failure. But what Shari'ati tried, unsuccessfully, to break into the Safavid and Alavid Shi'isms, in oppositional plural, is in fact the intertwined paradox that is Shi'ism itself. There is no breaking up Shi'ism into its constituent oppositional ends without breaking it up altogether, denying it its transformative energy, alternating mechanics. Because Shi'ism was born metaphysically by being denied politically, it always covets the political in order to reclaim itself metaphysically. Shi'ism has had to turn into its own worst enemy in order to justify its own historicity, its own place in the world. If the Sunni majority, the world at large, were the only Other that Shi'ism had to battle to prove and implicate itself, it would have long since been rendered obsolete, redundant, outdated. Shi'ism had to bifurcate itself into a site of insurrectionary revolt and then into its own negation in order to see itself in the speculum of its own defeat, so that it could always-already rise again and remember itself triumphantly. Shi'ism does not forget but mis-remembers itself. And that is the paradox definitive to its history.

This active self-remembrance always bracing itself for a mis-remembrance punctuates the interface of Shi'ism as a *conscience collective* and its proclivity to charismatic outbursts. If we put together the classical Durkheimian insight of religion as "a system of actions aimed at making and perpetually remaking the soul of the collectivity and of the individual,"[11] with the equally poignant Weberian insight that "it is recognition on the part of those subject to authority which is decisive for the validity of charisma,"[12] we begin to have a clearer angle on Shi'ism in its historical paradox. As a paradox, Shi'ism rests on its inaugural moment of being born as a refusal to let go of the charismatic moment of Muhammad's prophetic mission.[13] Islam itself was born as a religion of protest, a militant defiance of the self-paralyzed patrimonialism operative in the Arabian Peninsula, a moral mandate against the fragmented Arab tribalism. The death of the prophet for the majority of Muslims meant the systematic routinization of his charismatic authority in a multifocal set of institutions. But for the Shi'i minority the inaugural charismatic moment was to continue in first the figure and then the paradoxical institution of the Imam and the *Imamate*.[14] The disenfranchised community that was inevitably generated around the opulent center of the early Islamic empires became the fertile ground of Shi'i and proto-Shi'i sentiments and movements. Something of the early charismatic conscience of the early Islam, an agitated memory of its inaugural moment, remained in Shi'ism. As a *conscience collective*, Shi'ism thus remained persistent on the insurrectionary birth beat of Islam, its defining moment. Throughout its history, Shi'ism has dissipated its *conscience collective* in moments of historical atrophy and then recollected that insurrectionary memory in the figure of a charismatic persona, always on the prototype of the Prophet and the historical modulations of the infallible Imams.

Bringing Durkheim and Weber together and having them simultaneously observe Shi'ism will rescue Durkheim from the elaborate and superfluous arguments of trying to place the *conscience collective* on an epiphenomenal level which is post-material and pre-phenomenological,[15] Weber from the tiresome reformulation of the nature of charisma which ultimately collapses his sociology of charismatic authority to a pathology of power rather than elevating it to a hermeneutics of its historical manifestations,[16] and Shi'ism from its own blind-spot of not seeing itself as a self-propelling, self-paralyzing paradox. Thus located, we can see how Shi'ism is paradoxical at the moment of its inception because it wants to capture a fleeting charismatic moment, and that it is paradoxical at all moments of its potential destinations because its political success is *ipso facto* the metaphysical negation of its validity. Having been born as an insurrectionary *defeat*, Shi'ism cannot politically *succeed* without negating its own charismatic occasion. Shi'ism cannot be in a position of political power because the state that it thus forms will have to have a claim on a monopoly of violence,[17] and it cannot claim that monopoly without turning every mode of opposition to it as the *de facto* versions of Shi'ism. The reigning Shi'i state, a contradiction in terms, makes of all its mortal enemies a more legitimate contender to Shi'ism than itself. That is why the student uprising against the tyrannical institutions of an Islamic republic (institutionalized in the position of the Supreme Leader as well as the Guardian and the Expediency Councils) has a far more effective claim on Shi'ism than the reigning theocracy.

This predicament is not exclusive to the Islamic Republic and its failure to institutionalize an un-institutionalizable claim to charismatic authority. The whole gamut of Shi'i *scholastic* learning (the *ulama*) and the whole history of Shi'i *dynastic* rule (from the Fatimids in Egypt to the Safavids in Iran) have scarcely escaped or diverted this constitutional logic of Shi'ism as a paradoxical religion of protest, quite to the contrary. The most glorious achievement of medieval scholastic learning, Mulla Sadra Shirazi (d. 1641), who brought the entire spectrum of Shi'i learning to its epistemic finale during the reign of the Safavids, could not but translate in his Transcendental Theosophy the political ambitions of a Shi'i empire.[18] In his Transcendental Theosophy

(*Hikmat al-Muta'aliyyah*), Mulla Sadra tried to do what the Safavids had done in the realm of political order. The Safavid constitution of a Shi'i empire is reflected in Mulla Sadra's imperial attempt at a metaphysical metanarrative that would embrace all the diversity of Islamic scholastic learning. From the nomocentricism of the Islamic law to the logocentricism of the Islamic philosophy, to the homocentricism of the Islamic mysticism are brought together in Mulla Sadra's Transcendental Theosophy in a massive centripetal move to unite and unify all the opposing forces of a centrifugal discursive tapestry. All the repressed forces of greatness that come back to haunt the Safavid nightmarish dream of a Shi'i empire find their metaphysical counterparts in Mulla Sadra's equally imperial attempt at giving One Final Shi'i shape to the thunderous oppositional forces that animate the mediaeval scholastic learning. Mulla Sadra's Transcendental Theosophy is thus in metaphysics what the Safavid dynasty is in politics: the return of the Shi'i repressed to haunt its own dream of Otherness.

Because it has been the historical Other of Islam itself (as Sunnism), Shi'ism can scarcely conceal its dream of being the Same. But being the Same, whether represented in the dynastic apparatus of the Safavids or the scholastic apparatus of Mulla Sadra's Transcendental Theosophy, *ipso facto* disqualifies Shi'ism from Shi'ism. Shi'ism always has to remain the Other and yet dream of the Same. When it becomes the Same it atrophies into its own nightmare. This is exactly the opposite of what Levinas detected as the primacy of the Same in what he would call "the Western Metaphysics," and identify with Socrates: "This primacy of the same was Socrates' teaching: to receive nothing of the Other but what is in me, as though from all eternity I was in possession of what comes to me from the outside – to receive nothing, or to be free."[19] Whereas Levinas' counter-metaphysics is to reconstitute the primacy of the Other, as the site of morality (for him located in the naked face of the Other), against a history of the primacy of the Same, he never paid any attention to what would happen to a metaphysics that narrates itself as the Other of a reigning the Same. The paradoxical history of Shi'ism is a good lesson in the equally pathological primacy of the Other dreaming of being the Same. Shi'ism is the Other. Shi'ism is Alterity. By virtue of its own historical roots, it has always been the Islamic Other, dreaming itself the Same. The mere assumption or even illusion of power gives Shi'ism a sense of political identity and *ipso facto* it loses its sense of historical Alterity. Shi'ism can never be the Same. It has believed in its own Otherness. Before the first slogan or bullet is fired against a Shi'i government, it has lost its own legitimacy by being a "government," and thus having an exclusive claim on legitimate violence. The Shi'i claim on any "Islamic republic" is always tangential, paradoxical, an antithesis running before its own thesis, never near a synthesis. The Shi'is are the Jews of Islam, the Other that proves the Same. The opposition between Shi'i Fundamentalism and Jewish Zionism is not the opposition between two oppositional identities, but the opposition between two identical Others, identical in their Alterity.

It is with this paradoxical disposition, at once insurrectionary and tyrannical, *de jure* and *de facto*, that Shi'ism enters its colonially mitigated history in modernity. What has happened to Shi'ism in the process is endemic to Islam at large – the aggressive mutation under colonial duress of a multifaceted moral imagination into a singular site of resistance to colonialism. The history of Shi'ism in modernity is the chronicle of its gradual revival as a religion of protest. During the Safavid period (1501–1722), Shi'ism experiences one of the sharpest episodes of its active complacency with an aggressive reconstitution of Persian monarchy, being in effect turned into the state religion and as such instrumental in the brutal execution of power. It can no longer speak the truth to power because it *is* the power. In the material success of the Safavids as a Shi'i dynasty, the moral legitimacy of the faith is critically compromised. Between the decline of the Safavids in 1722 and the rise of the Qajars in 1789, which also coincided with the onslaught of colonialism in Iran, the Shi'i clerical establishment is gradually depoliticized and rendered rather irrelevant beyond its scholastic domains, which is in effect the best thing that could have happened for the insurrectionary disposition of the faith to recollect and resuscitate itself.

With the rise of the Qajars and the commencement of the European project of colonialism in the region, Shi'ism begins to resume its revolutionary posture. It is impossible to read the history of modern Shi'ism and its gradual remodulation into Islamic Ideology, except as a *response* to the encroachment of the colonial onslaught and the joint projects of the European Enlightenment and its colonial modernity that it precipitated not just for the Shi'i Iranians but for Muslims in general. Even events and developments internal and integral to the history of Shi'ism in the nineteenth and twentieth centuries were agitated by a direct catalytic effect from the colonial encounter. From the active consolidation of the position of supreme religious leader to the victory of one school of jurisprudence over another, to the aggressive involvement of religious authorities in the political fate of the society at large all took place in the immediate context of a critical encounter with European Enlightenment and its instrumental carrier colonial modernity. Shi'ism was reinvented in modernity under colonial duress.

The mutation of Shi'ism into an Islamic Ideology as a site of resistance to colonialism, however, initially began exactly in the opposite direction and by the leading clerical authorities being aggressively incorporated into the Qajar political apparatus. Shi'ism thus began its modern history in response to colonially mitigated modernity in its complacent, self-negating, mode, and not in its revolutionary posturing. It was during the reign of the Qajar potentate Fath Ali Shah (1797–1834) that he actively recruited the blessings and supports of the Shi'i clerical establishment in legitimizing his political authority. The Qajars were instrumental in the gradual ideologization of

Shi'ism by trying, once again and on the model of the Safavids, to turn it into a state ideology. From the collapse of the Safavids in 1722 to the rise of the Qajars in 1789, the Shi'i clerical establishment had gradually emerged as an independent entity, far more independent of the ruling monarchy than they had been during the heydays of the Safavids. This relative autonomy, sustained by an independent source of income from religious taxes, resulted in the autonomous authority of such prominent clerical figures as Seyyed Mohammad Baqer Shafti, the Sheikh al-Islam of Isfahan, who was extraordinarily powerful.[20] The rapid rush of colonialism initially facilitated the incorporation of the Shi'i clerics into the state apparatus, and this was by and large mitigated by the internal rivalries among the competing juridical factions among the Ulama. A critical case in point is already evident during the reign of Fath Ali Shah when Mirza Mohammad Nishapuri, a staunch Akhbari jurist (who were engaged in a life-long battle against the Usulis, a principally juridical disputation with marked theological and even political implications) promised the Qajar warlord the head of Tsitianov, the Russian general who was poised to take over Baku, if the Akhbari school of jurisprudence were to be made the state creed. Fath Ali Shah made that promise and Mirza Mohammad did in fact produce Tsitianov's head. But the monarch reneged on his side of the bargain.[21]

Shi'ism gradually assumes a more aggressively combative posture in the Qajar period, although still remains subservient to the state apparatus. In the course of Qajar wars in the Caucasus with the Russians, Abbas Mirza, the Crown Prince, solicited and received the support of the Shi'i clerics in his territorial battles. The increasingly aggressive Russian colonialism was desperately trying to be a rival with the more potent European forces like the British and the French. Even the Ottomans were now something of a local menace for the Qajars. In the course of 1804–1814 wars with Russia, which resulted in the humiliating Treaty of Golestan in 1813, Abbas Mirza wrote to such prominent Shi'i clerics as Sheykh Ja'far Kashef al-Ghita and Mulla Ahmad Naraqi and asked them to declare his wars against the Russian a Holy War, and they did.[22] The barbarity of the Russian army under such savage generals as Yermelov in abusing the Muslim population of the Caucasus gave ample reason to the Shi'i authorities to become implicated in the frontier wars between the Qajars and the Russians. Abbas Mirza may in fact have used the Shi'i authorities to compel his reluctant father, Fath Ali Shah, into war.[23] Whatever the case, the Shi'i establishment was manipulated by the Qajars to serve their dynastic purposes. As for the clerical establishment itself, they lacked leadership, vision, or even legitimate universal authority to be an effective and autonomous political force. Their effective complacency in the humiliating defeat of the Qajars implicated them in that dynastic disgrace. But the thunderous elevation of popular discontent, caught between the Russian aggression, Qajar incompetence, and clerical complacency, was gradually awakening the insurrectionary spirit of the Shi'i *conscience collective*.

The Qajars are squarely defeated by the Russians and lose much territory in the Caucuses and this gives the Shi'i clerics a new momentum to reclaim political power. Much against Fath Ali Shah's resistance, such prominent clerics as Mulla Ahmad Naraqi and Aqa Seyyed Muhammad Tabataba'i forced him to go to war again and in fact participated in the battles against the Russians. But still the relationship between the clerical establishment and the Qajar potentates is predicated on power politics and not on the Shi'i Ulama's awareness of and trust in their popular basis. As a result, the loud rhetorics of the Shi'i clergy while joining force with the Qajar aristocracy did not match their dismal performance on the battlefield. Soon after the start of the campaign, Aqa Seyyed Mohammad, the chief protagonist of war against the Russians, abandoned Abbas Mirza's advancing army, retreated to Tehran and died. Add to that discouraging valor the treachery of the entire clerical class of Tabriz under the leadership of Mir Fattah the son of Mirza Yusef, one of the most prominent members of the Tabrizi Ulama, who betrayed their nation and handed over Tabriz to the invading Russian army.[24] The result is a continued upsurge of Shi'i moral indignation to which the dismal capabilities of the clerical class is yet to reach.

Although the agitation of the clerical class resulted in yet another disastrous treaty, Turkamanchai of 1828, and even more losses of territory to the Russians, the ennobling anger constitutional to Shi'ism in moments of revolutionary crisis was now in full political throttle, ready to recast the ancestral faith into a site of ideological resistance to colonialism. The terms *fatwa* (religious edict) and *jihad* (holy war) now resumed their militant currency. In the judicious words of one historian of modern Shi'ism: "the importance of the second Russo-Iranian War from the point of view of the ulama ... was their emergence as a force capable of shaping national policy. This was, indeed, the first of a chain of episodes where the ulama were to have a marked influence on the course of Iranian history."[25] This still is giving too much credit to a class whose atrophied body was running out of breath trying to catch up with the revolutionary crescendo of their constituency. Even an unabashedly pro-clerical historian like Algar concedes that in the course of these defeats at the hand of the Russians, "the ulama had been used initially as instruments for the arousing of religious emotions; but their success in arousing these emotions revealed their potential strength as leaders of the nation."[26] What both these historians confuse is the arrested growth of the clerical class, best evident during the Qajar frontier battles with the Russians, and the far more revolutionary expectations of their constituency.

After these wars, the failure of the Qajars to defend their Muslim subjects, and the active presence of the Shi'i clerics in resistance to colonialism, begins to affect the emerging Iranian political culture. Shi'ism in effect enters the phases of its encounter with the colonially mitigated modernity on the battlefields of Turkamanchai and Golestan. The active politicization of Shi'ism in response to colonialism, and the colonially mitigated politics of expectation among the Shi'is, was immediately translated into the institutional consolidation of the supreme position of religious authority. When today we look back at the charismatic figure of a prominent Shi'i cleric like Bahr al-Ulum (d. 1797), it is hard to believe that the attribution of miraculous deeds to him by his contemporaries were not the earliest indications of the emergence of the position of supreme religious leader (*Marja'-e Taqlid*) as a figure of political authority responsible to his constituency at the threshold of the colonial advancements in the region. By the middle of the nineteenth century, and in the two prominent figures of Hojjat al-Islam Shafti (d. 1844) and Hajji Muhammad Kalbasi (d. 1845), the position of *Marja'-e Taqlid* had been thoroughly consolidated and spread over a multinational (Iran, India, Iraq) domain. Already we hear of such titles as *Ra'is al-Ulama* and *Na'ib al-Imam* attributed to these figures.[27] The active attribution of such superlative political titles was in effect the institutional expression of the emerging expectation of the Shi'i community at large. Foreign aggression coupled with domestic corruption had made the time pregnant with great expectations, and the clerical class would sink or swim in the rising tides. By investing these titles in their religious leaders, the colonially ravaged nation was setting them up against monarchs and colonial officers alike – and thus mandating for them an agenda of political action. Colonialism proper had now become the principal cause of Shi'i political revivalism, its main interlocutor.

While from the Golestan Treaty of 1813 to the Turkamanchai Treaty of 1828 we see the active politicization of Shi'ism in complacency with the Qajar dynasty and yet in resistance to the Russian colonial advancements, in the clerical opposition to the reforms of Mirza Hossein Khan Sepahsalar, which came to a critical point in 1873, we witness a midway transition to full revolutionary posture because this episode represents the clerical establishment's own vested interest preventing the full revolutionary potentials of Shi'ism to explode onto the political scene. As a reform-minded minister, Mirza Hasan Khan Sepahsalar (d. 1880) was instrumental in initiating some crucial administrative changes that rubbed the clerical establishment the wrong way. In 1872, for example, he tried to systematize and incorporate into a central administrative apparatus the appointment of high-ranking clerics, which in turn deeply angered the Shi'i establishment.[28] Even his attempt to establish a cabinet in Naser al-Din Shah's court was distasteful to the clergy because it disturbed the feudal political culture of the court. But most objectionable to the Shi'i clergy was Sepahsalar's attempt to modernize the Iranian judicial system, which would have resulted in the clerical establishment losing its power. In the words of one historian: "Unconditional submission to the primacy of European models would have made their religious learning irrelevant to the affairs of society and destroyed their whole raison d'être."[29] The vested economic interest of the Shi'i clerics cannot be underestimated either. During the famine of 1871, Hajji Mulla Ali Kani, the chief nemesis of Sepahsalar, made millions, as did many other high-ranking Shi'i Ulama. The opposition of Kani and other like-minded clerics to Sepahsalar taking Naser al-Din Shah to Europe in 1873 in order to encourage the monarch towards modernizing reforms is equally informed by their fear that such reforms would put their economic and political power in danger. The situation finally culminated in the clergy's aggressive assault against Sepahsalar while he accompanied the monarch on his trip to Europe. The concession that the Qajar court had made to Baron Julius Reuter in 1872 for the exploitation of minerals and forests as well as the construction of the railroad was the principal occasion that coagulated the opposition of the Shi'i Ulama. The opposition was strong enough that Naser al-Din Shah, having no will or vision of his own, summarily dismissed Sepahsalar in 1873.

The fact that such corrupt Shi'i clerics as Mulla Ali Kani opposed colonial concession of the Qajars to the British out of their own vested economic and social interests does not make the resistance an entirely misguided social event. Through these concessions, the nascent Iranian national economy was being aggressively incorporated into a colonial configuration within the global economy of the British empire and its rivals. At a time when the emerging Iranian national prerogatives needed to be predicated on a sovereign economic policy, the British colonialists were aggressively after incorporating it into their global interests, while the Qajar aristocracy and their liberal reformist courtiers like Sepahsalar were complacent in the design. The "secular" modernization track that Sepahsalar represented was so utterly enamored by the achievements of the British that it had not an iota of critical stand against colonialism. Thus the aggressive "modernization" of Iran had very little distance from its equally aggressive colonization. Despite such corrupt figures as Mulla Ali Kani and many other Shi'i clerics like him, they at least had a more critical stand *vis-à-vis* colonialism. That critical stand was principally out of a corrupt concern with their own pathetic interests. But the critical *conscience collective that* now Shi'ism embodied and the deprived Shi'i masses represented defied and surpassed that pathological barrier.

The Tobacco Revolt of 1891–1892 gave a far more precise definition to the emergence of Shi'ism as an insurrectionary movement against colonialism.[30] Naser al-Din Shah's giving the Imperial Tobacco Corporation the exclusive right to the sale and distribution of tobacco in 1891 resulted in such massive popular abhorrence that the revolutionary force of Shi'ism was in effect exorcised out of a complacent clerical establishment. The initial outburst of popular resentment against the tobacco concession was in the provincial city of Shiraz, and soon spread to other cities such as Tabriz and Isfahan. The revolt that ensued reveals a clear coalition between local merchants like Hajji Abbas Urduabadi and lower-ranking clerics like Hajj Seyyed Ali Akbar Falasiri.[31] The active presence of the merchant class in the Tobacco Revolt is the clear indication that the nascent Iranian national bourgeoisie was being directly threatened by the encroachment of the colonial interests and had implicated the Shi'i establishment in providing it with an ideological battle-cry. Economically, the revolt represented the resistance of the Iranian national bourgeoisie to becoming subordinate to the overriding logic of colonialism. Socially, the clerical establishment was resisting its privileges being compromised. But in the middle of these particular class and colonial interests, Shi'ism, as the iconic constellation of an insurrectionary disposition, was re-emerging with full revolutionary power, over which no particular group, not even the clergy itself, had full control. Rising from the depth of the Shi'i *conscience collective* is now again its moral protestation against injustice. No particular class, least of all the clerical establishment itself, was in full control of this subterranean defiance of tyranny constitutional to the very moral texture of Shi'ism.

The emergence of Mirza Hasan Shirazi as the prominent clerical figure leading the uprising against the tobacco concession in 1891 marks a critical point in the active repoliticization of the faith. The presence of such figures as Seyyed Ali Akbar Falasiri from Shiraz and Aqa Munir al-Din from Isfahan in Samarra, where Mirza Hasan resided, points to the aggressive pressure that the merchant class was exerting on the Shi'i authorities to raise the ideological banner against the British colonial interests. The pressure was effective. Between July and September 1891, Mirza Hasan Shirazi wrote two letters to the Qajar monarch and publicly declared his opposition to the tobacco concession. While Naser al-Din Shah was contemplating his response, Mirza Hasan wrote to a reputable cleric in Iran, Mirza Hasan Ashtiyani, in November and charged him with leading the protest on his behalf. What happened next is a brilliant indication of who exactly was in charge of the Shi'i revolutionary resurrection. Shirazi's communication with Ashtiyani in November is the last factual evidence that we have of his intervention. Early in December a religious edict (*fatwa*) appeared in Tehran that banned the use of tobacco and it was signed by Mirza Hasan Shirazi. Earlier versions of the self-same *fatwa* appeared in Isfahan in November. Suddenly there was a collective conviction among the masses of ordinary people that Shirazi had actually issued this *fatwa*. The fact of the matter, however, is that there is no evidence that Shirazi actually issued this *fatwa*. It is as if the collective will of the popular demand had exacted it. And it was issued. It was issued and signed far more by the collective will of the Shi'i insurrectionary disposition than by Mirza Hasan Shirazi.[32]

This is not to underestimate the power and influence of the merchant class in fabricating this *fatwa* in order to protect their own economic interest against colonial intrusions. But at this stage, the formation of a national bourgeoisie is constitutional to the economic interest of the nation at large. The constitution of that national economy is threatened by both the infiltration of the colonial powers and the active collaboration of the corrupt Qajar court (which of course included a healthy dose of such prominent Shi'i clerics as Seyyed Abdollah Behbahani who squarely sided with the Qajar monarchy and their colonial cohorts and defied the *fatwa* against use of tobacco) as well as the malleable liberalism of Reformists like Sepahsalar. The prominence of such high-ranking Shi'i clerics as Mirza Hasan Shirazi in Iraq and Mirza Hasan Ashtiyani in Iran derived its legitimacy not by representing the economic interest of the Iranian merchant class but by being the spokesmen of a far more universal claim on the wellbeing of a nation. The Shi'i ulama in effect become the personification of the collective will of the Shi'i nation. The people at large were in effect transferring legitimate sovereignty from the court to the mosque, from the king to the clerics. But at all times *they* were in charge of bestowing sovereignty and legitimacy, and it was in *them* that the insurrectionary will of Shi'ism was once again being born into history. Sympathetic historians of the clerical class[33] are quick to attribute the success of the Tobacco Revolt to the leadership of the clergy. But the fact is that the best and most revolutionary among the clerical class *followed*, not *led*, the movement. When Naser al-Din Shah wrote his threatening letter to Mirza Hasan Shirazi admonishing him for not allowing the use of tobacco, the leading Shi'i clergyman of Iran packed his bag and was about to leave the country on January 4 1892. It was the gathering of a massive crowd at his residence, protecting him and demanding that he stay that *turned* him into a leader. He did not *lead* the protest. He *followed* it. The revolutionary disposition of the *conscience collective* of a people, agitated at the moment of historical crisis, has a far more fertile ground to give birth to a militant memory than the vested interest of any given class can either stop or control it. The whole tobacco episode came to an end when Naser al-Din Shah repealed the concession and Mirza Hasan Shirazi lifted the boycott on January 6 1892, which was followed by Mirza Hasan Ashtiyani restoring calm to the capital on January 26 of the same year. By then the Shi'i insurrectionary disposition had come to full revolutionary recognition.

This succession of political events ultimately culminated in two cataclysmic courses of insurrectionary movements that marked and forever changed the history of Shi'ism in its critical conversation with colonial modernity. One is domestic to Iranian Shi'ism and marks the last pre-modern revolution that tested the doctrinal boundaries of the faith, while the other confronted Shi'ism fully fledged with the colonially mitigated project of European modernity. The first, the Babi movement of 1844–1850, carried Shi'ism to one of its most radical doctrinal conclusions, while the second, the Constitutional Revolution of 1906–1911, cauterized the predicament of colonial modernity on its forehead. What the active participation of the Shi'i clerics in the Qajar frontier wars with the Russians in the first three decades of the nineteenth century reveals, as does public uprising against the Reuter and tobacco concessions in the last three decades of the century, is the resurgence of the Shi'i *conscience collective* as a religion of protest. No particular class, least of all the Shi'i clerical elite, was in total control of this insurrectionary *conscience collective*. It had a reality *sui generis* and it invested and divested power and authority on revolutionary figures and movements that remained loyal to its hopes and served its aspirations.

What the Babi Movement of the middle of the nineteenth century and the Constitutional Revolution of the end of the nineteenth/beginning of the twentieth century ultimately reveal is how as soon as the insurrectionary spirit of Shi'ism degenerates in one case it resuscitates itself in another. As soon as the Babi movement of the middle of the century degenerated into the Baha'i religion, the Constitutional Revolution of the end of the century becomes the repository of all the hopes and aspirations that were brutally murdered with the execution of Bab in 1850. The collective spirit of protest that is in Shi'ism in its most insurrectionary moments divests its aspirations from the lofty but irrelevant and megalomaniac claims of Baha'ullah and invests them in local and anonymous figures far closer to their miseries and hopes. The Constitutional Revolution thus rises like a sphinx from the ashes of the Babi Movement.[34]

In its domestic, feudal, and pre-modern features, the Babi Movement marks yet another case of Shi'ism giving revolutionary momentum to an insurrectionary uprising and then degenerating, at the point of its success, into, in this case, a pathological universalism. The Babi movement was the last, universalized, revolutionary disposition of Shi'ism in its medieval terms before in Baha'ism it turned into a jaundiced reactionary negation of itself. As the last insurrectionary event predicated entirely on doctrinal developments internal and integral to Shi'ism in its scholastic predicates, Babism tested the inherited Iranian political culture at its outer limits. As such, Babism gave political momentum to yet another healthy, robust, and revolutionary potential before it was doctrinally transmuted by the onslaught of colonial modernity.

As a political movement that shook the Qajar dynasty to its foundations, Babism began ideologically in Shaykhism, by far the most revolutionary doctrinal event in Iran of the nineteenth century. The founder of the Shaykhi movement in Shi'i scholastic doctrines was Shaykh Ahmad Ahsa'i (1753–1826), a prominent jurist and philosopher of the late eighteenth and early nineteenth century. The origin of Shaykh Ahmad Ahsa'i's thoughts can be traced back to the rise of the School of Isfahan in the sixteenth century, particularly in the ideas of such prominent philosophers as Mulla Sadra Shirazi (d. 1641), Mir Damad (d. 1631), Mir Fendereski (d. 1640) and Mulla Rajab Ali Tabrizi (d. 1669).[35] These philosophers gave an unprecedented universalizing momentum to Shi'i scholastic thought and sought for the first time in Islamic intellectual history to produce a unified field theory, as it were, of Islamic metaphysics. Mulla Sadra Shirazi, the most towering figure of the School of Isfahan, set upon himself the monumental task of bringing together centuries of conflicting Islamic scholastic thought in juridical (nomocentric), philosophical (logocentric), and mystical (homocentric) terms and give it a sustained metaphysical field theory which he called *Hekmat e Mota'aliyyah* ("Transcendental Theosophy").[36] There was a remarkable correspondence between the transcendental claims of

Mulla Sadra's metaphysics and the universal claims of the Safavid state on a Shi'i empire. In his theory of Transubstantial Motion (*Harakat-e Jawhari*), Mulla Sadra sought to generate a metanarrative to embrace divergent forces of the metaphysical foundations of Islamic scholastic thought. Mulla Sadra was passionately driven by a constitutional conviction that a single set of metaphysical forces and principles were at work in both the manifestations and the material working of the sacred, and his lifetime project was to articulate this simple and elegant universe.

Shaykh Ahmad Ahsa'i was a direct descendent of these groundbreaking events in Islamic intellectual history. By far the most revolutionary aspect of Shaykh Ahmad's ideas was his active reconstitution of the very idea of "Imam" in Shi'i imamology, directly rooted in its prophetology and theology. Although there was nothing particularly new in his attribution of divine qualities to the very Light from which the Imams were believed to have been emanated, his distinction of the divine attributes into *Dhati* (Essential) and *Muhdath* (Created) gave material agency not only to the figure of the (Hidden) Imam but by revolutionary extension to the charismatic community of his believers. Suddenly in the ideas of Sheykh Ahmad Ahsa'i, the dormant, post-Safavid, Shi'ism once again resumed a doctrinally theorized revolutionary disposition that gave the Shi'i believers and their leaders charismatic cause to be historical agents in the absence of the Hidden Imam. By far the most politically significant aspect of Shaykh Ahmad Ahsa'i's imamology was the creative constitution of historical agency for the charismatic community of his believers. Although in Ahsa'i's own ideas this political implication remains dormant, it nevertheless was instrumental in the active restoration of historical agency to the charismatic community in expectation of its final delivery. Sheykh Ahmad gave that metaphysical finality historical immediacy. There was only one step from Shaykh Ahmad Ahsa'i, who died in 1826, and Ali Mohammad Bab (1819–1850), who led a revolutionary uprising against the Qajars, and their clerical companions in 1848. Bab (meaning "gate") abruptly announced that the dawn of a new revelation was upon the world and that he was its agent. The year 1848 on the Christian calendar corresponded to 1260 on the Islamic and marked the 1000-year anniversary of the Disappearance (*Ghaybah*) of the Muslim Messiah for the Shi'is. This Y1K occasion, as it were, had given the Shi'i world reasons to expect cataclysmic changes signified in the reappearance of the Hidden Imam. Bab was the figurative manifestation of that expectation and hope.

Through a disciple of Shaykh Ahmad Ahsa'i, Seyyed Kazem Rashti (d. 1843), Bab was closely linked to the Shaykhi movement. After the death of Seyyed Kazem in 1843, in 1844 Bab first proclaimed himself "the Gate" ("Bab" in Arabic, and thus his name) to the Hidden Imam and then soon after the Hidden Imam Himself. His claim won considerable approval among the peasantry and the urban poor, ready to follow any raised banner against the blinded tyranny perpetrated by the Qajar aristocracy and their clerical cohorts. Bab's theoretical articulation of his leadership was both simple and elegant, and as such squarely rooted in Shaykh Ahmad Ahsa'i's imamology. The figure of the Hidden Imam was alive and present in the realm of Archetypal Absolutes (*Hurqalya*). The earthly manifestations of that Archetypal Absolute was simply here to give historical agency to the Shi'i community.[37] The political result of these theological speculations was a critical bypass of the clerical establishment and their vested interest in the status quo. By claiming direct communication with the Hidden Imam through a moral conception of his will, Bab in effect personified the charismatic community of the Hidden Imam's followers. The revolutionary implication of these ideas is not merely in their resuscitation of Hermetic, Isma'ili, and Ghullat tendencies in Shi'i scholastic thought.[38] There is something far more dangerous to the status quo in these beliefs. Although Sheykh Ahmad Ahsa'i's close followers considered him personally as the one in communication with the Hidden Imam, and although Bab claimed that status openly for himself, the fact is that in these ideas were dormant the restitution of active historical agency for all Shi'is and thus in the Shi'i community at large. What is theorized in Sheykh Ahmad Ahsa'i is nothing other than the historical disposition of the Shi'i community, namely their collective constitution of a charismatic *Gemeinschaft* with historical agency. This is what was potentially evident in the Shaykhi school of thought, brought from *de jure* to *de facto* by Bab and thus most feared by kings and clerics alike.

The Babi Movement was one of the most glorious revolutionary uprisings and the very last insurrectionary protest to come out of the Shi'i charismatic disposition in the pre-modern period. Bab's movement embraced both the impoverished peasantry and the urban poor, suffering under the double jeopardy of feudal tyranny and colonial encroachment, and shook the tyrannical reign of the Qajars to its foundations. But the final predicament of the Shaykhi school and of the Babi Movement unfolded in the colonial consequences of the onslaught of European modernity and revealed the cruel fate of this noble uprising that gave birth to some of the greatest heroes of modern Islamic history. What happens to this movement at the end is yet another catastrophic example of Shi'ism collapsing on its own face upon success. Bab was arrested and executed in 1850. He had appointed one of his followers, Mirza Yahya Sobh Azal (1830–1912) as his successor. An attempted assassination against Naser al-Din Shah by Babis resulted in their massive persecution, which in turn culminated in their migration to Iraq in the Ottoman territories. The leadership of Yahya Sobh Azal was soon challenged by a number of other Babis, among them his brother Mirza Hossein Ali (1817–1892). The Ottoman authorities, under pressure from the Qajars, finally divided the two groups and sent Yahya Sobh Azal and his followers to Cyprus and Mirza Hossein Ali and his followers to Acre. Meanwhile, in 1866, Mirza Hossein Ali took the title of Baha'ullah ("Glory of God") and claimed to be the messiah promised by Bab. Soon he expanded his claim and thought of himself as the promised salvation of all religions, from Zoroastrianism to Christianity. Baha'ullah systematically eradicated every ounce of revolutionary energy from Babism and put it squarely at the service of the reigning monarchy and of Russian and then British colonialism. By the time that Iranians were getting ready to tear down the very foundation of Qajar monarchy in the course of the Constitutional Revolution, Baha'ullah officially sided with Muhammad Ali Shah. His son and successor Abd al-Baha went even further and was knighted by George V, and under the British mandate established the center of his vanity in Haifa. And thus Shi'ism succeeded once again in giving revolutionary momentum to one massive social protest in the form of Babism and then degenerating upon its success into Baha'ism.

By the time Baha'ullah and his successors were busy giving themselves obscene egotistical titles, the revolutionary momentum that had now degenerated into their personal vanity had dwindled into non-relevance in the birthplace of the movement. The revolutionary disposition of the movement had long since abandoned it and left it a graceless universalism with no material or moral claim on the fate of a charismatic community that had once invested it with that grace. Having come to the cul-de-sac of the personal vainglory of yet another self-proclaimed prophet, managing his fortune distanced from the predicament of the nation, the Shi'i community now turned to the most consequential event in its fateful encounter with colonial modernity: the Constitutional Revolution of 1906–1911.

The Constitutional Revolution of 1906–1911 was the ultimate event that fully implicated Shi'ism in the globalizing project of colonial modernity, bringing a century-long process to a cataclysmic turning point. The confrontation with the European colonial modernity transmuted Shi'ism once again into a site of ideological resistance to colonialism while exposing its doctrinal roots to the brutally corrosive onslaught of instrumental rationalism at the heart of the European Enlightenment. If the Babi Movement in Iran is the last medieval insurrection in the Iranian feudal society, the Constitutional Revolution is the first modern revolution upon its successful formation as a nation-state. The moral force of this revolution was predicated on the material basis of subterranean changes in the new Iranian social formations. A wide spectrum of forces and classes participated in the Constitutional Revolution and three distinct ideological formations divided their attention. Socialist, Nationalist, and Islamist persuasions are distinctly evident in the course of the Constitutional Revolution. The effervescence of these ideological formations, however, is only the evident index of far more serious subterranean movements. The Constitutional Revolution is the most significant development in modern Iranian history by virtue of its marking the collapse of the medieval Persian political culture and the simultaneous rise and expansion of the Iranian civil society. This dual development was squarely predicated on the progressive integration of the Iranian national economy into the global circulation of capital and its colonial ancillary. As it was struggling to pull itself out of its medieval fetters, the rising Iranian bourgeoisie was also in a fateful battle with the encroaching colonial interests and the dual encounter resulted in the measurable expansion of the material basis of the civil society. The constituent components of the civil society now were in full view of history. The landlords and peasants continued to form the principal class formations throughout the nineteenth century. They were dominated by and incorporated into the Qajar feudal monarchy and the network of their princely division of the country, along with their military apparatus and bureaucratic officialdom. The merchants, craftsmen, and shopkeepers were the nucleus of the expanding urbanization, soon to be augmented by a rising industrial, commercial, and financial bourgeoisie as well as an industrial working class.[39] These continuous and creative class formations were now in a nascent state of a revolutionary coagulation that would forever change the moral and material disposition of the society.

The active incorporation of the nascent Iranian national polity and economy into global capitalism and the semi-colonial status of Iran in that predicament had the unintended consequence of providing the nation with the material infrastructure of its civil society. The dramatic expansion and increased security of the highways (completed in the north by the Russians for their own colonial interests) as well as the improvement of the postal service and in particular the establishment of telegraph lines (completed in the south by the British for similar reasons) began to weave the warp and woof of the territorial texture together.[40] The simplification of Persian prose that had started early in the century, the proliferation of printing machines, and the emergence of a robust press gave color and texture to the national character of the civil society. The nationalization of Iranian history and culture, literature in particular and chiefly by European Orientalist, soon followed. Though inorganic, an aggressive group of what can now be called a "national intelligentsia" emerged and began to defy their moderate class interests and speak the harsh truth to the entrenched power and become the opened windows of the national consciousness. It is in the creative imagination of this national intelligentsia that the very idea of Iran as a nation begins to take shape. The significance of these intellectuals in theorizing the idea and ideal of a civil society as the social site of "the nation" cannot be overemphasized. In the careful wording of Said Amir Arjomand:

> The social background of the intelligentsia at the turn of the century was undoubtedly diverse and included clerical, bureaucratic, landowning, and mercantile elements. But this diversity of social background did not prevent their unification on the basis of a single ideology comprised of the philosophy of the Enlightenment, the Victorian conception of progress, and the political ideas of nationalism and of parliamentary democracy. Nor did it prevent the intelligentsia from acting as the agent of mobilization and political enfranchisement of the growing civil society on the basis of the same ideology.[41]

There thus developed an always massive discrepancy between the ideas and ideals of civil society as articulated by a national intelligentsia and the weak material basis of a national bourgeoisie that could never exact, but would only wish for, such ideals. The central significance of Shi'ism in the revolutionary disposition that resulted in the groundbreaking victory of the civil society over the Qajar court, as the symbolic citadel of Persian feudalism, was directly related to the jaundiced complexion of the Iranian national bourgeoisie. Again in Arjomand's words,

> in the early decades of the twentieth century, civil society, though growing in economic importance, was nevertheless quite small and weak. The mercantile bourgeoisie could not act effectively without seeking support from the hierocracy, and the urban alliance of the mosque and the bazaar could not fail to draw the military might of the tribal periphery into political arena.[42]

Shi'ism thus re-emerged as a revolutionary site of resistance by virtue of a historical mission it now had to perform in order to compensate for the material absence of a powerful bourgeoisie and the moral want of an ideological formulation of their ideals. Once again, as in the case of the Babi Movement, this revolutionary *conscience collective* had to release its critical creativity from the bondage of the clerical class. Contrary to the persistently infantilizing readings of Iranian history that considers the disenfranchised classes as the passive site of manipulation by the clergy,[43] the active site of this critical consciousness is nowhere else but among the dispossessed classes, the brutalized peasantry, the urban poor, the economically insecure artisans, shopkeepers, small manufacturers, as well as the disenfranchised tribal communities, all of which were actively represented among the dispossessed lower-ranking clerics. The triumph of the revolutionary *conscience collective* of the Shi'is over the petty rivalries of the Shi'i clerics is best evident in the hostilities between the seminarians of the two madrasas of Muhammadiyah and Sadr.[44] Being transformed from such degenerate competition for religious endowments and seminarian stipends to revolutionary leadership of a massive social protest in modern history was no small feat and certainly no work of the sort that "pretexts were sought and found for the excitement of popular religious emotions against the state,"[45] as the infantilizing, irrationalizing, readings of modern Iranian history would have it. The fact that the infamous picture of Naus, the Belgian Minister of Customs, in the Shi'i clerical robe became a focal point of attention for the revolutionaries has very little to do with exciting popular emotions and very much to do with the colonial target of the anger that now brought the clerical class closer to the economic interests of the rising Iranian bourgeoisie.

The weaker the Iranian national bourgeoisie in its material basis the stronger the need for the moral reconstitution of Shi'ism as a site of ideological resistance. The weakness of the nascent bourgeoisie was primarily rooted in its being pulled down by the Qajar feudalism and asunder by the overwhelmingly more powerful global capitalism in its colonial contingency. The massive influx and trading of the British and Russian consumer goods inside Iran could of course as much strengthen the rising bourgeoisie as stifle it if coupled with forced colonial heavy-handed interference. The anti-colonial disposition of the mercantile bourgeoisie was thus diametrically opposed to the proclivity of the corrupt Qajar court that had a banal ball giving out lucrative economic concessions to colonial powers in exchange for cash to finance their obscene trips to European capitals. The result is quite simple and forthcoming: in the absence of a robust political apparatus (political parties, organs, discourses, and contestations) to respond to its needs, a natural alliance developed between the nascent Iranian bourgeoisie and the clerical establishment. The clerical establishment itself was in general disenfranchised from its customary position of material power in the interregnum between the fall of the Safavids and the rise of the Qajars. Particularly under the reign of Nader Shah Afshar their control of the religious endowment was much curtailed. As late as the reign of Naser al-Din Shah, the Qajar court had the audacity of under Sepahsalar appropriating the religious endowments into its bureaucratic administration. With few prominent exceptions, such as the monumentally corrupt clerics like Mulla Ali Kani, who himself was among the major feudal landlords, the lower-ranking clerics suffered along with everybody else the consequences of an inept and corrupt Qajar court and their colonial potentates.

A few staccato events of crucial catalytic impact led to the success of the Constitutional Revolution and Mozaffar al-Din Shah granting his signature to the drafting of a constitution to his subjects while effectively on his deathbed. Among these events, the seminarian students' attack on the site of the Russian Bank of Tehran and then the governor of Tehran's public punishment and humiliation of a group of Tehran merchants on December 12 1905 are clear indices of the economic causes and the social significance of the revolution. By January 14 1906, the ailing monarch was forced to put his royal seal and personal signature on the establishment of an *Adalatkhaneh* ("House of Justice"). The persistence of the monarch's Prime Minister Ayn al-Dowleh in power and the procrastination in the implementation of the royal decree resulted in two other major events that are equally crucial in revealing the underlying forces of the Constitutional Revolution. First was the massive migration of the major ulama to Qom on 15 July 1906, and second the seeking sanctuary of some 30 merchants and clerics in the British embassy four days later and submitting their demands for (1) the return of the ulama, (2) dismissal of the stubborn prime minister, and (3) the establishment of the House of Justice to the monarch through the British chargé d'affaires, Grant Duff. By the end of the month they had achieved all their three objectives.

The result of the Constitutional Revolution, more than anything else, was the inauguration of the very idea of "Civil Society" and its ancillary expansion of the political community to include the new social formations in the Iranian social structure. The Shi'i clerics played a central role in the actual events leading to these groundbreaking conclusions. But at no point were they the sole historical agency of its achievement, or in full control of all its major events, nor did they have a complete conception of what a constitutional revolution had to achieve. A critical body of national intelligentsia, with waxing or waning religious sentiments, were equally, if not more, instrumental in translating the ideals of a constitutional democracy into the Iranian political culture. The road for this critical role to be played by a national body of lay intellectuals was paved as early as the early nineteenth century and in the writings of such prominent figures as Mirza Saleh Shirazi, Hajj Zeyn al-Abedin Maraghe'i, Mirza Fath Ali Akhondzadeh, Abdolrahim Talebof, Mirza Malkam Khan Nazem al-Dowleh, and Mirza Aqa Khan Kermani. As a result, in the course and certainly after the Constitutional Revolution, we can no longer see the Iranian social elite in its medieval composition of kings and clerics. Instead we witness the birth of a "nation" in direct response to the colonial domination, through which the joint projects of European modernity and the Enlightenment were now perceived.

The progressive formation of Iranian civil society was contingent on the active constitution of any number of "national" nuclei at symbolic, textual, and institutional levels. The gradual composition and nationalization of a progressive intelligentsia was a critical factor in this creative nationalization of the Iranian historical memory. From diverse social origins, Iranian intellectuals began to conceive of themselves as the unitary spokespersons of a new *national* reality. Their creative imagination became the very effervescent site of a *national* psyche, a *national* narrative, and a *national* self-projection. The nationalization of the Iranian history, culture, and literature in particular, was an instrumental development in this critical point. The scattered and dynastic history of the land began to be renarrated in national terms. The territorial integrity of a certain cultural identity began to be articulated in very certain terms. Persian literature, poetry in particular, became the literary and artistic location of a transcontinental claim on a national continuity of creative character. As highways, railroads, and telegraph lines began to chart and graph the land, as the shape of a sitting cat began to identify the cartographic appearance of a homeland cut to a shapely size by the cutting edge of colonialism, so did a national intelligentsia begin to narrate a national history, a national literature, a national poetry, in short a national claim on time and space. All of this was in direct response to colonialism. As colonialism was the hegemonic denial of national sovereignty of other nations, other nations began first by identifying themselves as nations, and nations became the territorial sites of resistance to the colonial denial of national sovereignty.

88 The end of Islamic ideology

But behind colonialism were European modernity and its Enlightenment. Through the prism of colonialism but in the mirror of European modernity did Iranians of the constitutional period begin to see and seek themselves as a nation.

It is all but obvious that Shi'ism, now the *de jure* and *de facto* religion of the overwhelming majority of Iranians, would not be spared of this universal *nationalization* of the emerging collective psyche. In the course of the ideological preparations for the Constitutional Revolution, Shi'ism itself is *nationalized* in Iran and increasingly identified with Persian elements in the Islamic culture. The successful nationalization of Shi'ism was so indisputable that it became something of a shock to generations of students educated in national curriculum to discover that the great figures in the Persian poetic pantheon were in fact Sunni. In order for the nationalization of Persian literature and the simultaneous nationalization of Shi'ism not to collide, contradict, and cancel each other out, the nationalization of Shi'ism inevitably accompanied a Shi'ification of the Persian intellectual, poetic in particular, legacy. Ferdowsi's presumed Zaydi affiliation became a particularly poignant point in case where in one iconic figure the nationalization of Shi'ism and the Shi'ification of Persian poetic imagination convened in each other. But the nationalization of Shi'ism was not merely reflected on the cultural constitution of a collective character. From the beginning of the nineteenth century, and as anti-colonial resistance began to take momentum in Iran, Shi'ism was effectively implicated in the nationalization of that resistance. The territorial losses to the Russians in the early part of the nineteenth century and the economic concessions to colonial powers in the middle and towards the end of the century all culminated in the constitution of a national mode of resistance in which Shi'ism was being actively implicated. By the commencement of the Constitutional Revolution in the late nineteenth and early twentieth century, Shi'ism was fully invested in the aggressive nationalization of anti-colonial resistance leading to the formation of a national polity. Here it really did not make a difference that some of the ulama were Constitutionalist and others against it. Both constitutionalist ulama, such as Mirza Hossein Khalil Tehrani, Mulla Mohammad Kazem Khorasani, and Mulla Abdollah Mazandarani, and those who opposed it, such as Sheykh Mohammad Kazem Yazdi, Hajji Mirza Hasan, and of course Shaykh Fazlollah Nuri, all contributed, in positive or negative terms, to the aggressive *nationalization of* Shi'ism, whereby the scattered symbolics, institutions, and texts of the faith coagulated into the iconic forces of a national religion. The actual constitution itself officially recognized Shi'ism as the state religion and as such gave ultimate legal status to the constitutional nationalization of a medieval faith.

The nationalization of Shi'ism meant its aggressive modernization, and its modernization meant the exposing of its medieval doctrinal roots to the corrosive elements of the joint projects of colonial modernity and European Enlightenment. The result was enduring and cataclysmic. But in the immediate aftermath of the Constitutional Revolution, Shi'ism managed to safeguard its potential revolutionary posture by *not being* politically successful. Had Shi'ism succeeded in dominating and singularly defining the Constitutional Revolution, the ultimate failure of the movement in establishing a representative democracy would have been immediately translated into yet another moment of crisis for Shi'ism. But fortunately for the revolutionary disposition of Shi'ism, it failed to monopolize the ideological discourses of the Constitutional Revolution and had to yield considerable space and leverage to alternative modes of mobilization constitutional to the colonially mitigated project of modernity. Two other simultaneous sites of ideological resistance to colonialism emerged in the course of the revolution: nationalism and socialism, in the broadest sense of these two terms. The nationalization of Shi'ism in the course of the Constitutional Revolution and the simultaneous exposure of its doctrinal roots to the corrosive elements of the joint projects of modernity and the Enlightenment meant its concurrent conversation with nationalism and socialism as the other two modes of ideological resistance to colonialism. Shi'ism thus entered the twentieth century completely mutated into a religious nativism that competed with the Iranian ethnic nationalism and third-world socialism as rival sites of resistance to colonialism.[46]

The competitive claims of nationalism and socialism to modernity *ipso facto* rendered the nationalized Shi'ism into religious nativism. The result of this fear of its two ideological rivals was catastrophic, not just for Shi'ism but for the nation at large. The fear of the Shi'i ulama that in the post-constitutional Iranian political culture they will lose the battle to the so-called "secular" nationalists and socialists forced them into an ill-fated alliance with Reza Shah in 1923 and the safeguarding of the Persian monarchy. Little did they know that they were now in the claws of a far mightier force. Reza Shah soon mounted a massive campaign towards the administrative centralization of power that would sweep away the clerical establishment of all but a shadow of the respect and responsibility they had gained and richly deserved in the course of the Constitutional Revolution. Soon after he ascended the Peacock Throne, Reza Shah commenced a massive process of administrative centralization that became the hallmark of post-Constitutional statism. In 1925, a succession of commercial, criminal, and civil laws began to codify and centralize the Iranian legal system, all at the expense of religious courts. In 1928, the Shah decided to give a new look to his subjects and by a royal decree ordered men out of their customary habits and limited the clerical habit only to those who could prove their legitimate claim to wearing it. In 1929, the government was put in charge of qualifying exams recognizing the juridical status of the clergy. In the same year Seyyed Hassan Modarres, a solitary voice of resistance to Reza Shah's megalomaniac consolidation of power was put in jail. Reza Shah had masterfully divided the Islamist, nationalist, and socialist forces that had come to revolutionary prominence in the course of the Constitutional Revolution and was destroying them one by one. In a pathetic degeneration of the revolutionary spirit of the Constitutional period, all forces of opposition receded to their tribal limitations and allowed a massive centralization of power by a tyrant to take root. In the name of *modernization*, Reza Shah mounted one of the most frightful manifestation of fascist statism in modern history, eliminating all autonomous centers of voluntary association, generating a *Gleichschaltung* program very similar to Hitler's in contemporary Germany.

In the 1930s, the totalitarian tendencies of Reza Shah's tyrannical statism only intensified. In 1931, even harsher limits were imposed on the operation of clerical courts. In 1932, the power to issue property titles and other notarization responsibilities was divested from the clerical courts. In the same year the king prohibited performances of the Shi'i Passion Play, *Ta'ziyeh*. In 1934, the curricular decisions of the religious seminaries were appropriated by the government. In the same year, the establishment of the Faculty of Theology at Tehran University created a *de facto* alternative to religious seminaries and critically compromised their autonomy. In 1936, Reza Shah carried his intention to give a new look to his subject further and ordered Iranian women out of their veils. A year later, in 1937, he had Seyyed Hasan Modarres murdered in jail.

When under pressure from the allied forces, Reza Shah was forced to abdicate in 1941, the clerical establishment was left in a state of total shambles, the insurrectionary spirit of Shi'ism nowhere in sight. The formation of the Fada'ian-e Islam in 1945 and the series of political assassinations for which they assumed responsibility between 1946 and 1951 were the most obvious evidence of the Shi'i insurrectionary spirit immediately after the abdication of Reza Shah and the Allied occupation of the country. Instead, it was the third-world socialism of the Tudeh Party that now singularly defined the political agenda of the nation between the abdication of Reza Shah in 1941 until the downfall of Mosaddeq in 1953. In the 1940s it was the massive appeal of Tudeh third-world socialism that tested Shi'ism as a site of insurrectionary mobilization. In the battle, Shi'ism was totally cornered and had to yield the banner of insurrectionary mobilization to one of its two principal secular rivals. The catalytic impact of the Tudeh Party third-world socialism, its successes and failures, was to radicalize Shi'ism even further in its revolutionary resolve. Whereas the experience of the Constitutional Revolution and its competition with Iranian nationalism were to nationalize Shi'ism in its political disposition, its competition with Tudeh Party third-world socialism had an enduring effect in its equally socialistic economic disposition. Another major catalytic impact of the Tudeh Party on the Shi'i political disposition was the translation of the trans-national third-world socialism of the Tudeh Party into the trans-national pan-Islamism to which now such prominent Shi'i figures as Ayatollah Kashani aspired.

In the 1950s, it was the turn of the nationalism of the Mosaddeq era to test and over-run the revolutionary potentials of Shi'ism. Although Ayatollah

The end of Islamic ideology 91

Kashani was instrumental in Mosaddeq's assumption of power in 1951, the increasing political presence of the Tudeh Party in and out of the nationalist Prime Minister's government frightened the top Shi'i clerics and other members of the clerical establishment. Kashani's anti-colonial position at the height of Mosaddeq's nationalization of the Iranian oil industry was an extraordinarily positive force in the 1950s. But once again the competitive edge between Shi'ism and its two "secular" counterparts in ideological resistance to power was turned against them all. When the CIA-engineered coup of 1953 brought the Shah back to power, Kashani led the clerical sentiment in welcoming the monarch back to power. Thus twice in the course of the twentieth century, once in 1925 and once in 1953, the Shi'i clerical establishment was instrumental in restoring monarchical rule to Iran, in both cases out of their fear for the rise and supremacy of alternative sites of ideological resistance, socialism in particular, to the Shi'i clerical position. What the experience reveals is that both nationalism and socialism successfully constituted themselves as alternative sites to Shi'ism and had their significant share of the insurrectionary *conscience collective* of the nation. They in turn had a catalytic effect on the nature and disposition of Shi'ism as an equally forceful ideological force. Whereas nationalism nationalized Shi'ism, socialism socialized it. Nationalized and socialized, Shi'ism, now in full conversational posture with two dominant ideological forces of anti-colonial modernity, was fully prepared for revolutionary mobilization, while at the very same time was massively exposed to the corrosive forces of instrumental reason, totally unbeknown to itself.

By the 1960s Shi'ism, now nationalized and socialized, was ready for an aggressive re-ideologization against both nationalism and socialism in order to reclaim its full revolutionary potentials. In the course of the June 1963 uprising, led by Ayatollah Khomeini, it momentarily regained that revolutionary posture, but now top-to-toe exposed to the corrosive elements of anti-colonial modernity, and wall-to-wall metamorphosed via its conversation with nationalism and socialism, plunging it even deeper into its predicament of Enlightenment Rationalism. That Khomeini's uprising in 1963 fails only reinvigorates Shi'ism as a revolutionary ideology. No sooner had Khomeini's uprising been brutally suppressed than the eloquent voice of Ali Shari'ati was raised to give by far the most powerful expression to the Shi'i insurrectionary disposition. When Shari'ati returned to Iran from Paris in 1965 – the eloquent, cosmopolitan, and flamboyant voice of a defiant generation in conversation with liberation movements all over the world – the suppression of the June 1963 uprising had totally demoralized the revolutionary disposition of Shi'ism. It is impossible to exaggerate the impact that Shari'ati had in single-handedly giving full ideological expression to all the suppressed revolutionary potentials of Shi'ism since the commencement of its fateful conversation with the colonially mitigated European modernity. By the mid-1970s, and before his forced departure for and subsequent death in London, Shari'ati had successfully transformed

Shi'ism into the triumphant site of ideological mobilization against the Pahlavi regime.

The consummate summation of a century and a half of exposure to the corrosive forces of modernity, Shari'ati finally delivered Shi'ism into Islamic Ideology, at the very same time delivering its *coup de grâce* too. Shari'ati's was the prophetic voice of Shi'ism in the course of its encounter with anti-colonial modernity. Having conversed with and subsumed nationalism and socialism, Shi'ism could not but see itself in the speculum of European colonial modernity as its supreme Other, and it became that Other. Shari'ati was the last Shi'i metaphysician and the first Shi'i ideologue, the very picture of a medieval faith in the mirror of colonial modernity. He was the culmination of a century and a half of persistent exposure to the colonially mitigated project of European modernity. He coagulated Shi'ism into Islamic Ideology and by that very act delivered its last, fatal, stroke. By the time Shari'ati attended Shi'ism in the mid-1960s, it had been effectively sidestepped by nationalism in the 1950s and by socialism in the 1940s and thus conversely nationalized and socialized in return. Khomeini's 1963 uprising was no ideological match for the combined attraction of nationalism of the National Front or socialism of the Tudeh Party and the Fada'ian-e Khalq Organization. Khomeini had to be defeated in 1963, as it were, for Shari'ati to emerge in the late 1960s and early 1970s in order to prepare the ideological foregrounding of Khomeini's second coming.

Shari'ati stole the show from both the nationalist and the socialist sites of resistance by out-nationalizing one and out-socializing the other in his fiery speeches at the Hosseiniyeh Ershad. In the concise wording of Ervand Abrahamian:

> The central theme in many of Shari'ati's works is that Third World countries such as Iran need two interconnected and current revolutions: a national revolution to end all forms of imperial domination and to vitalize ... the country's culture, heritage, and national identity; and a social revolution to end all forms of exploitation, eradicate poverty and capitalism, modernize the economy, and most important of all, establish a "just" "dynamic," and "classless" society.[47]

Shari'ati, however, did far more than merely appropriate the nationalist and socialist agenda and incorporate them both in a massive repoliticization of Shi'ism as Islamic Ideology. His years in Paris in the early 1960s coincided with the height of student activism on behalf of the Algerian and Cuban revolutions. His political maturation was thus instantly globalized in the French capital. His translations of Sartre, Fanon, and Che Guevara were the most critical indices of his active incorporation of Shi'ism into a global revolutionary disposition. With Sartre, he gave an existentialist twist to his historical defiance of the essentialized Muslim subject. With Fanon and Che Guevara his revolutionary persona expanded to cross-cultural proportions and assumed a sense of global camaraderie. The result was that he delivered Shi'ism to its full ideological formation not just by subsuming all other ideological products of the colonially mitigated encounter with colonial modernity but, far more importantly, with a sense of global significance and urgency. With Shari'ati, as a result, Shi'ism was not only ideologized in response to colonialism and its two ideological ancillaries, ethnic nationalism and third-world socialism, but far more significantly it was globalized beyond its native contingencies. Shari'ati took that historically globalized conception of Shi'ism as Islamic Ideology and brought it so critically close to the *conscience collective* of the Shi'i insurrectionary disposition that he almost completely de-authorized the clerical class as the custodians of that conscience. The clerical class, after Shari'ati, was no longer the chief defining force in charting the Shi'i revolutionary disposition. Much against the anger and frustration of the clerical class, Shari'ati successfully wedded Shi'ism to the historical agency of the Shi'is themselves, bypassing the wavering instrumentality of the mullahs.

By the dint of a historical accident, Shari'ati was interjected into this fateful mission exactly after the failure of Khomeini's June 1963 uprising and right before his triumphant return in February 1979. Shari'ati came to Iran in 1965 less than two years after Khomeini was forced into exile following his failed June 1963 uprising, and he left for London less than two years before Khomeini returned to finish the job he had left behind in 1979. Khomeini had to vacate the scene, as it were, for Shari'ati to come back to his homeland from Paris and read Shi'ism fully into its ideological modernity. Khomeini returned triumphantly back to Iran soon after Shari'ati left for London, to die less than a month later from a massive heart attack, and rode on the rising wave Shari'ati had set in motion. It is at this point that Khomeini becomes the sole defining factor of the Shi'i insurrectionary disposition. If one revolutionary figure were to personify the paradox of Shi'ism at its insurrectionary best and its tyrannical worst, it is Ayatollah Khomeini. For decades he was the very voice, the cathartic elegance, of the noble anger that is Shi'ism, and then at the moment of his success in establishing a diabolic theocracy he became the incubus nightmare that always awaits any Shi'i success. If in the course of the 1977–1979 uprising, Khomeini was the beacon of revolutionary hope, the 10 years of his tyrannical reign between 1979 and 1989 were an interminable nightmare in their medieval terror. The Iran–Iraq war of the 1980–1988 only postponed the self-evident: that Shi'ism had once again defeated itself at the moment of its victory. By the end of the war in 1988 and the death of Khomeini in 1989, the 1990s witnessed Shi'ism in full tyrannical swing, the return of its repressed. The clerical class now set upon itself the task of routinizing the terror minus the charismatic occasion of its inauguration.

Khomeini's revolutionary success was the simultaneous failure of Shi'ism as the insurrectionary conscience of a people. But this time around Shi'ism was so thoroughly conversant with colonial modernity that its medieval doctrinal

94 The end of Islamic ideology

roots were dangerously exposed. Colonialism was the historical conduit of exposing Shi'ism to modernity. As alternative sites of resistance to colonialism, nationalism and socialism were the two ideological surrogates of modernity. Whether it resisted colonialism or competed with nationalism and socialism, Shi'ism (at the heart of Islam in general) *ipso facto* exposed its medieval doctrinal roots to the corrosive elements of European Enlightenment and colonial modernity.

The paradoxical history of Shi'ism in modernity, constantly turning from a revolutionary ideology into an ideology of tyranny, has now ended in the cul-de-sac of the clerical establishment stubbornly holding on to power, while reform-minded Shi'is like Abdolkarim Soroush are trying to restore to Shi'ism its inaugurating authority.[48] On the two complementary poles of theory and praxis, Soroush is trying to expand the historical claim of Shi'i scholastic limits, while President Mohammad Khatami is trying to reign in the dialectical outburst of the forceful self-negation of Shi'ism as a historical paradox. They, Soroush and Khatami, in their complementarity, are contradicting each other. All the appearances are that they complement each other in theory and practice. But in effect they are negating each other. One is contracting the hermeneutic effervescence of Shi'ism against itself, whereas the other is expanding that very dialectic into a conversation with its historical others. Soroush is pulling the Shi'i paradox towards a metaphysical resubjection, Khatami is pushing the edges of the selfsame paradox to restore agential autonomy to its history. In the dialectic of their cross-negation is now inserting itself a youthful revolution that feeds on nothing but the raw testosterone of its material, anti-oedipal, revolt. Soroush and Khatami are the historical mutations of Shari'ati and Khomeini. One is trying to de-ideologize Shi'ism back into its metaphysics of certainty, whereas the other is trying to have it engage in a civilizational dialogue with its historical others. Soroush is trying to globalize Shi'ism into a hermeneutics of progressive changes, whereas Khatami is trying to engage in a politics of dialogical self-affirmation. They will not necessitate; they will negate each other.

The July 1999 student uprising in Iran is the final demarcation of the end of Islamic Ideology not because this massive outpouring of anti-governmental mobilization was *anti-Islamic*, but precisely because it was *non-Islamic, non-nationalist, non-socialist*, in one word: non-ideological, or post-ideological. It rendered not just the Islamic but any other form of ideological metanarrative irrelevant. The material force of their defiance exceeds and post dates the necessity of any ideological convictions. By appearing to reform the Shi'i state from within, in both moral and material terms, what Soroush and Khatami in effect are doing is to gloss over the fact that the age of Islamic Ideology is effectively over, that Iran as a nation and as a political culture is on the verge of an entirely new moral and normative agency, and that both the glorious and the catastrophic consequences of the Islamic Ideology have now resulted in an entirely different political culture, one that can no longer be contingent on the

The end of Islamic ideology 95

medieval vocabulary of a theocracy. From the very ideological predicate of the constitution of the Islamic republic on the supreme political authority of the Jurist (*velayat-e faqih*) to such repressive organs as the Council of Guardians and the Expediency Council, the pernicious mutation of a once-revolutionary reading of a cataclysmic faith is now in full view. The seeds of this mutation have been self-sprouting in Shi'ism itself. Because of its long and arduous battles against tyranny, from the tyranny of the early caliphs to that of the latest monarchs, Shi'ism itself easily collapses into the most ferocious form of tyranny of the most sacred severity the instant that it assumes power. Shi'ism has to be defeated in order to remain victorious. Shi'ism is a religion of protest. It can never succeed without negating itself. When it succeeds, Shi'ism is in double jeopardy. In the Islamic context at large, it partakes in the masculinism of its transcendental deity, as in the Iranian context in particular it exacerbates the monstrosity of a monarchical claim on our credulity.

The emerging claims of the so-called "Dynamic Ijtihad" that today we hear in Iran and among the expatriate Iranists is an entirely bogus claim to gloss over this critical moment in the demise of Islamic Ideology. It is hard to believe that some 200 years into the catastrophic consequences of an ideological formation that has resulted in a tyrannical theocracy, still serious people can talk about "Dynamic Ijtihad." Dynamic Ijtihad is yet another trap to plunge the cosmopolitan Iranian political culture even deeper into an exclusively *Islamic* discourse. Two decades into its success, Shi'ism has once again completely lost its revolutionary momentum and turned into an ideology of tyrannical suppression. What we have witnessed over the last two decades is global capitalism rendering all religious nativism, ethnic nationalism, and third-world socialism obsolete, exactly at a time when the constitutional paradox of Shi'ism is coming back to haunt it. This at a time that Abdolkarim Soroush is trying to *de-historicize* Shi'ism – and with it Islam itself – to rescue it from its current predicament, whereas Khatami is trying to *historicize* it through a forced dialogue with its already outdated civilizational others. The result is that Soroush and Khatami, who look compatible on the surface, will in effect work against each other. While global capitalism and the Shi'i paradox will corroborate each other and thus Shi'ism as Islamic Ideology will lose its discursive legitimacy, Islamic Ideology loses its claim on state legitimacy, and Shi'ism as religious nativism will join ethnic nationalism and third-world socialism as outdated ideological formations – once again letting go of the central paradox of Shi'ism to roam freely into its future history.

The end of Islamic Ideology is not the end of ideology, nor is it the end of history, or the appearance of the last man.[49] Such self-congratulatory assumptions at the presumed centers of globalizing power are nervous signs of the encroachment of the periphery, the fear of the foreign. The center can no longer hold, and the periphery is now the center, the center periphery, and thus the instantaneous collapse of all nervous bifurcations that have for too long divided the world to rule it. The end of Islamic Ideology is not "the failure of political Islam" either.[50] If an iota of self-respect and historical agency has remained for Muslims some two centuries into the ravages of colonialism, it is precisely because of their having successfully turned aspects of their ancestral faith into sites of resistance to colonialism. The remarkable common feature of all such diagnosis of *Islamism* as political failure[51] is their selective historical amnesia that the mutation of Islam into Islamic Ideology took place under duress and in the shadow of the extended guns of colonialism.

The Islamic Ideology exhausted, Shi'ism, as Islam's insurrectionary dream of itself, will recede back into the latent layers of Muslim collective memory, awaiting yet another charismatic occasion to reclaim itself, to come back and lead yet another revolt that will be defeated at the moment of its success: Sisyphus paramount. Neither Mulla Sadra Shirazi nor Shaykh Ahmad Ahsa'i, neither Abdolkarim Soroush, nor Aristotle himself can save Shi'ism from its historical predicament. Shi'ism is a paradox. It dies at the moment of its success. It succeeds at the moment of its failure. It is only alive when it speaks the defiant truth to the entrenched power. It dies the second it succeeds and assumes power. The bullet that at the conclusion of this paragraph was sitting in the spinal chord of Saeed Hajjarian, a reformist ally of President Mohammad Khatami who was the target of an assassination attempt in March 2000, is the most eloquent argument that I can offer in defense of my thesis.

In a moving phrase that characterizes the social evolution of Christianity, the father of Christian liberation theology Gustavo Gutiérrez speaks of a "historical pilgrimage" of the religion itself, a pilgrimage from which we ought to learn "its success, its omissions, and its errors."[52] This is a critical self-reflection that ultimately amounts to "our heritage" – or the way a religion historically understands itself. What I have sought to outline in this chapter is in the spirit of a similar "historical pilgrimage" in order to argue that such a heritage, particularly in its political articulation in Islam, is not given but earned, effectively rehistoricized and reassessed by way of clearing the air to see in what particular terms it has done its services, run its course, and is now ready for another dispensation. In the context of Christianity proper, Gustavo Gutiérrez speaks of a succession of attempts – ranging from *theology of temporal realities* to *theology of history, theology of development,* even of a *theology of revolution,* and ultimately of course of a *political theology* and a *theology of liberation.* He categorically dismisses the historical record of Christianity in having taken the realm of the political or what he calls the domain of "social praxis" seriously, and as of 1971 could write that "in Christian circle there was – and continues to be – difficulty in perceiving the originality and specificity of the political sphere."[53] He observes that Christianity was very much limited to the private sphere and that the public sphere was left outside the domain of Christian theology, or at best delegated to an abstraction called "common good."

There was, in the Islamic case, quite an overabundance of emphasis on that political sphere – so much so that there remained very little room for the non-political sphere. There has in fact never been a clearly articulated bifurcation between the private and the public domains in the Islamic political culture. If anything, Islam has been too much public in its demands upon the individual, particularly during the last 200 years and in its active interlocution with European colonialism. Gustavo Gutiérrez believes, "we must take a new look at Christian life; we must see how these emphases in the past have conditioned and challenged the historical presence of the Church." A similar assessment and moral inventory is obviously in order in the Islamic case as well and its combative encounter with colonial modernity. The positing of the political, as Gustavo Gutiérrez argues, will in fact generate and articulate a new kind of Christianity. In his own words, "in this participation [in the public domain] will be heard nuances of the Word of God which are imperceptible in other existential situations and without which there can be no authentic and fruitful faithfulness to the lord." He goes so far as radically posing the question, "what does it mean to be a Christian today?" and adds further momentum to this question by forcing it to face the existential dilemma posed by Albert Camus: "To decide whether life deserves to be lived or not."[54] Islam deserves and demands no less a vigorous question if it is to be rescued from the militant adventurism of Osama bin Laden around the globe and the vagaries of an Islamist theocracy in Iran alike.

To ask the similar question of "what does it mean to be a Muslim today?" and thus to face the identical question that Camus poses and remains valid is to have what Gramsci has called a historical inventory of how and when did Muslims come to where they are now. If we are able to escape the frightful nightmare that Bin Laden and his American/Israeli neocon counterparts have created, we will have that necessary sanity to rethink Islam in its most recent history. The history of Shi'ism over the last 200 years, in the way I have outlined it in very general strokes in this chapter, is the history of Islam in general, and indicative of a more pervasive rise of Islam as the site of ideological resistance to European colonialism and now American imperialism. In the course of this mutation, Islam as a cosmopolitan culture in and of itself was mutated into a singular political citation confronting a monumental abstraction called "the West." While Islam in general was stripped of its innate cosmopolitan disposition and systematically mutated into a singular site of ideological resistance to this "West," Muslims themselves were being increasingly incorporated into a cosmopolitan culture of different and entirely worldly nature. In specifically political terms, socialism, nationalist, or Islamist dispositions were the divergent ideological insignia of integration into a far more cosmopolitan nature in correspondence to which Muslims were at times not even considering themselves Muslims, and simply as human beings partook in the moral and normative imaginary of a planetary worldview to which they were integral but over which they had no complete or exclusive control. Any singular claim to absolutist authenticity – Islamist, nationalist, or socialist – was bound to distort and thus repress the more worldly disposition of this cosmopolitan culture of resistance to colonialism. Because Islamist ideologies emerged in dialogical contestation against colonialism and thus perforce in dialectical conversation with the two oppositional ideologies most responsive to the same malady – nationalism and socialism – Islam too became a metanarrative of absolutist salvation, a proclivity not entirely alien to its own premodern metaphysical disposition. The combination of its own innate absolutists tendencies and its combative contestations with colonialism, as well as with anti-colonial nationalism and socialism, inevitably pushed Islam towards the nomocentricity of its juridical disposition, rather than the logocentricity of its philosophies or the homocentricity of its varied forms of mysticism – and thus the jurists, Sunni or Shi'i, became the principal iconic spokespersons of political Islam. The exclusive and combative juridicalization of Islam in its entirety meant that political Islamism also became correspondingly juridical and thus was systematically corroded, not just the cosmopolitan disposition of Islam itself but in fact the emerging cosmopolitanism of Muslims in their renewed worldly *Weltanschauung* (philosophy of life). These tendencies towards absolutist certainties were not of course limited to Islam. As Islam was thus reduced to yet another form of nativism, so was nationalism degenerated into jingoism, as did socialism into Stalinism.

Among all the Muslim ideologues of the last two centuries, Ali Shari'ati was the farthest into a radical ideologization of Islam and thus (quite paradoxically) closest in seeing it through a breakthrough into a new cosmopolitan disposition – and that by virtue of his prolonged and transformative conversations with Fanon and Che Guevara, and through them with the larger world revolutionary movements. As a result, throughout his writings Shari'ati became worldly in his disposition and nearest in rescuing Islam from its nativism, which is precisely what his American counterpart Malcolm X was about to do after his break with the Nation of Islam, from the exactly opposite direction. If we take the two leading revolutionary figures of the latter part of the twentieth century as our iconic conclusion of what has happened to the faith in general, whereas Ayatollah Khomeini's revolutionary practices were ultimately trapped inside the paradox of Shi'ism, Ali Shari'ati's revolutionary ideas were emancipated from that disabling paradox and thus wedded the particularity of Shi'ism to Islam at large, and even further on connected Islam to a world revolutionary mobilization. It is now from that transitional vantage point, when Islamist nativism has all but forgotten its originary cosmopolitan moment and yet it is about to discover a renewed worldly cosmopolitanism, that I need to tell the rest of my story.

3 Blindness and insight

> Europe is literally the creation of the Third World
> Frantz Fanon *The Wretched Of The Earth* (New York: Grove Press, 1963: 208)

While studying in Paris in the 1960s Ali Shari'ati (1933–1977) carried the Islam within him into a fateful conversation with radical revolutionaries and revolutions around the globe – with those in Cuba and Algeria in particular. Just like his contemporary Malcolm X (1925–1965), Shari'ati was shedding one skin after another in exposing his faith to ever wider revolutionary circles, mobilizing his Islam to face potent insurrectionary uprisings – a global reconfiguration of power in which Islam had to play an integral, but never a definitive, role. It is in that role that Islam could have, and yet has not, discovered its renewed cosmopolitan worldliness. Shari'ati moving from Iran to Paris, just like Malcolm X moving from America to Mecca, connected two colonially divergent worlds to make room for a far wider domain of revolutionary engagements – one that would make no distinction between a center and its peripheries, between a Christian who had become a Muslim, and a Muslim who had gone global.

The only crucial advantage of Malcolm X over Ali Shari'ati is that Malcolm had never any delusional configuration called "the West" bog him down. For him "the White Man" was the bugbear of his noble anger, which apparition he finally overcomes towards the end of his short but glorious revolutionary career. The combined wisdom of Ali Shari'ati and Malcolm X bears fruitfully on Frantz Fanon's revelations. Not just *literally*, as Fanon has said, but *conceptually* Europe is the invention of the Third World, which is a far more insidious proposition; it is not just Europe, as Fanon has rightly proposed, that is the invention of the Third World, the Third World itself is the invention of Europe, which results in a far more pernicious dialectic in which "Europe" (and thus "the West") always wins and "the Third World" always loses. In the dialectical treachery of that reciprocity dwells the roots of where and when Muslim intellectuals and activists the world over have picked up their pen or gun and started shooting. Here in this chapter, I wish to give a detailed outline of why and how is it that at the most serious epistemic level, any intellectual engagement with Islam that is still conversant with the very centrality of the notion of "Europe," or more specifically with the European colonial modernity has hit a cul-de-sac – and how is it that in one particularly potent and persuasive figure, Abdolkarim Soroush, an ambitious intellectual manages to write with an astonishing intellectual proficiency and yet have absolutely nothing to say about the global predicament of Muslims today. My intention here is to examine Abdolkarim Soroush as the very last Muslim ideologue – the Muslim ideologue who is actively engaged in an Islamic conversation with a dead entity. In debunking the outdated project of Abdolkarim Soroush, with an aside on an even less relevant figure, Tariq Ramadan, I wish to resuscitate the moral outrage and revolutionary project of Ali Shari'ati, but this time around with the global spirit of Malcolm X running through his rebellious veins.

Thinkers such as Abdolkarim Soroush and Tariq Ramadan have brought the revolutionary projects of Ali Shari'ati and Malcolm X to a false, premature, and forced conclusion by either subjecting them to a scholastic hermeneutics (Soroush), or thinking the locus of the encounter shifted to a vacated neighborhood in "the West" (Ramadan), or above all once again refetishizing (both Soroush and Ramadan) "the West," a colonial concoction that had been all but surpassed in the works of Ali Shari'ati and which had never been even a factor in the more advanced project of Malcolm X. In thinking through the emerging terms of a new liberation theodicy, we need to cross over the recent works of thinkers like Soroush and Ramadan and go back to those of Ali Shari'ati and Malcolm X and resume a conversation with their unfinished projects, which are almost identical, though launched from two opposing ends of the fictive line of "the West." Any serious reconsideration of the emancipatory aspirations at the heart of Ali Shari'ati and Malcolm X's unfinished project will wash over and supercede the belated works of people like Abdolkarim Soroush or Tariq Ramadan.

In proposing a resumed conversation with the unfinished revolutionary projects of Ali Shari'ati and Malcolm X, I also intend a not so hidden warning against the notion of European modernity as presumably still an unfinished project. Jürgen Habermas, the distinguished German philosopher, still insists on considering the European (for the rest of the world colonial) project of modernity unfinished, seemingly unaware or indifferent to the fact that the rest of the world received this lofty project through the gun barrel of European colonialism. What I am ultimately proposing here is to posit Ali Shari'ati and Malcolm X's unfinished global revolutionary project, to which particular liberation theology Islam is integral (but never definitive), up against Jürgen Habermas' reading of European modernity as an unfinished project, to which "Europe" (and by extension "the West") is not just integral but in fact definitive. For us to reach, at the end of this book, a critical evaluation of Malcolm X's unfinished revolutionary project as a prophetic vision of a new liberation theology, we will also need to see how what Habermas calls the unfinished project of (European) modernity is itself a further and more insidious philosophical trap towards which the non-European world cannot have any attraction or interest.¹

For Habermas *the* critical point of departure in the philosophical history of European modernity is Kant, and by the time Kant had published his "What is Enlightenment" (1784), he had already long since initiated the philosophical discourse of modernity. The philosophical tradition of European modernity considers Kant the precursor of the Young Hegelians, the first philosopher to make a clean break with the European metaphysical tradition, the philosopher who made everyone after him suspect everlasting assumptions of the metaphysics. In his essay on Kant's "What is the Enlightenment," Foucault, who otherwise criticizes Kant for having made the whole range of human sciences and the will to knowledge possible, considers him the first to have initiated a philosophical preoccupation with modernity that makes Hegel, Nietzsche, Max Weber, Horkheimer and Adorno, and even himself possible.² The only objection that Habermas has with Kant is that the father of Enlightenment modernity opted for a *subject-centered* self-criticism as the inaugurating moment of modernity; while Habermas proposes an *intersubjective* alternative that is predicated on a communicative reading of reason, a perspective, he believes, that will ward off the postmodern critique of modernity, while saving it for posterity. The fact that this liberal-minded philosophical articulation of *intersubjectivity* is always-already predicated on a nasty political imbalance of power does not seem to bother Habermas.

But that is the least of Habermas' problem and his reading of Kant so far as the world beyond the Danube River is concerned. The marking of Kant as the inaugural moment of modernity is quite crucial when we take a look at another work of the father of European modernity, namely his *Observations on the Feeling of the Beautiful and Sublime* (1763), in which we witness Kant willing to perform certain moral surgeries on Arabs ("the Spaniards of the Orient"), Persians ("The French of Asia"), or Japanese ("the Englishmen of this part of the world") to endow them with the hope of becoming like Europeans – though everything about them in Kant's estimation is either "degenerate" or "grotesque." But alas no moral surgery can save other Orientals in Kant's book:

> The Negroes of Africa [believed the author of "What is the Enlightenment" (1784)] have by nature no feeling that rises above the trifling. Mr. [David] Hume challenges anyone to cite a single example in which a Negro has shown talents, and asserts that among the hundreds of thousands of blacks who are transported elsewhere from their countries, although many of them have even been set free, still not a single one was ever found who presented anything great in art or science or any other praiseworthy quality, even though among the whites some continually rise aloft from the lowest rabble and through superior gifts earn respect in the world.³

On another occasion, Kant quotes a statement about women that is attributed to an African and reported by a certain Father Labat, to which the author of *Critique of Pure Reason* adds, "And it might be that there were something in this which perhaps deserved to be considered; but in short, this fellow was quite black from head to foot, a clear proof that what he said was stupid."[4] This is the author of a modernity that Habermas considers still unfinished, but worthy of getting there. Habermas is known for his insistence that German's should come to terms with their Nazi past. But he is yet to see the evidence of Immanuel Kant on the ground of European concentration camps and the Jewish Holocaust.

In his *Dispute of the Faculties* (1798), Kant had considered if not the French Revolution itself then the enthusiasm with which it was perceived and received as the empirical indication that the general direction of the human condition had a "moral tendency" towards the better. Kant considered the French Revolution central to his theory of historical emancipation of the human condition for the better, "for that event is too great, too closely interwoven with the interest of mankind, not to be remembered by the peoples of the world under the inducement of favorable conditions and awakened for renewed attempts of this kind."[5] Habermas takes this as an indication that "Foucault discovers in Kant the *first* philosopher to take aim like an archer at the heart of a present that is concentrated in the significance of the contemporary moment, and thereby to inaugurate the discourse of modernity."[6] Both Kant and Foucault, and of course Habermas, are correct in detecting in the French Revolution the inaugural pause of a history of emancipation in modernity, but it is not quite clear from any of these glosses if Kant considers people who are "quite black from head to foot" ("a clear proof" of their stupidity) among what he considers "the peoples of the world" and thus worthy of this emancipation. In Kant's "world" humanity at large was de-worlded; in Kant's notion of "emancipation" humanity at large was worthy only of slavery. This does not seem to bother Habermas.

In Habermas' reading of Kant, he is principally responsible for "transforming thought into a diagnostic instrument," because "he entangles it in the restless process of self-reassurance that to this day has kept modernity in ceaseless motion within the horizon of a new historical consciousness."[7] From Hölderlin to Foucault, Habermas considers a genealogy of poets and philosophers who

> contribute to the sharpening of the modern time consciousness that made its entrance into philosophy with the question: What is Enlightenment?" The philosopher becomes a contemporary; he steps out of the anonymity of an impersonal enterprise and identifies himself as a person of flesh and blood to whom every clinical investigation of a contemporary period confronting him must be directed."[8]

The only problem with this entrance into the lofty contemporaneity of the European philosopher is that he (and they are all he) has an imperial notion of Europe by which the world has to abide or else be called a savage. "All these savages," Habermas seems to have neglected this part of Kant's wisdom, "have little feeling for the beautiful in moral understanding, and the generous forgiveness of an injury, which is at once noble and beautiful, is completely unknown as a virtue among the savages, but is rather disdained as miserable cowardice."[9] One must not for a second be distracted by the vicious racism of this passage, lest we will forget that as savages we non-Europeans have simply no entry into Kant's moral imaginary. It is not that we are just ugly, "degenerate," "grotesque," "quite black from head to foot," and thus incapable of grasping beauty. But we are so because we are part of the knowable world, at the benevolent mercy of the white European, who alone is for Kant the knowing subject. When predicated on his reading of Kant, Habermas generously offers the world the chance to engage in forming "intersubjectivity" he fails to understand that we colored folks are *the objects* of Kantian subjective observation and can never be the subjects to any intersubjectivity. This is the problem that the rest of the world faces even if we were to try to give Habermas a helping hand in finishing his project of modernity.

For Habermas, *modernity* is an unfinished project. It has a long way to go. He opposes Lyotard's critic of *modernity* because he believes that the dismantling of any project will ultimately have to rely on a rational discourse. Habermas equally criticizes Horkheimer and Adorno for their critic of the Enlightenment project by abandoning systematic theorization for what he calls "ad hoc determinate negation."[10] In Richard Rorty's words:

> anything that abandons such an approach [to generate universal theories] will be counted by Habermas as more or less irrationalist because it drops the notions which have been used to justify the various reforms which have marked the history of the Western democracies since the Enlightenment, and which are still being used to criticize the socio-economic institutions of both the Free and the Communist worlds.[11]

Rorty further adds that "abandoning a standpoint which is, if not transcendental, at least 'universalistic,' seems to Habermas to betray the social hopes which have been central to liberal politics."[12] One might still insist in seeing Habermas' point that the world needs to have "social hopes," for social hopes are good, and in order to have them we do indeed need to have at least "universalistic" if not "transcendental" standpoints. But the problem is that for the world to join Habermas (and Rorty for that matter) in entertaining such "social hopes," people must cross this particularly tall wall that the very father of European Enlightenment has erected between them and the fortunate white folks: "So fundamental," Immanuel Kant insists, "is the difference between these two races of man, and it appears to be as great in regard to mental capacities as in color."[13] So it is not just their unfortunate color that the black folk have no clue what to do with but their very mental capacities that stands between their wretched existence and the "social hopes" that on behalf of Kant, Habermas wishes to impart to them. People around the globe do indeed wish to partake in those "social hopes" and attest to certain universal principles by which they are to be attained. But alas, "the blacks are very vain but in the Negro's way, and so talkative that they must be driven apart from each other with thrashing"[14] – thrashing that is as in inflicting corporal punishment with repeated blows, as in whacking, beating, and such. So what Habermas calls "irrationality" is unfortunately written into our "Negro's way" and there is no way we can give a helping hand in finishing this particular project of modernity. If we were to open our mouth to say something in support of finishing this project of modernity we are afraid we will expose our tenacity in talking too much and thus necessitate a solid whipping to stop us from talking. The blindness of Habermas and the entire racist modernity he represents is solidly written into the insights that he shares with his fellow countryman Kant.

One can of course argue that the defense of European Enlightenment modernity and the cause of finishing its project must perhaps altogether abandon Germany and Immanuel Kant and go to the United Kingdom and John Stuart Mill and begin with his magnificent essay *On Liberty*. But here too, alas, we face an even taller citadel. "The sacred duties," this is John Stuart Mill talking, after 23 years in the service of the East India Company, "which civilized nations owe to the independence and nationality of each other are not binding towards those to whom nationality and independence are certain evil, or at best a questionable good."[15] We are, however, not at liberty to make such shifts because if we look at the same problem from a poststructuralist, postmodernist perspective, the principal *objection* of Foucault to Kant is in fact his having initiated this modernity. The postmodern critic of Kant considers him *the* epistemologist who initiated the age of anthropological thought and made the human sciences possible with his analysis of *finiteness*. In *The Order of Things*, for example, Foucault argued that the mode of knowledge prevalent in modernity is characterized by the cognitive subject becoming self-referential and aware of its finiteness and thus demanding infinite power. As Habermas puts it, Foucault believed that "Kant transforms this aporia [of the self-referential cognitive subject being aware of its finiteness and thus demanding infinite power] into a structural principle of his epistemology by reinterpreting the limitations of our finite faculty of cognition as transcendental conditions of a knowledge that progresses on into infinitude."[16] Thus the project of modernity is inseparable form Kant's epistemological project – nor is his racism.

Habermas, nevertheless, is relentless and uncompromising in his defense of European modernity. In his theory of communicative action he argues that *rationality* is a moral imperative that is social. The communication among social agents places them in a moral bond. This is the conceptual premise of his defense of modernity around the idea of "autonomous public spheres." Through the work of Habermas, the entire course of Western

European philosophy, in particular the Enlightenment, is actively relegitimated. In addition, Habermas' claim for the Western European project of the Enlightenment is no longer even culture-specific to this region but in fact constitutionally universal. Concerned about the rise of neo-fascism in Germany, Habermas has branded the entire sweep of poststructuralist developments, from Nietzsche to Heidegger and Derrida, as "neoconservatives" and politically dangerous. Habermas' critique of the postmodernists and the accusation of labeling them "neoconservatives," have to do with the fact that he considers *modernity* as a philosophical condition through which we have a critical stance towards the foundations of our beliefs. His critique of the postmodernists is that they deny the existence of a universally legitimate moral consciousness from which we can sustain a critical stance to these foundations. He indeed may be correct in calling postmodernists what he does. But what for the rest of the world is entirely unclear is what exactly this seesawing between European modernity and European postmodernity has to say about the particularities of a universal colonial condition that was first placed outside the fold of Enlightenment modernity by its very founding father and then again deemed demonstrative of the inapplicability of such metanarratives by those who were thought to be criticizing Kant. Enlightenment modernity had no room for the colonized world (the vast expanse of the world at large in Asia, Africa, and Latin America) because it thought that black folks are constitutionally stupid and that they talk too much. Postmodernity does have room for the colonized world but only as the exception that proves the rule of universal humanity false. So either way, the non-European world is placed outside the fold of both the European reason and the European un-reason. So it makes absolutely no difference for the rest of the world whether this debate between modernists and postmodernists goes one way or another. Either way, we are out.

To be sure, the postmodernists are not rolling back and pretending they are dead when it comes to Habermas' defense of modernity as an unfinished project. Jean-François Lyotard, for example, criticizes Marx, Freud, and Habermas, among others, for having produced "metanarratives" as the theoretical enunciation of "modernity." For Lyotard the term "modern" refers to "any science that legitimates itself with reference to a meta-discourse."[17] A "meta-discourse" is "an explicit appeal to some grand narrative, such as the dialectics of the Spirit, the hermeneutics of meaning, the emancipation of the rational or working subject, or the creation of wealth."[18] For Lyotard, the term "postmodern" is an "incredulity towards metanarratives." Lyotard criticizes Habermas for producing yet another metanarrative, this one of "emancipation," which is even more abstract than the Marxian or Freudian metanarratives. Lyotard considers any attempt such as Habermas' to generate universalizable "theory" as yet another "metanarrative" in the Enlightenment spirit of "modernity." This indeed is a crucial warning when it comes to any liberation idea, theory, or theology – and thus the necessity of understanding liberation theodicy as a mode of thinking and practice that is always narratively unsure but morally certain of itself – and it does so by working its shadows of doubt into the shades of its certainties.

Richard Rorty, too, criticizes Habermas for insisting on *theory*, and in turn opts for what he calls "ethnocentrism" and "social practice." Rorty opposes Habermas' attempt to argue that "Western democracies" are predicated on a sustainable *theory* that is traceable to the Enlightenment. He insists that "... whereas Habermas compliments 'bourgeois ideals' by reference to the 'elements of reason' contained in them, it would be better just to compliment those untheorethical sorts of narrative discourse which make up the political speech of the Western democracies. It would be better to be frankly ethnocentric."[19] This frankness on the part of Rorty is quite crucial and in fact necessary, and indeed closer to what Kant had in mind by his Enlightenment, and thus the rest of the world will not have any delusional fantasy, nor would there be any expectation from it, to come and join Europeans in achieving the ends of their modernity. As Rorty rightly says, these ideals and aspirations have been the "social practices" of Europeans and their "Western democracies," as in fact a definitive and a particularity of these democracies as slavery in Greek city-states and colonialism in European modernity.

Rorty's unabashedly ethnocentric references to "the political speech of Western democracies" and even more emphatically his confession that "it would be better to be frankly ethnocentric" are where the postmodern critic of the projects of modernity finally yields inroad into a postcolonial critic of modernity which is conspicuously absent from the argument of both the defendant and the opponents of the Enlightenment. Rorty's admission that what Habermas insists in universalizing into the status of *theory* is really nothing more than "the social practice" and "the political speech" of "the Western democracies" exposes the honest to goodness ethnocentrism of these democracies. Once that ethnocentrism is thus exposed, and once we altogether abandon Habermas' insistence that the whole world must swallow such ethnocentrism as "rational" and "theoretical," we are in a far better position finally to turn to Rorty himself and ask by what power, and by what authority, have these "Western democracies" been put in a position thus socially to practice their political speech. In other words, it is precisely in the relation of power constitutional to the colonial practice that "Western democracies" have been put in a position not only to define their social practices and deliver their political speeches, but also to borrow from both the metaphysics and the enlightenment to call their practice "reason" and name their privilege "theory."

Habermas' critique of the postmodernists and the accusation of labeling them "neoconservatives" have to do with the fact that he considers European modernity as a philosophical condition through which we have a critical stance towards the foundations of our beliefs. His critique of the postmodernists is that they deny the existence of a universally legitimate moral consciousness from which we can sustain a critical stance to these foundations. What Habermas is seemingly unaware of or indifferent to is the fact that whether we call it "Modernity," "Enlightenment," or a "Universally Valid Moral Consciousness," the philosophical discourse of modernity, from Kant to Habermas, has been concomitant, not just historically but in fact epistemically, to a period of Western European history in which a handful of countries in these regions have colonized almost the entirety of the human race. Such problems as domestic colonialism, as in the case of Northern Italy versus Southern Italy, or capitalist entrepreneurship versus the working class, or the catastrophic consequences of the rise of National Socialism in Germany, or the Nazi concentration camps, are troubles enough for a position that argues for the existence of a universally valid "moral consciousness" in the "public sphere," as issued from the very site of these atrocities. But if we open the Western European window of Habermas to the larger world a much more troubling vista will open for him, his philosophical project, and his wish for us to join him in finishing the European project of modernity. There we will see that the project of Enlightenment modernity is precisely where the power-based production of knowledge in the Western European age of empire-building puts Habermas and his philosophical ancestry in a position of power to define what exactly *rationality* is, and, *ipso facto*, places the rest of the world in a receptive passivity that has to be told what rationality is. Other than being a bit too talkative and otherwise constitutionally demented Habermas' philosophical parentage thought we were capable of no other thing. The absence of the monumental problem of colonialism in Habermas' project of defending modernity points precisely to where the rationalism he defends is rational only for white people (this according to Kant himself and *not* according to the critics of modernity) and thus entirely irrational. "For the native," as Fanon used to say, "objectivity is always directed against him."[20] In other words, when ever Habermas utters "modernity" the rest of the world hears "colonial modernity." This strange echoing effect is the byproduct of the way, to borrow from Heidegger's famous phrase, philosophy speaks German.

Habermas, however, is entirely correct in accusing postmodernism of neoconservatism and dangerous political ineptitude. Postmodernism, understood in its most populist sense, can indeed turn its devastating critic of modernity into a supercilious language game in which no moral position can be held about anything. But that corruption of the postmodernist critic into moral indifference is really a nihilistic reaction of the selfsame white people's (Kant's choice race) rationality that has ultimately opted to throw up its hands in exasperation and altogether give up on the universality of their ancestral claim to reason. A much greater and potent potentiality is evident and palpitating in the critique of the European project of Enlightenment modernity which has to do with the mounting of that project on the back of the colonized world. It is impossible to imagine the

Western European project of Enlightenment modernity without its destructive shadow cast over the entirety of the colonized world – and it is to that world, the world at large, that Habermas seems to be entirely indifferent.

There is one other crucial point worth noting here: it is quite crucial to note that Habermas' attack against postmodernism is garbed in implicitly Christian terms, though seemingly unbeknown to himself. Against Derrida, for example, he charges that he is merely saved from the "aesthetic tastelessness of a New Paganism" by unconsciously belonging to the Jewish cabalistic tradition.[21] What Habermas does not realize is that this very charge is a two-edged sword, and when he thus spotlights Derrida as a *Jewish* philosopher he has in fact done the same on himself and underlined the *Christian* elements of his own blindfold insistence on the universality of the European project of modernity. If it is Derrida's Jewish cabalism that saves him from the "aesthetic tastelessness of a New Paganism," is it not then the Christian ecumenicalism of Habermas that informs his own bravura insistence on the universality of the European Enlightenment – for him the supreme sign of human salvation? There is nothing wrong with being a Jewish, a Christian, or a Muslim philosopher. But the arrogant self-confidence with which Habermas speaks as a "German" or a "European" and yet claims to speak for a "moral universalism" is at issue here – a point not entirely lost to his critics. He has been asked, point blank, when he uses the plural "we" in speaking in the defense of modernity, what exactly he has in mind.

> Who is "we"? Is the "we" universal, or does it mean "we Germans." Or does it even mean that because of their historical experience Germans now carry the world historical burden of the universal. If so, Habermas would be in perhaps uncomfortably close proximity to Heidegger's claim that "When [others] want to philosophize they speak German." We should note that whoever is meant by the "we" here, it is at least "we Europeans." At the end of his book on modernity we find: "Who else but Europe could draw from its own traditions the insight, the energy, the courage of vision – everything that would be necessary to strip from the ... premises of a blind compulsion to system maintenance and system expansion their power to shape our mentality."[22]

The problem with using a "we" by a German philosopher and then implicating something called a "moral universalism" has perhaps, as Strong and Sposito think, something to do with Habermas' "unresolved complexities in his relation to Kant."[23] But something far more insidious is at work here. That claim has to do with the audacity of "the Germans," if we are to think like Habermas and Heidegger, because after all "we" (that is they) *are* philosophizing, first giving the world Auschwitz and then by virtue of that calamity claiming the sole authority in philosophizing the modernity that conditioned it. Suppose what Nazis gave Europe in the form of the Holocaust was a sample of what Europeans have given the world in the form of colonialism. What then? Can the subaltern, to borrow Gayatri Spivak's rhetoric, philosophize? If we were not to be reprimanded and punished by the father of Enlightenment modernity for speaking too much, we might venture to say how fortunate we think we are that the European project of colonial modernity has remained unfinished, for it would have finished only by finishing the rest of the humanity off.

The problem of the Muslim subaltern over the last 200 years has not been the permission to philosophize. What in face of a predatory history of European colonialism Muslims (as all other colonized people) have done is simply to find a refuge, and a manner of mobilization and resistance, in (among other revolutionary ideologies) a rereading of their ancestral faith. In positing itself against two mighty rivals of anti-colonial nationalism and socialism, Islamism has had an innate propensity towards nativism and even at times obscurantism. The hostility to colonial modernity and a turn to what they have invariably termed "the Real Islam" as an alternative to both "Western democracies" and "Soviet Socialism" is nothing new or exclusive to Muslims. Similar, or variations on the theme of similar, reactions are evident in the very heart of European capitalist modernity. Consider the post-Weimar Germany and the reaction of German intellectuals, thinkers, and philosophers to the social and economic ravages of World War I, which has assumed an almost mystical anti-technological anti-modernity. Almost half a century before the advent of the "Islamic revolution" in Iran, and just about the time when the collapse of the Ottoman Empire was beginning to teach Muslims their harshest lessons ever in their colonially mitigated reception of modernity, at the heart of European modernity Heidegger had sought refuge from the ravages of modernity in a mystical perception of National Socialism. Jalal Al-e Ahmad's return to Islamism in his *Westoxication* (1962) was predicated on Ernst Jünger's critic of technological modernity, who had an identical effect on Martin Heidegger.[24] The subjugation of Muslims to the military might of the colonial powers at times translated into varied modes of technophobia. This colonially mitigated technophobia is frighteningly similar to Heidegger's philosophically derived anti-modernity, which narrows in on his condemnation of the technological age. As early as 1937, as noted by Luc Ferry and Alain Renaut in their *Heidegger and Modernity* (1988), Heidegger had noted the "calculative reason" as a feature of the technological age. Heidegger's critique of technology focused on the resubjection of man as a functionary of the useful in the modern age. Technology had demystified the world by making it an inventory of useful energies. Modernity was this period in history where the successful resubjection of man had made technology that paramount spirit of the age. While in Heidegger's thought Ferry and Renaut have detected a reading of Nazism as "the achievement of Modernity," they have equally noted his conception of the movement as "a response to Modernity."[25] It is in this latter reading that

> Heidegger always saw in the Nazi endeavor the search for a third term irreducible to either Western democracies or Soviet collectivism. His 1935 *Introduction to Metaphysics*, which describes the globalization of technology as the "spiritual decline of the earth," conjures up the pincers of East-West conflicts in which Europe is caught: "From a metaphysical point of view, Russia and America are the same; the same dreary technological frenzy, the same unrestricted organization of the average man."[26]

The similarity of these passages to Khomeini's slogan of "Neither the East, nor the West, but the Islamic Republic" is frightfully familiar.

What Germany experienced in the aftermath of World War I was just a taste of what the rest of the world has experienced subject to the savageries of European colonialism forever. Global capitalism experienced perhaps its most fateful demise, as recent economic historians propose,[27] in the immediate aftermath of World War I, when the USSR was chiefly responsible for the degeneration of a succession of socialist revolutionary movement around the globe into soviet imperialism, while European fascism was reaching for quick fixes to varied social and economic crisis, and the USA had not yet entered world economic dis/order in full throttle. The genocidal horrors of Nazi Germany, the depth of Soviet corruption, the demise of the social movements of the 1960s and the criminal involvement of Americans in the Vietnam may also in part account for the rise of European postmodernism in which the capitalist modernity experienced yet another intellectual blowback in the form of postmodernism in the widest sense of the term. In this context we may also understand the reasons for Foucault's misreading of the Islamic revolution in Iran as well. He too detected in what he categorically identifies as an Islamic revolution a momentary pause in the ravages of the European project of (for him invariably flawed, for the world always colonial) modernity, a charismatic escape from the routinized mendacities of the instrumental reason.[28] But he too, just like Habermas, could never see the doubly catastrophic consequences of European modernity for colonized or semi-colonized societies like Iran. Whatever the malaise of modernity and its instrumental reason might be, colonialism had constituted the very subjectivities of the colonized person at the receiving end of the project. The anti-colonial reason and agency that these struggles have generated and sustained have been instrumental to a worldly cosmopolitanism that went completely over Foucault's head when he spent a few days in Tehran and wrote about "the Islamic revolution" in Iran.[29] The Islamicity of that Islamic revolution, even if we were to disregard the significance of a range of nationalist and socialist forces integral to that revolution, has always been in active and transformative conversation with other worldly visions of reality that has translated into a planetary cosmopolitanism that European thinkers like Habermas and Foucault have categorically failed to see.

In face of the ravages of capitalist modernity, Germans turned to Nazism and wreaked havoc in Europe. In face of millennia of European anti-Semitism, ranging from pogroms to the Holocaust, European Jewry turned to Zionism. Both these developments were domestic to European economics and politics – one wreaked havoc in Europe and among its other atrocities exterminated some 6 million Jews, while the other took its perfectly legitimate but entirely misplaced revenge on the broken back of Palestinians. The rise of worldwide socialism, anti-colonial nationalism and Christian and Islamic liberation theologies in Latin America, Asia, and Africa were the more global consequences of the selfsame capitalist modernity, initially in response to European colonial savageries throughout the world and subsequently, soon after World War I, to the rapid globalization of American imperialism. The site and citation of any reconsideration of Islamic liberation theology, in this context, and in a manner that resumes the thinking and activism of visionary Muslims like Ali Shari'ati or Malcolm X, will have to be similarly global in proportion and perspective – and certainly away from the limiting purview of the polar opposition posited between "Islam and the West," the binary axis on which such Muslim intellectuals as Abdolkarim Soroush and Tariq Ramadan continue, belatedly, to operate.

To posit and purpose the global stage of rethinking the unfinished project of Malcolm X, and thus to articulate the cosmopolitan disposition of his unfinished liberation theology, we must abandon and discard the colonial context in which such figures among his kindred souls as Ali Shari'ati were incarcerated, normatively severed, and framed – held tightly in pigeonholes like "Iran," "the Middle East," or even "Islam." As a colonially fabricated designation, the term "Middle East" is simply too obscene to be even considered critically. It is a recent vintage of European colonial imaginary and has no basis in any pre-colonial geography. It was invented by Bernard Lewis's colonial pedigree and is today as discredited as Bernard Lewis himself. As equally colonial categories, and the way mercenary Orientalists have used and abused them (and *not* as extended insignia of collective identities throughout the ages) both "Iran" and "Islam" were (re)invented in the shadow of European modernity and by the very logic of its colonial extension. If "Iran" was invented in a manner to incorporate a colonial outpost into the globalizing logic of capitalism, "Islam" was counter invented by insurrectionary rebellions against colonialism as an ideology to resist that incorporation – and these *Iran* and *Islam* have scarce anything to do with the collective identities of millions of people over millennial of moral and normative solidarity.[30] Neither "Iran" nor "Islam" was of course left to the malicious devices of mercenary Orientalists to make and manufacture them in a manner subservient to European colonial designs. Both "Iran" and "Islam" were counter-coined in a manner liberating and emancipatory in the course of more than two centuries of anti-colonial struggles. As the more overriding term, and as an ideology of resistance to incorporation into the globalizing logic of capitalism, "Islam" has now failed, and capitalism and its varied7d of the twenty-first century, and more than two centuries into the predicament of Iran, Islam, and modernity, there is absolutely no difference between that ideology of incorporation into global capitalism and that manner of Islamic resistance to it. Today, there is no difference between the Pahlavi Imperial Dynasty and the Islamic Republic that has succeeded it.

As all other nation-states in its immediate and distant vicinity, "Iran" was (re)invented in the nineteenth century in the course of the global project of capitalist modernity and its extended arm of colonialism. The term "Iran" or "Persia" and a sense of communal identity called "Iranian" or "Persian" of course pre-dates colonial modernity and has identified Iranians in a successive set of formulations.[31] But the idea of "Iran" as a nation-state, in a manner that is easily incorporated into a constellation of national economies, national polities, and national cultures, is an entirely new invention, immediately traceable to the rise of European capitalist modernity, the spread of the project of colonialism, and the constitution of national identities compatible with these two interrelated projects. From E. J. Hobsbawm to Ernest Gellner to Benedict Anderson to Partha Chatterjee all the major theorists of nationalism concur, in one way or another, that the invention of nation-state and nationalism as a political ideology is a modern, modernist, colonial, and/or anti-colonial project. Not only "Iran" but the whole panorama of modern nation-states, from the heart of capitalist modernity to the remotest colonial outposts in Asia, Africa, and Latin America, was a necessary political predicate to the rise of globalizing capital. Not just its political predicates but the very ideological roots of modern nation-states is squarely located in the rise of capitalist modernity and the European project of self-globalizing Enlightenment. Only a conceptual confusion between the enduring varieties of communal identities and the emergence of the modern national identities can lead to the assumption that "nations" are to be traced to their ethnic origins.[32] Communal identifies, through a variety of mechanical and organic modes of solidarity, have always existed. The rise of nation-states, however, is an entirely recent event with its political and economic reasons and causes immediately traceable to not earlier than 1789 and the events leading to the French and other bourgeois revolutions. Naturally, the modern conceptions of nations are predicated on traces and assumptions of pre-modern ethnic communities. The role of the intelligentsia in the construction of modern national identities[33] is an entirely secondary role, predicated on their organic or inorganic membership in an already-incorporated political community identified as "nation."

"The basic characteristic of the modern nation and everything connected with it," as E. J. Hobsbawm has accurately observed," is its modernity."[34] Even in Europe, where the project of capitalist modernity originated and where the very idea of "nation-state" took shape, not until 1884 was the term "nation" used in the sense of "a State or political body which recognizes a supreme centre of common government."[35] In such colonial outposts as Iran, terms like "Mellat,"

"Vatan," "Mihan," or "Keshvar" were neologisms based on their pre-modern uses but meant to match "nation" and by then had a range of meanings and connotations entirely distanced from the notion of "a State or political body which recognizes a supreme centre of common government."

Neither "will" nor "culture," as Ernest Gellner has argued,[36] in and of itself constitutes a legitimate defining occasion for any idea of the "nation" on the colonial edges of capitalist modernity. Quite to the contrary: in the course of the European Enlightenment historiography, Iran, or "Persia" to be more exact, among other civilizational others, was narrated as an infancy, a tangential idea, an arrested growth, a historical predicate – the way that Hegel for example, treats India, Egypt, and Persia as the precursor of history, which begins in earnest in Greece, takes momentum in Rome, and comes to its conclusion in Germany. Because we were thus the passive recipient of a condition in which the very subjectivity of our national identity, "Iran," "Islam," etc. were narrated by the Orientalist agency of capitalist modernity, and because we counter-coined anti-colonial nationalism or Islamism as competing ideologies of resistance under duress, we now need to de-narrate ourselves out of all such predicaments before we can think ourselves free from that historical predicament in which we were in fact party to having painted ourselves into a colonial corner.

That freedom will come with a clear recognition of the origin of modern nationalism in the formative logic of global capitalism. Underlining the roots of nations and nationalism in capitalist modernity, Benedict Anderson's notion of "imagined communities," which is predicated on a much longer tradition of the sociology of knowledge and the social construction of reality, posits the self-propelling mental pictures of a nation as the *modus operandi* of how a national collectivity normatively registers itself.[37] Anderson's notion of "print-capitalism" in the various vernaculars of the emerging nation-states traces the roots of this particular manner of nationalism to its economic modes of operation. The active mutation of nations into nation-states, Anderson further argues, is contingent on the decline and fading out of dynastic histories and the emerging need for collective polities – all of course predicated on corresponding economies and cultures. In his equally important study, *Nationalist Thought and the Colonial World*, Partha Chatterjee demonstrates how nationalist thought, even (or particularly) in its anti-colonial postures, has perforce operated precisely in the framework of a mimetic structure that does not repudiate but in fact emulates and thus exacerbates the structure of power it imagines dismantling.[38]

A critical awareness of the rise of nation-state as the *modus operandi* of global capitalism, predicated on the basis of national economies, polities, and perforce cultures, is a prelude to resuming a creative conversation with Malcolm X's unfinished revolutionary project. At the root of Habermas' notion of modernity as an unfinished project remains Kant's constitution of the white European male as the knowing subject, the rest of the thus racialized and colonized world as the knowable object, in the context of which no democratic constitution of an intersubjectivity is logically plausible and thus an entirely useless proposition. The received (racialized and nationalized) bifurcations between Malcolm X and Ali Shari'ati as having belonged to two different worlds is a byproduct of a pernicious colonial geography coterminous with global capitalism that is neither valid any longer nor even factually self-evident. The need for a new and entirely different imaginative geography is not only necessary but in fact self-evident. The momentous occasion when during his Hajj pilgrimage in 1964 Malcolm X recognized his global solidarity with a far wider constituency is fatefully replicated in Ali Shari'ati's similar discoveries in Paris, especially through his correspondences with Franz Fanon and active solidarity with the Cuban and Algerian revolutions, which as fate would have it would also culminate in 1964 when he received his doctoral degree from the Sorbonne. The pharmakon of globalism is in its own poison. In order to see the global south in evident solidarity with the immigrant, the racialized, and altogether disenfranchised communities in the global north, all sorts of nativism, regionalism, and tribalism will have to be abandoned in favor of a globality of learning and action that simply resumes the process by which Malcolm X emerged from a common criminal to become a Muslim believer and then a revolutionary activist with a global vision of his commitments, a process replicated in a similar manner by Ali Shari'ati as he traveled from a devout Shi'i Muslim to engage in a critical and creative conversation with liberation ideologies all over the globe and finally to become, just before his premature death, the ideological vanguard of a revolutionary uprising in his homeland and beyond. One must see the structural similarities between domestic economic hardship in the heart of "the metropolitan West" and the rampant savageries of colonialism and imperialism all over the world and thus not single out Islamic or Christian liberation theologies as odd or outlandish modes of resistance to globalized tyranny. In the context of Islamic liberation theology in particular, the evident cosmopolitanism of Islamic cultures over the last 1400 years are the effective blueprint of resuming that open-ended worldliness in the making of a liberation theodicy that welcomes the shadows of its own doubts into the shades of its momentary certainties. The necessary moral imagination to resume that conversation will have to be predicated on visualizing the normative emergence of a new geography of liberation that can no longer be bogged down on a debilitating East–West axis or framed and incarcerated within specific nation-states that have hitherto distorted the far more global potentials of such revolutionary Muslim liberation activist as Ai Shari'ati or Malcolm X. Modern nation-states, whether they were incorporated into a colonial mode of nationalism or in turn revolted in anti-colonial nationalism, in effect amounted to the same and in fact corroborated and exacerbated the *modus operandi* and the power structure they thus wished to dismantle, as Partha Chatterjee has successfully demonstrated. In the age of globalization of capital all matters of identity politics are a bit more than frivolous bourgeois pastime. Liberation theologies in particular will have to cultivate cosmopolitan and transnational solidarities, the way initiated by revolutionary visionaries like Ali Shari'ati and Malcolm X. Before we have de-narrated ourselves out of those nasty narrations that have divided people to rule them better we will not be able to renarrate ourselves in an emancipatory and liberating manner. The ideas of prominent examples of persistence in narrating our global whereabouts on an outdated, divisive, and disabling East–West axis, or else positing the defeatist ghetto mentality of something called "Islam *in* the West," a variation of "Islam *and* the West" will first have to be critically considered and dismantled, before we can proceed apace – and it is to that task that I now turn.

After the success of the Islamic revolution in Iran in the late 1970s, it became something of an academic exercise in futility to give an account of the cosmopolitan disposition of the country at large in the immediate decades preceding that cataclysmic event.[39] When Ahmad Shamlu, the most distinguished public intellectual of his generation, died on July 24 2000, his funeral had an air of an archaeological excavation about it, something quite mummified and eerie about the most elegant poetic voice of the last two centuries dying in his homeland now officially called "the Islamic republic of Iran." From participant observers, suddenly an entire generation of Iranian public intellectuals turned into chronographers and historians of their own demise. As the fortunes of the Iranian inorganic public intellectuals of the Pahlavi period declined, the stars of a new constellation of (as they now opted to call themselves) *religious* intellectuals *(Roshanfekran-e Dini)* were on the rise. With an Islamic shadow now cast on the entire history of the Iranian colonial encounter with modernity, these religious intellectuals excavated a long and illustrious pedigree for themselves. From Mulla Ahmad Naraqi, early in the nineteenth century, all the way to Ali Shari'ati in the wake of the Islamic revolution of 1979, the religious intellectuals sought and found a sustained and legitimate genealogy for themselves. The public intellectuals of the Pahlavi period either effectively went into hiding or else left the country altogether. Some of them were brutally murdered. The religious intellectuals became prominent, occupying official positions, and a vast spectrum of government-sponsored forums was put at their disposal. Pre-Islamic revolution public intellectuals no longer dared speak the truth to power. Decidedly religious intellectuals *were* in power.

Practically all the major religious intellectuals today have had official affiliations, in one capacity or another, with the Islamic republic. But, as it is in the very texture of critical intelligence of any denomination, religious intellectuals soon parted ways with the clerical circle in power. They assumed oppositional postures, and very soon they became subject to official censure (Abdolkarim Soroush), periods of incarceration (Akbar Ganji), vicious attacks by hoodlums hired by the religious right (Hasan Yousefi Eshkevari among scores of others), and even assassination attempts (Said Hajjarian). A quarter of a century into the successful institutionalization of the Islamic republic, the term "religious intellectuals" *(Roshanfekran-e Dini)* has now assumed complete discursive legitimacy.

What does it exactly mean to be a "religious intellectual"?[40] How can an intellectual be religious, and how can one metaphysically committed to a set of doctrinal certainties be a free thinker, an autonomous subject, a critical intelligence, an intellectual? No single person embodies this series of contradictions in contemporary Iran better than Abdolkarim Soroush.[41] The most eloquent and controversial public intellectual in post-revolutionary Iran, Abdolkarim Soroush was initially trained as a pharmacologist in England in the 1970s but soon emerged as the leading theorist of the post-Islamic revolution politics of radical hermeneutics. His intellectual ambitions matched his political engagements with the Islamic republic. He went so far as being a leading member of the Advisory Council of the Cultural Revolution, appointed by Ayatollah Khomeini to "purify" Tehran University of all its "undesirable" elements, that is, such members of the faculty that were deemed incompatible with the brutal "Islamization" of the curriculum. But very soon after the successful institutionalization of the Islamic republic, Soroush began to articulate theoretical positions on Islamic hermeneutics that have come against severe criticism by the clerical establishment.

The predicament of Abdolkarim Soroush as a religious intellectual is thus symptomatic of a larger phenomenon, at once liberating and arresting, in the colonial history of combative encounters with European modernity. By far the most significant public intellectual of post-revolutionary Iran, Soroush personifies the predicament of a much larger universe of failed ideas. Understanding him is thus not yet another exercise in futility, a Monday morning quarterbacking after the game of Islamic confrontation with colonial modernity is over. In his blindness dwells his insights, for Soroush represents some two centuries of bewildered attempts to locate a historical agency for the Muslim subject in colonial modernity. The colonial integration of Islamic societies at large into the project of capitalist modernity necessitated anti-colonial responses that could not but adopt global modes of social mobilization (Nationalism and Socialism) or create its own nativist sites of resistance (Islamism). The intellectual pedigree that Soroush now represents claims such illustrious luminaries as Seyyed Jamal al-Din Asadabadi, "al-Afghani" (1838–1897), Muhammad Abduh (1849–1905), Rashid Rida (1865–1935), A. H. Abd al-Raziq (1888–1966), Abu al-Ala al-Mawdudi (1903–1979), Shaykh Mahmud Shaltut (1892–1963), and, perhaps most significantly, a protégé of Sir Seyyed Ahmad Khan named Chiragh Ali (1844–1895). Soroush is the very last metaphysician in the Islamic colonial encounter with modernity, the very last ideologue in whose blindness and insights we can see the decline and fall of the most massive mutation of Islam in its long and languid history into an "Islamic Ideology."

The Islam of Soroush's birth and breeding was an Islam invented in colonial encounters with European modernity. Gradually code-named "Islamic Ideology," the Islam of Soroush's world and vision was coined and made current to match and balance "the West," by far the most massive manufacturing of a categorical concept in modern history. "The West" was the categorical conception of a world that had emerged in modernity to replace medieval "Christendom," substituting, *ipso facto*, its dynastic components with the aggressive formation of the European national cultures. As the most dominant categorical imperative of colonizing modernity, the selfsame "West" was in dire need of its alternating Others in order to authenticate and believe itself. "The East" in general and "Islam" in particular were invented by Orientalism, as the intelligence arm of colonialism, to match and mate "the West." Muslims themselves in turn categorically bought into this colonial game, whether they opposed "the West" and aggressively mutated Islam into a site of ideological resistance to it or else collaborated with it and sought to ape and emulate its manufactured ethos.[42]

Soroush is the last in a long and illustrious line of Muslim ideologues who have remained creatively oblivious to this dialectical constitution of their ancestral faith and have categorically failed to disengage its systematic counter-essentialization: "Islam and the West." But where Muslim ideologues have failed, history has succeeded. It is the fate of Abdolkarim Soroush to have articulated his particular conception of Islam in silent conversation with "the West" at a time that "the West" no longer exists. As the polar opposites of "the West" and "the Rest" are collapsing because the rapid globalization of labor and capital can no longer sustain their once-ideological necessity, Soroush has been busy de-historicizing "Islam" in a mute dialogue with an absent interlocutor. As the world and all its binary oppositions dissolve into the modular formation of one singular empire, Abdolkarim Soroush has been hard at work saving an essential Islamic *noumenon* to allow its phenomenological variations to have a historical conversation with a modernity that has long since vacated the scene. He is so late in the last round that some have taken him as early in the next and call him "The Muslim Martin Luther"![43]

Soroush's project sums up in the evident urge to save the sacred from its history. His principal proposition in his exceedingly lucid and massive body of work is what he has called the "Theoretical Contraction and Expansion of Religious Knowledge" *(Qabz-o-Bast Teoric-e Shari'at)*. This theory is predicated on a metaphysics that he considers entirely innovative, which is to say "hermeneutic" *(ma'refat-shenasaneh)* and "historical" *(tarikhi)*, as opposed to "theological" *(motekallemaneh)* and "interpretative" *(mofasseraneh)*.[44] The critical proposal of the theory of the "Theoretical Contraction and Expansion of Religious Knowledge" is to separate "Religion Itself" from the knowledge of religion, and to put forward the proposition of "the historicity" or "the subjectivity *(tabe'iyyat)* of the religious knowledge to other forms of human knowledge."[45] In this theory, Soroush argues for the contemporaneity of religious knowledge, its accountability, as it were, to its historical presence. According to Soroush, the purpose of his theory is to "give a new space and possibility to religious democracy."[46] He also admits that he has sought to "predicate the religious government on the religious society."[47] Epistemologically, and Soroush does consider his proposition epistemological in nature, he wishes to predicate what he calls "the current and collective hermeneutics" on "the collective reason," and "religious knowledge" on "anthropology and jurisprudence," and "religion on justice" and not "justice on religion." In principle, he wishes to propose "the fallibility of religious knowledge" but safeguard "Religion Itself."

Soroush's conception of the "Theoretical Contraction and Expansion of Religious Knowledge" is linked to an equally significant notion he calls the "Historical Constriction and Dissipation of the School of Thought" *(Laff-o-Nashr-e Tarikhi-e Maktab)*. What he means by this is that religious knowledge not only theoretically contracts and expands by being in dialogue with its contemporary modes of knowledge but it also fluctuates in response to its historical vicissitudes. Religious knowledge, to be carefully separated from "Religion Itself," is tested both theoretically and practically by being placed, *ipso facto*, in a historical location. Thus, he proposes that the perception that our contemporaries have of religion is at once a creature of history of the religious life and is placed in the geography of human knowledge. "Tomorrow, when the book of history is turned again to a new page, and upon the soil of knowledge newer flowers have grown, religious knowledge too will assume a different pigmentation and aroma. And this transformation of colors and aromas is an inevitable and endless phenomenon."[48]

Equally related to both conceptions of the "Theoretical Contraction and Expansion of Religious Knowledge" and the "Historical Constriction and Dissipation of the School of Thought" is Soroush's insistence on an "Ennobling Understanding of Religion" *(Dark-e Azizaneh-ye Din)*. What he means by that is the proposition that a religion can as much advance a people toward progress and dignity as it can compel them toward backwardness and misery. One's understanding of a religion must thus be geared toward an ennobling of its adherents, their being propelled into an active role in history. The religious hermeneutician, as a result, will have to have a *soda-ye sarbala*, or "the ambition of upper-mobility."[49]

Finally, the "Theoretical Contraction and Expansion of Religious Knowledge," the "Historical Constriction and Dissipation of the School of Thought," and the "Ennobling Understanding of Religion" are all capped by the "Collectivity and Currency of Religious Knowledge" *(Jam'i and Jari Budan-e Ma'refat-e Dini)*. What Soroush means by that is the historical facility of providing a "multiplicity of human understanding of the Silent Religion, [and thus] preventing the possibility of the ideologization of religion, and inhibiting the propensity to give one final, exclusionary, and official interpretation of it."⁵⁰

Thus separating "Religion Itself" from the knowledge of religion, the principal task of Soroush is to place the production of such knowledge in what he calls "the general geography of human knowledge." Hermeneutic in its stated ambition, Soroush's project is targeted toward a systematic epistemology. With a trace of Thomas Kuhn's conception of scientific progress, with the obvious exception of his paradigmatic constitution of the scientific truth, Soroush believes that human knowledge does not progress cumulatively, but exponentially and qualitatively. "Things we know do not accumulate unit by unit, but, instead, constitute a composition, atom by atom. The resulting composition is constantly in qualitative increase."⁵¹ Any new "intrusion" into human knowledge requires other modes and modalities of accumulated and systematized knowledge to negotiate a new position for themselves. Thus new discoveries in physics, for example, or in cosmology, or in astrophysics, require substantial epistemological remodulations in religious and philosophical thought. There is a domino effect to the neighborly relations among human and religious sciences. More specifically, we may conclude from Soroush's concern about the qualitative changes in human sciences that the Copernican revolution in particular and the substitution of a heliocentric conception of universe for a geocentric one has had enduring consequences for religious knowledge by having a destabilizing effect on its entire epistemological foregroundings.

The result of this challenge to the continued viability of religious knowledge is that unless one has a current anthropology predicated on a host of related sciences that animate and inform that anthropology, one cannot have a legitimate and current theology. But since in addition to anthropology, not in the disciplinary but in the etymological sense of the term, a whole host of other sciences are in a constant process of progression and development, then so must be the understanding of a religion.⁵² Resorting to the sixteenth-century Shi'i philosopher Mulla Sadra Shirazi's theory of "Trans-substantial Motion" *(al-Harakah al-Jawhariyyah)*, Soroush suggests that the changing notions of belief in accordance with the changing topography of human knowledge does not diminish the continued legitimacy and authority of religious knowledge. Quite to the contrary, it contemporizes and further authenticates the sanctity of religious knowledge. The medieval Islamic metaphysics was predicated on a historically specific physics. Now that that physics has changed, Soroush proposes, so must the metaphysics responding to and corresponding with it.

For the progress of the profane, human knowledge, Soroush believes in its reality *sui generis*. Humans are constitutionally disposed to discover things, and that is compatible with the Divine Will too.⁵³ If in "the West" (and here commences Soroush's sliding down towards an absolutist reading of the world at large) people have abandoned their faith, it is because they could no longer cultivate a legitimate theology that was compatible with their emergent, scientifically based anthropology. In Iran, Soroush points out, those who want to safeguard their faith and secure it against all historical odds and those who argue for a progressive theology are both responding to the onslaught of modernity and its threatening postures against the historically received understanding of their ancestral faith.

As humans are constitutionally disposed to progress in their discovering of new things, so are they also in possession of an absolute and abstract reason, Soroush adamantly believes. He accuses those who believe in the historicity of reason of Hegelianism. "Their judge is history not Reason. Because they have followed the command of the god-of-history and beheaded Reason."[54] Soroush exonerates himself from any attachment to Hegelianism or historical determinism. He believes reason and the progress contingent upon it are realities *sui generis* and immune to any subjugation to history. He denounces the Hegelians for the principality of history in their understanding of reason and of rationality. He maintains that his argument for contemporizing religious knowledge is not tantamount to collapsing his hermeneutics into what he considers to be the Hegelian historical determinism.

The theoretical development of the religious knowledge *(Shari'at)* thus assumes an acceptable meaning. The proposition is not to add an item to what is doctrinally enjoined, or subtract an item from what is doctrinally forbidden, nor is it to abrogate a Qur'anic verse, or to distort a Prophetic or Imami tradition. That which is being changed is the human understanding of the religious knowledge, and that which remains constant is the Religion Itself.[55]

Soroush then proceeds to suggest that the philosophical, juridical, or even literary orientations in Islamic intellectual history are precisely such examples of multiple readings of one Singular Sacred Reality. History is silent, but historians make it sing different songs. Nature is silent, but physicists and biologists make it tell different stories. One needs to have a theoretically consistent awareness of these multiple readings. It is useless to compare a stagnant jurisprudence with a progressive jurisprudence when we still lack the principles of a hermeneutics that inform us as to what exactly is stagnant and what is progressive and why. Soroush considers himself as having provided the foundations of that hermeneutics.

From this premise Soroush concludes that so far as the nature and function of religious knowledge is concerned, it cannot remain indifferent to changes that occur in other modes of knowledge. Since the knowledge of the material world is changing, so must our knowledge of the "Religion Itself." There ought to be a dialogue between religious and non-religious forms of knowledge. Here, Soroush gives primacy of action to the knowledge of the world at large and not to the religious knowledge, because that which rationally and practically comes first and stands first and designs the geography of knowledge in general are the human forms of knowledge, that is to say, one first has to have a conception of the world and of the humanity in it before one can place the function of Prophethood in that context. In other words, it is the human *Weltanschauung* which gives the permission of entrance and issues the license of legitimacy to the religious *Weltanschauung*, and not vice versa.[56]

Upon this extraordinary suggestion, Soroush then proceeds to argue that a comprehensive understanding of the human condition is the function and responsibility of what he calls "the religious intellectual" (*Roshanfekr-e Dini*),[57] who is to make peace between the two worlds and lead them to benefit from each other. Soroush obviously considers himself an example of that prototype of "the religious intellectual" operating on the borderline of religious and non-religious modes of knowledge. Guiding the religious intellectual in this project is what Soroush calls *'Aql-e Parsa*, or "the pious intellect." "The pious intellect" does not lead to the periodization or to the relativization of "Truth," the charge against which Soroush is particularly adamant, but to an active dialogue between the multiplicity of human knowledge and the singular, but ever-changing, nature of the religious knowledge. That task, Soroush confesses, is not easy. It is much easier to shut the doors and windows to one's fortress of belief and keep a simple conviction in certain eternalities, safe and sound against all active intrusions of doubt. But it is much more courageous and indeed inevitable to dwell in the transsubstantial motion of a religious knowledge that fluctuates and keeps itself afloat against the tumultuous sea of intergalactic changes in human forms of knowledge. To formulate a hermeneutic which corresponds to that difficult task, the religious intellectual must be as diligent, serious, comprehensive, and principled as the functionaries of the human sciences are.

Soroush summarizes the principles of his hermeneutics in three major steps: (1) a description of the developmental nature of religious knowledge, (2) a causal analysis of the reasons of and the mechanics behind this development, and (3) an encouragement that Muslims should engage actively in advancing this development.[58] He points out that a cursory look at any form of knowledge, or even a literary tradition, demonstrates that man's understanding of things is constantly on a course of steady progress. Without admitting as much, Soroush's is an essentially Hegelian teleology in which man's knowledge of things is on a perpetual course of progress. Soroush is emphatic that the kind of "progress" he proposes pertains to what he calls the "secondary" forms of knowledge that are produced on the "primary" sources of the religious tradition. This he emphasizes so that his clerical critics would not accuse him of considering the sacred texts and the sacred knowledge of the "Faith Itself" to be subject to historical progress. When the heavenly sanctity of the sacred revealed itself to mortals, Soroush argues,[59] then it inevitably became sullied by human reality, and it is a reading of the vicissitude of the dialogue between the sacred and the profane that is the subject of investigation for religious hermeneutics.

Soroush is equally careful to separate the essence of belief and the religious rituals related to it from the subject of his hermeneutic investigations.[60] These are eternal, sacred, and the signs of divine attention to the mortal creatures. The subject of Soroush's concern, in contrast, are the worldly, earthly, and historical vicissitudes of a knowledge of that sacred essence in the context of what he repeatedly calls "the geography of human knowledge." Here he demands an extraordinarily diligent observance from the religious intellectuals who ought to be both aware of the non-religious knowledge and actively read them against the principality of their "Religion Itself" and the forms of religious knowledge pertinent to it. Man, as a result, ought to be seen in the mirror of the faith, the faith in the mirror of man, but in both these cases, it is the developmental and progressive nature of the knowledge of the world that are the deciding factors. Soroush's theory of knowledge is neither accumulative nor completely Kuhnian. He does not believe that knowledge is incrementally accumulated, nor does he believe, as does Thomas Kuhn, that there are epistemic breakthroughs in the production of knowledge. He believes that every new item of knowledge that is added to our inventory of knowledge forces the other accumulated ones to resituate, redefine, and replace themselves.

Scientific discoveries, as a result, do not *ipso facto* discredit the accumulated forms of knowledge, but force them to redefine and replace themselves in accordance with the factual and epistemic assumptions of the new findings. This principle is as much applicable to religious knowledge as to non-religious knowledge. The Ptolemaic geocentric cosmology, for example, required one kind of consistency in all other related and non-related forms of knowledge, whereas the Copernican heliocentric cosmology another. If the climactic condition of the world, Soroush adds,[61] was limited to one season, there were logical consistencies of one sort operative in it. But as soon as the second, third, and the fourth season appear, all such consistencies need to be reworked. On the basis of this epistemological stipulation, Soroush then proceeds to examine some of the most recent Qur'anic commentaries by such contemporaries of his as Seyyed Mahmud Taleqani and 'Allamah Tabataba'i in order to begin to map out their underlying, but never articulated and theorized, hermeneutic principles.[62] These principles are presumed and followed by these Qur'anic commentators and yet not completely thought through or actively theorized. Such deliberate and conscious theorization and articulation of the already practiced incorporation of contemporary non-religious forms of knowledge into religious knowledge is the principal hermeneutic task of Soroush. In doing so, he does not occasionally hesitate[63] to demonstrate how such contemporary luminaries of Shi'i thought as 'Allamah Tabataba'i would hold one specific epistemological position in their Qur'anic commentaries and yet do not think through a systematic account of their hermeneutics, and as a result would have to hold totally unacceptable doctrinal positions. Because 'Allamah Tabataba'i, Soroush contends, did not think through a systematic and consistent hermeneutic apparatus, then in such problematic places as the male and female children of Adam and Eve he would run into difficulties. When Tabataba'i has to address the Qur'anic assertion that from Adam and Eve their male and female offspring emerged, and thus when they married then sisters and brothers must have been able to marry, Tabataba'i must believe, as he does, in the conventionality of religious laws and not in their essentiality *(fitri)*.[64] This is a constitutional problem in Tabataba'i's position, Soroush contends, because we cannot believe in the mere conventionality of religious laws. They are, Soroush believes, natural, quintessential, and essential. Tabataba'i falls into the trap of having had to consider incestuous or even homosexual relationships as potentially acceptable to a religion the moment he conventionalizes and de-essentializes the sanctity of the religious laws. He falls into that trap because he does not think through the implications of one epistemological assertion for the rest of his hermeneutic system. A hermeneutic "system" is precisely what Tabataba'i and all other religious thinkers of Islam have hitherto lacked and what Soroush is henceforth providing them with. In short, there is a juridical Islam, and there is a philosophical Islam. There is a mystical Islam, and there is a theological Islam.[65] The function of a hermeneutician like Soroush is not to judge between 'Allamah Majlisi, a tenth/sixteenth-century Shi'i traditionalist, and 'Allamah Tabataba'i, a fourteenth/twentieth-century Shi'i philosopher. The task of a hermeneutician is to see upon what hidden and unarticulated assumptions their respective readings of the faith are predicated, and then set himself the task of monitoring and articulating those principles. Soroush is that hermeneutician that the Shi'i (and the Islamic) intellectual history has lacked and now achieved.

To summarize, religious knowledge is a humanly achieved form of understanding and, as such, quite similar to other forms of knowledge in a constant state of flux. The contraction and expansion of religious knowledge is always contingent on fluctuations in other forms of knowledge. Religious knowledge, in other words, is not independent of our growing knowledge of nature. Thus in the same way that non-religious knowledge is progressing constantly so must religious knowledge.[66]

This sets an active responsibility of contemporizing the religious knowledge. To have a "contemporary" knowledge of a religion means a fourfold task: (1) our understanding of religion must be compatible with the current status of knowledge of the time; (2) our understanding of religion must be influenced and aided by the current status of knowledge; (3) it must be responsive to the theoretical questions of the time; and (4) it must be responsive to the practical questions of the time.[67]

To elucidate further his distinction between "Religion Itself" and the knowledge of religion, Soroush gives an account of historiography,[68] in which he argues that what remains constant is the historical events themselves, and what is changing is the reading of those events in light of new theoretical developments in historiography. In his account of the theoretical changes in historiography, which though without any footnote are nevertheless informed by the current status of the discipline, Soroush in fact goes far beyond anything achieved in the theoretical sophistication of Islamic historiography in either Persian or in Arabic. His principal purpose here, though, is to strike a similarity between the theoretically informed historian and the "Silent" nature of historical events, and the suggestion of a similar relationship between the changing character of religious knowledge and the immutability of "Religion Itself." As historical events and texts, religion, too, is sitting silently, waiting for us to question it. We will get to know it in correspondence with responses it gives to our questions. Imagine a scientist who is sitting silently, not uttering a word. It is our questions and his answers that gradually reveal his character to us. This character is constantly subject to reconstitution. The person who asks him only philosophical questions (because he himself is philosophically oriented) would get to know him as a philosopher, and the person who asks him only literary questions and hears in response literary answers puts upon him a literary cloak.[69]

Soroush's most ambitious intention is to argue for a similarity between nature and religion, and thus between the changing logic of knowledge produced on one and on the other. Natural laws are constant, but our understanding of them is subject to progress. God is unchanging and perfect, but our understanding of God is changing and imperfect. Religion and religious dogma are immutable, but our interpretation of them is subject to historical mutation. This is the principal proposition of the theory of "the Theoretical Contraction and Expansion of Religious Knowledge."[70] Religious knowledge is itself a human knowledge, despite the fact that its object of study is a non-human reality. This knowledge has a collective and current status, and is in a constant state of progress. Religious knowledge is located in the midst of other forms of human knowledge and has (or ought to have) a persistent dialogue with them. The more legitimately a religious knowledge is sitting among other forms of human knowledge, the more intelligent, current, and relevant the questions it can ask from the otherwise "Silent Religion." In addition, there must be a consistency between the interpreters' current understanding of nature and their understanding of religion. Religion and nature are the products of one creator.[71] Thus the understanding of them ought to be concurrently consistent. The religious intellectual must begin with a universal understanding of the history and the geography of contemporary knowledge of the historical person and the world in which she or he lives. The evolving understanding of religion must then be compatible with those other forms of knowledge. The concurrent correspondence of religious knowledge with non-religious knowledge will thus constitute the epistemological foregrounding of asking new, pertinent, and liberating questions from religion and making it continuously relevant to the contemporary modes of knowledge. Identical facts, such as the rising of the sun,[72] have different meanings when they are read in the context of different theories of cosmology, for example. The world is thus like a written text: "No written text reveals its own meaning. It is the language-knowing mind that reads meaning into it. Sentences are hungry for meaning, not pregnant with them."[73]

The simpler a mind, the simpler the meaning it reads into the world-as-the-text (this Soroush calls "raw realism"), whereas the more complicated the mind, the more sophisticated the meaning it reads into the world-as-the-text (this he calls "complicated realism"). How exactly is a text to be well understood? Soroush takes his readers through three successive steps. First, we need to understand the world and the worldview of the author; second, we need to understand the logical and historical antecedents of the subject of the text; and third, we bring our own theories and knowledge to the text.[74] This hermeneutic system anticipates and concludes a religious knowledge that originates in this world but targets the sacred, the "Religion Itself," that Soroush has delegated to the other.

Divesting agency from the subject – that perhaps inadvertent implication ultimately informs Abdolkarim Soroush's hermeneutics. Two sets of interrelated anxieties inform Soroush and his elaborate attempt to take "Islam Itself," as he calls it, out of history: (1) the general anxiety of facing European modernity, intensifying, and (2) the particular anxiety of being party to a political triumph of Shi'ism, which in the classical Shi'i paradox is tantamount to its moral defeat. Understanding Soroush, as a result, is understanding the final end of "Islamic ideology," as we have known and documented it over the last 200 years, the collapse of its political viability, the defeat of its aspirations to posit a legitimate location for itself once it was dragged into a combative conversation with European modernity. When today we look at Soroush's proposition about the "Theoretical Expansion and Contraction of Religious Law," closer to three decades into the success of the Islamic revolution in Iran and more than two centuries into the meandering history of the colonial consequences of the European modernity in the region, we see that his project comes at the tail end of some 200 years of actively mutating Islamic normative, institutional, moral, and intellectual history into a singular site of ideological resistance to colonialism, the venue from which we received the European project of Enlightenment modernity. Responding to those two anxieties, Soroush has two simultaneous projects, one global to Islam, the other local to Iran: first, to de-historicize what he calls "Islam Itself" in order to safeguard it for posterity and make it immune to political catastrophe every time it has to have a conversation with modernity, and second to separate the political success of Shi'ism in the Islamic republic from its instantly manifested moral collapse. The first project is flawed, for Islam *is* its history; the second is Quixotic, for Shi'ism too *is* its history.

The paradox of Shi'ism is constitutional to its doctrinal origin and has scarcely anything to do with its particular predicament in modernity, whereas the predicament of colonial encounter with European modernity is circumstantial to its global periphery, where Soroush receives it. Shi'ism is paradoxical. It morally fails at the moment of its political success. Soroush's attempt to separate "Islam Itself" from its history is to save its moral authority from its political success. Modernity, meanwhile, is paradoxical on its colonial edges, so Soroush has to save Shi'ism from its failures. Saving Shi'ism from its success (in order to break its constitutional paradox) and from its failure (in order to sever its link with modernity) combine to lead Soroush to suppose and suggest a "Religion Itself," which is immune to its own political success and moral failure internally, as it is immune to its ideological failure and moral success externally. If we take Shi'ism as the unfulfilled promise of Islam, as we may, Soroush's project as a Shi'i Muslim intellectual is to save Islam from a paradox constitutional to its formative doctrines and a predicament accidental to its modern history. At the hermeneutic core of his project, Soroush is no longer a mere Shi'i. He is a Muslim at large – conversant with its most enduring internal paradox: the Meccan (revolutionary) and Medinan (institution-building) polar opposites of its revelatory moment. He, though, has been too busy articulating his hermeneutic theory to recognize these subterranean anxieties that inform and sustain this ambition. That he ultimately fails is less an indication of his theoretical limitations than evidence of his historical tardiness. Soroush is simply too late, and he does not see it.

The most significant aspects of Soroush's work are his acute, however inarticulate, awareness of the constitutional paradox of Shi'ism, that it morally fails at the moment of its political success, and his attempt to break it. His entire hermeneutic apparatus is targeted toward an active separation of the political success of Shi'ism from its moral failure and thus safeguarding Shi'ism from its own success. Soroush's proposition to separate "Religion Itself" from the knowledge of religion is to keep "Shi'ism Itself" intact and yet subject the religious state, as a manifestation of the religious knowledge, to a historical dialectic. He believes that Iranian society is constitutionally religious and thus needs a religious government, and that religious government, by definition, will have to be Shi'i. But he does not want the political failings of an Islamic republic discrediting "Islam Itself" or "Shi'ism Itself." Thus "Islam Itself," or "Shi'ism Itself" will have to be segregated, quarantined, from the political failures of an Islamic republic. The critical move of Soroush to achieve that end is to expand the hermeneutic circle in charge of the historical articulation of religion. To do that, he deauthorizes the clerical establishment as the sole custodians of the sacred. The clerical establishment has been the exclusive organ of interpretation in charge of making the sacred accessible to its social constituency. Soroush, on the trail of a genealogy of lay ideologues that includes Ali Shari'ati, wishes to dismantle that privilege. But this time he does so from the middle of his historical hermeneutics:

> The [assumption of] the silence of the religious knowledge, contrary to what is imagined, will not render it susceptible to the whimsical imagination

of intruders. But of course it will prevent [its interpretation] from becoming the exclusive prerogative of a single group who thus have a claim on it, and who having reached one interpretation wish to prevent or proclaim as blasphemous all the others. Thus, understanding religion, and indeed understanding it well, is incumbent upon everyone, everyone being equally a participant in and responsible for the construction of religious civilization and of civility, which belong to everyone and which constitute a commonly received Divine Gift. The understanding of no one and no group excludes others from understanding religion and understanding it well, nor does [shrugging from that responsibility] excuse his ignorance. "We all stand alone in front of God."[75]

That expansion of the hermeneutic circle achieved, Soroush heralds and unleashes an avalanche of lay interpretations to usher his ancestral faith onto the battleground of modernity and yet save it from its historical failures. He has fully recognized that the premodern discourses authenticating the faith or fortifying it to face modernity are just too much invested in the "Religion Itself," and he wishes to dislodge that investment. He has a far more accurate conception of the devastating power of European modernity and its ability to corrode into the very fabric and texture of "Religion Itself." Left to decompose with its historical dismantling, the very core of the sacred will equally lose its metaphysical claim to legitimacy. Soroush wishes to save the "Religion Itself" against its successive failures to face European modernity, while saving Shi'ism in particular, which as a religion of protest is the very promise of Islam, from its incidental political success.

Soroush fails to achieve his objectives. That failure is less a matter of theoretical blindness than a measure of historical belatedness. Soroush is the last Muslim ideologue, the very last layer in a variegated site that was actively cultivated in colonial response to modernity, and precisely in its representation of the very last gasp for an air of legitimacy his writing marks the death of Islamic ideology. The Islam of Soroush's captive imagination was invented in dialogical contestation with European modernity, in response to European colonialism, and as such it matched and countered "the West," its paramount Other. As a global, and increasingly globalizing, movement, the European project of colonial modernity abstracted and universalized its bourgeois point of origin and code-named it "the West," and in turn unleashed an army of mercenary Orientalists to invent a succession of Eastern Others to originate and authenticate the otherwise false assumption of "the West," chief among them "Islam" – to this day the single most abiding counter-presence of this "West." Soroush does not seem to, or care to, know that dialogical genealogy. He takes the Islam of his colonized imagination for his ancestral faith. The result is a double jeopardy: the metaphysical foregrounding of what he calls "Islam Itself" and the equally metaphysical underpinnings of modernity (Itself), which to aggravate the result even more and make it more deadly he receives through the petrified imagination of a colonial subject, combine to give his expansive prose an absolutely terrorizing metaphysical certainty. But the problem is that with the dawn of globalization, the Islam of Soroush's colonized imagination no longer has an Other against which it can articulate itself, nor does it have the imperial power with which to assert itself. In the normative absence of that binary opposition ("Islam and the West"), which made both its parties possible, Soroush is in effect carrying on a heated debate with a dead interlocutor, with the ghost of an apparition once called "the West." What has remained after the death of that interlocutor is the phantom pain of "Islam and the West," still haunting the perturbed imagination of a Muslim intellectual long since rendered irrelevant by the world at large.

The reason that Soroush fails in his stated objective is that he is proposing what he calls a "progressive theology" in conversation with a modernity that no longer exists. Conversation with modernity is what Muslim intellectuals have been conducting over the last 200 years. Today that conversation is no longer viable or even possible, because one side of the dialogue is no longer there. The European project of modernity has now imploded epistemically from within, by its own succession of inner self-negations, long after it had already contradicted itself externally at its colonial borders. At the colonial edges of its claim to universality, Enlightenment modernity never had any claim to legitimacy. But now even for the European intellectuals, constitutionally blind to the colonial catastrophes of modernity, it is obscene to believe in the promises of a modernity that had the Holocaust up its sleeve. Soroush does not realize that the Islam that he now has in his mind is a dialectical outcome of a conversation under duress with a colonial modernity that has long since mutated its shapely relationship with the capital it systematically served. So in effect, that Islam that came into conception by virtue of that dialogue no longer exists, because it no longer corresponds with the lived realities of living Muslims. That Islam is dead. What Islam will emerge in a globalizing context where all binary oppositions have melted away is yet to be seen. "Islam and the West" mirrored, originated, and authenticated each other in the speculum of each other's reflection. Take one away, the other no longer exists. Soroush himself, as a result, is the phantom phenomenon of an intellectual who can only make sense of the presumption of two transparent realities that used to mirror each other but are no longer there.

Those two mirrors removed, the entire oeuvre of Soroush's writing is an exercise in futility, a ghostly apparition, real only in the removed mirror of a dialectical negation that no longer is. The world has moved beyond the presumption of a Western center and its Eastern peripheries. North and South for a while attracted a far more compelling division in world wealth and distribution. But massive pockets of poverty in the North (from suburbs of Paris to slums of New York, New Orleans, and Los Angeles) and the obscenity of Sheikhdoms like Kuwait or corrupt African warlords sporting European designer suits have long since destroyed that binary as well. The viability and usefulness of the categorical imperative code-named "the West" has now dissolved into the global formation of an empire that can no longer sustain the legitimacy of any nation-state, any national culture, or any mode of civilizational thinking.[76] Soroush does not seem to know any of these and as a mobile piece of archaeological curiosity can only simulate a dead duel, an outdated and stale redux of once a furious debate between "Islam and the West," as a particular brand of the entirely bogus game of "Tradition versus Modernity." We can no longer think in those terms. The world has left that false opposition behind. Even if its ghostly interlocutor was not dead, the "progressive hermeneutics" that Soroush proposes is simply too petrified by the European project of Enlightenment modernity to take it to task. It takes modernity ahistorically for granted, divests itself of its most sacrosanct, and thus most viable, elements, and punches with empty and vacated gloves. In fear of modernity destabilizing Islam, Soroush deposits "Islam Itself" in a metaphysical safe box and in the process inadvertently cross-essentializes modernity out of its own history. Modernity was a European project in the course of its colonial savagery around the globe – and the two events were coterminous. As such, modernity is very recent in its invention and coinage. The fiction of reason and progress that it invented was entirely recent in its coinage and currency. Michel Foucault in *Madness and Civilization* thought it necessary to have imprisoned the unreason in European mental asylums in order to define Reason in reasonable terms. But we know that this Reason needed a much bigger space to deposit its shadowy nightmares and exotic subconscious, and thus it invented the Orient as a much larger abode of unreason and backwardness in order to ascertain itself in reason and progress. So the interlocutor that Soroush wishes to engage is really a moving target, amorphous in nature – it may feign an existence in the peripheral anonymity of its colonial translations, but it has lost all credibility in its original claim to authenticity. We can no longer take it seriously, let alone be intimidated by it and hide our innermost vulnerabilities from its ferocious fangs. Disillusioned European intellectuals like Foucault, at their best, may seek in vain to detect a prophetic resistance (alternative) to the catastrophe of modernity that Khomeini once personified and Soroush now theorizes. But our historical facts no longer allow for any such illusions. Such illusions lead to the eloquent articulation of an "Islam Itself" that aggressively mutates in ever more miasmatic spaces – this at a time of predatory globalization of capital and labor. Taking modernity too belatedly seriously, Soroush is letting loose the self-abstracting metaphysical underpinnings of "Islam Itself," colonially conditioned, exactly at a time when the material world is expanding in ever larger disproportionality of globalized capital exploiting impoverished labor. Soroush, as a result, is pushing "Islam Itself," so far as it can have any meaning in a postmodernity beyond its feeble control, toward a metaphysical metastasis, a theological mutation, an epistemic vaporization, where it can signify absolutely nothing because it can mean just about anything.

In awe of European modernity and entrapped in its time and narrative, Soroush is petrified into a numbing positivism that lacks any conception of not just the range and topography but in fact the content and epistemic foundations of sciences being predicated on institutions of power outside their claims to autonomy. Absent in Soroush's conception of social and biological sciences, with which he believes the religious sciences ought to converse, is any awareness of the presence, force, and ferocity of power in their very epistemic and operative parameters. He has a numbingly positivist conception of knowledge formation devoid and independent of all human interests, completely autonomous in its operation, so much so that if the military conquest of space is epistemically conducive to the advancement of a certain astrophysics as opposed to others, Islamic theology becomes contingent on the whims of American generals at the Pentagon. This does not concern Soroush in the slightest – for his metaphysics of knowledge is entirely innocent of any sociology of knowledge. He believes that Islamic sciences need to be conversant with the changing discourses of scientific modernity. What constellation of global power and class interest informs and sustains the production of such scientific modernity – from medical research in AIDS to space sciences in astrophysics – is not of immediate or even remote concern to Soroush. His is an essentialized and dehistoricized conception of science as solid and eternal as his Religion Itself. By essentializing "Religion Itself" as a noumenon *sui generis*, Soroush equally essentializes "modernity" as a transhistorical reality – it has no European origin, no colonial consequence, no frightful instrumentalization of Reason. Blindfolded by modernity itself (otherwise how could he think of Islam Itself?), Soroush sees the dual imperatives of Reason and Progress as immutable and does not even see them as modern parameters in the course of Enlightenment modernity and in the full service of a certain mode of the economic production of reality. Tucking away "Religion Itself" from the slings and arrows of outrageous fortune, as it were, Soroush is also, negationally, dehistoricizing the European colonial modernity that has scared the sacred witless, as if this modernity is now so triumphant that the sacred has no recourse except running away into the bosom of an absolute irreversibility. Soroush is far too Hegelian for his own benefit.

All of these failures, in having a critical grasp of the origin and vicissitude of the European project of modernity, pale in comparison to the catastrophic anthropology that is contingent on Soroush's theology. Changing, he suggests, would be the human understanding of religion and constant "Religion Itself." In proposing this, Soroush is categorically oblivious to what will happen to the historical agency of the subject he has thus in his implicit anthropology depleted of all his sacred certitude rooted in historical experience, and waving in the air by the fluctuating wind of his ever-changing understandings. What use would that "Religion Itself" have for the historical person once it is ritually and piously tucked away in some sacred safe-deposit box? What an empty shell of wavering beliefs would humans be without their most sacrosanct convictions put on the line, exposed to historical elements? Faith, as in hope for an alternative to human misery, becomes a matter of private piety, publicly irrelevant. A precious piece of antiquarian interest, perhaps, a museum piece of incidental curiosity, but inconsequential on the battlefield of humanity in history, a single person's presence in the world. Trying to save "Islam Itself" from its doctrinal paradox and historical predicament constitutes the constellation of a very good set of intentions, paving the way for some catastrophic consequences. Soroush's project certainly succeeds in saving "Religion Itself" both from its political success and its ideological failures, but in the process he squarely manages to deplete Muslims, qua Muslims, from historical agency. Once their "Religion Itself" is squarely essentialized and safely deposited in some extraterrestrial domain, Muslims, qua Muslims, will have no historical investment in their faith or any historical agency in their world. Soroush's theology may indeed be quite clever, but his anthropology is positively disastrous. The "Religion Itself" is not particularly saved from this theology either. It too is cut off from its worldly presence, its historical relevance, as it is irrelevantly saved and deposited in the museum of dead certainties. Saving the sacred from its history means manufacturing an empty shell instead of a historical person with moral agency. The sacred that is saved from profanity of the historical person is a museum piece of exotic curiosity, quite expensive among the antique dealers of historical pieties, worthless though in the streets and deserts of human suffering.

Soroush is no Martin Luther (1483–1546) of his faith, as some have suggested him to be. Soroush is the Mulla Sadra (1571–1640) of his time, with half his philosophical genius, twice his metaphysical certainty. Like Mulla Sadra, Soroush has the creative courage of trying to combine two opposing forces in Islamic intellectual disposition, law and philosophy, the nomocentric and the logocentric proclivities effectively at war against each other throughout Islamic intellectual history. He equally inherits from Mulla Sadra his poetic prowess to fuse the nomocentricity of Islamic law and the logocentricity of Islamic philosophy, with the homocentricity of Islamic mysticism. Soroush's fascination with Rumi (1207–1273) is not a belated addendum to the massive output of his restless, yet alarmingly poised, writings. It is constitutional to his hermeneutically breaking the back of Islamic law by subjecting it to a philosophical distinction between its essence and its attributes, its noumenal certainty and its phenomenal doubts, its metaphysical otherworldliness and its historical mutations. The catastrophic difference between the two is that Mulla Sadra did most of his serious philosophizing in the privacy of his exile in a remote village in central Safavid Iran, whereas Soroush does his in the full publicity of an increasingly globalized space that is checked only by the nativity of his writing in Persian. The result might be irrelevant for the rest of the world that does not read Persian but is deadly for those who do – the captive audience of some 70 million Iranians who having barely survived a retrograde monarchy are now collectively tormented by a medieval theocracy, falsely promised by an eloquent prophet, while in the throws of the globalizing terror of capital and labor, of which they know very little, to which they have no choice but be victim. At a time when Iranians at large need to recognize the bestial barbarity of the globalizing terror of capital on labor, Soroush is intellectually leading them to ever more expansive spaces of a metaphysical thinking that evaporates the reality of Muslims themselves into the paradisiacal inanity of "Islam Itself." Instead of responding to the globalizing terror of the postmodernity of capital and labor, Soroush's "hermeneutics" corresponds to its metaphysical constitution of a digitized empire of abstractions.

The entire spectrum of Soroush's discursive universe is a locally outdated, globally irrelevant nativism rendering the very philosophical culture that generates and sustains it epistemically self-absorbed and universally exotic. Soroush is the very last relic from the "Islam and the West" archaeological site in whose insights we can see how the pathology of power divides to conquer, and in whose blindness we can imagine otherwise than being trapped in a false binary opposition. Separating the historical readings of Islam from "Islam Itself" seeks to safeguard an iconic conception of religion in order to save it for posterity and then offer a carbon copy conception on which history can leave its footsteps and traces. This, in a simpler language, is to try to have your cake and eat it too. This also is the final fear in facing European colonial modernity, the anxiety of a colonized, petrified mind writ large, and all of that at a time when the project of racialized modernity itself has self-destructed. Having failed to face this colonial modernity, and having mutated itself into the rotating mirror of realities originated elsewhere, Islam is finally made by Soroush to run for cover and leave behind a conceptual surrogate, a historical shadow, to face the world. This is worse than trying to have your cake and eat it too. This is postulating an agential impossibility, where historical agency is impossible because we are no longer real when we have checked ourselves out of history, imagined a hidden metaphysical haven to run to, where we never face the real because we are not real. We are the shadow of our own former faith.

If Abdolkarim Soroush is a belated nativist persisting on the false binary opposition between "Islam and the West," Tariq Ramadan is a cream puff by the mainly European media to play a variation on the similar theme of (this time around) "Islam *in* the West." The problem with Soroush, who is an infinitely superior intellectual force and formidable thinker, is that paramount in his hermeneutics remains the centrality of a time that is, entirely unbeknown to himself, a European time, a colonial time, a time out of joint, a time that is neither Islamic nor worldly. But Soroush's, with all its faults, is an immensely erudite mind, a vastly learned intellect, albeit caught in an entirely captured and colonized imagination, writing deeply informed and spectacularly learned essays and books in a principal Islamic language (Persian), which is not what one can claim for Tariq Ramadan. With Soroush we at least know that we are in the presence of a magnificent (however retrograde) intelligence, as we can also detect exactly where his epistemic problems originate, when, for example, we note that the interlocutor that he wishes to place in front of this "Religion Itself" is (subconsciously) an impersonator of "the West" – someone imagining what this "West" wishes him to say. None of these are even remotely applicable to Tariq Ramadan, who is far more a media hype than an intellectual force.

Tariq Ramadan is a product of Euro-American media sensationalism, especially after he was denied a US visa on the ludicrous charges of affiliation with a "terrorist" organization. His appointment at a teaching position at Notre Dame University and subsequent denial of an entry visa to move to the USA created an international spectacle from which Tariq Ramadan emerged as yet another candidate for this bizarre epithet of the "Martin Luther of Islam," hitherto given to any number of other candidates. "Tariq Ramadan is a Muslim Martin Luther" has declared Paul Donnelly at *The Washington Post*. "The work of Tariq Ramadan will take its place in the annals of Islamic thought" chimes in *Le Monde Diplomatique*. By what authority and on the basis of what evidence, and do Muslims around the globe need to have a Martin Luther of their own – no one dares to ask or cares to answer. To be sure, it is mostly European and American (Christian, Protestant) observers who seem to be in search of a Muslim Martin Luther and keep bestowing it on Soroush one day Ramadan another, and now even on Reza Aslan. The calamity of 9/11 has bizarre repercussions of a variety of vintages – only the least of them is the rise of fictive Martin Luthers to save Europeans and Americans from their fear of this chimerical creature they keep calling "Islam."

One looks in vain at Tariq Ramadan's work for the trace of any original idea, any sign of a pathbreaking suggestion, anything remotely resembling the catholicity of Soroush's hermeneutic or theological learning, anything that will touch upon the sufferings and repressed aspirations of people (Muslim or otherwise) around the globe. Swiss by birth and breeding, his conception of the (Muslim) world is from the vantage point of a belated European – provincial at heart, parochial in diction and disposition. As a media product, Ramadan is quite an oddity and has a particularly difficult time being taken seriously by any Muslim (or non-Muslim) readership. Such scholars, theorists, and activists as Nasr Hamid Abu Zayd[77] or Nawal El Saadawi,[78] to give two prominent global examples, cut far more formidable and compelling figures. Ramadan, though of Egyptian decent, does not write in any Islamic language – Arabic, Persian, Turkish, or Urdu. His writings are published in English, though evidently he is more at home in French than in English,[79] and yet his books are readily available in English – and yet (bizarre indeed) he does not write them in English but has them translated for him into English by a certain Claude Dabbak, on one occasion, and a Carol Bebawi, on another: translators whom he thanks in his acknowledgements but who do not receive credit on the cover of the book, thus creating the impression that Tariq Ramadan originally wrote his books in English.[80] English, French, whatever, the authorial voice of Tariq Ramadan is fabricated, concocted, oscillating, miasmatic.

Even bypassing all these bizarre circumstances and irregularities, the substance of what one reads over Tariq Ramadan's signature is singularly vacuous and useless – mostly a primer in an elementary knowledge of Islam mixed with yet another tiresome joggling of "Islam and the West" or "Tradition versus modernity." To be sure, on the surface what Tariq Ramadan is proposing is rather an innocuous reconsideration of some basic creedal and communal parameters of being a Muslim in a European context. In *To be a European Muslim* (1999), for example, he provides a handy and perhaps useful primer for young Muslims about the classification of various branches of Islamic juridical (and exclusively juridical) learning, a classification that is neither wrong nor particularly noteworthy. Muslims have been dividing and subdividing their various branches of knowledge at least since the time of Abu Nasr al Farabi's (870–950) *Ihsa' al-Ulum*. Ramadan's purpose here, however, is to give young European Muslims a generic exposure to various modes of knowledge production in Islam, though (and there is the rub) mostly in juridical terms, with a nod towards Islamic ethics.[81] What is particularly noteworthy in Ramadan's conception of Islam is that his reading of his faith remains at a quintessentially *juridical* level, with very little or non-existent awareness or notice of the non-juridical, in fact counter-juridical, dimensions of Islam? Beyond these innocuous preliminaries, Ramadan does raise some quite serious questions about the identity, the whereabouts, and the possibilities of coexistence of Muslims in Europe, somewhere "between assimilation and alienation."[82] But all these questions are predicated on his normative geographical worldview, the way he sees the world divided – and *that* precisely is where his problems dwell.

The problem with much of what Ramadan writes and proposes remains his astonishingly provincial and outdated conception of the globe, very much partaking in the European provincialism that embraces him and he embraces back as a "*European* Muslim." Central to this provincialism is his worldview as it is best articulated in his chapter on "Where Are We?" in his *To Be a European Muslim*, where he has an elaborate discussion about "Old Concepts."[83] Here lies Tariq Ramadan's captured imagination, oscillating between an old, useless, irrelevant, and entirely banal juridical bifurcation between *Dar al-Islam* and *Dar al-Harb*, on one hand, and a center-and-periphery conception of the world, with "the West" at the center and the rest of the world at its periphery.[84] A number of crucial consequences are contingent on this central blind spot of Tariq Ramadan – consequences that alas make him a central figure in the racist presumptions of the white-washed

Eurocentricity that has in turn opted to celebrate, embrace, and anoint him as a "Muslim Martin Luther."

At the very outset, Ramadan acknowledges that these two binary concepts, *Dar al-Islam* and *Dar al-Harb,* are nowhere to be found either in the Qur'an or in the Hadith literature. But nevertheless he proceeds to pick on the juridical distinction made between these two *abodes* (or *spaces*) for effectively legalistic purposes and functions (mostly the regulated and codified rituals of piety) incumbent upon a Muslim. From this point forward he is at great pains to prove that "a close study of these two definitions ... shows that the parameters on which the recognition of a specific and qualified *Dar* is based are not strictly antithetical."[85] He then goes so far as proposing that in fact sometime in fact the opposite is true, because "Muslims are sometimes safer in the West – regarding the free practise of their Religion – than they are in Islamic countries."[86]

Reviving an old, outdated, entirely irrelevant, and at its essence a matter of codifying the ritual obligations of Muslims in certain schools of law, with little to no particularly enduring effect in the course of Islamic civilization, though later revived and trumpeted up by some Orientalists dead set to essentialize, antagonize, and alienate an entire civilization, what in effect Tariq Ramadan is doing here first and foremost is revealing his own vertiginous juridical (legalistic) disposition. The man cannot breathe a word outside a strictly jurisprudential (Fiqh-based and Shari'ah-conscious) state of mind, which for him is "Islam" *in toto* and *par excellence*. That legalistic disposition marks just about anything and everything that Tariq Ramadan thinks of and writes about Islam, all underwritten by an evident piety which he flaunts in his subordinate clauses – greetings that he sends to the prophet and such – which in and of themselves are entirely innocent and innocuous but give his language and discourse a decidedly pietistic (and thus juridically binding) disposition. Within that disposition, in the domain of Islamic law proper, the Shari'ah, we are facing a medieval legal system that is, just like Jewish or any other sacred law, quintessentially, categorically, and at its very epistemic roots predicated on a gender-apartheid jurisprudence. In this law, half of the humanity is systematically barred from equal rights in the eyes of a Muslim judge. None of these facts seem to bother Tariq Ramadan as he goes about stripping Muslims of their cosmopolitan cultures (which includes Islamic law but is not limited to it) and reducing them to a *homo juridicus*. These facts do bother Nawal El-Saadawi and scores of other Muslim women scholars, theorists, and activists, which European sexist disposition cannot even imagine as the "Muslim Martin Luther."

Equally important is Tariq Ramadan's mental entrapment inside an Orientalist disposition which makes him effectively speak to an imaginary white European interlocutor pointing an accusatory finger at him and his faith, against which he assumes an apologetic and explanatory posture. In effect it is this fictive white supremacist European that narratively teases out ideas, concepts, meanings, and doctrines that Ramadan feels obligated to enunciate, explain, or dismiss and revise. The result is a dual essentialization of *Islam* (in an absolutist and irreducibly juridical reading) and *the West* (as an equally absolutist, essentialized, and ahistorical icon). Thus Tariq Ramadan's conception of "Islam *in* the West" is just another gyration of the same old colonial cliché – vintage Orientalist manufacturing company – of "Islam *and* the West."

Having posited a fictively binary and entirely outdated and irrelevant geography (*Dar al-Islam* and *Dar al-Harb*) to target and dismiss, Tariq Ramadan then moves to articulate what he believes is now the more compelling and legitimate picture of the world in which we now live – and here his case goes from bad to worse. "Westernization," which for this "Muslim Martin Luther" is

> the legitimate daughter of pluridimensional globalization, can be far better expressed through the notions of center (the West and its relay capitals in the South) and periphery (the rest of the planet), than by the representation of two "abodes" living the reality of a "con-frontation."[87]

Here lies the kernel of why is it that Europeans are so excited about Tariq Ramadan and have bestowed upon him the honorific title of "Muslim Martin Luther." It is impossible nowadays to imagine a more reactionary, retrograde, stale, parochial, mothball of a manner in which to see the world than this center-periphery, "the West and the Rest," that this "European Muslim" is proposing for the world to note. "Muslims settled in the West," Ramadan congratulates himself, "are at the *centre*, at the *heart*, at the *head* of the system which produces the symbolical apparatus of Westernization."[88] One can only resort to an assumption of intentional blindness (for the alternatives are simply logical fallacy and momentary delusion) when one sees Tariq Ramadan thus entirely oblivious to the fact the he has just posited a binary opposition between *the West* and *the Rest* when he proceeds to say, "For Muslims, at the heart of the West, what matters is not to fall back into the old bipolar vision by looking for foes, but rather to find partners who will, like them, be determined to select in what Western culture produces in order to promote its positive contributions and to resist its destructive deviations, both on the human and environmental levels."[89]

Having just dismissed the bipolarity of *Dar al-Islam* and *Dar al-Harb* as irrelevant and inappropriate on pages 125–126, he proceeds on pages 148–149 to place the privileged European Muslims at the *Center* of an even more inane center-periphery bipolarity – *the West* and *the Rest* – which he posits as the quintessential fact of the world, in fact "the legitimate daughter of pluridimensional globalization," without as much as a blink of a notice that he just fell from the frying pan into the fire, without even noticing it. Not only that – he in fact proceeds to admonish Muslims to stop thinking in old bipolar ways, while congratulating them for having made it into the "heart" and the "head" of "the West," and thus to an advantageous position in a superior bipolar phase. What Tariq Ramadan is effectively doing is asking the supremacist European country clubs if they would please not mind admitting a few "good European Muslims" into the center of their globalizing provincialism, which he believes in pious earnest that such clubs are Allah's gift to humanity. Perhaps what the European admirers of Tariq Ramadan mean by the "Martin Luther of Islam" is a European white-washed version of Islam that may help admit a number of "good Muslims" into their country clubs (please). But Ramadan's entire project, predicated on this noxious notion of the *West* versus *the Rest* means absolutely nothing for about a billion Muslims scattered around the globe, or even more importantly for their emancipatory part in the fate of billions of other, non-Muslim, people who share their predicament.

As a fabrication of mostly European media, Tariq Ramadan speaks more to the anxiety of those who have manufactured him as a "Muslim Martin Luther" – and thus aborting the infinitely more material and worldly reading of Islam evident in the short but compelling careers of someone like Malcolm X in Africa or Ali Shari'ati in Europe. In specifically Islamic learning with a superior hermeneutic implication, no one (Abdolkarim Soroush and Tariq Ramadan put together) comes even close to what Nasr Hamid Abu Zayd has done in his Qur'anic hermeneutics, or Nawal al-Saadawi in her revolutionary re-reading of Muslim sacred sources. Nawal al-Saadawi in particular speaks to the repressed realities of half of the humanity (Muslim and non-Muslim women) categorically absent in this "Muslim Martin Luther's" universe of imagination. But who outside the small circle of Islamic scholars ever heard of Nasr Hamid Abu Zayd, and who other than a small circle of transnational feminists ever cared for what Nawal El Saadawi has to say – or Fatima Mernissi, Assia Djebar, Nadia Yassin, etc., for that matter? Nawal al-Saadawi cannot be a "Muslim Martin Luther." She is of the wrong sex. The racism of the proposition is confounded by its unabashed sexism.

The point of all such fabrications of one "Muslim Martin Luther" or another seems to address the phantom fears of Europeans themselves, exceedingly nervous about Muslim (and other) immigrant communities in their midst. The fabrication also keeps the unfinished project of such Muslim revolutionaries as Malcolm X or Ali Shari'a buried under the dizzying ping-pong game between "Islam and the West," or alternatively between "Tradition and Modernity" – as if Muslim societies have fallen from some extraterrestrial abode and have not been integral to the global formations of cosmopolitan cultures of identity and defiance the world over. At a time that massive labor migration from various corners of the world into Western Europe and North America is bound to change the demographic disposition of nation-states and once and for all override the cartographies of racialized imperialism, the function of Tariq Ramadan seems to be precisely in the reverse direction, to re-authenticate the racialized bifurcation between *the West* and *the Rest* by congratulating the "European

Muslims" for having made it to the *heart*, the *head*, and the *center* of universe. There is no such center to this universe. European colonial racism assumed that central role to give its predatory capitalism a cultural claim to superiority over its colonial ravages around the globe – and generations after courageous revolutionary thinkers and activists, from Frantz Fanon to Malcolm X, having sought to override that presumption, Tariq Ramadan is here to revive and re-author it.

As I will demonstrate in some detail in the next chapter, precisely at a time when groundbreaking ideas and practices of revolutionary activists ranging from Jose Martí and W. E. B. Dubois, down to Frantz Fanon, Che Guevara, and Malcolm X are in dire need of revisiting in order once and for all to dismantle and discard this racist conception of "the West" – colonially constructed morally to belittle and subject the entirety of humanity – in comes Tariq Ramadan as a bizarre concoction called "European Muslim" to revive and re-authenticate, and in fact give an Islamic disposition to, the most racist conception ever manufactured in the history of colonial modernity. A more reactionary, retrograde, and self-delusional proposition can hardly be imagined. At a time when the very long, shameful, and barbaric history of European colonial ravaging of the globe has finally exposed the rotten roots of its very denominational formations – "Europe is literally the invention of the Third World" (Frantz Fanon) – suddenly a Tariq Ramadan has appeared, seeking admission into the European country clubs, and thus re-authenticating that idea, but this time around infusing an Islamic element into it.

Muslims are not the only immigrant community in Western Europe or North America, nor has their Islamic affiliation been the *prima facie* cause of their immigration to the *Western* corner of Tariq Ramadan's captured imagination. The massive poverty and the unraveling destitution caused by European colonialism and now by American imperialism (aided and abetted by International Monetary Fund and the World Bank) are the principal causes of such massive labor migrations to Western Europe or North America. Muslims immigrated to Europe not as Muslims but as immigrant laborers, and there is a fundamental, factual, and categorical difference between the Islam of an Algerian, Moroccan, or Afghan illegal immigrant washing dishes in the basement of a restaurant in Paris, and that of the Saudi, Kuwaiti, or Bahraini Sheikhs and their concubines strolling by Lake Geneva. Unaware, indifferent, or oblivious to such differences, Tariq Ramadan promotes yet another generic brand of juridical "Islam," while congratulating himself and other "European Muslims" as if they are the only immigrant group entitled to a dignity of place, or to positing themselves in a symbiotic relationship to this colonially manufactured spatial idea called "Europe" or "the West." "Europe," as they call it, is being increasingly creolized, as they say in Cultural Studies, and all for the right, and all for inevitable, reasons. Migration and diasporic communities have raised questions about the very idea of "Europe" and the assumptions of its cultural, religious, or even political unity, integrity, collectivity. Only in the mind of incurably racist assumptions is "the West" the center of the universe and the whole world its periphery. That periphery is already in the center, for that center was roaming through its peripheries causing calamities and stealing resources. Intermingling of diverse communities of sentiments having gathered in "the West" from all the colonized lands prevents any essentialist assumption about any collectivity anywhere in the world. Migratory movements, breaking of diasporic boundaries, the shifting landscape of continental divides have all made the world look like a quilt rather than an encircled center. Millions of refugees are now the permanent fixtures of world demographic distribution. Their *minor* literatures and cultures are *major* to them. Postcoloniality means very little to new forms of labor abuse and household slavery. Before he thinks of French for *Dar al-Islam* or *Dar al-Harb* (outlandish and irrelevant terms), Tariq Ramadan needs to think of Arabic for *mestizaje, creolization, lusotropicalism*, etc.

Massive labor migrations from scores of countries to Western European and North American domains have been definitive to their economic and demographic dispositions. Italian, Irish, Polish, Scandinavian, Eastern European, North African, South Asian, East Asian, and Latin American communities have immigrated in their millions into these domains over the last 200 years in particular in desperate search of job. Why should the fate and lot of Muslims as Muslims be any different from others like them? Why should North African, South or West Asian communities even be reduced to their "Islamic" identities? Do they lack any other aspect, equally compelling perhaps, equally formative, equally if not more binding in them than their having been born to a Muslim parentage. Suppose they are nothing but Muslim. Why should a blindfolded, vertiginous, and entirely *juridical* conception of Islam have an exclusive claim on their faith, despite its magnificent cosmopolitan character and culture over the last 1400 years throughout the Muslim world? Islamic philosophy and its various epistemically liberating branches, Islamic mysticism and its globally forgiving reach, Islamic political thoughts of diverse normative disposition, Islamic natural and biological sciences in various fields and domains – why not Arabic, Persian, Turkish, or Urdu literary humanism, why not exposure to and the active cultivation of a worldly cosmopolitanism, an anti-colonial modernity, throughout the Muslim world over the last 200 years alone, their exposure to an equally, more immediate, worldly and cosmopolitan culture be the defining moment of Muslims in their contemporary condition? Who decided, and upon what pulpit exactly, that Muslims – even these "European Muslims" – are nothing but inanimate objects at the cold and calculating mercy of a Swiss Muslim jurist (akin to and reminiscent of Calvin's brutally meticulous Protestantism) deciding their moral and normative whereabouts?

Reducing Muslims' worldly character exclusively to their Islamic identities, dwarfing their collective claim to a magnificent cosmopolitan Islam to a theologically pedantic juridical Islam, and then placing that naked *homo juridicus* (stripped of any claim to a cosmopolitan culture innate to her and his history) next to a fictive white supremacist European assumption that "the West" (wherever that is) is the Center of the Universe and thus Allah's gift to humanity, and whereby to re-authenticate the racist assumption at the root of the very notion of "the West" – *that* is Tariq Ramadan in a nutshell. The Islam of a contemporary world that does not place the immigrant Muslim laborer, in the full regalia of her and his claim to a worldly and polyfocal civilization, next to a poor Christian Mexican laborer, equally full-bodied and about to cross the border and yet at the shooting range of a redneck Minuteman, and both of them then placed next to an Indian Hindu cabdriver pulling a backbreaking 12-hour shift in New York, and then all of them next to a Hungarian Jew running from European pogroms and the Holocaust, and then add to them, above all, a pagan, a kafir, an atheist, and a shaman from the heart of Africa selling fake Gucci bags in Florence, and then underlining their illegal immigrant status and noting the ghastly gender imbalance of power among them all – an Islam that is thus not situated in the real world has not an iota of credibility with a decent vision of humanity at large, let alone a claim to the visions of a prophet whose very first messages of hope was for the homeless and the illegal immigrants of Mecca and Medina of his time. Muslims do not need a Martin Luther. If anything, they need to revisit the historical vision of their own prophet, or at least that of his trusted companion Bilal al-Habashi, or even in a shorter cut that of Malcolm X – or in his absence a resumption of the project he left unfinished.

Islam can no longer speak. It has no particular interlocutor. Its once "Western" interlocutor has now imploded, vaporized into the thin air of globalization. The world has no center, no periphery. In the absence of a civilizational other, Islam has become mute. Molla Omar and Osama bin Laden speak for nothing but a vacuous and vicious violence. Faceless, voiceless, praying in silent soliloquies, Muslims face an Other beyond their active imagination. And thus precisely in their amorphous wonder they mirror the phantasmagoric violence of a mode of globalization that the most devastating military machinery in human history, now led by George W. Bush, can barely begin to claim or control. The war is no longer, if it ever was, between "Tradition and Modernity," between "the East and the West," or between "Islam and the West." The war is not between US imperialism and the Taliban, or al-Qaeda either. The war is between a monstrous apparition called globalization and the mirror reflection of the terror it visits upon the world, now code-named "Terrorism." The US army may now fashion itself to become the military arm of globalization, as al-Qaeda is made to represent its carbon copy, "Terrorism." But the battle lines are far too amorphous and porous to yield their imaginative geography so early in the game. That remapping needs active agency, though in a manner yet to be envisioned, outlined, peopled with a faltering humanity.

The very ideas of the nation-state, of cultural identity, and of civilizational boundaries have long since lost their categorical legitimacy. After the events of September 11 2001, the retrograde ideas of such instruments of power as Samuel Huntington and Bernard Lewis were once again dusted off and taken for yet another tired ride. But they are wrong. Even louder microphones can be given to Huntington and Osama bin Laden. But civilizational thinking is over. Bernard Lewis can frequent the Pentagon even more often and Molla Omar may go into hiding to resurface again. But "Islam and the West" is today more an inane binary opposition than it ever was. The battle was never between "Islam and the West." Kuwaiti sheikhs and Enron executives are of the same ilk, culture, and disposition; so are the inner-city kids from Harlem and Bronx who join the US army and the Taliban fighters from Kandahar. Islam of the Saudi princes is not the Islam of Algerian migrant laborers in France, and there is no Western corner of any globe in universe that can bring together Park Avenue in New York City and the slums of Newark, New Jersey. Left to the ravages of Katrina, New Orleans looks uncannily identical to Baghdad.

"Islam and the West" was one particularly malicious invention of colonial modernity. With modernity dead and the postmodern infusion of globalization rampant, that ghostly opposition means nothing. Globalization means nothing other than the lifting of that smoke screen of civilizational divides that covered the vertical and horizontal colonization. What difference does it make if the British colonized India or Ireland, the Italians Mezzogiorno or Libya, or the French bourgeoisie the French or Algerian laborers? Colonization is colonization is colonization. Colonialism is integral to the operation of capital. Colonialism is the abuse of labor by capital writ global, times racism, multiplied by predatory warmongering. The capital colonizes labor, not cultures. Nike will sell shoes to American marines and the Afghan Taliban alike – no discrimination here. Formation of national cultures (the British, the French, the Germans, etc.) succeeded the European dynastic histories by way of giving ideological cohesion to the emerging national economies as the optimum unit for the maximum abuse of labor by capital. Formation of civilizational divides (constituting "the West" and separating it from the Islamic, the Chinese, the Indian, etc., all invented by an army of mercenary Orientalists) succeeded the medieval idea of Christendom and thus expanded the ideological cohesion of national economies to their colonial divides. The Germans thought they were Germans against the French so that they would not see the brutal class division that internally pulled them apart, as *the Westerners* saw themselves as *Westerners* against Muslims, Chinese, or Indians (*Orientals* in general) so the structural similarities between the ravages of capital on labor whether in Paris or in Cairo would not reveal itself. This was the historical smoke screen that is now lifted from the global face of desperation and destitution that the brutality of capital on labor has visited upon the world. It is far more than theoretical blindness to perpetuate and authenticate inanities such as "Islam and the West" by forgetting that the "Islam" of that opposition, as indeed its "West," is the figment of a tormented, colonized, and captive imagination.

From its very inception, Islam has been a religion of protest. What is called "Shi'ism" is nothing other than the very soul of Islam as a religion of protest. But Shi'ism has succeeded precisely because, as the very soul of the Islamic message, it is a paradox. It can never, and should never, succeed. It should always speak the truth to power. It can never be in power. A "Muslim ruler" is, as it has always been, a contradiction in terms. All the current rulers in the Islamic republic of Iran who have not been democratically elected are usurpers of power. The very constitution of the Islamic Republic, the very idea of *Velayat e Faqih*, is the usurpation of power. Democracy, as the will of a people to self-governance, is constitutional to Shi'ism and by extension to Islam as a religion of protest. The confirmation or denial of authority to their leaders is always the sole prerogative of Muslims. The source of legitimacy is from the ground up and not the other way around. The fancy footwork of belated and blind ideologues notwithstanding, the ordinary Muslims in the streets of Tehran, Cairo, Peshawar, or Ramallah, whether or not they even consciously recognize themselves as believing Muslims, are the sole source of revolutionary energy and moral aspiration. That has always been the case, before and after colonial modernity. That will always be the case, before and after postcolonial postmodernity.

4 Islam and globalization

Here lies a YM [Yellow Man], killed by a BM [Black Man], fighting for the WM [White Man], who killed all the RM [Red Man].

Malcolm X

Corporate globalization – or shall we call it by its name? – Imperialism. ... So this – all this – is empire. This loyal confederation, this obscene accumulation of power, this greatly increased distance between those who make the decisions and those who have to suffer them.

Arundhati Roy

So may I work the mills just as long as I am able
And never meet the man whose name is on the label
It be me and my machine
For the rest of the morning
And the rest of the afternoon
Gone to hell for the rest of my life.

James Taylor, "Millworker"

In a brief but powerful speech that Arundhati Roy delivered at the closing rally of the World Social Forum in Porto Alegre, Brazil, on January 27 2003, the defiant anti-war activist, award-winning novelist, and the recipient of the 2002 Lannan Foundation Prize for Cultural Freedom outlined the vicious circularity of the violence that US imperialism unleashes upon the world. Identifying the empire as the scattered constellation of the US government, its European allies, the World Bank, the International Monetary Fund (IMF), the World Trade Organization (WTO), and multinational corporations, she then declared that this empire "has sprouted other subsidiary heads, some dangerous byproducts – nationalism, religious bigotry, fascism and, of course, terrorism. All these march arm in arm with the project of corporate globalization."[1] One of the principal examples that Roy provides to illustrate her argument is her own country, India, where she reports that the government is divided into two arms:

While one arm is busy selling India off in chunks, the other, to divert attention, is orchestrating a howling, baying chorus of Hindu nationalism and religious fascism. It is conducting nuclear tests, rewriting history books, burning churches, and demolishing mosques. Censorship, surveillance, the suspension of civil liberties and human rights, the questioning of who is an Indian citizen and who is not, particularly with regard to religious minorities, are all becoming common practice now.[2]

The deadly combination that Roy identifies as the high mark of globalization – economic buccaneering (overnight robbery of national wealth on the high economic seas of transnational commerce) on one hand and cultural tribalism on the other – is evident all over the globe. As part of this schizophrenic scene, Roy describes what she calls "a state-sponsored pogrom" in which thousands of Muslims, women in particular, were gang-raped and slaughtered by Hindu fundamentalists. "More than a hundred and fifty thousand Muslims," Roy reports, "have been driven from their homes. The economic basis of the Muslim community has been devastated." What have Indian authorities done in response? "Narendra Modi, architect of the pogrom, proud member of the RSS [Rashtriya Swayamsevak Sangh = "a right-wing Hindu cultural guild with a clearly articulated anti-Muslim stand and a nationalistic notion of *hindutva* ... the ideological backbone of BJP, the Hindu nationalist party"] has embarked on his second term as the Chief Minister of Gujarat." And then comes Roy's principal point: "If he [Narendra Modi] were Saddam Hussein, of course each atrocity would have been on CNN. But since he's not – and since the Indian "market" is open to global investors – the massacre is not even an embarrassing inconvenience."[3]

The point of Roy's argument, pointedly observed, is that if the market to globalized capital is wide open and lucrative, the presiding imperial hubris could not care less if consumers are eating each other alive, so far as it can make a lucrative business out of the spectacle. Add those countless Muslims murdered by Hindu fundamentalist thugs in India to countless more murdered by the Jewish state in Palestine and the even more countless massacred by the Christian empire and its allies in Afghanistan and Iraq, and then bring Arundhati Roy's voice of moral outrage closer to the mournful testimony of Judith Butler and ask with her "what are the cultural barriers against which we struggle when we try to find out about the losses that we are asked not to mourn, when we attempt to name, and so to bring under the rubric of the 'human' those whom the United States and its allies have killed?"[4] We can of course, as Judith Butler knows only too well, easily name the nameless, for they all have a name. His name is Muhammad al-Durrah (1988–2000), cold-bloodedly murdered by the Israeli sharpshooters on September 30 2000 in the Gaza Strip at the beginning of the al-Aqsa Intifada. Her name is Abeer Qassim Hamza al-Janabi (1991–2006), the 14-year-old Iraqi girl from the village of Mahmoudiyah near Baghdad who on or about March 12 2006 was gang-raped by the US serviceman, Pfc. Steven D. Green and his company, before they burned and murdered her ravaged body along with her father Qassim Hamza Raheem, 45, her mother Fakhriya Taha Muhasen, 34, and her seven-year-old sister, Hadeel Qassim Hamza. They are not nameless. Like all other humans, they have a name. CNN anchorpersons may not know how to pronounce them. Fox News propaganda officers may not care to consider them human. *The New York Times* might be complicitous in giving its reporter Judith Miller wide-opened columns to help the Bush administration to cheat and lie its way to bombing Abeer Qassim Hamza al-Janabi's entire country to rubble. But they all have proper names.

The question though that Judith Butler raises, when she "attempts to name," is far more fundamental, far more disconcerting. In a mournful voice depleted by the power of its own fear in the face of the inhumanity she has witnessed, Butler questions the specter of anonymity cast upon the immediate and distant victims of a neoconservative–Zionist global terrorism. The veil of that anonymity is far thicker than the proverbial "burka" that the propaganda machinery of the US empire has cast upon Muslim women, a "burka" categorically different from the habitual garment of one form or another wore by women around the globe. Taking her lead from Chandra Mohanty's groundbreaking essay, "Under Western Eyes," Judith Butler reaches out for a manner of transnational feminism that is no longer contingent on an imperial succumbing to the white women's notion of agency. Suppose, Butler has learned from Mohanty, that this thing that Hillary Clinton mispronounces as "Boor-Kaa" had a multiplicity of functions entirely unbeknown to the white and white-identified women. What then? Suppose that there were certain aliens who had by hook or by crook smuggled themselves into the belly of this beast they call "the West" and who have actually grown up (played hide-and-seek for example or else sought protection from nasty flies in cool summer afternoons) under those multifunctional things that Lynne Cheney (now that we are naming names) cannot even bring herself to pronounce, will not "attempt to name." What then? Judith Butler's answer, predicated on Chandra Mohanty's timely intervention, is clear and concise:

> It seems to me now that the possibility of international coalition has to be rethought on the basis of this critique and others. Such a coalition would have to be modeled on new modes of cultural transaction and would be different from appreciating this or that position or asking for recognition in ways that assume that we are all fixed and frozen in our various locations and 'subject-positions.' We could have several engaged intellectual debates going on at the same time and find ourselves joined in the fight against violence.[5]

What Judith Butler is proposing here is the active mutation of a single, solitary, and fixed subject position (and she must never wear a veil) into a multiplicity of equally agential subject positions, each located on a different, differing, and superceding cartography that no longer recognizes the imperial mapping of the world, on which is acknowledged and revealed a few as worthy of life and liberty, while the majority of the inhabitants of the world are dismissed as unworthy of either life, liberty, or even death – and thus rendered anonymous and faceless behind a *burka* far thicker than what Hillary Clinton and CNN can fathom. The death of the foreigner will have to remain foreign and unmourned and the death of the familiar, familiar and mourned – "and the twain," in the classical British imperial thinking of Rudyard Kipling, "shall never meet." The geography of human emotions that this politics of mourning entails is contingent on a simultaneous emotive solidarity with the familiar and permanent estrangement from the foreign. What Judith Butler calls for, predicated on a pathbreaking reading of Levinas' notion of the "face,"[6] is the reversal of that order, where the foreign becomes dialectically familiar by way of the familiarity of one's own death becoming uncannily foreign.

The politics of mourning names the familiar victims and leaves the foreign nameless, faceless, countless, irrelevant, and thus covered under a veil of anonymity far thicker and more imposing than what it calls a "Boor-Kaa." Named or nameless, subject formations are the insignia of a cartography of motions and emotions, the bright or blighted colors with which we map the world. The problem that Judith Butler's generation of critical theorists and feminists have faced, and are now trying to overcome, is not naming the nameless – or "when we attempt to name" – but *pronouncing* the already named (Abeer Qassim Hamza al-Janabi), and thus re-imagining the globe on a more emancipatory map, a map on which Abeer Qassim Hamza al-Janabi has a home just before it is raided by US soldiers. The map of the world that George W. Bush seeks to rule is overridden by a schizophrenic bifurcation best captured by Arundhati Roy's description of India – rampant corporate globalization on one side and religious fanaticism on the other. In other words, the manner in which the US-led globalization of capital and its human and cultural subsidiaries seems to operate is the planetary expansion of a postmodern productive machinery on one side and the aggressive disintegration of cosmopolitan cultures into medieval tribalisms of one sort or another.

Reflecting similar tendencies around the world, that bizarre concoction of corporate-sponsored tribalism assumed a spectacularly jingoistic disposition in the USA soon after the events of 9/11. "The meanings attached to flag waiving," observes Susan Willis in her *Portents of the Real: A Primer for Post-9/11 America*, very much reflecting and expounding Arundhati Roy's insights about India, "have a lot to tell us about the America that emerged phoenix-like out of its ashes to remake itself for the twenty-first century."[7] Thinking of the flag as something of "a circulating signifier," Willis ultimately concludes that "in its power to evoke healing and perseverance over New

York and retribution over Kandahar this flag shows itself as an empty signifier." Concomitant with this contradictory evacuation of meaning from the American flag, Susan Willis observes, "we were told to shop. Shop to show we're patriotic Americans. Shop to show our resilience over death and destruction. Shop because in consumer capitalism shopping is the only way we can participate."[8] Shopping and showing the American flag, Willis continues her probing insights into the immediate semiotics of post-9/11 flag-waving, became effectively interchangeable, for sometime you shopped for just about anything, including a T-shirt you just bought and wore with an American flag on it, for "many turned to displays of the flag as the only available mode of proclaiming community."[9] That sense of community though was transregional, not just American, for in the course of "America's new alliance in the fight against terrorism ... every nation's own troublesome dissidents become a pretext to adopt America's search-and-destroy policy: Russia's war against the Chechens, China's repression of its Muslim population in Xinjiang province, and Israel's drive to exterminate the Palestinians – all implicitly fly the American flag of approval."[10] But in one crucial way, the waiving of the American flag remained a quintessentially American thing, for, as Susan Willis puts it, "we Americans show with our car-mounted flags that we know the war against terrorism is the code term for the preservation of our interstates, cars, suburbs, and the petro-chemical octopus that feeds and clothes us."[11]

Whereas in specifically economic terms, Americans seem to manufacture less and less and yet accumulate wealth more and more, in cultural terms "globalization" has amounted to their positively catapulting their proverbial parochialism abroad, and thus systematically barring the formation of any cosmopolitan culture in their midst by branding, stigmatizing, and dismissing it as "multiculturalism." The combined contradictions of vacuous globalization of capital and the incessant tribilization of sentiments against which Arundhati Roy, Judith Butler, and Susan Willis warn is not limited to India, the Muslim world, or the USA. Europe, the self-proclaimed paragon of "civilization" has its own version of this deadly mixture of an even more potent provincialism. Consider the manner in which Julia Kristeva speaks of "our Europe," where she believes *we* "must not lose sight of the crucial point: the effort to construct the European Union is more than that; it is a global civilizing effort."[12] This is not provincializing Europe, as Dipesh Chakrabarty is suggesting what we need to do.[13] This is globalizing European provincialism and calling it its civilizing mission – of all people proposed by a Bulgarian, herself historically cast out (along with Gypsies and Jews) as the Internal Other of the very idea of Europe. Somewhat reminiscent of Berlusconi and Fallaci's identical positions on the matter, Kristeva warns Europeans: "On the threshold of the third millennium, we Europeans are encountering a major challenge involving the values of civilization, values that, *for better or worse,* we have succeeded in establishing and that will or will not be transmitted to the societies that come after us."[14] That subordinate clause of "for better or for worse" is a bit too much in a hurry to gloss over who exactly got *the better* and who *the worse* over the last millennial galaxies of terror and robbery that "we (them) Europeans" have inflicted upon the earth. A global landscape left to ruins by a savage history of European colonialism may wish to raise an objection and flag that *"for worse"* in that subordinate clause and ask Kristeva, Berlusconi, Fallaci, and any other "we (them) Europeans" that there are millennial histories and ruined landscapes of humanity that could not care less that "societies that come after us" will not repeat what European colonialism did on the planet earth. Will a "European" today dare to ask if the legacy of European barbarism that caused countless pogroms and culminated in the Jewish Holocaust "will or will not be transmitted to the societies that come after us"? What European racists did to European Jewry in the course of the Jewish Holocaust, despite its unique and unfathomable criminal enormity, pales in comparison to what the selfsame "Europeans" have done to colonized continents for centuries and for generations. The Jewish Holocaust was just a local sample of what Europe did outside Europe – and the world is much better off making sure that these "Europeans" will not repeat what they have inflicted on planet earth.

One reads Julia Kristeva's blinded provincialism as if the remnants of a history oblivious to its own memory. "In this identification of the subject with freedom," she stipulates pointedly, "an identification that crystallized at the intersection of Greek, Jewish, and Christian experience before being formulated by Kant, resides the essence and the most precious advantages of European civilization."[15] Really? A whole pedigree of theorized and practiced slavery and misogyny marks the birth of the "Greek" in that trio, while an entire history of pogroms and a genocidal Holocaust distances that "Jewish" from that "Christian" duo, while at the very same time that "Jewish" has the denial and denigration of an entire people, the Palestinians, to account for, standing in line right behind that "Christian" and its complicity in the murderous extermination of Native Americans during the onslaught of the European conquest of the New World. Christianity is not all turning the other cheek. The testimony of Bartolomé de Las Casas on the massacre of Native Americans is also Christian in color and character. As for Kant, he systematically barred the entire humanity (minus "the Europe" of Julia Kristeva and Tariq Ramadan, who themselves – as a Bulgarian and an Egyptian – Kant will chuckle to embrace as a "European") from even entering the domain of the human. Does the world really care for this "essence and the most precious advantages of European civilization," coming out of that particular pedigree, to define the terms of its "globalization"? The Europe of Kant, Kristeva, and Ramadan is even more horrid, racist, and imperial than the nightmare of American neoconservatives, the thuggish savagery of Hindu fundamentalists, and the blinded and banal hatred of Osama bin Laden – all put together. This "Europe" can form a union as it wills, but considering that unification a "global civilizing effort," as Julia Kristeva supposes (and Tariq Ramadan endorses), is a tad too late, and ought to be a bit more embarrassing, in the postcolonial game.

Between Judith Butler's necessary critique of American provincialism, where you cannot name let alone pronounce Abeer Qassim Hamza al-Janabi, and Julia Kristeva's vertiginous flaunting of the European version of the selfsame provincialism stands Susan Sontag's attempt to cross the boundary. In an unguarded moment in an otherwise nostalgic rumination on the US–European relations from the time of Tocqueville and D. H. Lawrence to that of post-9/11 consternations, Susan Sontag uttered the inner anxieties of a revealing gaffe. Speaking of the various colorations of the US and European perceptions of each other, particularly exacerbated in the aftermath of 9/11, she observed:

> What the Americans see is almost the reverse of the Europhile cliché: they see themselves defending civilization. The barbarian hordes are no longer outside the gates. They are within, in every prosperous city, plotting havoc. The 'chocolate-producing' countries (France, Germany, Belgium) will have to stand aside, while a country with 'will' – and God on its side – pursues the battle against terrorism (now conflated with barbarism).[16]

Let's for a moment hesitate from reading what Sontag says fewer than two pages later as clearly contradicting herself – when she says, "Americans have got used to thinking of the world in terms of enemies. Enemies are *somewhere else*, as the fighting is almost always '*over there,*' with Islamic fundamentalism having replaced Russian and Chinese Communism as the implacable, furtive menace."[17] For here in this unguarded moment what we see the pre-eminent American literati doing is an act of flipped over anxiety, where her fear of the enemy abroad *(over there, somewhere else)* has been internalized into the immigrant communities inside *("The barbarian hordes are no longer outside the gates. They are within, in every prosperous city, plotting havoc.")*. The South Asian, North Africans, Arabs, Muslims, etc., migrant communities that have descended upon European capitals and are defecating on Italian architectural masterpieces, as Oriana Fallaci used to say, are also coming to the USA to generate the functional equivalent of the same sentiments among the liberal literati. Ordinarily, and when well-guarded, Susan Sontag would not have been caught dead in such company. But when drawn into a charming, endearing, and nostalgic mapping of the US–EU relationship over the centuries (at one point even invoking the image of a parent–child metaphor), then the *over there* and *somewhere else* mutate, reverse and become: "The barbarian hordes are no longer outside the gates. They are within, in every prosperous city, plotting havoc." Who exactly did the great, late American literary icon have in mind – Arabs, perhaps, Africans, South Asians, Latinos, maybe? Racism of the learned becomes so positively tasteless in their otherwise charming disposition.[18]

The problem with Julia Kristeva and Susan Sontag is not a mere garden variety parochialism, bordering inevitably with racism, disguised under the thin veneer of a *Hochkultur* eurocentricity. The far more important problem is the provincial imagination of an imperial cartography that cannot see the world except on a West–East axis. "In the twenty-first century," observes the distinguished American feminist scholar Zillah Eisenstein, "'the West' means the US more than Europe as well as the globalized forms of cultural capitalism which no longer have any one geographical location."[19] *That* is the beginning of an emancipatory wisdom, for that is a far more liberating manner of revisiting the world through a revised geography of emancipation. Dismantling that geography of domination, predicated on "the globalized forms of cultural capitalism," is the first step towards re-imagining the world in alternative and liberating manners. What Eisenstein has achieved in her extraordinary work, *Against Empire* (2004), is one such critical remapping that brings the crucial issue of women's liberation movements into an entirely new and pathbreaking light.

"The flows," by which Zillah Eisenstein means both labor and capital, and their miasmatic cultures, "travel from global capital to sites everywhere; yet there still are flows travelling in reverse against these developments from Seattle, Washington, and Johannesburg, South Africa." These crosscurrents of domination and revolt radically remap the world and draw new lines of human agency. What we understand by "globalization" can be thus as much the scattered instrumentalities of domination as the varied strategies of resisting it. "Given the relations of power, flows both ways are absorbed by power-filled discourses which appropriate and silence subversive variety." But that silencing is not a *fait accompli*. Eisenstein is of course correct in alerting us to "power-filled discourses." But those discourses, *ipso facto*, are invitations to assault. It is certainly a project aided and abetted by the corporate media of the North American variety. But that constellation of banality is far more a paper tiger than a formidable force. Eisenstein's point, to be sure, is clear and concise, echoing Arundhati Roy's "Global capitalism parades as globalization. Globalization holds out the probability of world poverty worsening along with repressive measures against those who suffer most. It also holds out the possibility of resistance against these forces." This latter point, however, is a site of contestation, where human will to defy complicity is loud and clear, particularly at the heart of this predatory barbarity, the USA itself, which is now *ipso facto* no longer the center of anything other than its own parochial imagination. "Growing criticism of global capital and its culture of domination," Eisenstein rightly observes, "has taken hold in places like Seattle, Paris, and Barcelona" – locations peripheral and central at the same time.

The critical con/fusion of the imperial mapping of the globe that Eisenstein notes dismantles the cartography of power we have received and points to a far more liberating manner of looking at and imagining the world – and thus marks the way humanity at large is creatively re-imagined. "Bourgeois culture," she pointedly notes, "is seductive and captivating and it is oppressive and isolating. Monitoring is needed and most of all, the US needs to surveil more and more of the globe in order to protect its own needs which extend well beyond its own territorial borders. So the US builds empire for itself and the globe be damned."[20] What Eisenstein identifies here is the imperial urge to dominate the world in a manner that safeguards the privileged classes not only within the US borders but just about anywhere else. Those who are the beneficiary of this imperial design are not just the American millionaires. The Saudi and Kuwaiti billionaires, just like Jordanian or Moroccan monarchists, or Latin American drug cartels, Asian entrepreneurs, Russian businessmen, Iranian clerical cliques, Chinese party apparatchiks, Indian Hindu fundamentalists, Israeli Zionists, European corporations, etc. – they are all, as Susan Willis would put it, flying the American flag.

Infinitely superior to both Julia Kristeva and Susan Sontag in her vision and insight into the critical remapping of the world is the extraordinary work of Amy Kaplan in *The Anarchy of Empire in the Making of US Culture*, in which she outlines and exposes the fabricated dichotomy between *the inside* and *the outside* in a far more convincing way. For Amy Kaplan, "manifest destiny" is "manifest domesticity," and "foreign policy" is written into the fabric of "domestic affairs," and thus the US wars against Native Americans, extended into the war with Mexico in mid-nineteenth century and then later against Spain, Cuba, the Philippines, Korea, Vietnam, etc. are all not just related but in fact integral and definitive to matters domestic to the imperial republic. "The anarchy of empire in its convulsive reach across the globe," Amy Kaplan argues, "both erects and destabilizes the geopolitical boundaries of nation-states and colonies and the conceptual borders between the domestic and the foreign."[21]

One of Amy Kaplan's most salient arguments in her *Anarchy of empire* is when she turns to W. E. B. Du Bois' pan-African internationalism as posited against the grain of American imperialism. "Du Bois not only condemned the United States as an imperial force in the world, but used the framework of empire to decenter America as a product of broader global forces, and at times to recenter his own international authority."[22] Concentrating on Du Bois' *Darkwater: Voices from within the Veil* (1920), Amy Kaplan demonstrates how "through seismic shifts of perspective, *Darkwater* expands the geographical terrain of "world war" to encompass the colonization of Africa and Asia, post-Reconstruction America, and the US empire abroad."[23] Amy Kaplan's own ambitious project echoes W. E. B. Du Bois': "Mapping the overlapping terrain of the foreign and domestic involves contests over writing of history. I am interested not only in how we write the history of imperialism, but also in how the participants and critics of the imperial projects historicized empire in their own time."[24] Precisely at a moment when US–European warmongering had termed their rivalries over who will get to rob the world of its resources "World War I," Du Bois wrote "The African Roots of War" (1915), in which, as Amy Kaplan puts it, he

> moves Africa from geographic periphery and historical backwater into the central vantage point from which to rewrite the history of the present and remap the terrain of the "World War." The essay offers more than the causal economic argument for which it is known. By grounding his inquiry in Africa, Du Bois exposes the way the representations of space and time have been structured by imperial maps and narratives of the world, and from this location he draws alternative maps and writes new historical narratives.[25]

The superiority of Kaplan's argument, predicated on Du Bois critical remapping of the world, puts both Kristeva's parochial Eurocentricism and Sontag's mothballing endearment to her European friends (both almost a century behind the creative intelligence of W. E. B. Du Bois) to shame.

The point though, when we connect Kaplan to Eivenstein, Willis, Butler, and back to Roy, is not to shame the obviated provincialism of imperial imaginings that is particularly (not surprisingly) evident in its most so-called progressive and liberal voices, when their guarded and studied demeanors fall and their inadvertent racism shows through. But to pick up where Du Bois left off, the way Amy Kaplan does, and then posit the idea that in his turn Malcolm X was the Muslim version of Du Bois in their mutual defiance of the imperial mapping of the world and their decentering of the American empire. "It is well known," Amy Kaplan points out, "that Du Bois drew a powerful link between 'segregation at home and colonialism abroad,' and that he connected these spheres through the common denominator of the color line."[26] This is also precisely what Malcolm X did following his break with the Nation of Islam and his historic Hajj pilgrimage, after which he began to cultivate a far more universal conception of his revolutionary project. Africa, as a result, was the identical site of the universal transformation of both Du Bois and Malcolm X in wedding the problem of racism at home to colonialism around the world. Objecting to previous generations of scholarship on Du Bois, Amy Kaplan suggests,

> by limiting Du Bois' treatment of empire to the European colonization of Africa, scholars of Du Bois often overlook the international role of the USA in demarcating and policing the global color line, as well as the way global imperial dynamics affect race condition within the USA. An analysis of Du Bois' complex representation of American imperialism, I contend, can enrich our understanding of how his internationalism deconstructs the bifurcation between racism at home and colonialism abroad.[27]

The gradual blurring and final crossing of that false bifurcation between domestic racism and global colonialism assumed for Malcolm X a specifically Islamic disposition when he had to face his own falsely racialized conception of his own faith and altogether abandoned the assumption that only black people could be Muslims, a recognition he reached while on his Hajj pilgrimage with millions of others of his fellow Muslims converging in Mecca from four corners of the world, where "the color line," if Du Bois were to be with him on that Hajj pilgrimage, meant absolutely nothing. What remains dormant in Malcolm X (1925–1965), but evident in W. E. B. Du Bois (1868–1963) – who was born 57 years before Malcolm X and died only two years before him, thus living an active and prolific life for about 55 tumultuous years more than Malcolm X – is the full revolutionary course of a manner of rethinking, remapping, and renarrating the world in a way that, as Amy Kaplan puts it, "imperialism did more than propel US domination abroad; it also struck at the heart of the domestic nation. Thus rather than just condemn the United States as a center of world power, Du Bois used the framework of empire to decenter American power and destabilize its national boundaries."[28]

Today, decades beyond both Du Bois and Malcolm X, the world desperately awaits a remapping of their unfinished projects the way, for example, that committed and visionary scholars like Amy Kaplan do. Kaplan's reading of Du Bois' conception of European colonialism and American imperialism very much anticipates the manner in which, for example, Antonio Negri and Michael Hardt propose the idea of empire[29] as a mode and manner of imperialism in which an integrated constellation of political and financial powers – ranging from powerful nation-states (such as the USA), to their client colonial settlements (Israel), to nauseating hubs of abusive treatments of immigrant laborers by predatory capital (United Arab Emirates) to transnational institutions (IMF and the World Bank), and above all major corporations and transnational civil society NGOs (non-governmental organizations) – sustain the benefits of a few at the astounding misery of the rest. Though still pathologically Eurocentric in the economic grasp of this empire, Negri and Hardt understand and propose the idea as the *modus operandi* of a capital that is no longer homebound, if it ever was, but is in fact amorphous and planetary in its ravages. "Partly for that reason," Michael Hardt has recently argued, "for being more purely capitalist, its forms of domination, social segregation and geographical divisions of the globe will be even more severe, its structures of poverty more brutal and its forms of exploitation more degrading."[30] The problem should not remain at a semantic level – is globalization merely Americanization of the globe or is it an entirely different creature, in which the USA is a more destructive and viciously driven force. As Hardt puts it:

> In light of recent events this notion of an emerging empire gives us, now more than ever, a framework for understanding why imperialism cannot succeed today, and specifically why the Bush Administration's unilateral projects in Iraq and elsewhere are failures. No single power can be successful in this situation without paying attention to the internal dynamics of empire and gaining the collaboration of others – not only the other dominant nation-states but also the subordinated nation-states, the supranational institutions, corporations and so forth. This does not suggest that the various collaborating powers in this network are equal. The USA undoubtedly is and will remain for the near future the dominant nation-state of the network. It simply means that no power can go it alone.[31]

The question thus at some point becomes academic and moot. There is no doubt that the conglomeration of forces and institutions that Negri and Hardt outline and call empire is globally evident. But does that constellation of forces in any significant way diminish the evidence of what the USA has been doing in Afghanistan and Iraq as anything other than imperialist? Certainly not. Thus within the notion of empire as Negri and Hardt propose and understand it, there is a predatory imperialism that on the classical conception of the practice – as we have understood it from Max Weber, to J.A. Hobson, Vladimir Lenin, and Joseph Schumpeter – has now built and put in gear hundreds of military bases around the globe to facilitate its smooth operation.[32]

The global reconfiguration of power, the ever-expansive geographical domains of the capital, massive labor migrations, the collapse of hitherto compelling binary oppositions (East–West, North–South, etc.), and above all a planetary reconception of the globe in unfamiliar terms are among the leading indices of an emerging condition in which Islam, among other metaphysical claims on people's credulities, will have to relocate and reconceive itself. The specific conditions in which the decline and demise of militant Islamism, as we have known it over the last two centuries, just before the success and failure of the Islamic revolution in Iran and ultimately the rise of al-Qaeda and the events of 9/11, is both socially visible and doctrinally inevitable is now fast upon us – thus setting the stage for a new liberation theology that will correspond and converse more specifically with the globalized condition of Muslims living in the shadow of a postcolonial and postmodern empire. The political fragmentation of the social basis of militant Islamism as we have hitherto known it is now in full view under the conditions we call *globalization*, the premise upon which we must consider the emerging modes of revolutionary resistances to any manner of planetary imperialism.

On Thursday, October 12 2000, Iran's Foreign Minister, Kamal Kharrazi, met with Sheikh Hassan Nasrallah, the leader of Hezbollah in Beirut. The prestige of Hezbollah for having just scored a singular victory against Israel in southern Lebanon had increased its status among the revolutionary aspirations in the region. At this time, the Islamic republic, as represented by Foreign Minister Kharrazi, had a lot to boast about this decisive victory. At the wake of the Israeli withdrawal from southern Lebanon, Sheykh Hassan Nasrallah and other leaders of Hezbollah had journeyed to Tehran, met with Ayatollah Khamenei, the Supreme Leader of the Islamic Republic, and sought his advice and of course financial backing in the aftermath of their victory. The Iranian dailies sympathetic to the Supreme Leader reported jubilantly as to how he had delineated for the Shi'i guerilla movement the outline for a final liberation of Jerusalem.[33]

The configuration of Sheykh Nasrallah of Lebanon and Ayatollah Khamenei of Iran poses a particularly troubling picture for someone who is as much delighted in the revolutionary heroism of the Shi'is in the liberation of southern Lebanon as deeply troubled with the reign of terror and intimidation the clerical clique has imposed in the Islamic Republic of Iran. As a signifier, albeit with two slightly different inflections in Arabic and Persian, the term "Hezbollah" today signifies two diametrically opposed meanings. In Lebanon and in the rest of the Arab world, both in 2002 and then again in the aftermath of the savage Israeli invasion of Lebanon in July 2006, the term "Hezbollah" rightly signifies the heroic effort of a band of Lebanese fighters who liberated their ancestral homeland from foreign occupation, and then defended it against yet another barbaric invasion, for which they have the love and admiration of any human being with a grain of decency. In Iran, though, the term "Hezbollah" signifies an entirely different range of association: club-wielding bands of thugs, mercenaries hired by one of the most tyrannically repressive regimes on earth, violent forces recruited from the most retrograde elements to suffocate the most elementary forms of democratic behavior, brutal executioners barring the most innocent expressions of youth (beauty, sensuality, love, affection, friendship), political assassins, moral militia, social psychopaths, economic mafia, cultural pathologies. Utter the name "Hezbollah" in Iran and that is the range of its factual meanings.

How did that happen? How could one term signify two such radically different sets of meanings in such a tight neighborhood? Ayatollah Khamenei of today was Sheykh Fazlollah of yesterday. Shaykh Fazlollah of today might become Ayatollah Khamenei of tomorrow. And precisely in the certainty of that possibility dwells the paradox of Shi'ism as a religion of protest. Shi'ism is a religion of protest. It cannot succeed without contradicting itself. As the prototype of the noblest sentiments definitive to its doctrinal texture and history, Shi'ism is triumphant at the moment of its insurrection, defeated at the moment of its success. Because it has historically spoken the truth to power, it cannot be in power, because it then robs itself of speaking the truth to power.

Whereas Shi'ism (as a particular branch of Islam) is a religion that is insurrectionary in its very historical soul, what today we call "Islam" was re/invented across the colonial divide as a metanarrative of resistance opposing a European project of colonial domination. As a religion of protest predicated on a paradox of power, Shi'ism was aggravated in its historical encounter with the colonial shadow of European modernity. As the collective faith of a colonial by subjugated people, from India all the way to North Africa, from Central Asia to the Malaysia and Indonesia, Islam was categorically re/invented as a site of ideological resistance to European colonial modernity. The gradual mutation of Islam, as the ancestral faith of a people, into "Islamic Ideology," as the site of political resistance to colonialism, from the earliest decades of the nineteenth to the latter part of the twentieth century, corresponded to the two complementary projects of capitalist modernity and the European Enlightenment. Both these projects reached the farthest corners of the world through their extended arm of colonialism. Inevitable and justifiable reactions to European colonialism were in turn conducive to the production of the nation-state and of national economies, national polities, national societies, and ultimately national cultures. Anti-colonial nationalism, revolutionary socialism, and religious nativism (Islamism) were the direct result of various ideological and political resistances to the aggressive encroachment of the European colonial adventures. Whereas anti-colonial nationalism borrowed the very modular imagination of the "nation" from the centers of capitalist modernity and used it against colonialism, religious nativism recast the ancestral faith of the natives at large and sought similar ends. Partha Chatterjee has articulated in some detail the manner in which nationalism in the colonial world was colonially remodulated in response to capitalist modernity.[34] Nationalism was the ideological predicate of the political claim to the nation-state and as such corresponded with the modulation of national economies best suited for both capitalizing *and* colonizing the world economic order. It was the *substance*, not the *form*, of nationalism that provided the colonial world with a site of resistance to colonialism.

In the course of European colonial encounters with Muslims, "Islam" was invented as the civilizational other of "the West" by the massive project of Orientalism at the service of the colonial interests that had both occasioned the very idea of "the West" and necessitated an "East" to match, balance, and authenticate it. But the material misery of Muslims occasioned by colonialism took precisely the supposition of that civilizational bifurcation and changed it into an ideology of resistance. But ultimately in the binary opposition thus constituted between "Islam and the West," Islam was the loser, the West the winner. "Islam versus the West" was the originary trap in which "the West" was made to believe in its own veracity and "Islam" was made to counteressentialize itself. If "Islam" (or "the East" in general) were to be severed from that binary fabrication, "the West" could hardly recognize or believe itself. If "the West" were to be exposed for the empty trap that it was, "Islam" would have no nemesis to find and there and thus to define itself. As we understand it over the last 200 years, Islam has been re/narrated as an insurrectionary ideology (adjacent to anti-colonial nationalism and revolutionary socialism) in its colonially contingent encounter with European modernity.

The mutation of Islam into a site of categorical resistance to colonialism was a specific episode in the contemporary history of its encounter with European Enlightenment modernity. While the operation of capital culturally constituted itself on the premise of "the West," the working of the colonial was culturally delegated to the realm of "the Rest," and in this particular case that of an "Islam" which was only there to other and thus authenticate "the West." The rapid circularity of capital and labor code-named "globalization" in its most recent spin has finally exposed the fabricated ideology of domination constitutional to the binary opposition between "Islam and the West," from which both illusions were made possible. The collapse of the presumed centrality of the capital and its colonial periphery into one globalizing spiral of capital and labor chasing after each other has exposed the naked relation of power for long concealed under the smoke screen of civilizational divides and national cultures, all narrated around the fictive bipolarity of "The West and the Rest." The collapse of the smoke screen of the ideology of domination code-named "the West" has not just dismantled the fiction of its civilizational ipseity; it has, as a result and far more important, collapsed the horizontal (external) and vertical (internal) modes of colonialism otherwise categorically disjointed. We can no longer hold to be self-evident the fictive presumption of national cultures and civilizational divides that falsely separated the working of the capital and the colonial and called it "the West and the Rest." The event code-named *globalization* has made that chronic disease transparent. The imperial mapping of the world, in other words, and as we learn from Amy Kaplan's reading of W. E. B. Du Bois, has lost all its hegemonic ordering of the globe and such power-basing binaries as "Islam and the West" no longer holds any validity.[35]

Two simultaneous developments have now changed the global configuration of power and as a result the continued validity of nativist ideologies, like the Islamic Ideology as it emerged in response to classical European colonialism, is no longer a viable mode of emancipatory movement. The rapid globalization of capital, on one hand, and the massive critique of the project of European modernity, on the other, has changed the material and moral foregrounding of both the constitution of the relations of power and of insurrectionary resistance to it. The increasing attention to the emerging significance of *the city* in economic production is already pointing to the collapse of the nation-state as a unitary category in matters not just political but far more importantly economic.[36] The total collapse of national economies into the overpowering globalization of the economic production has now led to a more critical consideration of smaller, subnational, units that can gauge and monitor the global economy in more accurate measures. In answer to the question, "Why does it matter to recover place in analyses of the global economy, particularly place as constituted in major cities?" Sassen responds that: " ... it allows us to see the multiplicity of economies and work cultures in which the global information economy is embedded. It also allows us to recover the concrete, localized processes through which globalization exists and to argue that much of the Multiculturalism in large cities is as much a part of globalization as is international finance."[37] Whether or not the direction of this new geography of economic production of power is towards a transnational politics, as Sassen suspects, or towards a more local insurrectionary resistance, as I suspect, remains to be seen. What is certain, though, is the outdated economic relevance of both ethnicized nationalism and religious nativism as legitimate modes of resistance. What is critical in Saskia Sassen's studies of globalization is the aggressive transnationalization of labor migration that has more than ever turned the world into an ever-contracting factory floor. But the factory floor is now entirely invisible. Far more effectively than the suburban shopping malls, electronic space (shoppingmall.com) has radically suppressed the economic production of reality into subterranean levels. "Whether in the geography of its infrastructure or in the structure of cyberspace itself," Sassen has argued, "electronic space is inscribed, and to some extent shaped, by power, concentration, and contestation, as well as openness and decentralization."[38]

The globalizing economics of domination is now completely amorphous and no political organ is in effective control of its operation. Now we face the monstrous abstraction of the industrial capital mutated into the finance and then re/modulated into the electronic capital. The capital constitution of national cultures and the colonial fabrication of civilizational divides have long since exhausted their ideological uses. We have now completely entered a post-national dominance of cultures and the post-civilizational collapse of capital and colonial divides. The fabrication of "Islam and the West" as a particularly poignant variation on the theme of "The West and the Rest" no longer holds valid. "Islam," as a site of ideological resistance to classical colonialism no longer corresponds with the predicament of Muslims in the age of globalization. The factual evidence of globalization, by which we ought to understand nothing more than the lifting of the smoke screen that categorically separated vertical and horizontal, internal and external, colonialism has dismantled all binary oppositions. As we have understood it over the last two centuries in its colonial resistance to European modernity, the "Islam" of that binary can no longer function as a metanarrative of resistance. As colonialism enters a new phase of its globalizing metamorphosis so do all its contrapuntal narratives of resistance are rendered obsolete, and thus in dire need of revamping.

In the event called *globalization* we witness the possibility of the final collapse of the state as the monopoly of violence. The US presidential election of 2000 is by far the most serious indication of the crisis of the state – when the US electorate was shown to be completely paralyzed in its choice and the matter had to be decided (quite controversially) by the US Supreme

Court. The "war on terrorism," in full swing since 9/11/01, has visibly robbed the state of its exclusive claim to (legitimate) violence, the way we have understood the notion of the state at least since Max Weber. In the post-revolutionary Iran of the Khatami presidency we have the peculiar situation that the state is actually in opposition to the ruling clerical clique. In Iran, Afghanistan, Pakistan, Saudi Arabia, and elsewhere in the Arab and Muslim world, we also witness a reconstitution, a complete reversal, of the private and the public domain. As the private domain has become publicly legislated by the Islamic codes of conduct, the public domain has been increasingly privatized. The exchanging of the private and the public, the mutation of the state into opposition, the implosion of imperialism into the empire, the supremacy of the finance over industrial capital, the increasing mutation of the national into expatriate (and mostly compradorial) intellectuals, the lifting of the smoke-screen of the difference between horizontal and vertical colonialism, all equal a state of globalization which requires an entirely new mode of confronting the imperial proclivity that seeks to dominate and control it.

The possibility of that new mode of resistance, however, is thwarted by an outdated, exhausted, and globally irrelevant nativism. What we know as "Islam" today has been a metanarrative of resistance to a metanarrative of domination. That domination no longer works via a metanarrative, so it cannot be resisted via a metanarrative. The metanarrative of European modernity required and exacted an "Islam" as a site of resistance to its colonial shadow. The dialectics implicit in "Islam and the West" cross-referenced, cross-essentialized, metastasized, and thus corroborated each side of the two polar opposites. Post-structurally de-sedimented, globally circuitous, self-mocking itself as postmodern, the amorphous nature of the beast no longer requires an essentialized resistance, and thus all essentialized resistances it has created are now materially outdated, politically moot, culturally obsolete. But the phantom pain of "the Islamic Ideology" is yet to recognize its amputated legs.

Almost immediately after the success of the Islamic revolution (the watershed of Islamist movements in modern history), the most serious ideologues who had actually precipitated it began to worry about its success. There are indications that even Morteza Motahhari, who was a principal theorist of the Islamic revolution (before he was assassinated soon after it success), began to worry about its theocratic consequences. But the revolutionary momentum and the war that immediately followed it prevented any serious reflection on the predicament of an Islamic republic. Soon after the end of the Iran–Iraq war, when the charismatic terror of Ayatollah Khomeini had lifted its shadow and neither the revolutionary fervor nor the national defense had created a smoke screen for the brutal institutionalization of the theocracy, people like Abdolkarim Soroush began to realize what had happened and began a monumental project to dissociate "Islam Itself" from the factual evidence of an Islamic revolution predicated on an

Islamic Ideology. As a devout Muslim intellectual, Soroush's concern was not the active theorization of Iranians' or Muslims' predicament as a people, and what they should learn from such historical experiences. His concern, instead, was to separate what he proposed to be "Islam Itself" from its historical predicament. In other words, he wanted to safeguard Islam for posterity, and blame the present condition on our human fallacy. This is how he came up with his theory of "the theoretical contraction and expansion of religious knowledge." It is within that context that he and a few other reform-minded Muslim intellectuals are trying to give alternative readings of Islam that are pluralistic, liberal, and compatible with democracy (and of course with neoliberal economics).

The principal problem with Soroush's project and that of his reform-minded colleagues, however, is that they are theorizing a "democratic Islam" at a time when Shi'ism is in power (always a contradiction in terms). This is constitutionally different from when Shari'ati was theorizing Islam at a time when Shi'ism was the site of resistance to tyranny. Today in Iran, Shi'ism is the site of tyranny. As Shi'ism is paradoxically triumphant and defeated, Soroush and his colleagues are after a metaphysical quarantine to safeguard "Islam Itself." But "Islam Itself" has been out in the open for a very long time. The Islam of the last 200 years was formed in conversation with colonialism. Whenever it opposed colonialism and tyranny (as it is now doing in southern Lebanon and occupied Palestine) it has revealed its revolutionary potentials. As soon as it came to power, as in the Islamic Republic of Iran or in Afghanistan under the vicious Taliban rule, it has revealed the most monstrous tyrannical tendencies. So what Soroush and other are addressing is really a nineteenth-century problem as we are entering the twenty-first century. The Islam that will inevitably emerge in conversation with the colossal consequences of globalization that has entailed massive labor migrations from Muslim communities across the globe will be a markedly different Islam than the one we had in conversation with classical colonialism.

Islamic liberalism of the sort that Soroush propagates is trying to extend the thinnest, pulled-to-the-point-of-break, end of nativist Islamic Ideology to the most monstrous end of global capitalism. The point of this tie is ludicrously lopsided. The end of Islamic Ideology is the end of ideology. But it is not the end of history. The radical critic of the project of European modernity and the instantaneous incorporation of all national economies into a post-national, organically global, logic has posed a new condition and logic of material resistance. The dominant discourse of the most successful material constitution of political uprising against the conservatives in Iran is Melli-Mazhabi (nationalist-religious). Neither ethnic nationalism nor religious nativism are any longer legitimate modes of thought and operation at the threshold of the twenty-first century. They are both dead, collapsed on their face with the triumphant surge of global capitalism. The political production of the nation-state and the ideological construction of nationalism are both post-Napoleonic units of identity production compatible with the collective unit of the "nation" as the most optimum unit of economic, social, political, and cultural units. The Napoleonic generation of colonizing and anti-colonial nationalism has now epistemically *aufgehoben* (dissolved) into George W. Bush's "war on terrorism" (war without end, war without borders).

Globalization has rendered the Islam that the colonial encounter with European modernity had crafted obsolete. The paradoxical disposition of Shi'ism is one critical example of how urgent it is for us to retrieve and re/articulate the polylocality of Islamic cultures, in their pluralities of historical unfolding. In articulating the specific terms of Muslim polylocalities, the postmodern critique of the Enlightenment itself needs a postcolonial critique so that we stay clear of both a belated fixation with European modernity and a belabored attraction to postmodernity, both of which have been narrated from the falsely presumed centers of the material and cultural production of capital. There is no, and there has never been any, center, and thus no periphery, to the operation of capital and its colonial shades and shadows. The national constitution of cultures and the colonial constitution of civilizational boundaries were both the ideological machination of capital to sustain the optimum level of its operation intact. The assumption of a cosmopolitan *center* to the operation of capital, code-named "the West," and a vernacular *periphery* to it, code-named "the Rest," "the East," or "Islam," can no longer be held legitimate. But the postmodern critique of the European Enlightenment project continues to operate from the presumption of that center because its theorists are color-blind (or a Du Bois is missing in their Lyotard).

To find our way towards the multiplicity of resistances that ought to collectively constitute our emancipation in face of a predatory empire we need to have a strategic foot in the destruction of the very metaphysical foundation of "the West" as much as we do another in the material basis of our localities. Today in the critique of the Enlightenment, Immanuel Kant is read as the very "paradigm of the internal incoherence of the enlightenment."[39] We need to enter that moment of metaphysical crisis that this statement announces. We ought to know in what particular way are we entering a post-historical condition? The condition is perhaps post-historical for those who had and wrote a history, not for those whose histories were underwritten. From that perspective, the European Enlightenment is not the contradictory encounter between Newtonian science and political freedom. That freedom was complementary to that science, to exploit it and dominate the world. Perhaps the beneficiaries of knowledge as Enlightenment had to follow the beast all the way to the Holocaust to realize that their pursuit of freedom had led them to slavery. The rest of the world did not. Reason (as both *Vernuft* and *Verstand*) has always been an artifact of history for the rest of the world,[40] and not vice versa. But the history that reason, and the reason that history, made possible had a shadow of un-reason and non-history, which is the rest of the world, the non-European world, the un-American world.

In that shadow, the colonized and brutalized world did not have to wait for the advent of postmodernity to find fault with the promises of reason and progress. The world at large was the failure of that promise. The condition code-named postmodernity in Europe has nothing to do with the rest of the world at the receiving end of the project. It is the chickens of the European Enlightenment modernity coming home to roost. The world did not have to wait for postmodernism to know the self-destructive nature of the instrumental reason. European intellectuals from Adorno forward had to wait for the Holocaust to taste the bitter fruit of the tree of knowledge Kant had planted. The very heavy root of that tree was on the broken back of the world at large. The condition called postmodernity has opted to oppose that instrumental rationalism by reading freedom as spontaneity. For the rest of the world, freedom is not an apposite occasion for spontaneity. Our freedom has a cause, a purpose, a direction. There is a method to our madness. For the custodians of the European Enlightenment, even those who detect a contradiction in the project,

> a call for the liberation of humanity from the domination of the anthropological tentacles of the Enlightenment is at once a call to anarchism, since politics as we know it is inevitably enacted by the "rationalist" state. [41]

We cannot see it that way from the receiving end of the project. In the shadow of the European Enlightenment things appear rather differently. The European Enlightenment, both then and now, always assumes to speak for "the humanity." It does not. If the latter-day custodians of the Enlightenment consider our emancipation from the shadow of the Enlightenment, aka colonialism, as anarchism, then we are indeed anarchists. We will have to be allowed to seek our own order in that anarchy. The hitherto beneficiaries of the European Enlightenment may indeed engage in name-calling:

> Thus someone like Foucault, for example, who lapsed into a flirtation with Maoism during his later years, despite the perception that not all forms of domination are undesirable, was immobilized by the contradictions inherent in his own version of Enlightenment.[42]

or:

> archeological science is replaced by a genealogical transvaluation of values, or a paradoxical, but today almost obligatory, left-wing Nietzscheanism.[43]

These may indeed be all true. But it is nothing short of astonishing so late in the game for the leading theorists of post-Enlightenment angst to continue to play the game on the Western corner of their imagination. The debate and the disenchantment may indeed be accused of "flirtation with Maoism" or "left-wing Nietzscheanism." But in both these occasions, in practice and theory, dwells the full exposure of the very idea of "Europe" to a global responsibility. The idea of Europe (not just its material well-being) is chiefly responsible for the global catastrophe of the Enlightenment modernity, whether people have opposed that modernity on the colonial site of its ravages, or else self-Orientalized themselves by being Westernized, they have authenticated that claim and are thus head-to-toe implicated in that catastrophic project. But at their worst (their compradorial bourgeoisie) people around the globe are the accomplices. The primary perpetrator is the power-basing project of the European reign of terror visited upon the world. There is no difference between being disenfranchised by the idea of Europe internally as subaltern European or externally as colonial non-European. Globalization means the lifting of the smoke screen of the East versus the West, the capital versus the colonial, the center versus the periphery and the full exposure of the naked power relations that structurally link the internal and external colonization. The prevalent theories of globalization assume some major ruptures and definitive epistemic shifts in the operation of the capital and its concomitant culture. But none of these are applicable. It only appears that way because the smoke screen was so successful.

Globalization has made the categorical essentialization of Islam as a meta-narrative of resistance obsolete. Though Muslims have collectively benefited from that categorical essentialization of Islam in their anti-colonial struggles over the last 200 years, they have also suffered the continental pacification of their constitutionally polylocal histories and polyfocal cultures into a totalitarian claim on their credulity. Within the doctrinal contours of Islam, Muslims have collectively produced a historically polyvocal tapestry of cultures articulated on a map of polylocal texture. If Muslim jurists have opted to legislate the *nomocentric* disposition of their culture, Muslim philosophers have articulated the *logocentricity* of their intellectual disposition. If both the jurists and the philosophers have demanded too much of Muslims' law- and logic-abiding weaknesses, their mystics have opted for the *homocentricity* of an agential defiance. These are all in the domain of Muslims' intellectual oscillations with truth. In the literary disposition of their cultures, Muslims have checked and balanced the transcendental unity of that sedimented fixation with truth and celebrated the narrative undecidability and literary contingency of the transcendental signified – all in the making of their multifaceted literary humanism *(Adab)*.

Against the forsaken background of a polyfocal Islam, anti-colonial Islamism had mutated Islam into a monolithic proposition. Globalization has made a monolithic Islam impossible. With the collapse of classical colonialism and the rise of globalization, Islam as a metanarrative of resistance no longer commands any credulity. From the history of Shi'ism in colonial modernity we learn that only a small band of guerrillas can resist the amorphous beast locally and that the declaration of revolutionary insurrection should never collapse into a constitutional formation. Shi'ism, as a paradox of power that should always be in an insurrectionary posture and yet never completely succeed, becomes the prototype of a permanent revolutionary posture with no ideology, a local configuration of resistance that never collapses into a metanarrative of salvation, a forgetful amnesia that is condemned to remember its own history but never forget it.

A whole new mode of resistance movement, neither ethnically nationalist nor religiously nativist, is now needed to confront the predicament of Muslim peoples at large. While postmodernist critique of the project of European modernity is paving the way towards a moral reconstitution of the very idea of the nation, global capitalism has already changed the material basis of that moral reconstitution. It is useless to speculate what precisely the particular disposition of these modes of post-national and post-nativist resistance would be is. But its dominant features are already evident. A total distrust of ideological meta-narratives is by far the most critical feature of this emerging mode of resistance. It is crucial here to carefully consider the case of the Iranian student and press uprisings – all in the aftermath of a massive revolution that Islamism exclusively misappropriated. Such movements are not only non-ideological, they are decidedly anti-ideological. Not only the vested interest of the Islamic republic but its chief nemesis the Mujahedin Khalq organization are ludicrously wasting their time trying to win this mass movement over. Neither *Western* nor *Eastern*, neither *Modern* nor *Islamic*, these movements fly in the face of any metanarrative claim on the credulity of its moral and material defiance of empty abstractions, categorical imperatives, and constitutional claims. Two millennia of stupendous modulation of a dangerous liaison between two utterly empty abstractions, "Islam and the West" mean nothing to these movements. Morally and materially, these are the children of a world the Internet has made impossible to divide and rule.

Consider the neoliberal economics of Mohammad Khatami's Reform Movement. More than 38 million Iranians, as the inhabitants of an Islamic republic, aged 16 and up, were eligible and poised to vote in the new round of parliamentary elections in February 2000. In what was shaping up as a referendum on Mohammad Khatami's reforms, some 6000 candidates ran for the 290 seats of the parliament. Meanwhile, on the eve of the Iranian parliamentary elections, the news from Bangkok, Thailand, was that after seeing the oil prices surge quickly to their highest level in nine years, Iran had suggested that OPEC might want to try to slow things down. The Iranian Commerce Minister Mohammad Shari'atmadari was quoted as having said that a "suitable mechanism"[44] needed to be found before the world oil market was allowed to spin out of control. The

Iranian position was an obvious one: "Iran wants higher prices, but the minister said he does not want to see them come through such a quick rise that could prove disruptive to the global economy."[45] The rise of the oil price from $11 per barrel in February 1999 to about $30 per barrel in the New York futures trading on Monday February 14 2000 had given the Iranian Commerce Minister reasons to fear the consequences of the gain. He obviously had vivid memory of the Asian economic crisis of 1998 that in combination with overproduction by OPEC threw the industry into a deep crisis.

When President Khatami submitted his balanced budget on Wednesday December 15 1999 to parliament, he had outlined his next five-year plan for the economic revival of the nation. The 13 billion dollars (at the market rate, 36 billion dollar at the official rate) budget was geared specifically to "reduce the dependence of the country on oil receipts."[46] According to Khatami's own figures, only 49 percent of the revenue would derive from oil. The five-year plan was based on an oil price of 14 dollars per barrel. The plan equally called for wholesale privatization of the railways and telecommunications, an end to state monopolies in tobacco, sugar, and tea. Khatami had also added that he intended "to reduce the role of the state in the Iranian economy and increase that of private sector."[47] Ayatollah Reza Ostadi, spokesman for the Council of Guardians, was meanwhile quoted as having said that his organization is radically opposed to such privatization. The railways, telecommunications, civil aviation and the key sectors of the industry, he said, are to remain under state control.

The five-year plan of Khatami was geared to lower the Iranian rate of unemployment, now officially set at 15 percent, to 10.5 percent, an ambition for which Khatami's government had to generate at least 750,000 jobs per year. Seventy-five percent of Iran's exports consist of oil and gas. The 112 billion dollars in state revenue is broken done as 56 billion coming from oil exports, 44 billion in non-oil exports, and 12 billion in foreign loans and credits. As the editorials in the hard-line *Jomhuri Islami* had warned its readers, a vote for reformists would deal an "irreparable blow" to the principles of the 1979 Revolution.[48] The result of Khatami's neoliberal economics, hidden under the fanfare of a "Reform Movement," is very simple. A coalition of political forces will result in these reforms to be a mode of economic Neoliberalism that will continue to keep the 350 billion dollars in GDP (gross domestic product) and the per capita income of 5000 dollars economy centrally planned, predicated on the state ownership of oil revenues, large industries under state control, lucrative business under the control of private clerical order. Nowhere near the 750,000 jobs that are needed to keep the rate of unemployment at the present level will be achieved. And the sixth Majlis will have a monument social crisis on its hand.

But none of these political groupings effectively represents the coagulation of discontent, symbolically represented by the university student organizations, tapping on the raw energy of millions of young people who have been at the cutting edge of the catastrophic decades under clerical rule. Such events as the student uprising in July 1999, such newspapers as *Asr-e Azadegan*, and such catch-phrases as civil society or dialogue of civilization represent the emerging sentiments of this vocal majority. With over 60 percent of the Iranian population of nearly 70 million under the age of 25, it is not surprising at all that the overwhelming majority of this population has no active or consequential memory of the Islamic revolution of 1979, and it could not care less about that deficiency. By far the most startling fact about the student uprising of July 1999 is the absence of any ideological affiliation in it, neither left nor right, religious or secular. Even at its most radical moments, the anti-Khamenei slogans were not targeted against the constitution of the Islamic republic. The absence of any ideological affiliation, combined with a vociferous anti-establishment sentiments, is by far the most critical indication of the end of Islamic Ideology in Iranian political culture.

Young Iranian women with 80 percent of them literate, 51 percent of them in 1998, 57 percent of them in 1999, and up to 62 percent in 2006, as the university entrants are a particular force that can no longer be taken for granted or kept under control. Faezeh Hashemi and Jamileh Kadivar were among scores of other women candidates running for two of the 290 seats, one a daughter and the other the wife and the sister of prominent figures in the Islamic Republic. Both Hashemi and Kadivar have taken the very constitution of the Islamic republic to task and demanded more freedom. They are as a result among the elite Islamic ideologues who are engaging the dominant regime even further dragging the political culture in the direction of the Islamic Ideology. Faezeh Hashemi, however, is far more political (like her father) to be too ideological. By advocating the cause of women's freedom in such symbolic gestures as wearing jeans, engaging in sports, and initiating marriage proposals she is trying to tap in to the larger youth movement of whose needs and aspirations she remains, like everyone else, unaware.

There is a raw body of material evidence of absolute and final disenchantment with the age and appeal of ideology on which a spectrum of ideological movements is trying to ride. But such belated ideologies are entirely misplaced. They will of course benefit from the youthful trust of one band of discontent or another. But the youthful force in its entirety cannot be compromised. The fifth Majlis, even with the presence of as many as 14 women deputies, has the distinction of having ratified legislation that has resulted in gender apartheid in hospitals. Under circumstances that the Iranian medical resources have been systematically eroded, this was nothing short of a criminal act, putting female patients in disadvantage and danger. Hashemi had the ambition of becoming the iconic voice of young women. But her name and her politics are no match for the reality they are trying to tap. Under circumstances that Rafsanjani himself is under severe criticism, Rafsanjani's paternal name recognition is no longer an asset but a definite liability. But religious intellectuals like

Abdolkarim Soroush, Mohsen Kadivar, and Abdollah Nuri continue to engage with the constitution seriously. Their engagement is far more detrimental to the Iranian future than the students' disengagement.

From Shi'ism as a religion of protest, paradoxical to the core of its doctrinal disposition, and Islam as a metanarrative of ideological resistance to colonialism we learn one abiding lesson as we enter the age of globalization. Given the amorphous nature and disposition of the electronic capital, no head-on collision with the amorphous empire that seeks to sustain and ride on it is even possible, even if advisable. As in the postmodernity of its globalizing logic, the capital has relinquished all its claims to metanarrative legitimacy, as must all forms of ideological resistance to it. Today only guerilla warfare, the strategic locating of a target to hit, and the instantaneous tenacity to run marks the polylocality of our presence in our rebellious history – and by this "us" I mean the brutally colonized world now at the mercy of the USA, the EU, the IMF, the World Bank, and the conglomerate of military industrial complexes that seeks to sustain their collectively violent disposition. Today more than ever, we need to retrieve the polylocality of our local cultures before they are homogenized, nationalized, categorized into a binary opposition to a figment of colonial imagination called "the West." The articulation of the polyfocality of our cultures inevitably leads to the critical formation of pockets of resistance beyond and above a single metanarrative claim on our emancipatory credulity. "Islam," as a metanarrative of salvation and resistance, totally unconscious of its colonial construction is now historically undone. Instead will have to emerge an entirely new political culture that no longer assumes its secondary status as an ideology of resistance to "Western domination," because neither "the West" nor the methods of its colonial domination have any further legitimacy.

The collapse of the binary ideological formation (*à la* "Islam and the West") points to a far more material collapse of the center-periphery dichotomy that has for long bifurcated the global logic of free-market economy. A full and final recognition of the complete and final integration of the colonizing and postcolonial states into the embracing logic of global capitalism is yet another prominent feature of the postnational, postnativist world. There is no longer a center and a periphery to this stage of global capitalism. In the constitution of that center and periphery, people in the colonial world had no say whatsoever. It was none other than the greatest critic of globalizing capital, Karl Marx himself, who delegated the non-European world to the backwaters of history. But today that power-basing bifurcation is no longer valid, evident, or material. Endemic moments of crisis at the headquarters of capital are almost identical with their regular occurrences in the field – *the fields* and the *headquarters* have become interchangeable sites. The world, from the surface of the globe to the planetary navigation of its cosmic location, is now more than ever one big factory floor where a hurricane in the Gulf of Mexico has an immediate effect on the result of parliamentary elections in Tehran.

The result is a total and final collapse of the First, the Second, and Third worlds into one world, ruled supremely by the faltering logic of globalizing capital, sought desperately to be regulated (through the IMF and the World Bank) via economic and political neoliberalism – and thus in dire need of an emancipatory remapping of the sort that W. E. B. Du Bois initiated and Amy Kaplan has revived and theorized. The collapse of the binary opposition between the center and the periphery of global economic production, of the colonizer and the colonized, the imperialist and the colonized, is matched by the by the collapse of the meta-narratives of emancipation, mobilization, Islamism, nationalism, liberalism, etc. The result is an atomized state of affairs ready to accept the factual reality of moral and material pluralism, the blueprint of a collective, planetary defiance of the manufactured will of the US-led global domination.

Historically multifocal, multilocal, multivocal, and inherently cosmopolitan, the Islam that survives the end of Islamic Ideology, the Islam that is hidden to Bush and Bin Laden alike, has a renewed rendezvous with history – side by side and embracing all other emancipatory ideas and movements equally at odds with this predatory empire. The end of Islamic Ideology is the end of Ideology but not the end of history – for the history of a renewed struggle to oppose and end this predatory empire is yet to begin. It is the beginning of a *history* in the lower case. As a particular branch of Islam, Shi'ism as a metaphysics of protest now recedes into the hidden corners of its once and future adherents, always there as a tempestuous template of revolt, no longer a drawn saber, but always ready to draw. The strategic articulation of a paradox of power that immediately negates itself at the moment of its success is a colonial critique of European modernity that ought to stay clear of a formal critique of modernity that proposes a global condition for postmodernity. We are not implicated in that presumed globality. We are not postmodern.

From Arundhati Roy to Judith Butler and Susan Willis, bypassing Julia Kristeva and Susan Sontag's provincialism, we reach a cosmopolitan remapping of the world best represented in the groundbreaking scholarship of Zillah Eisenstein and Amy Kaplan. Theirs is the rebellious cry of a visionary recital imagining a different world. At the end of Islamic Ideology, a new Islamic liberation theodicy awaits its long and languorous history. This promise carries the limits of Islam as a liberation theology to its far more emancipatory domains of a theodicy yet to be articulated, written, and promised, on a location where *Islam* willingly embraces its shades and shadows of doubt, welcomes its others and alternatives, and helps in the making of a global liberation movement beyond color lines and gender apartheid – for if we were ever fool to think that the global, transnational, abuse of labor by capital were matters of colonizing the yonder lands or else colored men, here is the superior wisdom of an ordinary, an extraordinary, American singer and songwriter from the heartland of its perils and promises, placing a single white mother (and with her the rest of Americans as ordinary people) at the center of the world consciousness:

"*Millworker*"

Well, my grandfather was a sailor
He blew in off the water
My father was a farmer
And I, his only daughter
Took up with a no good millworking man
From Massachusetts
Who dies from too much whiskey
And leaves me these three faces to feed
Millwork aint easy
Millwork aint hard
Millwork it aint nothing
But an awful boring job
I'm waiting for a daydream
To take me through the morning
And put me in my coffee break
Where I can have a sandwich
And remember
Then it's me and my machine
For the rest of the morning
And the rest of the afternoon
And the rest of my life
Now my mind begins to wander
To the days back on the farm
I can see my father smiling at me
Swinging on his arm
I can hear my granddads stories
Of the storms out on lake Eerie
Where vessels and cargos and fortunes
And sailors lives were lost
Ya, but its my life has been wasted
And I have been the fool
To let this manufacturer
Use my body as a tool
I can ride home in the evening
Staring at my hands
Swearing by my sorrow that a young girl
Ought to stand a better chance
So may I work the mills just as long as I am able

And never meet the man whose name is on the label
It be me and my machine
For the rest of the morning
And the rest of the afternoon
Gone to hell for the rest of my life

James Taylor

5 Shi'i passion play

In July 1863, the introduction of the military draft provoked four days of rioting in New York City. A mob composed largely of Irish immigrants assaulted symbols of the new order being created by the war – draft offices, the mansions of wealthy Republicans, industrial establishments, and the city's black population. Black men, women, and children were lynched on the streets of the nation's commercial metropolis. Many black New Yorkers fled to New Jersey and Brooklyn or took refuge in Central Park.

Eric Foner, *Forever Free: The Story of Emancipation and Reconstruction*
(2005)

You simply get chills every time you see these poor individuals ... so tragically, so many of these people, almost all of them that we see, are so poor and they are so black...

CNN Wolf Blitzer, *covering the aftermath of Hurricane Katrina*
(1 September, 2005)

So I am not here as a Republican or a Democrat, not as a mason or an elk, not as a Christian or a Jew, not as a Catholic or a Protestant, not as a Baptist or a Methodist. Not even as an American. For if I was an American, the problem that confronts our people today would not exist. So I stand here and speak this evening as what I was when I was born – a black man. Long before there was any such place as America, there were black people. And after America has long passed from the scene there will still be black people. I represent that which has no beginning or ending. That which is endless. That which is eternal. The black man himself.

Malcolm X (1961)

In late February 2005, I was contacted by a freelance American journalist named Steven Vincent, telling me that he had just brought back from Iraq a number of posters with themes related to the Shi'i Passion Play (*Ta'ziyeh*) and was now writing a piece on them for *Harper's Magazine*. He wondered if I would meet with him and help him understand the significance of the posters and what they meant. After a few email and phone exchanges, he finally came to my office at Columbia with a handful of these posters, which he said he had collected while he was in Iraq.

I remember we spread Mr. Vincent's posters on the floor of my office and began to talk about their various historical and contemporary significance – their symbolic references, color codifications, storylines, etc. Mr. Vincent seemed quite a learned man who had done some initial reading on the Battle of Karbala, which had happened in the year 680 on the Christian calendar and ever since had remained the central drama of the Shi'i Passion Play. He was at home in early Shi'i history, and judging from the range of probing questions he had for me he was mostly interested in connecting the historical significance of what these posters were depicting with the contemporary condition of Iraq. Among the various questions that Mr. Vincent asked me, mostly about the symbolic references of what was depicted on the posters, one was concerning the location where I thought they had been manufactured. In response to which, and as I was speculating how they might have been printed in the basement of a mosque or some printing shop in Basra or Karbala, I casually looked at the bottom of a couple of these posters and noted the address of a printing house in downtown Tehran (written in a Persian font markedly different from the Arabic font on the actual poster). "Here," I pointed out to him, "here it says that this poster was printed in downtown Tehran."

Soon after my meeting with Mr. Vincent, I received an email from Ms. Emily Hyde from *Harper's Magazine,* who was fact checking on some of the issues Mr. Vincent had raised in his article, as well as a couple of quotations he had from his interview with me. I responded to Ms. Hyde's queries, and later in the May issue of *Harper's Magazine,* Steven Vincent's article appeared, "Every Land is Karbala: In Shiite posters, a fever dream for Iraq" (*Harper's* May 2005). The article was quite elegantly written, nicely laid out and illustrated with the posters Mr. Vincent had procured from Iraq, and altogether, I thought, quite informative for a general reader.

This was the last I heard of Steven Vincent, until 3 August 2005, when I was shocked to read in BBC News Website:

> A US freelance reporter, Steven Vincent, has been shot dead by unknown gunmen in Basra, southern Iraq, police have said. Mr. Vincent was abducted with his female Iraqi translator at gun point by men in a police car on Tuesday. His bullet-riddled body was found on the side of a highway south of the city a few hours later. He had been writing a book about the city, where insurgents have recently stepped up their attacks.[1]

I was startled, deeply saddened, and could not believe the news. This was the first time that someone I had come to know personally was so savagely murdered in Iraq shortly after I had helped him publish an essay – the subject of which had brought him to me and one of my scholarly interests. To learn more about the incident I went to *The New York Times* site and discovered that indeed:

An American journalist from New York who was writing about the rise of conservative Shiite Islam and the corruption of the Iraqi police was abducted and shot to death Tuesday evening in the southern port city of Basra, American and Iraqi officials said today. The reporter's interpreter was also shot and is hospitalized in serious condition. The incident involving the reporter, Steven Vincent, an art critic and freelance writer who had worked in Basra for months, was the first time an American journalist has been attacked and killed during the war. A handful of American journalists have died in vehicle accidents or from illness.[2]

From the BBC report I had also learned that "in a recent *New York Times* article, Mr. Vincent wrote that Basra's police force had been infiltrated by Shia militants." I had never read this article. According to *The New York Times* article too, "on Sunday [before his death], *The New York Times* printed an article on its op-ed pages that Mr. Vincent had written about the British military in Basra, in which he sharply criticized the British for allowing religious Shiite parties and clerics to take control of Basra and populate the security forces with their followers." I went online and read this article of Steven Vincent, "Switched Off in Basra," in which the following sentence caught my attention:

> Nor did I see anyone question the alarming number of religious posters on the walls of Basran police stations. When I asked British troops if the security sector reform strategy included measures to encourage cadets to identify with the national government rather than their neighborhood mosque, I received polite shrugs: not our job, mate.[3]

Presumably these were the same posters that Mr. Vincent had previously procured and on the basis of which he had written that article for *Harper's Magazine*. I read more on and by Steven Vincent, and the more I learned about him the more I realized that he indeed was a staunch pro-war journalist, heavily invested in what he believed was a US-led "liberation of Iraq." I learned that he used to be an art critic who after witnessing the horrid events of 9/11 from the roof of his house had decided he wanted to write about what he believed was called "Islamofascism" and who had indeed traveled to Iraq, soon after the US-led invasion of that country, and written a book on his experiences.[4] As a journalist, he was embedded with the British in southern Iraq, considering the US-led invasion and occupation of Iraq a noble cause, finding fault with antiwar activists, whom he dismissed as having failed to understand that the Americans and the British were there to liberate the Iraqis. In a blog he had written I read him expound on how "words matter. Words convey moral clarity. Without moral clarity, we will not succeed in Iraq. That is why the terms the press uses to cover this conflict are so vital."[5] He objected to such words as "insurgents" or "guerillas" to describe the Iraqis opposed to the US-led occupation of their country and thought they ought to be called "murderous thugs" or alternatively "masked reactionary killers." He encouraged the media to call the Iraqi resistance "right wing paramilitary death squads." If that were to happen, Steven Vincent, the man I had helped understand Shi'i posters, "not only would the description be more accurate, but it would offer the American public a clear idea of the enemy in Iraq. And that, in turn, would bolster public attitudes toward the war." These were not the only words to which Steven Vincent had objected. "Instead of saying that the Coalition 'invaded' Iraq," he had written in the same blog, "and 'occupies' it today, we could more precisely claim that the allies liberated the country and are currently reconstructing it." He blamed the "supporters of the conflict in Iraq" for not having done their job properly and allowed "the terminology – and, by extension, the narrative – of events to slip from our grasp and into the hands of the anti-war camp." These were not mere matters of cosmetics, Mr. Vincent insisted. "More than cosmetic changes, these definitions *reflect the nobility of our effort in Iraq*, and steal rhetorical ammunition from the left."[6] He categorically dismissed people fighting against the military occupation of their homeland as "Saddamites and foreign jihadists" and blamed "the left" for calling them "resistance." This he thought was "an example of moral inversion." What was endangering Iraqi people, Steven Vincent believed, was not the US-led occupation but what he thought was the "Islamofascists," which he alternatively clarified as "evil men" bent on "turning the entire nation into a mass slaughterhouse." He then concludes: "Anyone who cares about success in our struggle against Islamofascism, or upholds principles of moral clarity and lucid thought – should combat such Orwellian distortions of our language."[7]

About four months after the tragic death of Steven Vincent, on the morning of November 19 2005, the town of Haditha in Iraq was the scene of a roadside bomb attack against a US military patrol. An agricultural community near Baghdad, Haditha had been a major site of resistance to US-led occupation. In the course of this particular roadside attack, Lance Corp. Miguel ("TJ") Terrazas, who was driving one of the four Humvee in the US military convoy, was killed. A US military statement issued soon after the incident simply said: "A US marine and 15 civilians were killed yesterday from the blast of a roadside bomb in Haditha. Immediately following the bombing, gunmen attacked the convoy with small arms fire. Iraqi army soldiers and marines returned fire, killing eight insurgents and wounding another."[8]

What the US military was telling the world about the Haditha incident was far from the truth. It was a flagrant lie. It was not just a lie. It was a deliberate cover-up, a falsification of truth. This is not what had happened. What had happened was the single most defining moment of what the US-led invasion and occupation of Iraq have meant for millions of ordinary and innocent Iraqis. A day after the incident, and the subsequent cover-up by the US army, an Iraqi journalist named Taher Thabet takes a camera and goes to the scene of this incident and starts shooting – shooting not bullets and lies, but films and truth. What he captured on his camera were the dead bodies of Iraqi women and men, adults and children, young and old, all seen in their blood-stained nightclothes, all indiscriminately shot and cold-bloodedly murdered in their own homes, under their own roof, not knowing what had hit them, or what they had done to deserve the wrath of the great liberators of their homeland.

The evidence that Taher Thabet had captured in his camera led to an investigation by an Iraqi human rights organization called Hammurabi. Against the cover-up of the US army, the truth of the Haditha massacre (reminiscent of the My Lai massacre the US army perpetrated in Vietnam on March 16 1968) thus reached from Taher Thabet to Hammurabi and from Hammurabi to *Time Magazine* in January 2006. In the grand tradition of American journalistic ethics, *Time Magazine* sat on this truth from January to March 2006 – almost three whole months. Instead of publishing the truth, *Time Magazine* passed the evidence of the gruesome massacre to the US military, giving it ample time to begin the whitewashing of what had actually happened. The US military, thanks to the journalistic dignity of *Time Magazine*, now had ample time to change its story and admit that "after the roadside bomb, the 15 civilians had been accidentally shot by marines during a gun fight with insurgents."[9]

This is the best the US military could do – heaping even more lies on evident deceit. Based on the investigative reporting of Taher Thabet, the documentation of Hammurabi human rights organization, and additional eyewitness accounts, it soon become clear that an enraged band of US military went on a rampage in Haditha, house to house hunting down and cold-bloodedly murdering innocent civilians who had nothing to do with anything other than being the innocent Iraqis who were being liberated by the US-led invasion of their homeland.

Iraqi eyewitnesses of the massacre reported to Iraqi authorities the details of how the US troops entered their houses and began indiscriminately killing entire families. "They knocked at our front door," one eyewitness reported, "and my father went to open it. They shot him dead from behind the door and then they shot him again. Then one American soldier came in and shot at us all. I pretended to be dead and he didn't notice me."[10] Children as young as two years and as old as 14 were among the victims of the massacre. In an adjacent house yet another child and his 70-year-old grandfather were shot dead. Four brothers in the same family, aged from 24 to 41 were also shot dead. "Eyewitnesses said they were forced into a wardrobe and shot."[11] This is not all: "Outside in the street, US troops are said to have gunned down four students and a taxi driver they had stopped at a roadblock set up after the bombing."[12] At the end the US military "confirmed that 24 Iraqi civilians died in Haditha that day, none of them killed by a roadside bomb."[13] Colonel Stewart Navarre of the US army finally admitted on December 21 2006: "The reporting of the incident up the chain of command was inaccurate and untimely."[14]

I remember my encounter with the late Steven Vincent as a singular occasion when two people standing on two opposite ends of a politics of warfare temporarily suspended their politics and were drawn into the miasmatic labyrinth of an art that at once embraced and transcended their politics. I had not the foggiest clue as to Mr. Vincent's politics when he came to see me. He too seemed either entirely oblivious to my politics or else his fascination with these Shi'i posters transcended his undoubtedly serious objections to my stand on President Bush's predatory warmongering. By the time the late Mr. Vincent came to see me early in March 2005, my antiwar activism was not only known locally in New York but known all throughout the United States, Latin America, Europe, the Muslim and Arab World, and as far as Australia because of news reports and even documentaries. I doubt that the late Steven Vincent did not know of my politics when he came to see me. My name and face had been on the front page of the leading Zionist tabloids in the city. But, and there is the rub, the courteous, humane, I would not even hesitate calling it collegial and friendly, manner in which the late Steven Vincent solicited my help and I happily provided it bespeaks of a superior disposition, of a more compelling urge to understand what those posters meant and signified.

Everything that I remember from my email, phone, and person-to-person encounter with the late Mr. Vincent I remember fondly, dearly, and with profound sadness when I recall his brutal and vicious murder; and yet everything I later learned from his politics places me at exactly the opposite poll of where he believed he stood. In person and so far as my short encounter with him is concerned, Steven Vincent was kind, gentle even, caring, curious, exceedingly intelligent, quite learned, and easily at home with materials he wanted me to clarify further for him. I felt in fact grateful that he had fished out those posters from Iraq for the two of us to come and read them together for a larger audience. And yet in print, and based on what I later read from and on him, he was so exceedingly rash, superficial, indulgent, and outright racist in his presumption of Americans and Europeans going half way around the globe to "liberate" Iraqis. I will never be able to reconcile between these two images of Steven Vincent, for paramount in my mind remains that existential moment when he and I pored over the posters he had brought along from Iraq and we were helping each other read them better – he with his first-hand knowledge of the location and circumstantial details of their whereabouts, and I by virtue of things I had learned as a subject of my lifetime scholarship, which had brought him to my office in the first place. He was the eyes and ears of the moment that had occasioned these posters, and I a guide to the universe of their meandering meanings. We corrected each other's lenses.

My encounter with the late Steven Vincent very much signifies the peculiar dramaturgical disposition of the Shi'i Passion Play (*Ta'ziyeh*) and the manner in which it has historically mixed and meandered with history of the Shi'is in their medieval and modern history. Our encounter too, just like the porous borderlines of *Ta'ziyeh* and history, oscillated between our opposing politics and our shared fascination with the esthetics of Shi'i dramaturgy. As a theater of protest, *Ta'ziyeh* commemorates the traumatic historical events that took place near the city of Karbala in the year 680 on the Christian calendar. The Prophet's grandson Hossein ibn Ali (d. 680) thought he was the legitimate heir to the caliphate representing him. Others did not – and they killed him. Commemorating that fateful event early in the Islamic period, *Ta'ziyeh* is thus a redemptive ritual at once rooted in history and branching out and back into history – past and present, factual and mythic. Not just at the time of Hussein ibn Ali, but ever since that fateful 10th of Muharram when he was beheaded in Karbala. By the time that Steven Vincent's article appeared in May 2005 in *Harper's Magazine*, the Shi'i Passion Play was in full historical swing and the sectarian violence in Iraq was well under way. The posters he had collected were not covering the walls of Basra for nothing. They were the commemorative canvases of a history remembering, remarking, and registering itself.

The immediate history of sectarian violence agitating the dramaturgical tropes and performative memes, one interlacing into the other, of the Shi'i Passion Play in Iraq can (and should) of course be traced back to the reign of Saddam Hussein himself, long before the US-led invasion, when he had forbidden any sign or signal of Shi'i collective consciousness. The doctrinal roots of the conflict between the Sunnis and Shi'is can indeed be traced back even deeper into medieval hostilities that have existed between the Sunnis and the Shi'is from the immediate aftermath of the death of Prophet Muhammad in 632 AD.[15] But in the more immediate context of Iraq proper, the Shi'is have been a persecuted majority throughout the reign of Saddam Hussein, which commenced in July 1979, and even before that since the July 1968 Ba'thist coup that ousted Colonel Abd-al-Salam Muhammad Arif and brought General Ahmad Hasan al-Bakr to power, and even before that when in July 1958 the Iraqi monarch King Faysal was ousted by Brigadier Abd-al-Karim Qasim. The Iraqi Shi'is have thus remained a majority with a minority complex for much of modern Iraqi history – almost identical with the fate of the Shi'is in Lebanon. Their historical grievances against the Sunni majority have thus been wandering, waxing, and waning into mythic, doctrinal, and ritual terms in one direction and into episodic rebellions on another. As a paradigmatic pattern of protest, *Ta'ziyeh* has been, and is thus consistently, fed on such histories of dispossession and disenfranchisement.

Despite the fact that the origin of Sunni–Shi'i sectarian violence in Iraq predates its modern history, or the US-led invasion and occupation of Iraq since March 2003 (very much on the model of the British colonial occupation of Iraq in the 1920s), it is always the necessary factor of an extraneous political force that agitates and ignites such latent hostilities. The assumption of a so-called "Shi'i Crescent," extended in sectarian solidarity from Pakistan through Iran and Iraq and all the way to Lebanon, as jointly proposed by the

Jordanian monarch King Abdullah and the US navy scholar Seyyed Vali Reza Nasr, is logically flawed, historically untenable, and thematically reductionist.[16] It reduces the cosmopolitan complexity of a succession of political cultures to an absurdly monolithic reading of people's sectarian identity-politics and it deceptively glosses over the factual evidence that speaks otherwise. Consider the fact that Iran and Iraq, two presumably Shi'i nations, were at a horrid war against each other for eight long and brutish years in which they killed hundreds of thousands of their fellow Shi'is. There are fundamental differences – ranging from social and political to cultural and historical – among the Shi'is of the world that pulls them as much (if not more) apart as their varied identification with Shi'ism pulls them together. That the resistance of Iraqis against the colonial occupation of their homeland has assumed added sectarian elements does not mean that such factors are the primary cause of violence in Iraq. The illegal, immoral, and barbaric US-led invasion of Iraq is the first, foremost, and final cause of all violence that has ensued after the US Secretary of Defense Donald Rumsfeld's campaign of "shock and awe" – a perfectly clear *English* phrase, and *not* an Arabic, Islamic, or Shi'i concept or doctrine.

What has reignited the dramatic tropes of the Shi'i Passion Play is the general condition of violence in Iraq, a condition that has restaged the drama of Karbala under the full foreign occupation of a Shi'i homeland, in which there is only one army and one army only that can be categorically identified with the army of the arch villain Yazid and that is the US-led army that invaded Iraq. Consider how in the immediate aftermath of the first US-led invasion of Iraq in January 1991, following the Iraqi invasion of Kuwait in August 1990 (itself predicated on a green light by the US government), the Shi'is in southern Iraq were encouraged by President George H. W. Bush (1989–1993) to revolt against Saddam Hussein. They did indeed do so, and when Saddam Hussein sent his army to slaughter them in March–April 1991, the US government let the carnage proceed apace while it was in complete military and economic control of Iraq. With that history in their collective mind, do Iraqi Shi'is have any reason to trust Americans more than they did Saddam Hussein? "The Army of Yazid" is a floating signifier. It can be identified with the army of Saddam Hussein today, that of the US-led occupation forces in Iraq the next, and yet again with the Israeli army stealing the Palestinian homeland in the bright daylight of history the following day. Sunni, Shi'i, Socialist, Ba'thist, or nationalist, Iraqis have had a longstanding solidarity with the brutalized Palestinians. Does, perhaps, the US unconditional support for its colonial outpost it calls "Israel" add another element integral and definitive to the Iraqi collective uprising against the US-led occupation of their homeland, precisely on the model of the Israeli occupation of Palestine – entirely independent of the so-called Sunni–Shi'i hostility? The point is not to dismiss the millennial-old hostilities, at once doctrinal and political, between two factions within Islam. The point is to place that history in the immediate context of its renewed resurgence and thus to see under what specific historical circumstances has the Shi'i dramaturgical disposition been reactivated. Donald Rumsfeld's campaign of "shock and awe" will go a long way explaining what has happened in Iraq and caused the resurgence of the Karbala paradigm since the US-led invasion of March 2003, before we need to resort to any enduring – modern or medieval – hostility between the Sunnis and the Shi'is in order to explain and understand any residual balance in that explanation.

The same culpability in agitating the Sunni–Shi'i hostility (very much on the model of the British agitation of similar hostilities between Muslims and Hindus in India, or Catholics and Protestants in Ireland, in the heydays of their colonial thieveries of nations, or the Belgian instigation of hostilities between the Hutu and the Tutsi in what later became Rwanda and Burundi) is true in the aftermath of the US-led invasion of Iraq in March 2003, when the US Secretary of Defense Donald Rumsfeld's campaign of "shock and awe" unleashed a magnitude of violence rarely matched and never surpassed in modern warfare. As early as July 2003, only a few months into the US-led occupation of Iraq, the commander of the US forces in Iraq said that his troops faced guerrilla-style war, which at the time was of an entirely generic anti-colonial disposition and had not yet fragmented into any particular denomination of a Sunni, Shi'i, or Kurdish kind. About a month later, by August of that very first year of the US-led occupation of Iraq, a car bomb in Najaf killed 125 people,[17] including the prominent Shia leader Ayatollah Mohammed Baqer al-Hakim, and thus sectarian violence had become integral to the US-led occupation of Iraq and Iraqis of various sorts fighting against that colonial occupation.

To break down the delusion, fed to the US military establishment by the US navy scholar Seyyed Vali Reza Nasr's psyop (psychological operations) pamphlet, *The Shia Revival: How Conflicts within Islam Will Shape the Future*, it is also imperative to keep in mind that the sectarian violence in Iraq has never been limited to the Sunni–Shi'i divide. In February 2004, for example, more than 100 people were killed in Irbil in suicide attacks targeting Kurdish factions. The anti-Shi'i disposition of the violence, to be sure, became particularly evident in March 2004 (coinciding with the Moharram ceremonies sacred to the Shi'is), when suicide bombers attacked the Shia pilgrims in Karbala and Baghdad, killing some 140 people. When in April–May 2004, Shia militias loyal to Muqtada Sadr confronted the US and UK forces, the Iraqi rebellion against the occupation of their homeland assumed a decidedly Shi'i character. At the same time the US massacre of Iraqi resistance in Falluja had Sunni Iraqis as the principal target of its wrath, while the criminal atrocities that American soldiers were perpetrating in Abu Ghraib torture chambers did not discriminate against Sunni or Shi'is and tortured them equally. In August 2004, when Muqtada Sadr's militia engaged with US forces, this was a decidedly anti-colonial uprising by a major Iraqi faction rebelling against the colonial occupation of their homeland, identical to similar uprisings by people around the globe against British, French, Spanish, Portuguese, Belgian and now above all American old and new colonialism.

The Iraqi Shi'is uprising against the foreign domination of their homeland is thus integral to their share and participation in the democratic aspirations of their country. Were there any of those people whom the late Steven Vincent opted to call "murderous thugs" among the massive millions who on January 30 2005 participated in elections for a Transitional National Assembly? How are we to distinguish between the people that the late Steven Vincent thought were "murderous thugs" and those who elected Prime Minister Nouri al-Maliki, or the prime minister himself? The Shia faction of the United Iraqi Alliance won a majority of assembly seats, followed by the Kurdish parties. One cannot completely bracket the principal source and cause of violence in Iraq – the US-led campaign of "shock and awe" – and then find fault with the people who in one way or another are resisting the military occupation of their homeland. When on February 28 2005 some 114 people were killed by a massive car bomb in the Shi'i-dominated city of Hilla, nothing but Donald Rumsfeld's campaign of "shock and awe" was in full swing. "Shock and awe" is not an Arabic phrase, a Qur'anic reference, or a Shi'i doctrinal concept. It is in plain old English. The late Steven Vincent need not have learned any Arabic, Persian, Turkish, or Urdu to know what it meant. One need not point to the fact that President Bush appointed a diplomat globally infamous for his insidious support of right-wing death squads in Central America during the 1980s, the US UN ambassador John Negroponte, as the highest ranking US official succeeding Viceroy Paul Bremer, as the possible (potential, probable) source of the resurgence of sectarian violence in Iraq. One can simply suggest that the unleashing of such a vicious volume of violence suggested by the phrase "shock and awe" is bound to ricochet and swing and self-perpetuate itself in more than one way. The rise of Shi'i dramaturgical disposition trying to cope with the encounter of Muslim Shi'is with the foreign occupation of their homeland is only one performative ritual among many other traumatic measures of coping with unfathomable violence. Akira Kurosawa spent a lifetime of filmmaking trying to cope with the consequences of the Americans dropping the atomic bomb on his homeland. The *Ta'ziyeh* is a variation on that very theme, as Palestinian cinema in its entirety is the creative effervescence of a nation trying to cope with the grand thievery of their homeland by the European Zionists.

In the same month that Steven Vincent's noble and admirable attempt to understand Iraq under US-led occupation was brutally cut short and he was murdered in Basra, more than 1000 Shi'is were stampeded to death in the course of a religious ceremony in Baghdad. By the time that in February 2006 a bomb attack on an important Shia shrine in Samarra destroyed a major landmark of the Shi'is, people just lost count of how many hundreds of thousands of Iraqis – Sunnis, Shi'is, Kurds, or otherwise – had been murdered since Donald Rumsfeld's campaign of "shock and awe" had commenced. A team of American and Iraqi epidemiologists, according to a report in *The Washington Post* in October 2006, estimated that 655,000 people had been killed in Iraq since Donald Rumsfeld's campaign of "shock and awe" had started in March 2003.[18] How many more thousands were killed after that report? How many were missed by that report? After this report, would it be too much of an exaggeration that the war that Mr. Vincent believed was "a noble" attempt "to liberate Iraq" from its won evils murdered about 1 million Iraqis, wounded many more, made millions more homeless refugees, massacred them in their multitudes in Falluja, Najaf, or Haditha, tortured them in hidden dungeons of Abu Ghraib and a whole network of interrogation cells in Europe and Almighty only knows where else, raped and burned their ravaged bodies as they did Abeer Qassim Hamza al-Janabi (1991–2006), the 14-year-old Iraqi girl from the village of Mahmoudiyah, gang-raped by the US serviceman, Pfc. Steven D. Green and his company, before they burned her violated body along with her father Qassim Hamza Raheem, 45, her mother Fakhriya Taha Muhasen, 34, and her seven-year-old sister, Hadeel Qassim Hamza. One can of course dismiss Abeer Qassim Hamza al-Janabi and 655,000 other Iraqis killed in the aftermath of the US Secretary of Defense Donald Rumsfeld's campaign of "shock and awe" as "murderous thugs," as the late Steven Vincent did, undeserving of the gift that Mr. Vincent's elected officials were giving to Iraq. But where would that leave humanity at large – and what would be the point of knowing anything about anything, let alone about something called *Ta'ziyeh*? *Ta'ziyeh* stepped out of its own mythic memories and exited people's collective consciousness and walked in mourning through the streets and alleys, mountains and valleys, of Iraq. The US-led invasion of Iraq was the meltdown point of a millennial old metaphor. The blood of some 1 million people – Sunnis and Shi'is, guilty or innocent – is running through the veins of a human calamity for which we are yet to find a proper sentence to utter, a mimetic measure to grasp, to comprehend, to convey, or simply to mark, mourn, register.

The Haditha massacre was not the exception. It was the rule. The Haditha massacre of November 2005, the Falluja carnage of November 2004, and the Nasiriya and Najaf slaughter of May 2004 were chief among a whole spectrum of atrocities that commenced with Donald Rumsfeld's campaign of "shock and awe" in March 2003 and defined the US-led invasion of Iraq for people at the receiving end of it. The Abu Ghraib torture chambers, where the US soldiers systematically – sexually and otherwise – abused Iraqi inmates, were not the exception. They were the rule. The Abu Ghraib Prison, the Bagram Air Base, Guantanamo Bay, and a whole network of subterranean detention and interrogation dungeons scattered around Europe were definitive to the US-led terrorism perpetrated upon the world, forcing humanity at large into submission to its whimsical will.

The systematicity, banality, and wide-eyed gangster mentality with which the US warmongers and their neocon ideologues go about maiming and murdering people has more than one set of victims. The least visible of the "collateral damage" they fail even to note is the spectrum of people's sacred memories they habitually disregard and transgress. US imperialism very much operates on the model of Steven Spielberg's Indiana Jones character, in *The Raiders of the Lost Ark* (1981) in particular, where a gung-ho professor of archeology, not having a blasted clue as to where and what it is he is getting himself into, by hook or by crook, and with a helping hand from cliché-ridden scripts from Hollywood, USA, manages to save the day, "get the girl," and run away with the hidden treasure. What inner sanctum of people's sacred history the Indiana Jones of American imperialism manages to butcher, snatch, or destroy neither Steven Spielberg nor Indiana Jones nor Donald Rumsfeld could care less. It's Hollywood, it's Pentagon, anything goes, everything is possible. The US invasion of Iraq opened a miasmatic Pandora's box, where things hidden and things sacred to people's sense of who and what and where they are were all blasted out into the open for the whole world to see, for an entire history yet to be written. The criminal looting of the Iraqi national museums and the museums of antiquities by mercenary antique dealers from Western Europe and North America pales in comparison and is only the outward sign of what inner sanctum of how many millions of believing Muslims the US-led invasion of Iraq has managed to defile and deform. Beyond the moral and material, human and environmental, calamities that it has caused, the Operation Iraqi Freedom, as the Orwellian Newspeak has it, sent a bunker buster nuclear device into the inner sanctum of a people's most inviolable memories.

What the tragedy of the late Steven Vincent (and millions of other ordinary and decent Americans trying to understand what their government is doing in Iraq) and the victims of the Haditha massacre (and hundreds of thousands of other equally innocent Iraqis murdered after the US-led occupation of their country) share frames a cognitive and mimetic dissonance at the heart of *Ta'ziyeh* as a theater of protest – for Mr. Vincent and other Americans, to be sure, a matter of passing (though ultimately in his case fatal) curiosity, while for millions of Iraqis a matter of collective identity, communal dignity, agential autonomy, national sovereignty, and above all memorial habitat, where people hold their dignity tightly close and call the covered cracks of their vulnerabilities home. *Ta'ziyeh* dwells on the intersection of myth and history, where in the streets of Basra an American journalist meets his tragic death while collecting the evidence of an atrocity he may have misread in its origin and proportion but cannot escape in its full unfolding and tragic drama. *Ta'ziyeh* as a paradigm of human suffering and moral rectitude has history as its site of citation, the material of its variegated evidence. *Ta'ziyeh* notes and stages a *mimetic dissonance* between what it sees and what it shows – the memory of Karbala it remembers and the streets and back alleys of Baghdad and Basra it thus resignifies. The mimetic dissonance that *Ta'ziyeh* signifies leads to a suspended sense of history, where events mean more than meets the eye, where events signify less than they invest and project for a posterity yet to come. The suspended sense of history is contingent – always – on a expectant delivery, where a promise is made, an almost (but never completely) cosmetic promise, and whereupon history can never end, or begin, for *history* is but a mimetic trope in a story that is eternally retold.

Ta'ziyeh is a dramaturgical paradigm conjugated like a verb that never exhausts its grammatology. On that paradigm history is nothing but a passing exemplar, an illustration, there to make a point, the point that *Ta'ziyeh* dramatically makes – that the world is but a stage and we the passing shadows that make it move and mean. The formation of the mimetic dissonance at the heart of *Ta'ziyeh* suspends it in time, hangs it on the sense and sensibilities of a miasmatic place, a suspended and suspenseful conception of the history that it thus makes meaningful, trustworthy. Imam Hossein is any one who says no to tyranny and injustice. Shimr is just about any militant thug who launches a campaign of "shock and awe." Karbala is right where the US-led invading army has landed. No metaphor is needed there. The metaphor has come to meet the naked aggression, where history attests to the veracity of the allegory. In deference to that allegory, history is always in a state of flux, waiting to be delivered, as all Shi'is always are, waiting for the Expectant Deliverer, the Imam of the Age. If *Ta'ziyeh* as metaphor fails narratively to absorb and esthetically to sublate the barbarity of the US-led invasion of Iraq, and there is only so much abusive terror and Indiana Jones imperialism a metaphor can take, then Donald Rumsfeld's campaign of "shock and awe" has destroyed something far more crucial and precious than a people's homeland. It has brought a people's epic narrative to the tip of a meltdown, the point where all its dwelling allegories run away from its mimetic measures of meaning and significance. At that point people become moral zombies, *homo sacer* as Georgio Agamben calls them, sleepwalking into a normative coma where nothing means anything any more. The 14-year-old Abeer Qassim Hamza al-Janabi that the US serviceman, Pfc. Steven D. Green and his company gang-raped before they burned her violated body was already the *homo sacer*, the stripped body, by virtue of an illegal war that abrogated the legality of her personhood. The violated inviolability of an innocence murdered in the *homo sacer* of Abeer Qassim Hamza al-Janabi is also a boomerang, and it is yet to come back to haunt Americans for generations to come (mark these words). No people can just go around the globe raping and murdering people and get away with it. There is a brutal justice in the universe of things, a vindictive justice rooted and driven from the heart of darkness itself.[19] Abeer Qassim Hamza al-Janabi, as *homo sacer*, as bared life, was made an exile in the domesticity of her own homeland, by an invading army, a gang of which went and raped and murdered her and her family. The illegal war that turned Abeer

Qassim Hamza al-Janabi into a *homo sacer* is the war that also denied her protection. Her natural/biological life (*Zoë*), exposed and stripped by Donald Rumsfeld's campaign of "shock and awe," pre-empted her political life (*Bios*). At the moment of her being raped, she was already denied her *political life* by virtue of a moral depravity that turned her, *ipso facto*, into a *homo sacer*, a sacrificial lamb.

What has happened in the streets, back alleys, and even private homes in Baghdad, Basra, Najaf, or Karbala is yet to become meaningful. Will *Ta'ziyeh* as a paradigm of suffering and redemption absorb the US-led invasion of Iraq into the bosom of its millennial history and make it mean and signify something by way of overcoming it when all the colonial officers of "shock and awe" have packed and left – or will the US-led invasion overwhelm the Karbala metaphor and forever make it meaningless?[20] The calamity of Bush's Babylon is still meaningless – it has no point of reference. Statistics means nothing. They are good for epidemiologists, useless to propagandists who are thinking otherwise. Thomas Friedman and Charles Krauthammer, as everyone else, will sooner or later die and disappear – and the ignominies they have committed in publicly supporting the mass murder of a nation-state will degenerate into footnotes of a history no one will care to read or remember. The cosmic timing of *Ta'ziyeh* is on a Sarmadi scale (Thomas Friedman and Charles Krauthammer cannot know and will not know what that means – they cannot google it). Somewhere between pre- and post-eternity, between *Azal* and *Abad*, the events of Iraq are yet to mean anything. Sold to the delusions of an empire, and yet drawn to the miasmatic labyrinth of a visual regime of suspended meaning, the late Steven Vincent died the art critic that he had originally (always) been, temporarily distracted by a politics he tragically failed to understand. He was, perhaps intuitively, perhaps by cultivation, a far superior art critic than a journalist embedded with the army of Attila the Hun, Donald Rumsfeld of a reckless, corporate-corrupt, and misplaced empire. The late Steven Vincent's misreading of the Iraq war is infinitely superior in intelligence and nobler in honesty than the accuracy of Dick Cheney in anticipating the business windfalls of US-led invasion of an oil-rich nation.

For an Islamic liberation theodicy to be rooted in the creative crisis of a world at mimetic odds with itself, it is impossible to ignore the dramaturgical blueprint of *Ta'ziyeh* as the single most important theatrical manifestation of Islam as a religion of protest. The specific conditions in which the decline and demise of (legitimate and purposeful) militant Islamism is both socially visible and doctrinally inevitable has now set the stage for a new liberation theology that will correspond and converse more specifically with the globalized condition of Muslims living in the shadow of an amorphous, postmodern empire and its colonial outpost (apartheid state) called "Israel." As a revolutionary template of such actual and potential movements, *Ta'ziyeh* sublates the historically most militant Islamic sect, Shi'ism, into a symbolically most explosive repertoire of its insurrectionary dispositions, its theater of protest, its conventional tropes and transformative memes of sublated anger, its drama of salvation, epic of uprising against tyranny and injustice. As the single most performative evidence of Islam as a religion of protest, a religion that can never lose its revolutionary disposition without at once contradicting – and thus getting ready to redeem – itself, *Ta'ziyeh* is a theater of redemption and protest inundated with sustained revolutionary potentials. The asyncretic mimesis operative at the dramaturgical heart of *Ta'ziyeh* (that there is no one-to-one correspondence in its iconic acts of representation) corresponds to a manner of liberation theology in which a mode of permanent but inconclusive revolution, a mimetic dissonance that can face the amorphous empire by remaining always on the offensive but never in power.

What had most probably brought the late Steven Vincent to meet with me and discuss his Shi'i posters was a book that Peter Chelkowski and I had written on the iconic and dramaturgical dimensions of the Islamic revolution in Iran. What we had done in that book, *Staging a Revolution: The Art of Persuasion in the Islamic republic of Iran* (1999), was to collect the most compelling visual and performative aspects of the Islamic revolution in Iran (1977–1979) and the eight grueling years of war with Iraq that followed (1980–1988) and then begin reading through the semiotic repertoire of what we had collected. We thus narrated the course of the Islamic revolution in Iran as if the dramatic unfolding of a *Ta'ziyeh* performance, using the revolutionary occasion as the location of that unfolding.

Some two decades before the twentieth century came to an end a massive revolution shook an ancient land to its foundation.[21] What was later to be called "the Islamic revolution" in Iran took much of the world by surprise. It did so far less by the fact of its occurrence than by the manifestly religious signs of its mobilization. The revolution was led by a high ranking cleric, Ayatollah Khomeini, mostly organized by the clerical class, and demanded (and exacted) the establishment of an Islamic republic. Some two centuries into the commencement of the European Enlightenment modernity, a project that its colonial shadow had extended it to the four corners of the globe, a religious revolution of sudden and inexplicable ferocity brought a corrupt monarchy and its military might to their knees.[22] Why and whence a religious revolution? Now? At this particular juncture in history, when God had been for long proclaimed dead, at the heart of Enlightenment modernity, and thus by extension at its colonial edges? In the figure of none other than Michel Foucault himself, the world dispatched, as it were, its leading theorist of power and critic of European modernity to Iran to figure out what in the world was happening. In a series of dispatches he sent to the Italian daily *Corriere della Sera*, Foucault sought to explain the Islamic revolution to himself and to the rest of the world. The supreme critic of modernity was off to see how it was being challenged from one outlandish colonial shadow of the Enlightenment.[23]

By the early 1980s an Islamic Republic was established in Iran and an all-out war was under way with neighboring Iraq. As the ravages of the war wreaked havoc on both nations, the institutions of an Islamic Republic were brutally consolidated in Iran. Some 200 years into the Iranian colonial encounter with European modernity, and almost 100 years after a massive revolution that had replaced an absolutist state apparatus with a constitutional monarchy, the organs of a repressive theocracy were now solidly in place. The defining moment of the Islamic revolution in Iran was Shi'ism and its political updating by a succession of revolutionary ideologues. As a religion of protest, and as an ethos of speaking truth to power, Shi'ism was put to full revolutionary use in overthrowing a corrupt monarchic government and then mobilizing the masses against an invading army, before it was equally put to use to consolidate a repressive theocracy. That today the Islamic republic is an entirely discredited and illegitimate state apparatus, held together by a bizarre combination of militant thugs, entrenched clerical establishment, and the contradictory consequences of such nonsensical rhetoric as "The Axis of Evil" is nothing but a historical testimony to the doctrinal paradox at the heart of Shi'ism, that it succeeds when it is defeated, and defeated when it succeeds.

At the end of the twentieth century, Shi'ism was thus put to immediate and enduring use in a momentous historical uprising in order to topple a monarchy, consolidate an Islamic Republic, and institutionalize a repressive theocracy. True to its doctrinal paradox, Shi'ism has been instrumental in the first and the second task, and entirely useless in the last. In both its suggestive symbolics and enduring institutions, Shi'ism has been the paramount ideological force in revolutionary and military mobilization, before it has categorically abandoned the clerical establishment to their own graceless devices to continue their illegitimate reign of terror and intimidation.

Nowhere is the central paradox of Shi'ism, in both its mobilizing and demobilizing contradictory forces, more vividly evident than in its most spectacular visual manifestations, namely in the thematics of *Ta'ziyeh* and all its visual and performing variations. By *Ta'ziyeh* we should not just mean a Shi'i version of the Christian Passion play similar to the Miracle plays of Oberammergau, though it has a striking similarity to it, particularly with Bach's cantatas. *Ta'ziyeh* is more a thematic of mourning, as its name clearly indicates, that has historically spread over a whole constellation of dramatic and ritual performances. *Ta'ziyeh* will have to be considered in its more generic and thematic sense that includes the location-based *Ta'ziyeh* proper, extends into the less elaborate recitatives like *Shabih-khani*, includes one- or two-man recitations in front of an illustrated canvas as *Shamayel-gardani* and *Pardeh-dari*, and can be stationary like *Rozeh-khani* or mobile like *Dasteh*, and invariably extends to mild or brutal rituals of self-flagellation in the form of *Sineh-zani*, *Zanjir-zani*, and in extreme cases *Qameh-zani*. *Ta'ziyeh* is the constellation of all these variations on the thematics of mourning the death of the Prophet's grandson, Seyyed al-Shohada, Hussein ibn Ali, "the Prince of Martyrs." It is in that thematic sense that *Ta'ziyeh* became a paramount mode of mobilization in the course of the Islamic revolution (1977–1979) and immediately after that during the war with Iraq (1980–1988).

As a theater of protest, *Ta'ziyeh* is a Shi'i ritual of dramatic redemption.[24] Although its dramatic and ritual roots are traced to such pre-Islamic Iranian origins as *Seyavashan*, today *Ta'ziyeh* is a thoroughly recodified act as a specifically Shi'i practice with multifaceted expressions in South Asia, Iran, the Arab world, and even the Caribbean, where it was taken by South Asian communities and then mixed with Latin American carnivals.[25] *Ta'ziyeh* is a theater of protest, based on the most dramatic event in early Islamic history. As a theater of protest, *Ta'ziyeh* is integral to Shi'ism and its paradox of power. Whatever its dramatic or ritual roots might be in ancient Iranian or Mesopotamian practices, *Ta'ziyeh* today remains a quintessentially Islamic and more specifically Shi'i practice.[26] The defining moment of *Ta'ziyeh* is its destabilizing dramatics, that it keeps the charismatic moment of Shi'ism mimetically alive and symbolically suggestive. Today it is impossible to understand *Ta'ziyeh* outside its Islamic and Shi'i context. To exoticize it as "traditional theater," the way classical Orientalism has done it, to isolate and sever it from the rest of the creative culture that generates and sustains it, the way contemporary anthropology has done it, or else to assimilate it backward to its possible Iranian roots in *Seyavashan*, as the Iranian nativist reading is wont to do, all rob *Ta'ziyeh* of its integral location in the entirety of its immediate cultural universe.[27] Above all else, *Ta'ziyeh* is a communal act of collective redemption – its performative, dramatic, mimetic, and dramaturgical dimensions all integral to this its most defining significance.

The central thematic of *Ta'ziyeh* as drama is the notion of *mazlumiyyat*, which is the presiding moment of Shi'ism itself. What is *mazlumiyyat*? As the originary concept of Shi'ism, and by extension *Ta'ziyeh*, *mazlumiyyat* constitutes the moral/political community in terms of justice and its aberration. *Mazlumiyyat* is the absence of justice that signals the necessity of its presence. In Shi'ism, the originary promise of Islam to deliver earthly and eternal justice to the world is kept doctrinally alive in the charismatic figure of the Imam. In *Ta'ziyeh*, Yazid and Imam Hossein, the two arch nemeses, are metaphoric representations of unjust power and revolutionary mobilization against it. *Mazlumiyyat* is more an assumption than a notion. It means, "having been wronged." Hossein's epithet is "Mazlum," he is called "Hossein-e Mazlum," or "the Hossein who was wronged." But the trilateral root of *mazlumiyyat*, ZLM, means "tyranny" and "injustice" at one and the same time, collapsing the political and the moral. Thus two paradoxical principles are instantaneously summoned and metamorphically collapsed in the assumption of mazlumiyyat. First, it is a *weakness* that constitutes *power*, a *passivity* that entails *active* agency, and second it is a *morality* that surmises the *political*, a *politics* that summons the *moral*. As the supreme symbolic figure of Shi'ism, Hossein is cosmogonically *Mazlum* – and as such he is a permanent revolutionary. He can never be *in* power, because that, *ipso facto*, makes him a *Zalem*, a tyrant, and that can never be, that would be a contradiction in terms, the undoing of Hossein, and with Hossein Shi'ism – and thus the central paradox of Shi'ism in its historical unfolding. *Ta'ziyeh* is the dramatic register, the suggestive symbolics, of that doctrinal paradox at the heart of Shi'ism.

Whatever its pre-Islamic dramatic and ritual origins, *Ta'ziyeh* is now thoroughly recodified in Islamic terms, and as such it carries within its dramaturgical tension the central paradox of power constitutional to the Qur'anic revelation itself. The Qur'an consists of two major parts, each at narrative and normative odd with the other. The 114 *surahs* or chapters of the Qur'an are divided into those revealed in Mecca between 610 and 622 (or ten years before the commencement of the Islamic calendar until the prophet's migration from Mecca to Medina), and those revealed in Medina between 622 and 632 (or from year 1 on the Islamic Calendar to year 10). The Meccan *surahs* correspond to the rising crescendo of the Prophet's mission and are revolutionary and destabilizing in their moral defiance of injustice and tyranny, as he brings the Meccan pariahs and the downtrodden together around his insurrectionary revelations. The Medinan *surahs*, on the contrary, are the record of the prophet's consolidating his power in Medina and the establishing of his a political community. Between the Meccan and the Medinan chapters of the Qur'an, the moral uprising of a revolutionary movement and the political consolidation of power, there is thus a narrative and normative tension. This tension has remained definitive to Islamic doctrine and history. To the degree that Shi'ism in general and *Ta'ziyeh* in particular act out that central Qur'anic tension they are both constitutional to Islam itself. "What you see here is the real Islam," a Nabatiyya resident told Augustus Richard Norton during an Ashura ceremony in Lebanon in 2000, "Islam is not found in books, it is here."[28]

Immediately after the death of the Prophet, the routinization of his charismatic authority into Islamic caliphate is the most immediate and suggestively metaphoric expression of this definitive paradox at the heart of Islam.[29] What was gradually called the Sunni branch of Islam identifies the overwhelming majority of Muslims who opted for the eventual institutionalization of Muhammad's charismatic authority in the juridical institution of the *ulama* and the political power of the *caliphs*. A small minority of Muslims, however, sought to perpetuate that charismatic moment and doctrinally transfer it from the institution of Prophethood to that of their saintly figures they called their Imams. The Shi'is, as they were gradually identified, related to the figure of their infallible Imams with the same charismatic spontaneity as they once did to the Prophet himself. While in Sunni Islam the paradox of power constitutional to the nascent faith was disentangled and pacified in the dual institutions of the ulama and the caliphs, in Shi'ism the charismatic undecidability of the faith was kept allegorically alive. That charismatic undecidability is centered on the principle of justice (*adl*), as the defining moment of the faith. The charismatic figures of the Imam personifies the principal of speaking truth to power, upholding the Meccan spontaneity of the Qur'an over and against its Medinan propensity to institution-building, transferring the Prophet's prophetic spontaneity to their Imams over his political prowess in consolidation of power. It is precisely this enduring and definitive *charismatic spontaneity* at the heart of Muhammadan message that in *Ta'ziyeh* is esthetically sublated into a mode of *mimetic dissonance* that never allows a fixed and sedated correspondence between reality and representation.

This preference of spontaneous charisma over enduring institutions of legitimate power has given Shi'ism a doctrinally paradoxical disposition reflective of the normative tension hidden in the very heart of Islam and constitutional to the Qur'anic narrative itself. Shi'ism, as a result, has encapsulated the insurrectionary moment of the nascent Islam and remained categorically a religion of protest. It must always speak truth to power. It can never be *in* power. That constitutional paradox at the heart of Shi'ism is of course first and foremost theorized in its doctrinal articulation of Imamah, or the succession of a series of infallible saintly figures, but also dramatically staged in *Ta'ziyeh*. *Ta'ziyeh*, as a result, carries within its dramatic tension the central paradox of Shi'ism, and in turn the principal doctrinal anxiety of Islam itself. Carrying within itself the very seed of Islam and Shi'ism as a religion of protest, *Ta'ziyeh* collapses the dual supposition of the moral and political communities together, disallowing the narrative and normative separation of the two. In the same vein, reality and fiction are counter-narrated, bringing the tragedy of Hossein home to bear on the contemporaneity of its actual performance. This in turn mutates the creative and critical dimensions of the drama much closer together than ordinarily allowed. The two moments of the act, its historical roots and its momentary remembrance, are equally collapsed into each other, preventing a sympathetic distancing of the audience from the fact of the event. The diachronic and synchronic separation of history and reality are equally fused into each other, making art and politics almost impossible to separate, making the world its performative stage.

This doctrinal tension at the roots of *Ta'ziyeh* as ritual drama gives the nature and disposition of its *mimesis* an entirely different modulation from that of the Aristotelian Greek, which as *mimesis* or "imitation" it is immediately tantamount to onomatopoeia, or the actual making (*poiein*) of the naming (*onoma*) of the mimetic act. We have no such presumtions in *Ta'ziyeh*. Quite to the contrary. In *Ta'ziyeh*, *acting* is not mimetic (in the Aristotelian sense) and entirely suggestive (or only momentarily mimetic), with a full contractual agreement, performatively stipulated, between the actors and the audience that they are *just* acting. Actors hold their script in their hands, not because they don't know the lines but because they want to gesture a distance and suggest a dissimilitude. If the Aristotelian mimesis is based on *similitude*, *Ta'ziyeh* is predicated on *dissimilitude*. The director of *Ta'ziyeh* is always present (and often deliberately visible) on the stage, not because the actors don't know what to do, but because the audience needs assurance that this is just acting. The stage is not really a stage, not because the villagers and townspeople who staged this play were poor and could not afford an amphitheater, but because the stage must be an extension of the rest of the physical habitat of the actors and the audience. The actors in fact come on stage directly from the middle of their houses, alleys, streets, and markets. The stage never loses the sight of its not-being-the-stage. Non-actors can frequent it easily, while the actors fall in and out of their character without a cue. There is fluidity between reality and representation because the actors are acting no act of fiction. They are acting reality. Imam Hossein and his companions were really killed in the battle of Karbala in October 680 by Yazid and his cohorts. You cannot pretend acting that as if it never happened and you are just acting a work of fiction; and yet you cannot pretend that you are Imam Hossein either. That would be sacrilegious. This, as a result, necessitates an active vigilance on part of the audience to know when you are acting and when you are not. This is substantially facilitated by the fact that *Ta'ziyeh* actors are not actors. They ordinarily have other professions. They used to be greengrocers, butchers, carpenters, and now they may be dentists, lawyers, and teachers. If one sees a *Ta'ziyeh* with a built-in Aristotelian conception of mimesis, one is terribly disappointed. One has to understand how in a doctrinally charged collapse of the *then* and the *now*, the moral and the political, the real and the ideal, the charismatic paradox at the heart of Shi'ism informs the dramatic tension at the heart of *Ta'ziyeh* and all its suggestive symbolics of acting, staging, showing, representing.

As a performative art, though, *Ta'ziyeh* is never totally under the control and authority of its own verbal memory. There is a verbal memory to *Ta'ziyeh* to which its performative drama is alluding but to which it is not totally obligated. This is the *performative paradox* at the heart of *Ta'ziyeh*, which is itself located within the *memorial paradox* of Shi'ism as a religion of protest, which itself is located within the narrative and normative paradox of the Qur'an, as the textual anamnesis of Muhammad's prophetic charisma. *Ta'ziyeh* is thus a theater of protest whose moral parameters break and intrude into the boundaries of the political. The result is the peculiar status of *Ta'ziyeh*, which is neither fictive theater nor stylized ritual, neither real nor unreal. It is located on a tertiary plane between the real and the representational, the factual and the fictive, from which both the evident and the imaginative sustain their relevance.

Shi'ism and *Ta'ziyeh* as Religion and Drama of Protest reflect and replace each other. That *Ta'ziyeh* as a universe of creative imagination should lend itself to political uses is immediately rooted in its originary character as a theater of protest, performing and visualizing the most dramatic moment, the very historical birth, of a religion of protest. As a theater of protest, *Ta'ziyeh* is coterminous with Shi'ism, commemorating its very doctrinal disposition as a religion that was born at the death of its saintly figures of first and foremost Ali, the prophet's son-in-law and one of his staunchest supporters, and then his son Hossein. *Ta'ziyeh* remembers and re-enacts a doomed battle between a small band of revolutionaries and an entrenched and deeply corrupt political power. There is a universality to the battle of Karbala that can easily be extrapolated to implicate any small band of revolutionaries fighting against any entrenched political power. *Ta'ziyeh* in effect provides the bands of revolutionaries across time and space with the opportunity to change the course of history, as it was unjustly determined in the battle of Karbala. "We are not the people of Kufa," read some slogans during the revolutionary mobilization that invited Khomeini back to Iran, meaning that this time around, these Muslims were not going to betray their saintly leader Imam Hossein/Imam Khomeini by inviting him to Kufa/Tehran and then not helping him out fight against Yazid/Shah. The characters of *Ta'ziyeh* drama are not just metaphorical. They are metamorphic. They easily mutate into contemporary historical figures. The transfiguration of *Ta'ziyeh* characters is historically multi-metamorphic, from historical to metaphorical, and from metaphorical to historical. That multi-metamorphic aspect of *Ta'ziyeh* characters makes them at once extremely potent allegories of cosmic significance and yet instantaneously accessible to contemporary remodulations.

In the course of the Islamic revolution, the figure of Khomeini was immediately identified with that of Hossein, or even more poignantly with a conflated figure of Muhammad, Ali, and Hossein, which is to say with the most combatant saintly figures in the Islamic universe of creative imagination. With the same token, the late Shah was identified with Yazid, a usurper in power, corrupt, tyrannical, banal, and demonic. The configuration of the protagonist and the antagonist in this drama transformed the battle between Khomeini and the Shah into the simulacrum of the battle of Karbala, in which this generation of Muslims could actually participate. We have to remember that *Ta'ziyeh* is much more than a mere passion play commemorating the battle of Karbala. There is a profound element of redemptive suffering involved in its multifaceted self-flagellation that can assume mild forms of *Sineh-zani* (rhythmic beating of the chest) to very violent forms of *Qameh-zani* (cutting your shaved head with a saber). There is a real sense of angry regret in *Ta'ziyeh* that Muslims mourn their historical inability to have aided their Imam. The *Ta'ziyeh* of Hor in fact is replete with potential participation in absentia, with which contemporary Shi'is vicariously identify. Every time forces of good and evil face each other, the extension of the *Ta'ziyeh* thematics into real time history provides the Shi'is with an opportunity in effect to participate in the battle of Karbala and help their Imam Hossein win the battle against Yazid. There is a scene in the battle of Karbala, when one of Imam Hossein's companions asks him why does he not solicit divine intervention in his fight against Yazid. He opens his proverbial fingers in a V-shape in front of the interlocutor and asks him to look. Armies and armies of angelic and demonic forces are visible through the Imam's fingers, mounted on their celestial horses and ready at his command. But, he says, he will not summon them because this battle is an historical test of his followers. In any kind of revolutionary mobilization of the forces of good against forces of evil, there is an immediate, trans-metamorphic identification of the band of revolutionaries with the forces that this time around the living Imam Hossein is summoning to the battle. There is a Manichean element of cosmogonic forces at war about the battle of Karbala that gives it its enduring metamorphic potency.

The summoning of the metamorphic battle of Karbala in revolutionary mobilization against the Shah soon after the success of the Islamic revolution mutated into the war mobilization against Saddam Hussein. While Saddam Hussein was left to such historical devices as the battle of al-Qadesiyyah (in which the Sassanid army was defeated by a band of Muslim warriors in 650) to be invoked in his war against Iran, for Khomeini the battle of Karbala was a far more potent metaphor, judged by hundreds of thousands of young Iranians who marched to their death. It is a telling example of the power of these two respective metaphors that while Saddam Hussein had to hire some Egyptian filmmakers to aid and abet him in his propaganda and to make a film about al-Qadesiyyah, while Khomeini's propaganda was made much easier by generations of *Ta'ziyeh* performances having paved the way for his battle of Karbala. The physical location of Karbala in contemporary Iraq, and Mesopotamia being the actual battleground between Imam Hossein and Yazid, made the identification of Saddam Hussein with Yazid and by implication Khomeini with Imam Hossein, that much stronger. Given the more regional and global context of the Iran-Iraq war, such figures as Menachem Begin, then the Prime Minister of Israel, and Jimmy Carter, then the President of the United States, were equally drawn into the cosmogonic battle between the forces of good and evil fought on the frontline between Iran and Iraq.

Somewhere half way through the Iran-Iraq war, the legitimizing grace of *Ta'ziyeh* began to abandon Khomeini and his cause. Here we need to resort to the Iranian notion of "divine charisma," *farrah-e izadi*, as the best possible mode of explanation, with the legendary king Jamshid in Ferdowsi's *Shahnameh* as the model of first receiving and then losing this gift of grace. Jamshid was one of the earliest kings in Iranian legendary imagination who was principally responsible for crafting civilization and making life as we know it possible. He lived a very long life and achieved many marvelous deeds, and precisely because of the wonders he had brought about, including the secret of immortality, which he shared with his subjects, arrogance overcame him and led him to proclaim himself Divine. Precisely at that moment, the Divine gift of grace abandoned him and the evil king Zahhak, an Arab, invaded his kingdom and ultimately destroyed him. The Divine gift of grace can be as arbitrarily given as instantly taken back. In the Islamic universe of the same imagination, Shi'ism as a religion and *Ta'ziyeh* as a theater of protest have a legitimizing force only to the degree that a small revolutionary band of rebels are speaking truth to power and leading a just cause against tyranny. The moment Khomeini refused to agree to a ceasefire, when young Iranians were brought back in their shrouds in their hundreds and thousands to be buried, and ultimately when these innocent bodies were abused to consolidate the foundations of a tyrannical theocracy and the brutal suppression of all and every voice of reason and protest, neither Shi'ism as a religion nor *Ta'ziyeh* as a theater of protest would lend themselves as the doctrine and drama of legitimacy.

Today, close to three decades into the brutal consolidation of power by the entrenched clerical establishment, both Shi'ism as a religion and *Ta'ziyeh* as a theater of protest have categorically abandoned the organs and institutions of the Islamic Republic. As the dramatic nucleus of Shi'ism, the thematics of *Ta'ziyeh* served the revolution to de-legitimize the Pahlavis and then wage a defensive war against Saddam Hussein. But long before even Khomeini died it could do absolutely nothing to legitimize a discredited theocracy. Shi'ism is a religion of protest. It can never succeed politically without failing morally. As a cosmic carnival of a constitutional injustice, *Ta'ziyeh* is the mourning of a loss that must always fail in its stated objective if it is to be successful. No mourning could or should ever be successful. The success of mourning is its failure. It is successful only to the degree that it fails. In commemorating the death of a martyr we are seeking to identify with absolute Otherness, with saintliness in the midst of sin and with death at the moment of living, with dual, absolutely incongruent, Otherness, with the face and the body of the saintly and the dis-eased. In that impossibility, mourning choreographed and staged as *Ta'ziyeh* is made possible.

As Shi'ism as a religion of protest retreated from the streets of Iran and was secluded to the practice of private pieties, and as *Ta'ziyeh* went for a tour of the "Great Satan," as the US used to be called,[30] both Shi'ism and *Ta'ziyeh* resumed their more potent relevance in the battlefields of Iraq, Palestine, and Lebanon. As Shi'ism was retreating to private pieties in Iran, and as *Ta'ziyeh* was being thematically theatricalized, overtly estheticized, Orientalized, anthropologized, and ultimately museumized,[31] both Shi'ism and *Ta'ziyeh* had a far more momentous rendezvous with history elsewhere in the Muslim world. Passivity and museumization have never been the fate of either Shi'ism or of *Ta'ziyeh*. Powers that be have always sought to appropriate Shi'ism (as did once the Pahlavis and now do the clerical cliques in Iran), and then either ban or neutralize *Ta'ziyeh* (as did once Reza Shah and do now the Islamic republic). During the Shah's time Shi'ism was sought to be officially neutralized and *Ta'ziyeh* overtly theatricalized at Shiraz Art Festival. They survived them both. As Shi'ism retreated to private pieties in Iran, in exile Ayatollah Khomeini was taking it out for a massive political showdown. As *Ta'ziyeh* was staged in Shiraz Art Festival, *Ta'ziyeh* leitmotifs were fomenting revolutionary mobilizations in the streets and alleys, markets and squares, of its multiple habitats. If Shi'ism and *Ta'ziyeh* are to be found at all today, they are neither in the circles of the ruling clerics in Tehran, nor indeed in the circus ring at the Damrosch Park in the Lincoln Center, nor indeed in the Museum of Modern Arts in New York. They are both to be detected smack in the middle of a student-led uprising against the reigning Yazid and all his cohorts in Tehran – as they are even more widely evident in the battlefronts of Iraq, where Karbala, Najaf, and Samara have assumed a renewed significance, and as they are also visible in the cities and alleys of Palestine, and all over Lebanon, in one combatant posture or another.

In *Ta'ziyeh* history is suspended. The mimetic dissonance at the heart of *Ta'ziyeh* makes the history mean things it otherwise conceals – even to itself. A liberation theodicy that must announce and embrace (rather than denounce and dismiss) all its shades and shadows of uncertainty can take its clues from the mimetic dissonance of *Ta'ziyeh*, where things mean enough to mobilize moral conviction, but never long enough to dismiss the worldly polytheism of the universe it tries to understand.

For *Ta'ziyeh* to suggest and sustain itself as the mimetic template of a manner of liberation theology at ease with its shades and shadows of doubts and uncertainty, and for that liberation to remain liberating beyond its own dead certainties, we need also to remember the danger of anthropological distancing evident at the heart of all cross-cultural spectatorship. Evident in the asymmetrical mimesis of *Ta'ziyeh*, I have argued in this chapter, is an exemplary model for a liberation theology that does not degenerate into its own nightmare. For that not to happen, and for *Ta'ziyeh* to sustain and exude the creative confidence of its free-floating mimesis it will have to be left to its own performative palimpsestics – consistently rewriting itself against the grain of history. The obstacle we face in that direction does not come from the untranslatable dramaturgy of *Ta'ziyeh* itself, but in fact from its too frequent translations into objects of anthropological observations and museumized curiosity. The prolonged attraction of European Orientalists and American anthropologists to *Ta'ziyeh* has now been followed by the equally blasé curiosity of museums and art festivals. The unwarranted attention has produced the uncanny sideshow of procreating false familiarities and dangerous liaisons as to what and wherefore is *Ta'ziyeh*.

As a perfect example of a crisscrossed metaphorization of *Ta'ziyeh* I offer a bizarre but perfectly telling incident. I remember in Spring 1988, I was invited to attend a *Ta'ziyeh* performance and conference staged and organized at Trinity College in Hartford Connecticut. The event was organized by Professor Milla Cozart Riggio of Trinity College, supervised by Professor Peter Chelkowski of New York University, and attended by quite a number of scholars in the field. The centerpiece of the event was the staging of a modern adaptation of *Ta'ziyeh* by the distinguished Iranian director Mohammad Ghaffari.[32] The following November, during the MESA

(Middle East Studies Association) annual meeting, there was a follow up panel on this event. In the course of this panel, Professor Riggio shared with her audience an anecdote about how after screening a documentary on *Ta'ziyeh* done by a French filmmaker, a member of the audience in Connecticut had come to her and asked, in a perfectly caring and yet matter-of-fact manner: "But how do they chose these children?" The reference of "these children" was to a scene in the documentary in which a child actor was being "beheaded" in the course of a *Ta'ziyeh* episode. "What do you mean how they are selected," Milla Riggio had wondered, thinking the question was about the selection of actors in the play. "I mean do their parents consent?" The questioner had wondered. "Of course they do," Milla Riggio had answered, "it is considered an act of religious duty, something of a privilege," she had added. The questioner was quite amused and yet still looked bewildered, trying politely to hide her horror. It had taken Milla Riggio and the person asking the question quite a number of additional missteps for Professor Riggio to realize the nature of the misunderstanding. The innocent American asking the question had thought that the head of the kid being "beheaded" in the play was actually cut off, and that this was a religious sacrifice of some sort, of young boys being offered as sacrifice to some deity of a sort.

Professor Riggio was offering the anecdote by way of explaining the cultural distance between the staging of *Ta'ziyeh* in the United States and an audience unfamiliar with its most basic facts – in this case simply the fact that *Ta'ziyeh* is after all a play and no one is actually being killed on stage. These sorts of innocent misunderstandings that the staging of *Ta'ziyeh* can and does generate have an added significance, which has to do with the assimilation of cultural oddities backward into familiar references. As to what spectacle was it that a theatrical performance of *Ta'ziyeh*, anthropologized and taken out of its context, can generate, I may have to resort to a passage about lynching black people in the Southern United States. "Some lynchings," according to historians

> occurred secretly at night; others were advertised in advance and attracted huge audiences of onlookers. In 1899, Sam Hose, a plantation laborer who killed his employer in self-defense, was brutally murdered near Newman, Georgia, before two thousand onlookers, some of whom arrived on a special excursion train from Atlanta. The crowd watched as Hose's executioners cut off his ears, fingers, and genitals and burned him alive, and then fought over "souvenirs," such as pieces of his bones. Law enforcement authorities made no effort to prevent the lynching or to bring the assailants to justice. Like many victims of lynchings, Hose was retrospectively accused of raping a white woman, a deed almost universally considered by white southerners as justification for extralegal vengeance.[33]

6 Liberation theodicy

I had a jungle mind, I was living in a jungle.

Malcolm X

My examination of Ta'ziyeh as the mimetic template of a mode of liberation theology that ultimately does not degenerate into an absolutism of convictions and allows for the shades and shadows of its own doubts and uncertainties brings us down to the most fundamental failure of militant Islamism over the last two centuries. In combative conversation with "the West" (the code-name for European colonialism that culminated in American imperialism), "Islam" was systematically mutated (more than by anyone else by Muslims themselves) into a singular site of ideological resistance to foreign domination in Muslim lands. The militant Islamism that ensued was obviously not the only mode of ideological resistance to attempts at global domination. Anti-colonial nationalism and revolutionary socialism (of pre-Soviet, Soviet, and post-Soviet sorts) were equally instrumental in mobilizing people against the barefaced robbery of their homeland and dignity. Constitutional to both sides of this binary – both European colonialism/US imperialism and the varied forms of ideological resistances to them – was a metanarrative of absolutist certainty that in the case of militant Islamism meant a constitutional intolerance for opposing or alternative points of view sharing the very same struggle. The wholesale robbery of the Iranian revolution of 1979 by the Islamist faction is perhaps the most blatant example of a militant Islamism that for 200 years had been a legitimate and integral component of anti-colonial mobilization, and yet upon the moment of its political victory it viciously eliminated all its ideological rivals and established a horrid theocracy. That theocracy notwithstanding, we cannot altogether ignore or dismiss the positive role of militant Islamism as a cogent and perfectly legitimate mode of resistance to global domination by Western Europeans and North Americans just over the last 200 years alone. That theocracy, however, that Islamic Republic, is the nightmare at the heart of militant Islamism, which was historically exorcised and thus categorically concluded a mode of revolutionary opposition to global domination that had systematically created manners of resistance to it identical in their proclivity for metanarrative absolutism. With "the West" having now finally exhausted its historical calamities and conceptually imploded, and with the rise of a mode of globalized empire with no particular center to any presumed periphery, the emerging cartography of global resistance to US-led military adventurism, and the calamities that it causes, requires a radically different mode of participation by Muslims in planetary resistance to this predatory empire. My reflections on a mode of *liberation theodicy* that accounts for the success and failures of militant Islamism over the last 200 years, and thinks through the possibility of a mode of resistance that itself does not degenerate into an absolutist term of metaphysical propositions, is geared towards this end.

This new mode of liberation movement, which is better understood as a *theodicy* than a *theology*, is predicated on the necessity of a new strategy of resistance at a moment when Islam has spread into a new global configuration of its historical habitat. While Osama bin Laden's militant adventurisms, following the nightmares of the Taliban in Afghanistan and the reign of the clerical cliques in the Islamic Republic of Iran, have finally dismantled and concluded legitimate *Islamism*, Islam is yet again emerging as the *tabula rasa* of political resistance to the globalizing empire. The result of this new condition is the possibility of a *liberation theodicy* that corresponds to the geographical transmutation of Islam beyond its imaginary, hitherto compelling, boundaries. The dangerous liaison colonially manufactured between "Islam and the West" having now fully exhausted its historical usefulness, both the US empire and the emerging pockets of resistance to it will have to cross over presumed cultures and their corresponding countries, one in seeking to dominate, the other in assuring resistance to that domination.

What the precise contours of this liberation theodicy will be is still too early to say. But the sites of its emerging disposition are now evident among such battlefields of critical crisis as those of the Hamas movement for the liberation of Palestine, Hezbollah in defending the territorial integrity of Lebanon, and the Shi'i community resisting the colonial occupation of their homeland in Iraq. Reading these revolutionary movements as they are putting up heroic resistances against a predatory empire and its mini-imperial cloning called "Israel" will have to be placed next to a reading of old and emerging Muslim communities in Europe and the USA before we can map out the contours of this emerging liberation theodicy (on a model thought through but left unfinished by Malcolm X). Paramount in giving an outline of this liberation theodicy is to find out in what particular ways can these movements and communities overcome the dangers of their corruption into perpetrators of senseless violence and indiscriminate murder of innocent people (on the model of the US/Israel and its "coalition of the willing" on one side and that of Osama bin Laden and the so-called "al-Qaeda" on the other). Against the backdrop of that categorical degeneration of revolutionary projects into miasmatic acts of senseless violence on both sides of the Bush–bin Laden divide, national

(Palestinian, Iraqi, Afghan, Lebanese) and regional (South Asian, West Asian, North African, Central Asian, etc.) liberation movements will have to assume a polyfocal disposition that resists their degeneration into the mirror image of the US–Israeli tribalism. Resisting the US empire is integral and coterminous with dismantling the discredited and failed Zionist project that has culminated in the racist, apartheid, colonial settlement they call "Israel" – in favor of a one-state solution for all inhabitants of historical Palestine: Jews, Christians, Muslims, agnostics, and atheists alike. This objective, the ultimate aspiration of any liberation theodicy one might propose, is the only legitimate solution to the most enduring sore at the heart of the regional politics over which presides the predatory US imperialism. The cosmopolitan political culture that will thus ensue will then become the exemplary model of similar state apparatus for the entire region, so that instead of an Islamic Republic at one end of the neighborhood, a Jewish state at another, and a Hindu fundamentalism at yet another, all seeking to clone themselves in the region, the democratic republics of Iraq, Lebanon, and particularly Palestine – free, cosmopolitan, multi-ethnic, and equitable, with constitutional rights for *all* its citizens – will be exported to all the backward and retarded Arab and Muslim states, chief among them the Islamic Republic of Iran.

9/11 was the end of Frantz Fanon, the end of George Sorel, the end of our received understanding of what Max Weber called "legitimate violence" as the modus operandi of politics. 9/11 was the end of politics, and the commencement of a meltdown in both progressive and retrograde acts of violence. Frantz Fanon (1925–1961) was the last great theorist of revolutionary violence, a measured and judicious violence at the service of a revolutionary cause, a stated social and political project, geared towards the emancipation of multitudes of the humanity from the barbarian domination of European colonialism throughout the globe, in Africa in particular. In his *The Wretched of the Earth* (1961), Fanon extensively theorized the colonial cause, the measured proportions, and the emancipatory power of violence that he thus circumscribed.[1] The question of violence however was long the subject of theoretical reflection before Frantz Fanon. In his sociology of authority, particularly in his groundbreaking essay, "Politics as a Vocation" (1919), the prominent German sociologist Max Weber (1864–1920) identified the defining moment of politics as a claim over "the monopoly of the legitimate use of physical force," considering the state as "a relation of men dominating men, a relation supported by means of legitimate (i.e. considered to be legitimate) violence."[2] Even before Max Weber, the French social philosopher Georges Sorel (1847–1922), in his *Reflections on Violence* (1908), militantly celebrated the creative power of proletarian violence and its ability to overcome the coercive economic force of capitalism.[3] Georges Sorel's celebration of violence of course goes back to Lenin, and before Lenin to Marx and their espousal of revolutionary violence, and even of "the dictatorship of the proletariat": "Between capitalist and communist society lies the period of the revolutionary transformation of the one into the other. There corresponds to this also a political transition period in which the state can be nothing but *the revolutionary dictatorship of the proletariat.*"[4]

From Karl Marx, through Georges Sorel and Max Weber, and down to Frantz Fanon, the legitimate, measured, and judicious use of violence has been integral to all revolutionary projects with a stated social and political program. For over 200 years – from the active commencement of Russian, French, and British colonialism in Muslim lands – militant Islamism has opted to use a legitimate (i.e. considered to be legitimate, to keep Weber's parenthetical correction in mind) measure of violence in opposing the colonial domination of Muslim homelands. With the events of 9/11, militant Islamism, as we have known and understood it over the preceding two centuries, ceased to have any claim to measured and judicious use of revolutionary violence and degenerated into an absolutist, anarchist, nihilistic, and self-annihilating triumphalism with no legitimate claim to any principled project of revolutionary uprising.

The degeneration of Islamism from a legitimate mode of revolutionary mobilization into a vile array of senseless and murderous violence corresponds to the decline and collapse of the binary opposition presumed between "Islam and the West" and the emergence of an amorphous mode of imperialism. Militant Islamism, like anti-colonial nationalism and revolutionary nationalism that were coterminous with it, drove its legitimate use of revolutionary violence (on the model suggested and theorized from Marx to Fanon) within the binary context of "Islam and the West," which made such measured, judicious, and purposeful uses of violence legitimate, and meaningful. The collapse of such hitherto compelling binaries as those presumed between "Islam and the West," as a particularly potent *modus operandi* of capitalist economy, colonial domination, imperialist tendencies, and, *a fortiori*, revolutionary resistances to them, has amounted to the categorical disappearance of the meaningful measures of such uses of violence.

The demise of "Islam and the West," as the *modus operandi* of colonial domination and revolutionary resistance to it, and thus the measure of what was legitimate and what illegitimate violence, however, does not mean that identical or alternative binaries are not manufactured to sustain the selfsame relation of domination – and thus (and there is the rub) perpetuate a mode of outrageous violence by both the US imperial hubris and the militant adventurism of the Bin Laden variety that feigns to oppose (but in fact corroborates) it. The rhetorical use of the term "crusades," for example, by both President Bush and Osama bin Laden, or the narration of a tale of (women's) emancipation by, for example, Azar Nafisi, Ayaan Hirsi Ali, Irshad Manji, Fouad Ajami, and Ibn Warraq, or the persistence of global polling, most recently by the BBC, asking Muslims and "Westerners" (as they call themselves) how they feel about each other, all come together to generate and sustain a phantom force field in which a binary opposition that has long since lost its generative disposition will go on manufacturing Manichean dualities where none exists.⁵

The problem, however, is not limited to the manufacturing of a continued validity to the assumption of an "Islam and the West" binary. The problem is deeper. Perhaps the most pernicious mode of presumed binaries that are instrumental to sustaining the selfsame relation of power between a small white (identified) minority and the rest of the humanity at large is the one manufactured between local communities that are thus divided in order to be ruled better. Reminiscent of the hostilities that the British, for example, manufactured between Muslims and Hindus in India, or the French did between the Tutsi and the Hutu in Rwanda and Burundi in central Africa, or again the British did between the Catholics and Protestant in Ireland, or yet again the French did between Christians and Muslims in Lebanon, is the hostility fomented and enflamed between the Sunnis and the Shi'is in Iraq in the aftermath of the US-led invasion and occupation of Iraq. Perhaps the most pernicious template of these sorts of vicious manipulations by colonial powers is the one exercised by the British over the so-called Indian caste system. As Nicholas Dirks has aptly demonstrated, the Indian caste system was far more the result of British colonial rule than an intrinsic aspect of the land and culture they so savagely plundered. In his *Castes of Mind*, Nicholas Dirks demonstrates that the British colonial rule and administrative apparatus in India was very much contingent on an active manipulation of a caste system that was far more a ruse of their domination than an inherited class system.⁶

The chief psyop pamphlet promoting a quintessential and millennial hostility between the Sunnis and the Shi'is in the aftermath of the US-led carnage in Iraq, very much reminiscent of similar services that native informers had provided British colonialism in previous incarnation of the selfsame barbarity, is by a certain Seyyed Vali Reza Nasr, whose *Shia Revival: How Conflicts within Islam Will Shape the Future* (2006) was published some three years into the US-led occupation of Iraq and while the author was in the employment of the US navy. The sociology and politics of knowledge production in the USA, particularly in the catastrophic aftermath of 9/11, is of central significance in understanding how binary oppositions are generated and sustained as a *modus operandi* of an eternal conflict beyond the pale of history – in the name of an *ancient* history whitewashing the compelling facts of the *current* history. Teaching at the Department of National Security Affairs of the Naval Postgraduate School, Seyyed Vali Reza Nasr's principal audience in this book, his military superiors and students combined, are his employers at the US navy, and by extension the US Commander-in-Chief, President George W. Bush. His book on Shi'ism, as a result, is a peculiar case of knowledge produced at the service of the US military, its naval officers perhaps in particular. The publication of Seyyed Vali Reza Nasr's *Shi'i Revival* thus opens a whole new chapter in sociology of knowledge, whereby the US military, while engaged in a major imperial conquest, produces the terms of public debate about its adventures. In this respect, Seyyed Vali Reza Nasr is a case not of an otherwise respectable academic embedded with the US army, but in fact the other way around: a US intelligence agent embedded with the public.[7]

The central function of Seyyed Vali Reza Nasr's pamphlet is to shift the terms of debate about "Islam" and the presumed Islamist confrontation with "the West" (the US in particular) away from the barefaced fact of the US-led invasion and occupation of Iraq and into the millennial but internal rivalries within Islam itself. Beginning about 1400 years ago, Professor Nasr reports to his military superiors and students at the Department of National Security Affairs of the Naval Postgraduate School, the sectarian hostilities between the Sunnis and Shi'is has now reached the regional rivalries between the Islamic republic of Iran and Saudi Arabia, one leading the Shi'is and the other heralding the Sunnis.[8] The central thesis of Seyyed Vali Reza Nasr, that the Shi'is have staged a comeback against the Sunni ascendancy in the region, is predicated on a rather clichéd history of Shi'ism and the Sunni–Shi'i sectarian bifurcation from the earliest Islamic history. But everything in that forced narrative is geared towards the proposition that over the last two to three decades the Shi'i communities from Pakistan to Lebanon have assumed a militant posture against their Sunni rivals. Thus everything up to Chapter 6 of *The Shia Revival*, "The Tide Turns," is a blasé and flat reading of Shi'i history, with a particularly vindictive take on Khomeini's Islamist revolution (which, incidentally, forced Seyyed Vali Reza Nasr's monarchist father, Seyyed Hossein Nasr, and the rest of his family out of Iran and made them all quite dependent on the munificence of the exiled Pahlavi court, which the father and son continue to serve in exile). Beginning with the US-led invasion of Iraq, which Seyyed Vali Reza Nasr of the Department of National Security Affairs of the Naval Postgraduate School never ever identifies as an invasion and whenever even synthetically is forced to use the term "occupation" he diligently places it inside a qualifying quotation mark,[9] the Shi'is have regained a prominence that both the Sunni states, thus identified, and Professor Seyyed Vali Reza Nasr of the US navy sternly apprehend. Here is the gist of the fear they share:

> What Iran's revolution had failed to do, the Shia revival in post-Saddam Iraq was set to achieve. The challenge that the Shia revival poses to the Sunni Arab domination of the Middle East and to the Sunni conception of political identity and authority is not substantially different from the threat that Khomeini posed. Iran's revolution also sought to break the hegemonic control of the Sunni Arab establishment. The only difference is that last time around the Shias were the more radical and anti-American force, and now the reverse seems to be true.[10]

The problem with this thesis, also known as the threat of "the Shi'is Crescent," as King Abdullah of Jordan has put it, is manifold. To take the very proposition on its face value, that an entire array of cosmopolitan cultures in the region can be reduced to its sectarian identities, still Nasr's thesis is deeply flawed. Suppose we take the people of this region as being nothing but actively and singularly Muslim, and those who are Sunni or Shi'is as nothing but Sunni and Shi'i. As a religion, Shi'ism in such diverse settings as in India, Pakistan, Afghanistan, Iran, Iraq, Bahrain, Saudi Arabia, Iraq, or Lebanon is cast upon vastly different social, political, and economic landscapes. In Iran, for example, they are the overwhelming majority, whereas everywhere else either a tiny minority (Saudi Arabia) or else integral to a mosaic of sectarian and ethnic pluralism (Lebanon and Iraq). Any assumption of a transnational solidarity among all Shi'is of all ranks in all these nations is a piece of fictitious nonsense that can persuade wide-eyed navy officers in sunny California perhaps but amounts to catastrophic consequences when they are dispatched to kill and get killed on far-away lands. If the purpose of the US navy scholar is to create a smoke screen where people cannot see the principal culprit responsible for the carnage in Iraq (his employer), this may indeed buy the Bush administration some time to figure out how to drag itself out of the Iraq debacle. But if this is offered as a cogent intelligence of the geopolitics of the region, as a US tax payer one can only wish to have had the option of a "money-back guarantee."

What separates the Shi'is of this region is far more important than what holds them presumably together. The most important of these differences is that in Iran Shi'ism is the religion of the overwhelming majority (more than 90 percent), whereas in both Iraq and Lebanon the slight majority of the Shi'is has to contend with very powerful non-Shi'i forces – with the Sunnis, Maronite, Druze, etc., in Lebanon, with the Sunnis and Kurds in Iraq. This does not mean sectarianism, this means cosmopolitanism. In other words, Seyyed Vali Reza Nasr sees and casts the entire region in the image of Israel – a religiously fanatic state *par excellence*. The real threat to Israel and its religious polity is not Shi'ism (or Hezbollah). The real threat to Israel is the Lebanese political cosmopolitanism, civil society, economic prosperity, cultural pluralism, in short a deeply rooted civility in character and disposition that the colonial settlement itself constitutionally lacks, for at its roots is a tribalism of the most ancient disposition and cannot but see the world in the image of its own clan. That the medieval notion of a Jewish state (identical in its religious disposition to an Islamic republic) has been confounded by the most enduring form of European colonialism and then underwritten by a militarism of unsurpassed savagery gives an altogether postmodern disposition to the settler colony that in the age of the so-called postcolonialism makes a mockery of the very notion of postcoloniality.

More than anything else, Seyyed Vali Reza Nasr's is a diversionary tactic, shifting the point of emphasis away from where the real problem is and directing it towards a fictitious point of sectarian references. The point here is not that the Shi'i–Sunni hostilities are not domestic to Islamic sectarian history. The point here is how that history is incorporated into the US-led military occupation of Iraq, and how Seyyed Vali Reza Nasr is narrating that history in a manner conducive to American military and strategic interests. To demonstrate this point, we can put Seyyed Vali Reza Nasr's thesis to a very simple test: What are the three most dangerous sites of warfare in the region? Iraq, Palestine, and Lebanon. Let's take them one by one. In Iraq everything that has happened since March 2003, including the rise in sectarian violence, is directly the result of the illegal and immoral military thuggery of the USA, about which criminal atrocity the US navy professor remains entirely silent. To the degree that Iraqi Shi'is (as Shi'is and as nothing else) are politically engaged in Iraq, they are part and parcel of a national liberation movement against a predatory empire and its warmongering. Whether they are Sunnis or Shi'is, or even Kurds, the Iraqis are united in their reactions to the continued presence of an occupying force in their homeland. Only a propaganda officer committed to the cause of US imperialism can disregard this fact and send the public after the wild-goose chase of Sunni–Shi'i rivalries.

The next stop is Palestine, occupied brutally for decades now, and against all international law and acceptable norms, by the Jewish apartheid state of Israel, the military settler colony on which the US relies heavily for its regional domination, and about which in Seyyed Vali Reza Nasr's world the word is "mum." The Shi'is have absolutely no indigenous presence in Palestine and are not part of the Palestinian national liberation movement. Seyyed Vali Reza Nasr of the US navy has absolutely nothing to say about the Jewish settler colony or its criminal thuggeries for more than half a century in the region – nor does he have anything to offer about the Zionist robbery of Palestinians of their homeland in the broad daylight of history. Then we come to Lebanon, yet another theater of operation for the military adventurism of the Jewish state, repeatedly invading, occupying, fomenting civil war, or else destroying the economic infrastructure of an entire nation-state with total impunity. Here the Lebanese Shi'is have organized in order to defend themselves into such militant groups as Hezbollah and Amal, who have historically been as much against each other as against Israel. Be that as it may, both Hezbollah and Amal are integral to a Lebanese national liberation movement fighting against the Jewish colonial settlement to their southern borders. On none of these violent and critical sites has Shi'ism (or Islam for that matter) been the primary cause of violence, and in fact Shi'is (and Muslims) have been the principal target of a predatory violence launched either by the USA (in Afghanistan and Iraq) or its client settler colony Israel.

The main argument of Seyyed Vali Reza Nasr, that what we are witnessing is a global rise of radical Shi'ism in the region, is equally flawed, but exceedingly timely in crafting a new bugbear from within Islam itself. Constitution of Shi'ism as the primary enemy of the US interests in the region,[11] is predicated on yet another misguided notion that prior to this rise of radical Shi'ism, Muslim societies were by and large under the influence of Sunni Islam. To be sure, Sunnis and Shi'is have been at each other's throat for 1400 years – but there has always been an extraneous factor agitating and exacerbating these medieval feuds. True to his employment terms, Seyyed Vali Reza Nasr never asks the far more fundamental question of what precise campaign of "shock and awe" was it that initiated this particular round of animosity between Sunnis and Shi's. Instead, he opts for two entirely inane explanations – a blasé and sophomoric rehearsal of the doctrinal differences between Sunnis and Shi'is and then heaping of a world of abuse on Ayatollah Khomeini, whose revolution forces he, his father and family and their monarchical supporters into the USA. It is of course true that there are medieval factors and that no litany of abuse on Khomeini is long enough. But in the immediate context of this particular rise of Sunni–Shi'i animosity there is a much bigger bully in the neighborhood that Nasr leaves completely off the hook: his own employer, the US military.

Seyyed Vali Reza Nasr's detection of a Shi'i factor, internal to Islamic history and the geopolitics of the region and yet detrimental to the US military and its strategic interests in the area has another, exceedingly important function. What this diversionary tactic also does amounts to giving agential primacy to the USA as the arbiter of truth, harbinger of freedom and democracy, and thus shifting the blame of the failure of the US to achieve anything other than death, destruction, and mayhem in Iraq to internal dynamics domestic to these Muslims who cannot get along with each other.[12] Here the native informer appears as an adviser to the imperial officers informing them as to how to shift the blame to the natives, correct their course of action, save face, and continue their colonial occupation of a sovereign nation-state on an adjusted course of action whereby it gets all the credits and none of the blame.

But by far the most crucial aspect of Seyyed Vali Reza Nasr's thesis is his active participation in a pervasive analytical malady that is best manifested in the widespread metastasis of such religious states and movements as the Jewish state, the Islamic republic, the Christian empire, and the Hindu fundamentalism – all gathered in the same region – into the very definition of political cultures at large. Discounting, forgetting, ignoring, diminishing, or denigrating (it ultimately makes no difference) the cosmopolitan cultures of these regions and movements, Seyyed Vali Reza Nasr's analysis of the Sunni–Shi'i differences in the region takes the Jewish state of Israel (or the Islamic republic of Iran) as the template and blueprint of his reading of the region and in effect becomes a self-fulfilling prophecy that nothing but religious fanaticism of the most pernicious kind matters in these countries. This assertion is the sign of the mind of Nasr himself and does not correspond to lived experiences of people in this region and their evident realities. The assessment is really in the mind of Seyyed Vali Reza Nasr himself and in the best interest of the Jewish state and Christian empire that he thus serves, as much as in the interest (paradoxically) of the Islamic republic that has forced him and his family out of a very lucrative life in Iran.

Above all, Seyyed Vali Reza Nasr's sectarian reading of the geopolitics of the region is Samuel Huntington's thesis of the "Clash of Civilizations" running amuck. What Nasr's thesis amounts to is the corroboration of a systematic reduction of multifaceted peoples and their cosmopolitan cultures and lived experiences into an absolutist conception of their religious denomination – thus Iranians are nothing but Shi'is, and Iraqi or Lebanese Shi'is nothing but their religious identities. The diverse and at times clashing class and gender differences of people, or their materially based and widely evident cosmopolitan cultures are all reduced to their just being "Shi'is." The *Jewish* state, the *Islamic* republic, the *Hindu* fundamentalism, and the mutation of the American republic into a *Christian* empire are all exceptional maladies in the region and beyond, against which there is a sustained course of resistance by people domestic and integral to these societies. These states are not the rule. The rule is otherwise. The evident fact of these societies is a worldly cosmopolitanism, based on the factual evidence of their having battled a vicious succession of European and American colonial and imperial domination. The cutting edge of the sorts of arguments that Seyyed Vali Reza Nasr puts forward is at the service of the European/American colonial robbery of a cosmopolitan Palestinian reality for the creation of a Jewish state, thus counter-corroborating the theocracy of an Islamic republic, the vicious barbarity of a Hindu fundamentalism, and the imperial hubris of a Christian empire. Arguing against the self-fulfilling prophecy of Seyyed Vali Reza Nasr is not only necessary in order to restore the cosmopolitan political culture of the region but equally importantly to warn against the gradual mutation of the American polity into a Christian fundamentalist theocracy, as evidenced in the extraordinary study of Kevin Phillips, *American Theocracy: The Peril and Politics of Radical Religion, Oil, and Borrowed Money in the 21st Century* (2006).

The sectarian-driven imagination of both the regional powers and military scholars like Seyyed Vali Reza Nasr speak of a transnational Shi'i alliance against the grain of material history and lived experiences. Digging out the "deep roots" of the Shi'i alliance among Iran, Iraq, and Lebanon ignores the more immediate, multifaceted disposition of cosmopolitan cultures that inform, animate, and preoccupy people – Shi'i or otherwise. Such sectarian reductionism is principally informed by a provincialism that is modulated in the immediate aftermath of the Orientalist fantasies – fantasies that see Muslims in utter isolation from the worldly and cosmopolitan context of their historical character. There are fundamental and irreconcilable differences between *Shi'ism* in Iran, Iraq, and Lebanon – and there are far more compelling similarities among *Shi'is* so far as they have all been the target of a predatory imperial adventurism and as such integral to a spectrum of diverse and divergent moral and normative ideas and aspirations.

The ideological manufacturing of an everlasting divide within Islam, and as such independent of the US imperial violence, ultimately fails to cover "the state of exception," as Giorgio Agamben has theorized it, that now prevails upon the whole spectrum of the campaign of "shock and awe" that Donald Rumsfeld had unleashed. From Karl Marx, through Georges Sorel and Max Weber, and down to Frantz Fanon, the judicious use of legitimate violence has been seen as integral to all state apparatuses and revolutionary projects alike. Perhaps the most perceptive theorist of violence after all was Max Weber, for having made no distinction between state-sponsored or insurrectionary violence and for having simply placed a parenthetical "legitimate" ("i.e. considered to be legitimate") at the cutting edge of his theory of violence. The crashing of civilian airplanes, full of innocent and helpless passengers, into public targets, for immediate and spectacular results, is a singular act of senseless and murderous violence that categorically ends any notion of violence either as means of legitimizing a state apparatus or else to dismantling that claim and replacing it with another. To capture the momentous occasion of that state of exception where violence is at once spectacularly evident and yet categorically lacking legitimacy, we need to enter the uncharted zone of illegal wars and spectacular acts of violence – variations on the identical themes of violence without ends, violence with any means, violence as pure violence.

What is "pure violence"? It was Walter Benjamin who for the first time sought to theorize the notion of "pure violence." It is thanks to Giorgio Agamben that we now have a renewed reading of Walter Benjamin's premonitory essay "Critique of Violence" (1920–1921).[13] Quite persuasively, Agamben argues that Benjamin's "Zur Kritik der Gewalt" – "the only explicit exposition of Benjamin's political philosophy that has survived," as Agamben calls it – was known to Karl Schmitt and instrumental in his conception of "the state of exception," as formulated in his *Concept of the Political* (1927).[14] Be that as it may, Benjamin and Schmitt used and meant the notion of "pure violence" in two diametrically opposed manners, and premised it on two violently opposed domains. For Walter Benjamin, the idea of "pure violence" was a space where revolutionary use of violence goes beyond the two legal modes of violence, or what he called "law-making" and "law-preserving" violence. Schmitt, on the other hand, was after a theorization of the exercise of extra-juridical violence by the state (read the Nazi concentration camps, Israeli extra-juridical assassination of Palestinians, and the US torture chambers in Abu Ghraib and Bagram air Base) as the abyss upon which the very edifice of "Western" juridico-political system is predicated. "Though external to the law," for Schmitt (as Agamben reads him with Benjamin on his mind) "the state of exception" (*Ausnahmezustand*) "creates the normal situation in which the law can be in force." This state "does not simply mean anarchy or anomie." The state of exception for Schmitt "is not simply outside the juridical order, but that paradoxically this legal vacuum – insofar as it is not identical to anarchy – constitutes a sort of threshold between outside and inside."[15]

For Benjamin, any critic of violence that does not recognize the distinction between the legitimate and illegitimate violence or between the function of violence as "lawmaking violence and law-preserving violence," amounts to "a quite childish anarchism."[16] For Benjamin, violence was either "lawmaking" or "law preserving." If violence "lays claim to neither of these predicates, it forfeits all validity."[17] The bifurcation between "lawmaking" and "law-preserving" violence very much limits the exercise of violence within the boundaries of a given law – either to make it or to preserve it. "But if the existence of violence outside the law," Benjamin stipulates, "as pure immediate violence, is assured, this furnishes proof that revolutionary violence, the highest manifestation of unalloyed violence by man, is possible."[18] Agamben's point in invoking Benjamin while reading Schmitt is to pinpoint "the sense in which Schmitt's definition of sovereignty can be considered a response to Benjamin's 'Kritik der Gewalt.' The state of exception is precisely the space in which Schmitt tries to capture and incorporate Benjamin's conception of pure violence that exists outside the law."[19]

This "capture and incorporation" of Benjamin by Schmitt is a misappropriation – a theoretical shoplifting, abusing Benjamin precisely in the opposite direction of his point of departure. For Benjamin, the notion of "pure violence" went in revolutionary, or what he called *mythic*, or *divine*, directions – and certainly *not* as a domain where "the state of exception" suspends the law by way of preserving the status quo and safeguarding the interests of the privileged class. On the theoretical premise of "pure violence," revolutionary outburst has a claim to legitimate violence. What Schmitt does in *The Concept of the Political* is misappropriating Benjamin's notion of revolutionary violence and makes it the cornerstone of his theory of "the state of exception," a misappropriation that Karl Schmitt's subsequent interlocutor Leo Straus in turn philosophizes, takes out of Schmitt's theological domain, and brings it as a gift to America and gives it to his neocon followers – Paul Wolfowitz et al.[20]

Agamben's take on Benjamin and Schmitt is more directed at proving the influence of the former on the latter. He is of course correct in proposing that "just as in 'Zur Kritik der Gewalt,' pure violence could neither be recognized nor decided a priori, so too is the state of exception undecidable."[21] But what Agamben leaves unattended is the fact that that *undecidability* errs on the side of the revolutionaries for Benjamin and on the side of Fascism for Schmitt. Agamben is far more accurate in his assessment that "Benjamin seeks to ensure violence's existence outside the law, while Schmitt attempts to capture pure violence through the fiction of the state of exception."[22]

Agamben concludes with a very provocative question that he opts to leave unanswered: "Why does the Western juridico-political order constitute itself through a contention over a legal vacuum in exactly the same way as Western metaphysic presents itself as a struggle over pure being?"[23] Should we look for that answer (perhaps) in Christianity, in the hidden Christianity of the European political philosophy, or more precisely (perhaps) in the not so hidden Christian Christological absence of the Father, or the Son, or the

Holy Ghost – a dangerously nostalgic abyss at the heart of Christian Europe? Instead of going in that speculative direction, Agamben is moved to make the following observation: "What I find interesting here is that, like in the imperial *iustitium*, a state of exception is appropriated and transformed into a ceremony; but while in the imperial *iustitium* the feast was performed in the mournful form of military mobilization, here the state of exception is transformed into an unrestrained feast in which *pure violence is exhibited and enjoyed as such*."[24] Here in Agamben's aside comment dwells *the spectacle* of 9/11 violence and Donald Rumsfeld's "campaign of shock and awe" alike – two identical cases of Benjaminian "pure violence" degenerating into two identical cases of Schmittian "state of exception." What holds the two amorphous modes of violence together is their common visuality (what Agamben fails to theorize), their lifting the exercise of violence out of the political state, out of the revolutionary project, and right into the realm of sheer pornographic voyeurism of spectacular acts of violence – for Bush and bin Laden alike. The Schmitt–Agamben "state of exception" is thereby the rule, the state of the meltdown of enduring binaries ("Islam and the West"), the site of the emergence of strategic and ephemeral binaries (Seyyed Vali Reza Nasr's bifurcation between "the Sunnis and the Shi'is"), where violence is no longer regulated either within the law or within a revolutionary project – and thus precisely where "the falcon cannot hear the falconer;/Things fall apart; the centre cannot hold;/Mere anarchy is loosed upon the world. . . . "

In April 2000, the Heinrich Böll Foundation hosted a conference in Berlin to which were invited a number of prominent Iranian public intellectuals. They were asked to take advantage of this opportunity and away from the censorial policies of the Islamic republic to reflect collectively on the predicament of democracy in their homeland. The conference was particularly poignant in the wake of the February 2002 parliamentary elections, which had resulted in a landslide victory for the reformist supporters of President Khatami. A wide spectrum of public intellectuals, both religious and secular, accepted the invitation of the Heinrich Böll Foundation, came to Berlin, and engaged in heated debates among themselves and with their cantankerous audience about the historical obstacles to democracy in their ancient land. In the course of the conference, a few women in the audience staged a protest by taking off articles of their clothing – among other more spectacular manifestations of their anger and frustration with the Islamic republic – and disrupting the conference. When the meeting ended and its participants returned to Iran, they found out that a manipulated videotape of the incident had made it to their notorious national television. They were subsequently summoned to the revolutionary court, tried behind closed doors, and sentenced to various terms of imprisonment.

I would like to offer this episode as one among many other signs of the climactic closure to the tumultuous history of the rise of Islamic ideology not just in Iran but in fact in the more global context of colonial modernity – and then upon that closure the commencement of a postmodern liberation theodicy. The end of Islamic Ideology, as a *modus operandi* of nativist Islamism, anticipates the rise of a new mode of resistance that is yet to be articulated. What today we call "Islam" was invented across the colonial divide as a metanarrative of resistance in order to oppose a metanarrative of domination. As a religion of protest predicated on a paradox of power, Islam was politically agitated in its historical encounter with the colonial shadow of European modernity. As a world religion, Islam was categorically re/invented in the course of the nineteenth and the twentieth centuries as a site of ideological resistance to colonial modernity. The gradual mutation of Islam, as the ancestral faith of a people, into Islamic Ideology (or Islamism), as the site of political resistance to colonialism, corresponded to the two complementary projects of capitalist modernity and the European Enlightenment. Both these projects reached the farthest corners of the world (including the Muslim world) through their extended arm of colonialism. Colonialism was in turn conducive to the political production of the nation-state and of national economies and polities. Ethnic nationalism and religious nativism were the direct results of anticolonial resistance to the aggressive encroachment of predatory capital. Whereas ethnic nationalism borrowed the exemplary model of its ideology from the centers of capitalist modernity and used it against colonialism, religious nativism recast the ancestral faith of the natives at large and sought similar ends. Nationalism was the ideological predicate of the political claim to the nation-state and as such corresponded with the modes of national economies best suited for both capitalizing and colonizing the world economic order. It was the substance, not the form, of nationalism that provided the colonial world with a site of resistance to colonialism.

The mutation of Islam into a site of categorical resistance to colonialism was a specific episode in the contemporary history of its encounter with Enlightenment modernity. While the operation of transnational capital culturally constituted itself on the premise of what it called *the West*, the working of its *colonial* extension was geographically delegated to the realm of *the Rest*, and in this particular case that of an *Islam* which was only there to other and thus authenticate *the West* – facilitating a new phase of civilizational thinking in modern social thought.[25] The rapid circularity of capital and labor code-named *globalization* in its most recent spin has finally exposed the fabricated ideology of domination constitutional to the binary opposition of *Islam and the West*, from which both illusions were made plausible. The dismantling of the presumed centrality of *capital* and its *colonial* periphery into one globalizing spiral of capital and labor chasing after each other has exposed the naked relation of power for long concealed under the smoke screen of civilizational divides and national cultures, all narrated around the fictive polarity of *The West and the Rest*. The disappearance of the smoke screen of the ideology of domination code-named

210 *Liberation theodicy*

the West has not just discredited the fiction of its civilizational authenticity. It has equally discredited the artificial distinction made between the horizontal (external) and vertical (internal) modes of colonialism. We can no longer hold to be self-evident the fictive presumption of national cultures and civilizational divides that has falsely separated the working of the capital and the colonial. The event code-named *globalization* has made that chronic disease transparent.

Today the crisis of a post-Islamic Ideology manifests itself in a variety of simultaneous symptomatics – at once local and global, political and pathological. Counterintuitive as it may seem to speak of an end to Islamism in the phantasmagoric macabre carnival of the post 9/11 world scene, the fact remains that the ideological fervor and political power germane and constitutional to the making of Islamism (as we have known and documented it over the last 200 years) have long since lost their material ground and exhausted their political energy. Today we are at the threshold of a whole new mode of Islamic consciousness. What could some of its emerging thematics be is entirely contingent on a clear conception of the demise of Islamism as we have known it over its last 200 years of resistance first to European colonialism and then to American imperialism.

Although the rise of Islamism has been a collective site of resistance to colonialism in much of the Muslim world since the early nineteenth century, it was principally in Iran that it ultimately resulted in a theocracy, in an Islamic republic. The successful institutionalization of the Islamic Republic was predicated on the work of generations of Muslim ideologues instrumental in the gradual mutation of Islam into militant Islamism – from Muhammad Abduh, Jamal al-Din al-Afghani, and Rashid Rida to Ali Shari'ati, Morteza Motahhari, and Ayatollah Taleqani. After the success of the Islamic revolution in 1979, Ayatollah Khomeini led his tormented nation through a ghoulish US hostage crisis and then nearly a decade of war with Iraq (1980–1988), foregrounding a brutal suppression of all alternative voices and visions to his tyrannical rule and the constitutional consolidation of an Islamic republic. While much of world attention was distracted by the American hostage crisis of 1979–1980, the ideologues of the Islamic republic quickly ratified an Islamic constitution at a massive cost to civil liberties and human rights. Almost a decade later, and when the country was left to ruins after the Iran–Iraq war, again while the focus of the world media was distracted by the notorious Salman Rushdie Affair, Ayatollah Khomeini engineered yet another constitutional coup and changed the terms of succession to his charismatic authority in a way that guaranteed the institutional continuity of the Islamic republic (and the silencing of all its rival ideologies and movements).

Soon after the death of Ayatollah Khomeini and the end of the Iran–Iraq war, the early 1990s witnessed a rapid dissolution of the terror of his charismatic memory and the rise of massive discontent with the medieval texture and totalitarian disposition of his legacy in the Islamic republic. The presidential election of June 1998, the massive student uprising of July 1999, the parliamentary elections of February 2000, and again the presidential election of 2002 clearly and unequivocally demonstrated the catastrophic collapse of all claims to legitimacy of the Islamic Republic and even beyond that the categorical failure of Islamism as a legitimate revolutionary ideology. What has now been dubbed *The Berlin Conference* of April 2000 is chief among a succession of brutal crackdowns on freedom of expression that includes the serial murder of secular intellectuals traced to the highest-ranking officials of the Islamic republic. The categorical failure of President Khatami to deliver on any of his twice-repeated campaign promises, a systematic suppression of the most basic civil rights by the Islamic judiciary, a wide range of brutal public tortures and executions, a severe crackdown on the press, official death sentences issued against the slightest suggestions of ideological disobedience, clandestine trials and illegal incarceration of political activists, forcing millions of Iranians out of their homeland because of their religious and/or ideological affinities, and an official campaign of defamation and character assassination targeted against political dissidents are chief among a broad array of developments marking the definitive delegitimation of any claim to an Islamic republic and the categorical failure of the very idea of an Islamic Ideology. The overwhelming will of a nation to secure enduring institutions of democracy in their political culture is now brutally thwarted by a constellation of undemocratic institutions woven into the fabric of the Islamic constitution, which include the Expediency Council, the Guardian Council, and ultimately the office and the doctrine of the Supreme Jurist – in and of itself an insult to the collective intelligence of an entire nation. A constitutional crisis of historical proportions has now split the will of a nation from its ruling oligarchy and its merciless despotism.

The appeal of militant Islamism as a site of political resistance to colonialism has not been limited to the Islamic Republic of course. Historically, a far more universal application has been contingent on this anti-colonial ideology. But the successive failures of this political reconstitution of Islam – in critical confrontation with European colonialism once and with American imperialism now – to result in any successful political revolution with a viable economic or cultural program has finally degenerated into what is now summarily code-named Osama bin Laden or al-Qaeda. The phenomenon, not just the person, of Osama bin Laden and al-Qaeda emerged from the proxy war that the Wahhabis from Saudi Arabia and the Iranian revolutionaries were fighting initially in Afghanistan, sponsored at the time by the US government during the Soviet occupation, and subsequently waged throughout Central Asia. What is now called al-Qaeda (or alternatively "the Taliban") is of course a figment of Pentagon imagination, a blueprint of its own military designs for global control. But the person and phenomenon of Osama bin Laden and the guerilla operations attributed to his so-called al-Qaeda organization are the last desperate gasps of a once revolutionary movement that has now degenerated into militant but futile adventurism, lacking any grass-roots popular support, economic agenda, political ideology, or social cohesion. If the Islamic Republic of Iran today represents the institutional conclusion of militant Islamism as a once potent anti-colonial ideology, the phenomenon of Osama bin Laden and his so-called al-Qaeda signify the final, dying, flames of a bitterly outdated political imagination on a far more global scale.

These two political indices of the end of militant Islamism are matched by the most important hermeneutic attempt to give it yet another lease on life. Almost immediately after the success of the Islamic revolution, the most serious Muslim ideologue instrumental in its articulation began to worry about its success and sought to find a way out of its cul-de-sac. There are indications that before his assassination, Morteza Motahhari (d. 1979), a major ideologue of the Islamic revolution, had in fact articulated his fears of the theocratic consequences of an Islamic ideology. But the revolutionary momentum and the war that immediately followed it prevented any serious reflection on the predicament of the Islamic republic and the ideological Islamism on which it is predicated. Soon after the end of the Iran–Iraq war, when neither revolutionary fervor nor national defense had created a smoke screen thick enough for the brutal institutionalization of the theocracy, such Muslim ideologues as Abdolkarim Soroush began to realize what had happened and initiated a monumental project to dissociate "Islam Itself" from the factual evidence of an Islamic revolution predicated on any Islamic Ideology. As a devout Muslim intellectual, Soroush's concern was not the active theorization of the predicament of his nation, and what it should learn from this historical experience. Instead, he wanted to safeguard *Islam Itself* for posterity, and blame the present condition on the vicissitudes of human fallacy. This is how he came to his theory of "the theoretical contraction and expansion of religious knowledge." It is within that context that he and a few other reform-minded Muslim intellectuals have tried to give alternative readings of Islam that are more liberal and compatible with democracy – leading to the designation of Soroush as "the Martin Luther of the Islamic World!" The problem with Soroush and his supporters, however, is that they are about two centuries behind the globalizing operation of capital and are thus trying to re/articulate the particulars of an Islamic hermeneutics quintessentially outdated in its epistemic correspondence with the end of the centralized capital, as well as with the colonially nationalized economies, polities, and cultures. The result is a museumized conception of their ancestral faith, seductive in its hermeneutic appeal but nativist in its intellectual disposition and thus entirely useless in the globalized reconfiguration of labor and capital and all its cultural and hermeneutic consequences for the living Muslims.

The political, ideological, and hermeneutic end of militant Islamism is also complemented by a superannuated and yawning *mysticism* now best represented by a bizarre amalgamation that ranges from Seyyed Hossein Nasr's tireless but tiring beautification of "Islam," particularly perambulated into soothing nursery rhymes since 9/11, to Deepak Chopra and his therapeutic industry of Hollywood *spirituality*, which partakes heavily in the recent American giddiness with Coleman Bark's trying Rumi's patience in his grave.[26] This is a particularly pathetic end for once a towering civilizational universe now degenerated into therapeutic gobbledygook for the incurably bored and boring. But what this jaundiced beatification of "Islam" by Seyyed Hossein Nasr and Co. indicates is the whiplash effect of the global demonization of a faith that it seeks to rectify but that in effect reciprocates and perpetuates in a complementary way. A dialectics of reciprocity thus emerges between the political atrocities that a delegitimated ideology perpetrates (Osama bin Laden) and the pathological compensations that it occasions for the misplaced gurus and their lucrative *spirituality* industry (Seyyed Hossein Nasr). Osama bin Laden and Seyyed Hossein Nasr are thus the two sides of the same coin: one degenerating the legitimate use of violence in revolutionary projects (Islamist or otherwise) into militant adventurism of the most barbaric forms, and the other corrupting the moral imagination of a world religion into a jaundiced spirituality of immense and useless vacuity. The result is a false sense of continuity in the discourse and disposition of a civilizational universe, which by now has vacated these shallow shells and transmigrated along with global labor migrations into an entirely different space, light years distant from these parallel pathologies.

On the other side of the born-again Muslims stand the post-Muslim modernists who lack even an iota of a critical bone in the body of their love and admiration for the European Enlightenment. The sad sliding of a people's ancestral faith into mystical nonentity is matched by the public self-flagellation of those who stand in awe of the Enlightenment modernity – from Bassam Tibi to Aziz al-Azmeh, Fatima Mernissi, Fouad Ajami, and Daryush Shayegan, to name just a few – all mesmerized by a pious devotion to an ideal they celebrate with total disregard for the colonial context of its rise and reception. No account of the rise and demise of Islamic Ideology is possible without a simultaneous critique of Enlightenment modernity and the colonial shadow of its extension and function in and within the non-European world. Much of the critique of modernity that has been launched from postmodernist positions – having occasioned Jürgen Habermas' famous defense of modernity as an unfinished project – is in fact a self-contained debate within the European project and categorically lacking a colonial site and citation. The same can also be leveled against most of the postcolonial theorists, many of them limited in the range of their reflections to the South Asian colonial scene, where the Persian and Islamic elements are conspicuously absent from the purview of their consideration. What is needed is a double-edged, simultaneous, critique of *both* the colonial context wherein Islam was politically mutated into a site of ideological resistance *and* the historical catastrophes contingent on the failures of that ideology. Without a colonial take on Enlightenment modernity, we will lose sight of the historical function of Islamic Ideology as a site of ideological resistance to colonialism; and without a critique of the Islamic Ideology itself we will tend to blame the fact and features of colonialism for failures internal to the logic of the postcolonial predicament.

As these dying days of once a powerful religion, colonially transmuted into a potent ideology of resistance, are coming to an ignominious end, Islam as a religion of protest is taking root in an entirely different set of material circumstances, giving rise to a radically different Islamic liberation theodicy. To notice the growth of this new consciousness, first we have to understand that at the heart of Islam and its revelatory language is a quintessential paradox, that Islam from its very inception has been a religion of protest that can never completely deliver its promises without simultaneously negating itself. At the heart of Islam as a religion of protest stands a proto-Shi'ism, which is more endemic to the faith than a small sect within it can claim. As a religion of protest, Islam cannot completely succeed without instantaneously contradicting itself. As the template of the revolutionary sentiments definitive to its doctrinal texture and history, Islam is triumphant at the moment of its insurrection, defeated at the moment of its success. This is a creative contradiction constitutional to the very text of the Qur'an and its schematic division between the Meccan (revolutionary) and Medinan (state-building) chapters. Because it has historically spoken the truth to power, it cannot be in power, for it then robs itself of speaking the truth to power. The defining moment of Shi'ism – and with it Islam in general – is the doctrinal sanctity of *mazlumiyyat*, of having been wronged, subjected to tyranny – a theory I have extensively outlined in my *Authority in Islam* (1989). From the controversy over the succession of the Prophet, to the caliphate of Ali, and ultimately to the battle of Karbala, constitutional to the historical memory we call Shi'ism is the condition of its subalternity, its perpetual terms of disenchantment, its having been deprived and wronged. It ought to remain that way. The instant it succeeds in power it negates itself. Islam is thus either a religion of perpetual insurrectionary disposition or the very negation of itself.

The exemplary cases of how Islam is finding its way back into the most vital political sites of struggle in contemporary history are the crucial instances of the Hamas in Palestine, the Hezbollah in Lebanon, and various Shi'i forces in Iraq. These insurrectionary cases have far-reaching implications beyond their immediate limitations. In all these cases, Islam is now integral to liberation movements by definition polyvocal in their texture and multicultural in their disposition. In the case of the Hezbollah, the Shi'i faction of a national liberation movement has had to negotiate a politically viable position for itself in Lebanon. In this particular context, Shi'ism has had to articulate its political posture in ideological conversation with Sunni, Greek Orthodox, Roman Catholic, Protestant, and even patently Marxist variations of the same thematic resistance to that foreign occupation. In a similar vein, the Hamas contingency of the Palestinian national liberation movement has had to articulate its political stance in a similar ideological conversation with other – both religious and non-religious – components of the Palestinian liberation struggle. The same holds true for the Iraqi Shi'i forces that will have to negotiate a viable political position for themselves in peaceful or combative conversation with the Iraqi Sunni, Kurdish, Ba'thist, and nationalist forces.

Other exemplary sites will have to be added to these to make a solid global case for the emergence of a new mode of Islamic consciousness. Another critical site, adding to the combative cases of Hezbollah (national) and Hamas (pre-national), respectively, is the Muslim population of the former Yugoslavia, now mainly in Bosnia and Herzegovina, where after the November 21 1995 Dayton, Ohio, Agreement the 40 percent Muslim population is part of a post-national configuration that also includes more than 30 percent Orthodox, 15 percent Roman Catholic, and 4 percent Protestant Christians. Add to this factor the pending inclusion of Turkey in the EU and the sizeable presence of European Muslims, considerably increased by the massive labor migration of South Asian Muslims to England, Turks to Germany, Algerian and other North Africans to France, and Moroccans to the Netherlands, all evidencing a picture of a considerable transnational Islamic presence in Europe. The same phenomenon is repeated of course in the USA and the rest of the Americas, including, for example, the largest community of Palestinians outside of Palestine residing in Chile, which results in a cross-national and transcontinental conception of the Islamic communities. Once we add the Muslims of South Asia to those of Central Asia, to the combatant Muslim communities of Chechnya, and from there to China, and then down to sub-Saharan Africa, we will have a geographical conception of the fact and phenomenon of Islam no longer limited to a definable geographical space extending from Morocco to Pakistan, historically identified with the so-called Islamic World – or the so-called *Dar al-Islam*.

The implications of this geographical expansion of Muslims into the four corners of the world, ranging from sizeable minorities to a considerable majority, facilitated and factored in by massive labor migrations over the last half a century, are far above and beyond the European fear for their *cultural identity* and the American anxiety of *the end of history* and *clash of civilizations*. What this geographical re-imagining of Muslims occasions is a re-emergence of Islam in correspondence with seismic changes and epistemic ruptures marking global transformations in the historical circumstances under which from early in the nineteenth century forward Islamic Ideology emerged as a site of political resistance to colonialism. That Islamic Ideology was by definition territorially exclusive to what was categorically called *Islamic societies* or *Dar al-Islam*. That territorial designation is no longer valid; this emerging conception of Islam-in-the world can no longer thus geographically delineate itself.

Under colonial conditions, a pre-Modern set of Islamic binaries – *Dar al-Islam* and *Dar al-Harb* – led credence to a modern colonial divide – the

West and the Rest – and resulted in the most fatal and distorting binary opposition in modern history, that between Islam and the West. The current, massive, dispersion of Muslims throughout the world – occasioned by enormous labor migrations, territorial dispossession, and displacement of refugees – has categorically confused the doctrinal division between *Dar al-Islam* and *Dar al-Harb* on one side and the West and the Rest on the other. Right now the forces of rapid globalization have forced Muslims to live with non-Muslims in all parts of the world, whereas post-Muslims continue to live in their own homeland but are no longer identifiable in any meaningful way as *Muslim*. The categorical assumption of so-called *Islamic societies* can no longer conceal the globalizing formation of international civil societies and the dominant force of the constitutionally cosmopolitan middle class in much of the so called *Islamic world*. The result is a categorical confusion that eats into the very core of the double-binaries – *Dar al-Harb* and *Dar al-Islam* and *the West* and *the Rest* – liberating the factual evidence of people no longer limited by these outdated categories to redefine and relocate themselves differently.[27]

What we are witnessing today is the end of Islamic Ideology, as indeed the end of all liberation theologies formulated as sites of resistance to classical European colonialism, and the simultaneous rise of an *Islamic liberation theodicy, ipso facto* in creative conversation with other transregional and multicultural liberation movements. The difference between a *liberation theology* and a *liberation theodicy* is, very simply put, the difference between an emancipatory movement in categorical isolation from the rest of the world and one integral to the global collapse of all binary oppositions. Today all liberation theories will have to be formulated above and beyond all binary oppositions, first and foremost the one between the religious and the secular. Immediately contingent on that collapse is the recognition that no singular *liberation theology* can be speculated in a hermetic seal and categorical isolation from the rest of the world – and only in a fictive and combatant conversation with a "West" that simply no longer exists. The result is a *liberation theodicy*, in which the god-terms of an emancipatory movement will have to account for the existence of worlds and ideas, modes of imagination and manners of being, entirely alien to their received limitations. It is in that sense that the *Islamic liberation theodicy* will be at once true to the material evidence of its revolutionary potentials, cognizant of the cultural heritage of its ancestral faith, and yet fully aware of the necessary negotiations it will have to make and incorporate into the making of its *theodicy*. In the case of *the Islamic liberation theodicy*, what will immediately have to be noted is the collapse of the binary assumption held between *Islam* and *the West* or *Dar al-Islam* and *Dar al-Harb* and the rise of a critical and creative consciousness in hermeneutic conversation with its presence in a polyvocal context and multicultural world, astonishingly reminiscent of its own pre-modern intellectual universe before it was robbed of its own innate polylocality and regimented into a singular (and necessarily authoritarian) site of ideological resistance to colonialism. In other words, Islamic liberation theodicy replaces Islam back where it was, in the world, cognizant and conversant with the world: Islam-in-the world. The real world, and not the fabricated binary between "Islam and the West" will now again become the home of a cosmopolitan and worldly Islam, with its other-worldly claims on its adherents matters of private piety and public tolerance.

Today the predicaments of nations are no longer narrated and negotiated within their colonially constituted national boundaries. The very birthplace of the idea and practice of the nation-state has now officially abandoned both the idea and the practice for a cross-national unification. In both economic and political terms, the EU is emerging as the principal contender against US imperial designs for the world. With the euro a stronger currency than the dollar, and a market at its disposal as populated and lucrative as that of the USA, the EU is now a major economic force, mirroring and corroborating its political prowess. Meanwhile in the USA, the crowning achievement of Enlightenment modernity, labor migrations in the successive decades of the 1970s and 1980s have drastically altered the demographic disposition of the country, resulting in phantasmagoric theses about the end of history and the clash of civilizations, ostensibly targeted toward a global market but decidedly local to the American anxiety of the loss of their manifest destiny.

Massive millions of laborers are moving around the globe in search of job opportunities. The economic logic of capitalism has long since overridden the political rhetoric of the nation-states. Within the larger body of the labor migrations, according to the latest UN report, there are more than 20 million refugees, asylum seekers, and others of concern around the globe. The US-led wars on the Muslim world have significantly added to this number and made Muslims a major component of these crucial statistics. For millions of Muslims dispersed around the world, they are no longer at home in an imaginative geography called *the Islamic world*. The most prominent public intellectuals of an Islamic republic come to the globalized space of a conference in Berlin where they argue and analyze the specifics of their no longer national destiny. The space of the Heinrich Böll Foundation categorically transforms the political discourse of the *nation* and mutates it into a *transnational* language of globalized consequences. The proceedings of this conference are neither limited to Iran nor barred from Germany. They are articulated in a third space that transcends and includes both. What happens in Berlin among a handful of Muslim intellectuals has obvious and immediate consequences in Iran, as it does for the Muslim population of Europe in general and the Turks of Germany in particular. But there are hermeneutic consequences to such proceedings mapped out on an entirely different geopolitical imagination – polyvocal and heteroglossic in its nature and disposition.

This gathering of Iranian intellectuals in Berlin in April 2000 was in marked contrast from yet another group of prominent Iranian literati who almost 100 years earlier, immediately after the commencement of the First European (World) War, gathered in Berlin in 1915 and began the publication of a now legendary journal called *Kaveh*. Mohammad Qazvini, Ibrahim Pour Davoud, Seyyed Mohammad Ali Jamalzadeh and Mirza Hossein Khan Kazemzadeh were chief among a group of Iranian intellectuals whom their principal doyen and sponsor, Seyyed Hasan Taqizadeh, had brought together and financed, all courtesy of the German government, to publish a journal in Persian to combat the British influence in their homeland. At the time, the defining moment of these Iranian intellectuals was the colonial rivalries among the British, the French, the Russians, and the Germans, in the midst of which they were articulating the terms of their own national polity and culture. Almost a century later, no Iranian or Muslim intellectual could have the perils or promises of any such limited *national* destiny confined within his or her territorial imagination. They now have to narrate and negotiate their collective destiny in dialogical conversation with a reality neither adversarial to their wellbeing nor indifferent to their location in history – and yet constitutionally polyfocal in nature and disposition.

In an astonishing turn of events, the recent rise of Iranian cinema to global prominence provides a serendipitous esthetic template for what is about to happen hermeneutically to Islamic *liberation theodicy*. As a national art form of now global significance, Iranian cinema has articulated a mode of *para-realism*[28] for itself in creative conversation with the other exemplary models of national cinema – Italian neorealism, French New Wave, German New Cinema, and other masters of the craft from Russia, India, China, and Japan. As a major artistic adventure now in full fruition, Iranian cinema commands a global appeal that has thematically influenced much of what is now happening in world cinema. It has achieved that status precisely by having a creative conversation with the best of world cinema, while standing confident at the center of its own esthetic take on reality. By cross-metaphorizing with mimetic possibilities foreign to their own esthetics, Iranian filmmakers are moving toward the next phase of a conversational presence in the world that denies the false comfort of insular piety, prevents further binary oppositions, and at the same time enables an emancipatory esthetics from which the politics of *liberation theodicy* will have much to learn. In the global rise of Iranian cinema to prominence, its whole-hearted reception and spectacular celebration, the rising Islamic *liberation theodicy* has a tested template. Iranian cinema made it to global reception *not* in binary opposition to any other national or regional cinema but in creative conversation with all of them, thus securing for itself a liberating esthetics at once local and immediate to its domestic sense of the beautiful and the sublime, and yet global to a multiplicity of voices and visions that can only add yet another color of hope to life.

The particulars of that Islamic liberation theodicy – at once local and global to our historical predicament – will have to articulate its terms of

Liberation theodicy 219

deliverance in the real battlefields of history, and for that final test we must visit where revolutionary Islamism has had a rendezvous with history, and where the terms of national, regional, and global liberations need rethinking.

"Mulahaza" suggested the small print at the bottom of the electronic flyer, "*La mubarayat Mundial fi hadha al-waqt.*"[29] The timing of the conference that Samah Idriss had organized at al-Saaha Club, on Thursday June 29 2006, at precisely 7.30 pm, was carefully calculated that it would not coincide with any game during the crucial quarterfinals of the World Cup 2006. The previous round had just ended on June 27, when Brazil defeated Ghana 3–0, and France defeated Spain 3–1. The Lebanese (and Palestinians) were very happy indeed, for judging by the number of colorful flags at full blast all over residential and commercial Beirut (and all over the Palestinian refugee camps even), were mostly rooting for Brazil and France, and scarcely a flag of Ghana or Spain was in sight anywhere in the city. People were now getting ready for June 30, when Germany was to play Argentina and Italy Ukraine. So Samah Idriss, the Editor-in-Chief of *al-Adab* magazine and the convener of the conference at al-Saaha Club, had planted his event right between these four crucial soccer matches, hoping to get the maximum audience – and he was right. The medium-size hall of al-Saaha Club in Wata al-Musaytbeh was standing room only, with Ahmad Dallal, Rania Masri, and As'ad Abu-Khalil, three distinguished Lebanese academic intellectuals, taking it in turn to reflect on the US empire and strategies of resisting it.

The joyous confidence and the playful frivolity of attending to by far the most urgent political calamity of contemporary history (the bugbear of the incompetent US empire) while mindful of the dramatic vagaries of the World Cup takes a certain kind of imaginative panache, predicated on an unsurpassed generosity of spirit, that only a few urban intellectual cultures around the globe can fathom, muster, and demonstrate. The cosmopolitan grace and the thriving political culture of Lebanon, characteristically evident to any casual observer or seasoned visitor to Beirut up until June 2006, must be traced back to the normative and moral courage of a nation now poised to play a pivotal role in its regional history.

Perhaps the most salient feature of this cosmopolitan urbanism at the roots of the Lebanese political culture is that it is squarely rooted in the hard and fast historical experiences of a nation deeply traumatized by generations and decades of successive Palestinian refugee migrations, savage Israeli invasions, belligerent Syrian occupation, insidious interference by the Islamic republic, chronic sectarian strife, all of which underlined by ostentatious class differences, evident in the seasonal Saudis and Khalijis obscenely flaunting their wealth, against the background of dilapidated Palestinian refugee camps and a rising subaltern underclass of Sri Lankan and other modern-day slaves crowding the Lebanese underclass. Lebanon thus exudes a cosmopolitan political culture not despite the calamities that inform and agitate its modern history but in fact through those calamities. The imaginative grace and defiant disposition of the Lebanese political culture is thus far from skin-deep, and is squarely rooted in an urbanity of moral imagination exemplary in its courage and proverbial in its steadfastness.

In its most recent history, Lebanon has endured much political calamity and yet managed to maintain a level of social maturity and defiant demand for pride of place among its poorest and most disenfranchised communities entirely unrivalled anywhere else in the Arab and the Muslim world.[30] At the very least, one might trace this cosmopolitan disposition of Lebanese political culture, and its unusual ability to survive political calamities of one brand or another, to May 2000 when following the disintegration of the mercenary army of Major Saad Haddad, the SLA (The South Lebanon Army), their sponsor and benefactors, the Israeli military forces, collected their belongings and withdrew from Lebanon in humiliation and disgrace. By October of that year, and literally within months after the Israeli withdrawal, Rafik Hariri took office as the Lebanese prime minister for a second term and thus commenced in earnest a massive project of reconstructing Lebanon in both political and economic terms.

By June 2006, and just days before the unsurpassed savagery of the Jewish state was unleashed on the Lebanese, the cosmopolitan urbanity of Lebanon was written all over its face – from its poorest and most disenfranchised communities to its richest and most opulent neighborhoods. Over the course of some six years – from the disgraceful defeat of the Israelis in southern Lebanon in 2000 until his assassination in 2006, Prime Minister Hariri had managed to bring in massive foreign investment, while the cosmopolitan disposition of the Lebanese political culture began to work its magic out and belligerent political factions began to work together toward a government of national reconciliation following a period of destructive civil war. The commencement of the period of post-war reconstruction in Lebanon of course did not mean that the Jewish state had left the country to its northern colonial borders to its own constructive course. The January 2002 assassination of Elie Hobeika, a key figure in the massacres of Palestinian refugees in 1982, soon after he had disclosed that he was in possession of videotapes and other evidence challenging the Israeli account of the massacres, indicated that the Israeli army may have been defeated and forced to retreat from Lebanese territories but that the treacherous interference of the Jewish state in Lebanese affairs was far from over. In a similar vein, in September 2002, the Jewish state threatened Lebanon with military action if the Lebanese went ahead with a plan to use the water of the Wazzani River for their own benefits. To make their point quite clear, by August 2003, the Israelis managed to assassinate a member of the Shi'i guerilla movement, the Hezbollah. All of these were in addition to the innumerable Lebanese freedom fighters who remained suffering in Israeli jails, the Israelis refusal to hand in the map of the minefields it had left behind in southern Lebanon following its historic defeat, and its illegal occupation of the Shebaa Farms in Lebanese territories.

Lebanon has always been the postcard picture of what is fundamentally wrong and what is potentially hopeful about the Arab and the Muslim world in general – its divisive and factious politics oscillating fatefully between destructive sectarianism and thriving cosmopolitanism, and the year 2005 brought this historic paradox to perfect realization – a year that brought both grief and solidarity to Lebanon, both outspoken demands for freedom and democracy and heavy prices paid for those ideals. In February 2005, Prime Minister Rafik Hariri was killed by a car bomb in Beirut. The assassination of Hariri, admired by the business community and middle class Lebanese, although severely criticized by the progressive left, ignited both pro- and anti-Syrian sentiments and resulted in the resignation of Prime Minister Omar Karami's cabinet. By March 2005, hundreds of thousands of Lebanese joined pro- and anti-Syrian rallies in Beirut. By the following month, in April 2005, Omar Karami resigned as Prime Minister, having failed to form a government, and yielding to the moderate pro-Syrian MP Najib Mikati. Pressure on Syria to withdraw its forces from Lebanon was now intensified, and finally Bashar al-Asad yielded to the collective will of the Lebanese – endorsed by the UN, and abused by the USA and France – and ended the Syrian occupation of Lebanon. This was not to be the end of the Lebanese woes. In June 2005, the prominent journalist Samir Qasir, severely critical of the Syrian presence in Lebanon, but curiously silent on other forms of military occupations in the region, was assassinated. His death was a major trauma in Lebanese consciousness. Posters and even an oversize statue of Samir Qasir sprang all over Beirut, and his diehard followers pushed for a UN investigation and the punishment of those responsible for his murder.

What was now dubbed a Cedar Revolution by the US neocons and a Gucci Revolution by the progressive Lebanese left was fully under way. The middle class Lebanese bourgeoisie was now fully in line with a pro-American, pro-French, anti-Hezbollah, and anti-Palestinian (and thus effectively pro-Israeli) disposition. Under these circumstances an anti-Syrian alliance, led by Rafik Hariri's son, Saad al-Hariri, won control of the Lebanese parliament. The new parliament elected the major Hariri ally, Fouad Siniora, as prime minister. But the political circumstances in Lebanon were still purgatorial. George Hawi, an anti-Syrian former leader of the Lebanese Communist Party, was killed by a car bomb. But despite all the turmoil, by July 2005, the Lebanese Prime Minister Siniora met with Syria's President Assad, working towards a new, bilateral relationship. By September of that year, four pro-Syrian generals were charged with the assassination of former Prime Minister Rafik Hariri, and before the year ended, a prominent anti-Syrian MP and journalist Gibran Tueni was assassinated. Whoever was behind these assassinations, whatever one might think of the pro- and anti-Syrian sentiments among various Lebanese factions, a fragile parliamentary democracy seemed to have held Lebanon together not just despite its factious politics but in fact, paradoxically, because of it.

By the time Israel launched its savage attack on every inch of Lebanese territory, with the occasional exception of the heavily Christian sections of Lebanon that were ethnically cleansed during the Lebanese civil war, in mid-July 2006, there were every reason to believe that Lebanon was on its way to survive its historic woes – with civility, grace, and hope – leave behind and forgive the previous barbarisms of its Zionist neighbor, and the vicious civil war that it had deliberately instigated and fueled with evident and conniving treachery. There was hope for Lebanon in the aftermath of the Israeli withdrawal from its southern territories. The invasion and occupation had happened and ended in disgrace. The civil war had exhausted all internecine factionalism and Lebanon was still intact – in body and soul. The Syrians had packed and left. The Gucci revolutionaries had demonstrated in their hundreds of thousands in March against Syria and made their presence felt, as had the poor and the disenfranchised of Lebanon, the Shi'is in particular – that they too were a force to contend with. There seemed to be a fair balance of classes and interests, a fairly representative coalition from across the political divide. The bizarre combination of pro-American, Francophone, bourgeoisie, (not even hiding their Sri Lankan maids), were met and matched by the wretched of the Lebanese earth, the poor Shi'is, the disenfranchised Palestinians, and an array of temporary slaves heralding from Syria, Iraq, Bangladesh, Sri Lanka, and all across the Arab, the Muslim, and the poor world.

The road and the struggle ahead of the Lebanese seemed to sustain a proactive economy and a thriving political culture. Whatever the late Prime Minister Hariri did or did not do, and however he did or did not do it, downtown Beirut looked and exuded an emerging confidence – shops were full of goods and customers, fruit and vegetables were in full abundance, cultural activities, TV programs, the rambunctious press, the university campuses, the art scenes, the money that Ford and other American and European foundations were investing in the Lebanese creative imagination – all indicated that there was not just hope but a trust in what was happening – and what was happening was good, promising, beautiful, hopeful. Between the enterprising bourgeoisie (and their colorful SUVs) and the accumulated suffering of the labor class a difference was evident, a struggle was in process, of which history is made, political parties are formed, ideological formations take place – and in the midst of that a people are named, a nation of common sentiments collected, a country is called home. You could tell by the number of native Lebanese living outside their country but going back for their summer holidays, the money and gifts they brought back to their families, and those members of the same family who were leading a happy and satisfying life inside Lebanon, that Lebanon was collecting itself and once again calling itself a homeland. In Lebanon, Islam was in the world – integral to a political culture but not definitive to it, where it best belonged. What a ground-breaking difference with a *Jewish state* or an *Islamic republic*, where Judaism and Islam had degenerated into a state ideology.

By April 2005, Syria was forced to collect its military and leave Lebanon. Pressure was mounting on Hezbollah to distance itself from the corrupting influence of the Islamic Republic and perhaps even to disarm, now that it was part of the post-Hariri government. Pressure was also evident for those huge posters of Khomeini and Khamenei in the al-Dahiya neighborhood of Beirut to come down, get packed, and go back where they came from and leave Lebanon alone – they were the nightmare of another nation and it was enough. No Islamic republic of Lebanon – thank you very much. One Islamic republic of Iran was enough in the neighborhood of the Jewish state, mirroring the Christian empire, echoing the Hindu fundamentalism. Lebanon had no sign that it would be party to such corrupt calamities. Quite to the contrary – it exuded the promises of a syncretic and cosmopolitan political culture that is precisely the opposite of such monolithic (ethically cleansed) theocratic nightmares.

All indications came together in the summer of 2006 that there was hope for Lebanon. Syria was out, Hezbollah was part of the government, religious factions were regrouping, Gucci revolutionaries were adamant, the white-washed bourgeoisie were visibly invisible, the progressive left was challenging the complicitous anti-Syrian, pro-American air of the older generation of Lebanese intellectuals – so all was well. Lebanon could have been a contender as a model of ecumenical balance (if not tolerance), ideological diversity, political pluralism, societal syncretism. The walk by the Mediterranean coast of Lebanon, on the Corniche between the Rawda restaurant and Gamal Abd al-Nasser's monument in Beirut, had as many veiled women as women in their bikinis, songs of Abd al-Halim Hafez and Fairuz out loud, nargilas at full blast, huge TV screens on which people were watching the Algerian–French striker Zinedine Zidane headbutting the Italian defender Marco Materazzi. Lebanon was no hotbed of religious fanaticism – neither a Jewish state, nor an Islamic republic, nor indeed a Christian colony of the American empire was evident in the graceful but balanced countenance of Lebanon.

If this sounds a bit too innocent a reading of Lebanon before the savages descended upon it, then it is precisely that innocence that Israel is hellbound to murder.

Things could have been different in the summer of 2006 even in Palestine, very much on the Lebanese model. Hamas had won a democratic election and was now part of the government. The USA and EU came together to punish Palestinians for the unforgivable crime of exercising their democratic rights by withdrawing their financial help, thus seeking to starve Palestinians into submission and acceptance of the Euro-American colonial settlement in their homeland. Disregarding this weapon of the rich (starving poor people to submission), Hamas representatives had been signatories to the so-called "Prison Memorandum," thus implicitly accepting the existence of the Jewish state in their homeland. Hamas had initiated a unilateral cease-fire for almost three months, while Israelis continued to maim and murder Palestinians in both Gaza and the West Bank – busy as usual with their targeted assassinations, extra-juridical arrests, killing or kidnapping Palestinians activists, murdering at least 85 civilians in the process – including the members of a family whose only surviving child was captured in a picture screaming heaven-ward, why?

Why indeed? Why would Israel invade Lebanon, while engaged on another front in destroying the Palestinian infrastructure in Gaza, and barefacedly continuing to steal Palestinian land on the West Bank?

A quick look at the vicious savagery with which Israel invaded Lebanon, particularly at the bombing pattern of the Israeli air force, navy, and army that commenced on July 12 2006 and continued apace despite a global call for ceasefire – every country in the world except the US, the UK, and Israel itself – indicates that the Israeli invasion was (1) long in preparation; (2) nationwide and by no means limited to Hezbollah targets; and (3) intended, on the Rumsfeldian model of "shock and awe," to cripple the Lebanese national sovereignty, polity, society, and economy for yet another generation. As verified by world press and confirmed by Amnesty International, Israel mounted "more than 7,000 air force attacks and 2,500 naval bombardments particularly concentrated on civilian areas. ... The majority of the 1,183 Lebanese deaths were non-combatants, and about a third were reportedly children."[31] The Israeli invasion of Lebanon was of course not limited to these civilian casualties (an Israeli trademark in Palestine) and included the other Zionist pastime of forcing more than a million people to flee their homes and create a refugee crisis in Lebanon. While "destroying thousands of home in mainly Shia Muslim parts of the country," Amnesty International reports, the Israeli military blew up some 80 bridges around the country. "Amnesty also criticized attacks on fuel and water storage sites with no obvious military value."[32] The extent of this vicious savagery becomes evident even more in the way the Jewish state went after the economic infrastructure of Lebanon. "Israel's air force," the *Financial Times* reports,

> has directed its sophisticated arsenal of precision weapons at the fabric of Lebanon's economy. At least 45 large factories have been hit by Israeli air strikes according to a list compiled by Lebanese businessmen. On the list are factories for furniture, medical products, textiles, paper and a milk plant. Proctor and Gamble warehouse in Beirut was bombed, with damage to $20m of stock. In total, 95 percent of industry has ground to a halt, according to the Association of Lebanese Industrialists. Those companies not directly targeted have been halted by the Israeli blockade. ... Until fighting broke out last month, Lebanon's economy was on track for its best year in more than a decade. Exports

were up over one hundred percent on 2005 and tourism was booming. "Israel is taking advantage of the war to destroy what it can of the infrastructure as well as the basic sectors of economy," said Adnan Kassar, president of the Lebanese Economic Organization grouping the country's business associations. "They want to destroy everything – even pick-up trucks loaded with potatoes or watermelons. People on motorcycle have been killed like birds."[33]

As far north as Tripoli and Halba and their surroundings, the easternmost regions of Baalbek, virtually all the major and minor ports of Lebanon up and down the Mediterranean coast, from Tripoli down to Beirut and then to Tyre, with anything south of Saida, Jezzine, and down to Nabatiyeh, and Hasbaiya, effectively the shooting gallery of the Israeli army, navy, and their air force, there remains little doubt as to what exactly the Jewish state was up to. With hundreds of murdered civilians, more than a million refugees, the deliberate murder of the UN observers, the equally intentional massacre of women and children in Qana in southern Lebanon, which according to Amnesty International are "deliberate war crimes,"[34] and a cold-blooded criminal ability to cheat and lie that it has agreed to a temporary ceasefire (to investigate the Qana massacre) and then immediately ignoring it, the sadistic intensity of this particular Israeli invasion of Lebanon surpasses all the records of the racist settlement with a criminal record of savagery unsurpassed in recent and rarely matched in human history. The enormity of this Israeli crime against humanity, however, must not blind us to trying to see through the barbarism as to what the Jewish state, with the full and flaunted support of its patron Christian imperial godfather, is up to.

On the evidence of the facts on the ground, the death and destruction and the rubble and ruin that this wild European beast has left behind in Lebanon, it is quite evident that the purpose of this latest criminal atrocity was to destroy the very possibility of any kind of cosmopolitan culture in Lebanon. The failed launch of "Israel" as a mini-empire, modeling itself clumsily on the pattern of the neocon artist in Washington DC (as AIPAC tries to prove to Washington that it can be useful in Bush's war on "terrorism"), has an evident agenda far beyond Palestine and Lebanon – and the fact that it has miserably failed to achieve it must not blind us to the projected agenda that this mutated stage of Zionism is projecting. The mutation of the Zionist settlement into a mini-empire wannabe means that all the positive and hopeful developments in both Palestine and Lebanon, that both Hamas and Hezbollah were now part and parcel of a more embracing political process, were in fact inimical to the Israeli imperial aping of the USA in the region. In that respect, all the hogwash of European and American so-called liberals that the Israeli response to Hezbollah was "disproportionate" is sheer nonsense. Israeli's war crimes in Lebanon were perfectly proportionate to what it wanted to do – to bomb Lebanon back to sectarian warfare, to reduce the cosmopolitan character of Lebanon to Muslims and Christians fighting against each other in order to make the Jewish state look normal and at home in the neighborhood. That Israel miserably failed to achieve that malicious objective speaks volumes both to the medieval tribalism that is at the heart of the Jewish state and the cosmopolitan character of the Lebanese national resistance.

The rapid incorporation of Hezbollah into Lebanese civil society and political culture, almost identical with a similar incorporation of Hamas into the Palestinian national liberation movement will create a prototype of democratic pluralism that both the American neocon artists and their Zionist counterparts in Israel find frightening to their strategies of state terrorism and imperial hubris. The Lebanese and Palestinian model can very easily be emulated in Iraq and all its fabricated sectarian strife, generated and sustained in the aftermath of the US-led invasion, turned around towards the creation of a government of national reconciliation, which would be *ipso facto* against the very presence of the US-led occupying forces. Three factors are against the possibility of such a constructive formation in Iraq: (1) the US and its European allies and Israeli partners; (2) the US-generated Afghan-based al-Qaeda; and (3) the Islamic republic – each one of them for their own respective reasons and degenerate interests. In the Islamic republic itself, the fledgling reform movement can assume a renewed momentum if it were to be wedded to progressive national liberation movements in Lebanon, Palestine, and Iraq. The same holds true for the corrupt and retrograde patrimonial tribalism of the Ba'th party in Syria and the obscenely outdated autocracy of Bashar al-Asad. The legitimate anger of Syrian dissident intellectuals has so far degenerated into a pro-American stand that makes strange bedfellows of them with the US and Israeli neocons. But that legitimate dissent itself can be equally integral to a national uprising against the Syrian autocracy. In short, Lebanon and Palestine might very well export their grassroots, materially evident and historically tested cosmopolitan political culture to Iraq and Iran rather than the Islamic republic (or the backward Syrian patrimonialism for that matter) exporting their tribalism and theocracy the other way around.

But Israel (and by extension the USA) is the sworn enemy of any such cosmopolitan culture. Israel sees the world in its own tribal image. The Jewish state sees only Islamic republics in its vicinity – and can only deal with theocratic dispositions akin to its own. The Jewish state thus protests too much against the Islamic Republic; and the Islamic Republic protests too much against the Jewish state. It is imperative for the rest of the world to distance itself from the delusional reading of the current condition and see how Israel and the Islamic Republic are in fact identical regimes – two sides of the same coin, and as such they need, require, and cross-essentialize each other. They want the world in their own image: patriarchal tribalisms writ large into a theocratic state apparatus. The USA and Israel, one a Christian empire and the other a Jewish state, are the global enemies of syncretic and cosmopolitan political cultures. They much rather have al-Qaeda and Islamic republics about them, for they confirm their own medieval banalities, the us-versus-them mentality. The Jewish state confirms the necessity of not just an Islamic Republic of Iran but also (and if it has to) an Islamic Republic of Palestine and an Islamic Republic of Lebanon. The more Islamic republics in the neighborhood the more the Jewish state will look normal and feel at home.

The key question in drawing any enduring lesson from Lebanon in the aftermath of the July 2006 Israeli invasion is how do we read the phenomenon called Hezbollah. Not just in the heartland of US neocons, Washington DC, where Hezbollah is synonymous with terrorism, but even more pointedly among the supposedly more progressive European observers there is a palpable unease, a bit of a bafflement, and a conspicuous hesitation to identify with the Lebanese national resistance to the military adventurism of the Israeli mini-empire. In practically every dispatch he has sent from the war-torn Lebanon, and as the Lebanese of all walks of life were putting up a heroic resistance against the predatory killing machine called "Israel," the veteran British journalist Robert Fisk did not lose a single opportunity to vilify Hezbollah and squarely blame it for the commencement of the war, at times in a language identical with the right wing of the Israeli Likudnicks, the US neocons, put together with the erstwhile Phalangists, unabashedly equating "Hezbollah atrocities" with "Israeli atrocities,"[35] insisting that "it was Hezbollah which provoked this latest war," and warning that by invading Lebanon, Israelis "are legitimizing Hezbollah, ... a rag-tag army of guerillas"[36] – as if this "rag-tag army" lacked such legitimacy before it represented and defended the dignity of an equally "rag-tag" multitude of poor and disenfranchised Lebanese masses.

From the neocon operations in the USA to Robert Fisk, the phenomenon of the Lebanese Hezbollah has been the chief focal point of exonerating Israel from its violent disposition in the region – all behaving as if this thing they call "Hezbollah" fell off from the sky on the innocent Lebanese, preventing them to live in peace and prosperity with their splendidly democratic, peaceful, and generous southern neighbor. But aren't the Hezbollah fighters and the mass of Lebanese they represent Lebanese too? In all such dismissive assessments of Hezbollah, there has been a misplaced concreteness, a pervasive surrogate confusion, as to what exactly this Hezbollah thing is. Hezbollah is not a band of Martians who have landed in Lebanon. Hezbollah in Lebanon is what Hamas is in Palestine, and what the Mahdi's army is in Iraq – the political manifestation of the historically denied and politically repressed subaltern components of three national liberation movements. Too much emphasis on Hezbollah, Hamas, and the Mahdi's army as three political organizations confuses a subaltern political reality (the poor and the disenfranchised in Lebanon, Palestine, and Iraq) with its accidental organizational manifestation. Israel can kill Hassan Nasrallah in Lebanon and Khaled Mashaal in Palestine, as the USA might Muqtada

Sadr in Iraq, tomorrow (if they only could) and 10 more Nasrallah's and Mashaal's and Muqtada Sadr's will emerge from the Dahiya neighborhood in Beirut and from Gaza in Palestine and from Najaf in Iraq. Hezbollah and Hamas and the Mahdi's army are three accidental expressions of three deeply rooted political and demographic realities. The poor of southern Lebanon (who happen to be Shi'is) have historically been denied their fair share in Lebanese politics; as have the poor and the disenfranchised among the Palestinians (who happen to be Muslims), and the poor and the disenfranchised among the Iraqis (who too happen to be Shi'is). Hezbollah, Hamas, and the Mahdi's army are not manufactured banalities and militant adventurers like al-Qaeda, created and crafted by the US–Pakistan–Saudi alliance to fight the Russians and prevent the spread of the Iranian Islamic revolution eastward. Hezbollah, Hamas, and the Mahdi's army are grassroots movements – the shame of the national liberation movements in Lebanon, Palestine, and Iraq that had historically failed to include the most disenfranchised subaltern communities in their emancipatory projects.

As for Hezbollah specifically in Lebanon, the second that the Israelis dropped the very first bomb on their Lebanese targets, Hezbollah sublated from a factious Shi'i guerilla movement into an army of national liberation. This fundamental fact, missed miserably as much by the US and Israeli neocons as by the so-called European left, rests on the miasmatic disposition of all national liberation movements, all guerrilla organizations that fade in and out of their national and subaltern dispositions. From Vietnam to Africa to Latin America, the history of all national liberation movements testify to this fact – they can degenerate into violent malignancies or else sublate into emancipatory national liberation movements, all depending on the circumstances of their historical unfolding, and nothing can help a guerrilla operation assume national leadership than a military invasion by a colonial or imperial power – Pol Pot's Khmer Rouge in Cambodia as opposed to Ho Chi Minh's revolutionary army in Vietnam are prime examples here.

Consider the fact that halfway through the Israeli bombardment of Lebanon, in an interview with Jon Snow of the British television station Channel 4, on August 3 2006, the Lebanese Prime Minister Fouad Siniora, a Hariri ally, stated clearly and categorically that Hezbollah's demands for the condition of its disarming itself – namely, the return of the Lebanese freedom fighters incarcerated in the Israeli prisons, the return of the Shebaa farms, and the map of the minefields Israel has left behind after its withdrawal from Southern Lebanon in 2000 – were indeed his own government's terms for a comprehensive treaty with the Jewish state.

The Zionist propaganda machinery commenced this war by insisting that Hezbollah had miscalculated the Israeli response, that it did not know what terror the Jewish state would unleash on an entire nation. As always such propaganda clichés take the historical fact and by simply turning it around thinks it suppressed. It was Israel that miscalculated its military capability and made a global fool out of itself by trying to catch the butterfly of Hezbollah on the graceful face of Lebanon – destroying an entire country in the futile hope of catching and killing that butterfly. At the end, Israel "liberated" Lebanon exactly the same way that its Christian imperial sponsor, the USA, was liberating Iraq and Afghanistan – except neither Hamas is Taliban, nor Hezbollah is Saddam Hussein. There is a fundamental difference here – a difference not between the identical savageries of the USA in Afghanistan and Iraq and Israel in Palestine and Lebanon, but between the natures of the enemy they purport to fight. Both Saddam Hussein and the Taliban were the handmade creatures of the USA, whereas Hezbollah and Hams are grassroots national liberation movements integral (but not definitive) to Palestine and Lebanon. The US manufacturing of the Taliban and Saddam Hussein in Afghanistan and Iraq, respectively, and by way of curtailing the political appeal of the initial stages of the Iranian revolution of 1979, had corrupted the miasmatic nature of two legitimate national liberation movements into a senseless, pointless, and globalized violence called al-Qaeda that in its adventurous pursuit of spectacular violence mirrors and reflects the vacuous disposition of its chief nemesis, the US empire, while the Israeli savagery against Palestinian and Lebanese will make Hamas and Hezbollah even more integral to their respective national liberation movements.

The USA and Israel and their European and Arab allies are thus dead wrong that Syria and Iran are the main culprits and the principal villains and those who have in fact instigated Hamas and Hezbollah to act. There is no doubt that the Syrian military would love to come back and occupy Lebanon and the Islamic Republic would be only too happy to clone itself and see an Islamic republic in Lebanon or even in Palestine. But Syria is a corrupt, degenerate, and impotent bureaucracy hardly capable of holding its own illegitimate reign together, while the Islamic republic is an equally bankrupt, incompetent, and degenerate regime hardly capable of saving its own skin should push come to shove, except through medieval measures of repression, torture, human rights violations, gender apartheid, and scores of other criminal activities. Assimilating the Lebanese Hezbollah and the Palestinian Hamas to the corrupt and corrupting Syrian and Iranian model is in fact a self-fulfilling prophecy for the USA and Israel (US/Israel would in fact be the proper name for this twin tower of calamity let loose upon the world), who wish nothing more than cloning their own Jewish and Christian fanaticism in their Islamic versions.

The real struggle, the real resistance, and thus the battlefield of the exemplary national liberation movements are currently neither in Iraq, nor in the Islamic Republic, nor in Afghanistan – one degenerated into sectarian violence, to the US neocons heart's desire, the other in the tight grips of a medieval theocracy, and the last having collapsed back to a narcotic stronghold for drug dealers, highway bandits, and US- and UK-sponsored mercenary private contractors. The real battlefield is now in Lebanon and in

Palestine, in Beirut and in Gaza – where Islam is in the world, forced to negotiate its emancipatory terms in conversation with non-Islamic terms. For here is where two grassroots Islamist movements have had to come to terms with the multifaceted and cosmopolitan fact and disposition of the national liberation movement of which they are but one component. The lead role here is with Palestine, and in particular in the historic signatures of Marwan Barghouti, the leader of Fatah in the West Bank, Sheik Abd-al-Khaliq al-Natshe, a Hamas leader, as well as the signatures of the leaders of Islamic Jihad and the Popular Front and the Democratic Front for the Liberation of Palestine on the so-called "Prison Accord." The formation of a cross-section of Palestinian national liberation movement is unprecedented in its history. By virtue of this document, Hamas has achieved something far more important than an implicit recognition of a colonial settlement on Palestinian homeland. With this document, Hamas has joined the formation of a historical balance between all the factions and forces integral to the national liberation of Palestine – and as such has learned the art of political compromise for a larger and more significant goal. The conditions in Lebanon were not half as ready and were just in the embryonic stage and a contingent process of fermentation when the Israelis made the monumental stupidity of invading Lebanon hoping to destroy Hezbollah. This was not a mere military folly, for a conventional army cannot defeat a guerrilla operation fighting to defend its homeland. The Israeli invasion of Lebanon in July–August 2006, and particularly in the enormity of death and destruction it rained on civilians, instantly turned Hezbollah from an erstwhile Shi'i guerrilla operation into the chief organ of a national resistance. Israel has always been a gargantuan military with a colonial state apparatus built around it. But this time around it committed the monumental stupidity of thinking that with military thuggery it could impose its will on the region – not just in Palestine and Lebanon, but through the evident logic of US/Israel, the degeneration of two state apparatus (one imperial, the other colonial) into one imperial design, in Iraq and Afghanistan and by design in Iran and Syria. They cannot. The US/Israel has just expedited the sublation of Hezbollah into a national resistance in Lebanon – and as such a model of syncretic and cosmopolitan revolutionary uprising in the region.

In the realm of political possibilities there is of course nothing impossible. Is there thus the danger that the Lebanese Hezbollah might degenerate into an Iranian Hezbollah and opt thoroughly to Islamize the Lebanese national liberation movement and work towards the creation of an Islamic republic of Lebanon (the way that the Khomeini Islamists did early in the course of the 1979 Revolution) – or, extending the same argument, could Hamas equally Islamize the Palestinian national liberation movement and degenerate into demanding and exacting an Islamic republic of Palestine, or, just to complete the regional picture, is it possible that the Mahdi's army (in collaboration with other Shi'is factions in Iraq) do the same and demand and exact an Islamic republic of Iraq? Nothing will make Israel and its US supporters happier than such a nightmare, and they will do anything in their power to achieve precisely that – the self-fulfilling prophecy of degenerating syncretic and cosmopolitan national liberation movements into tyrannical religious fanaticism that *ipso facto* justify the existence of a Jewish state in their vicinity and the Christian fundamentalism that informs US imperialism in the region. The Israeli propaganda treachery has already started conniving for such an eventuality in Lebanon by sending its commandos to fight the Hezbollah fighters while dressed in Lebanese army uniforms. But one fundamental fact articulated in three diverse settings speaks against such a possibility and promises the creation of three pluralist and cosmopolitan political cultures that would be the identical nightmare of the Jewish state, the Islamic Republic, and their Christian imperial arbiter. That single abiding fact is the demographic disposition of Lebanon, Palestine, and Iraq. In Lebanon and in Iraq the Shi'is are a slight majority with a significant minority complex, and in Palestine Hamas is but one of four major political factions. With a historical draw of luck for Lebanon and the entire region, Hezbollah has to (*has to*, not that it might or should or could – it simply *has to*) share power and contend with the Sunnis, the Christians, and the Druze with almost exactly the same logic that in Iraq, the Shi'is have to share power and content with the Sunnis and the Kurds, and in Palestine Hamas has to share power and content with Fatah, the Islamic Jihad, the PFLP and DFLP. In this respect, the Islamists in Lebanon, Palestine, and Iraq are exactly the opposite of the Islamists in the Islamic republic of Iran, where the Shi'is constitute the overwhelming majority of the population. The fortunate demographic diversity of Lebanon, Palestine, and Iraq works much to the advantage of a pluralistic society and a cosmopolitan political culture. Whereas in the Islamic republic the 95 percent plus Shi'i population projects the false assumption that the society at large is an "Islamic" society and nothing but an "Islamic" society – a false assumption that both the Islamic republic and even its so-called opposition among the reformists corroborate and put to a brutal political use to destroy and dismantle the cosmopolitan Iranian political culture that certainly includes the Islamists but is by no means limited to or defined by it. This sectarian reading of the regional politics is only pertinent if we think of these nations in terms of their sectarian breakdown and religious disposition and disregard the long and arduous history of their anti-colonial national liberation movements. In Lebanon, Palestine, Iraq, and even Iran, the Islamists have had to garb their religious sentiments in blatantly nationalist terms – and thus the emancipatory power of national liberation movements that still mobilizes these nations to rise up against all colonial and imperial designs targeting their sovereignty.

Perhaps a not so dissimilar warning is also due for the Lebanese Gucci revolutionaries, for the Rafik Hariri-Samir Qasir diehards who in their legitimate call for the Syrian withdrawal from Lebanon have degenerated into believing that the USA was their ally. Let the 34 consecutive and brutal days that the USA, UK, and even France dragged their feet while men, women, and children of Lebanon were massacred by the Israelis and their entire economic infrastructure was viciously destroyed be a lesson to those Gucci revolutionaries in Lebanon and their Syrian counterparts that their absolutely legitimate liberal concern for the cause of the middle class must be institutionally wedded to the cause of their national liberation – targeted against Syria and the Islamic republic as much as it must be articulated against Israel, the USA and the EU (UK in particular – remember how the US-made missiles swiftly dispatched to Israel to murder more Lebanese were given passageway through British airbases and airspace). These neocon artists – American, Israeli, or of the Tony Blair variety – are no friends of any national liberation movement, middle class or otherwise. Those huge posters of Rafik Hariri and that oversize statute of Samir Qasir in downtown Beirut are in dire need of revisiting by a grassroots, progressive, overarching and cosmopolitan national liberation movement in Lebanon – a movement to which Hezbollah must always remain integral but never definitive.

The single most important lesson from the latest military thuggery of Israel in Lebanon is the fact that the Jewish state wants to see the region in its own traumatized image: Jewish tribalism running amuck, for in effect the legitimacy of the Jewish state is entirely contingent not just on one but preferably on a multitude of Islamic republics in the region, so that with the Christian empire that presides over them all and the Hindu fundamentalism that lurks in its background the European Zionist colonial settlement finds itself in a natural habitat and is thus *ipso facto* legitimized – and so that with a *Jewish* state, a *Christian* empire, an *Islamic* republic, and a *Hindu* fundamentalism the whole world can go to hell in a hand-basket. With the same logic that the US neocons manufactured al-Qaeda in their own tribalist image, Israel wishes to project the Lebanese Hezbollah and the Palestinian Hamas as its own mirror reflection. The problem for Israel, however, as it clumsily tries to ape the USA and become a mini-empire in the region, is that neither Hezbollah nor Hamas is al-Qaeda – the figment of an over-militarized imagination of a miasmatic empire that needs an equally amorphous nemesis. Hezbollah and Hamas are and will remain two grassroots movements integral to two national liberation movements syncretic, pluralist, and cosmopolitan in their quintessential nature and disposition – and it is precisely that cosmopolitanism which is the nightmare of the medieval tribalism of the Jewish state, and that is precisely the reason that the Israeli warlords unleashed their unsurpassed military savagery on Lebanon with such vicious vengeance. To defeat Israel in terms emancipatory not just to the entirety of the region but in terms that in fact includes the 6 million plus inhabitants of Israel itself, and thus liberate them from the claws of their own tribal fanaticism, nothing can be more effective than generating and sustaining a multitude of pluralist civil societies and cosmopolitan political cultures in which grassroots Islamist movements like Hamas and Hezbollah will always be integral but never definitive. Islam thus in the world will mirror and reflect other religions in the world – so that Judaism, Christianity, Islam, Hinduism, Buddhism, etc., will no longer be world religions, as we have habitually known them, but religions-in-the-world. Any otherworldly claim these religions may have on their followers is ultimately tested by this worldliness.

7 Malcolm X as a Muslim revolutionary

> The shadow of a mighty Negro past flits through the tale of Ethiopia and of the Egypt the Sphinx. Throughout history, the powers of single blacks flash like falling stars, and die sometimes before the world has rightly gauged their brightness.
>
> W. E. B. Du Bois

I write this chapter under the bright light of a single shining star – the memory of Malcolm X and his dazzling flash of memorial insight into our collective predicament – not just as Muslims, or Americans, but for the historically disenfranchised and the defiantly determined peoples around the globe, and all of that from a decidedly Muslim perspective. To pave my way to this point, my principal concern in the previous chapter was for us to see through the false binaries – such as the Sunni–Shi'i divide – that have succeeded that of "Islam and the West" and continue to maim and mark the terms of a new revolutionary dispensation in which Islam (re-imagined) will have a positive role to play. Today Islam – in its global public perceptions – has been effectively degenerated into a whimsical plaything between Bush and Bin Laden, Blair and Berlusconi, Hirsi Ali and Azar Nafisi, Irshad Manji and Ibn Warraq – defining the terms of an ancient civilization and the pieties that define millions of human beings around the globe. Islam though at the very same time is also a freed and emancipated signifier (a moment that we should happily embrace and celebrate) – waiting to be renamed, reclaimed, resignified, placed squarely at the service of a legitimate resistance to an illegitimate imperial disposition that uses and abuses native informers and their white supremacist employers alike. Today, Islam has been narratively placed outside the world, in the contested rhetorical domain of the American neoconservatives and their terrorist cohorts – Bernard Lewis and Ayatollah Mesbah Yazdi are the mirror image of each other, as are Osama bin Laden and Hirsi Ali. Islam though at the very same time is also the emerging sign of a Muslim participation in a global struggle – from Asia to Africa to Latin America to the very heart of the US and Europe – that will have to abandon all its absolute and absolutist terms of self-righteous assertions if it is to reach for a more open-ended and cosmopolitan conception of itself, of the very foundation of any religion, any culture, any claim to worldly reason and social justice.

In the previous chapter I wanted to dwell on the climactic closure of "Islam and the West," for the simple reason that the "Islam" that "the West" had colonially crafted by forceful interlocution has now ended, as has that "West" that occasioned it. Under conditions code-named globalization, the rise of a renewed Islamic liberation theology, or an Islamic liberation theodicy, to be more exact, I wanted to argue, will have to be worked out from the ground zero of the most vital battlefields of our contemporary history – in Afghanistan, Iraq, Palestine, and Lebanon in particular. A realistic dream for Islam to have a positive and emancipatory role to play in these adjacent and interrelated regions will have to be integral to a cosmopolitan political culture in which Islam will remain integral but never definitive – as in the catastrophic case of the Islamic Republic of Iran – to the entirety of a political culture. This is one crucial lesson that Afghanistan, Iraq, Palestine, and Lebanon can learn from the criminal takeover of power by the Islamists in Iran against all other alternatives to their theocratic reign – and thus seeking to dismantle an entire cosmopolitan political culture. An Islamic republic is as, if not more, catastrophic in its essence and attributes than the Jewish state and the Christian empire it may pretend to fight but in effect mirrors, corroborates, and authenticates. Islam-in-the world is the worldly Islam in which Muslims re/think their most sacrosanct otherworldly tenets for a place in the world in which the face of their enemies – in a manner in which Emmanuel Levinas becomes a Muslim theologian – is the principal site of their emancipatory and embracing theodicy. An Islam in which a Muslim cannot look straight at the face of a Jewish Zionist settler in the occupied Palestine and see the face of his own brother and the countenance of her own sister, and the fate of their common folly, and then factor in and incorporate in the vision of its future the fact of their common claim to humanity, is an already discredited and lost Islam. When Islam is thus located in the world, the only Islamic liberation theology that makes perpetual sense is a cultivated theodicy that is always *on the case* of power but never *in power*, and in the liberating dialectic of that paradox dwells the share of an Islamic liberation theodicy for a global resistance to the persistent US imperial proclivities.

For Islam once again to become a theology of liberation, it first had to be liberated from the paralyzing binary of "Islam and the West." As a dialogical dyad, "Islam and the West" has ended, "the West" has imploded, and Islam is now a free and floating signifier in search of its own meaning and significance – with a much maligned countenance and in a much troubled world. Bush and Bin laden are too ephemeral historical nuisances to define anything, let alone the economy of meaning in the enormity of an ahistorical claim on history – for which purpose we need to pull back and look at one occasion when the fate of Islam and the fact of a visionary Muslim became one and the same.

How would have Malcolm X read the current world condition and explained it to an African American solider serving in the US military and stationed somewhere in Iraq? This simple exercise is not too hard to imagine or too futile to undertake. Resurrecting the defiant soul and the probing intellect of Malcolm X as a Muslim revolutionary, the problems that the word faces today have increasingly assumed an Islamic disposition, though they are not all of an Islamic provenance. The presence of the US-led forces in Iraq and Afghanistan, and the predominance of the Israeli military adventurism in the very same region spell out the modes of resistance to both in precisely Islamic terms. The persistence of a Jewish state, the vagaries of a Christian empire, and the belligerence of a Hindu fundamentalism cannot but color any mode of resistance to any and all of these adventures as Islamic. The systematic transmutation of American civil liberties, the overwhelming presence of African American and members of other disenfranchised communities in the US army, the evident racism at the root of American poverty, as best evident in the course of the Hurricane Katrina in August 2005, would have been the principal point of contact and conversation between Malcolm X and any African American soldier now serving in the US military.

First and foremost, there is no face-saving scenario for the USA or its European allies to pack and leave Iraq – the Baker–Hamilton report of the Iraq Study Group notwithstanding, and while the astounding accumulation of lies and deception at the commencement of this war are staring glaringly at any casual observer. The potential US/Israel invasion of Iran or Syria, and the continued Israeli occupation of Palestine and its warring posture against Lebanon are bound to exacerbate this state of war. The US-led invasion of Afghanistan was equally wrong and targeted the wrong people for the atrocities of 9/11 – the perpetrators of which had all perished along with their victims. Premised on that ill-fated invasion, in Afghanistan, the US/NATO/ISAF forces are entirely useless (except for periodically managing to kill scores of Afghan civilians)[1] and may indeed be forced to accept elements of the regrouped Taliban back inside the Afghan government – yet another exercise in futility, thousands of Afghan lives and millions of refugees in surrounding countries and around the globe later.

As George W. Bush's "long war against Islamofascism" (a term the powerful Zionist contingency of the US neocons has successfully sold him)[2] moves on from one disastrous year to another, the attention span of Americans is subdivided into an Osama bin Laden for their breakfast cereal, a Saddam Hussein for their sandwich at lunch, and an Ahmadinejad for their dinner table. In Iraq, the USA might in fact opt to side with the Shi'a faction led by Abd al-Aziz al-Hakim, the head of the Supreme Council for the Islamic revolution in Iraq in order to opposes the rabblerousing threats of Muqtada Sadr, in an ill-fated attempt to face the

Sunni-side of the anti-American insurrection – and thus effectively give birth to an Islamic republic of Iraq, right next to the Islamic Republic of Iran. This is of course in case the Saudi government (along with those of Egypt and Jordan) will abandon the Sunnis of Iraq to their own devices – a quite unlikely scenario, and thus the catastrophic prospect of the Iraqi civil war. The US-led departure from Iraq will certainly diminish the anti-colonial insurgency of the Iraqi resistance, but it is bound to procure even more sectarian violence, looming large on the horizon of an Islamic republic of Iraq. What did the Bush administration achieve in Iraq – Malcolm X would have likely asked and wondered: a mega-billion dollar military adventurism indefinitely casting the whole world into a perilous disposition – for which the world is infinitely less safe and Americans (innocent or guilty) infinitely more despised.

The catastrophic consequences of US/Israel military adventurism is not limited to Iraq of course and is cast widely over the entire region – not as the "birth pangs of a new Middle East" as the US Secretary of State Condoleezza Rice put it in a moment of hyperbolic mendacity, but in fact in its exact metaphoric opposite and as the death trap of everything decent and hopeful in the region. The uncharted and miasmatic violence that the US-led invasion and occupation of Iraq has caused, conditioned, and sustained is in danger of spreading widely in the region. Afghanistan is still simmering with the violence that the US-led invasion in October 2001 had generated, sustained, and prolonged. As a major military subcontractor for the USA and Saudi Arabia, Pakistan is itself full of political and religious tension – both within itself and *vis-à-vis* India. The same is true about the Islamic Republic of Iran, fearful of a US/Israel invasion, exceedingly intolerant of reformist moves by its own citizens. Palestine continues to be the killing field of Israel, with Lebanon always at the mercy of the Jewish state and its military whims. The Turkish repression of its Kurdish population, its denial of the Armenian genocide, and its wishes to be included as part of EU all go hand in hand. The degenerate and backward conglomerate of Saudi Arabia, the Persian Gulf states, Kuwait, and Jordan suffer under medieval potentates masquerading as modern nation-sates. The rest of the Arab and North African scene continues to defy the will of its progressive and cosmopolitan cultures under one form of authoritarian regime that the US fully endorses (Egypt and Morocco) or another that it does not (Syria, Sudan, or Libya). Thus the war in Afghanistan is organically connected to the war in Iraq, each exacerbating the other, most probably dragging Iran into the quagmire, with Israel, Saudi Arabia, and all other illegitimate state apparatus like them as the sole beneficiaries of any scenario of conflict and mayhem. The theater of warfare may well extend into Africa, with Somalia, Ethiopia, Eritrea, Sudan, and Chad as the most obvious sites of confrontation between a senseless and miasmatic Islamist adventurism and the US-led war of terrorism that in fact generates and exacerbates that very Islamism it claims to oppose.

The legacy of the Bush administration in the region, all articulated, theorized, and executed with the intellectually bankrupt and morally degenerate ideologies of the US neoconservative movement, is going to wreak havoc – and the USA and its European and regional allies are singularly responsible for the calamity. Starting from the East, nobody is now holding successive American administrations responsible for (along with the Saudis) funding, arming, and managing the anti-Soviet Afghan Mojahedin, including Osama bin Laden, in Afghanistan in the 1980s. The Pakistani intelligence was chiefly responsible for the creation of the Taliban. Despite its long and proud anti-colonial history and widely held cosmopolitan culture, Pakistan is reduced to a military client state of the USA, performing military duties and getting paid for it.

The same ignoble record is the history of the USA in Afghanistan, where the US-manufactured Taliban and al-Qaeda are now poised to stage a comeback and put their perfected tactics in Iraq to effective use in ousting the ridiculous puppet regime of Hamid Karzai, "the Mayor of Kabul." The woes of Afghanistan meanwhile have intensified – poor, desolate, riddled with tribal factionalism of the most retrograde and criminal sort, all endemic to a colonially manufactured state and yet all radically intensified in the aftermath of the first Soviet and now the US-led invasion – with the civilian population the principal victim of all these varied forms of military thuggery. Every inch of any infrastructure of a civil society or even a hope for a cosmopolitan political culture have been systematically destroyed, if not by the Soviets then by the Taliban, if not by Taliban then in the aftermath of the US-led invasion and NATO-led occupation, and by the reckless and enduring legacy of the globalized al-Qaeda, headquartered on the ruins of Afghanistan. Every single American who voted for President Bush, including those who did not and yet thought the US-led invasion of Afghanistan was a "just war" is responsible for the total destruction of a nation-state and the subsequent creation of a globalized terrorist network. Half a decade into its "liberation," Afghanistan is a zest pool of religious fanaticism, tribal conflict, peppered with US-led torture chambers, a thriving narcotic terrain of warlords whose sense of morality is only slightly better than American and European corporate chief executive officers. The US–NATO forces will be defeated there, as were the Russians – and Afghanistan will be back where it was, a desolate landscape of poverty and fanaticism, a major supplier of hashish and heroin for the suburban boredom of Europe and the USA.

The fate of 70 million Iranians and their continued struggles for political liberty and economic justice has suffered a major setback precisely in the aftermath of the US-led military adventurism in Afghanistan and Iraq. In the eyes of the US military analysts (e.g. Seyyed Vali Reza Nasr of the US Naval Postgraduate School), the entire moral and political universe of Iran is now reduced to a Shi'i state apparatus hunting for power in the region. The only manner that the illegitimate reign of the clerical clique can be sustained, throughout its beleaguered recent history, has been via an assumption of a warring posture vis-à-vis the USA and/or Israel, an excuse that the US neocon imperialism has offered on a silver plate to their clerical counterparts in the Islamic Republic. Whether via economic embargo, military maneuvers in the Persian Gulf, Arabian Sea, and the Indian Ocean, or insidious instigation of ethnic unrest in southern provinces, the USA is pulling out some of the oldest colonial tricks in the British hat to weaken and or/intimidate the Islamic republic.

Moving westward from Iran, Iraq is the singular site of shame if those responsible for this egregious act of criminal invasion and occupation of a sovereign nation-state were to have any notion of shame. Malcolm X would have had no difficulty demonstrating to an African American soldier serving in Iraq that Iraq is now reduced to nothing more than a constellation of US military bases guarding the flow of oil to provide gas to the alleviation of its bored suburban population getting into their SUVs and going for a ride. First Afghanistan and now Iraq, the region is one sovereign nation-state at a time being reduced to a shooting gallery for the enduring entertainment of Zach Snyder's generation of computer-generated imagery (CGI)-infested militarized imagination.

Meanwhile Palestine remains the killing field of a racist, supremacist, apartheid Jewish state systematically stealing, occupying, and appropriating the homeland of another people. The principal partner of US imperialism in the region and beyond, the European colonial settlement wants to reduce the entire region into medieval sectarian division on its own fanatic image – Islamic republics, a Christian empire, and a Hindu fundamentalism that makes the Jewish state feel at home in its neighborhood. Extending its thuggish operation beyond Palestine and into Lebanon, Syria, and possibly even Iran, the historical calamity called "Israel" is now completely divorced even from its own original Zionist ideals and degenerated into the military extension of the USA's imperial operations in the region.

The circle of misery that the US-led militarism in the region has drawn, Malcolm X would explain, is not limited to what Bernard Lewis has taught them to call "the Middle East." The USA is now actively aiding the corrupt leadership of Ethiopia (the Pakistan of North Africa) so that it does its dirty work in Somalia (the Afghanistan of North Africa). The result is simple and obvious: more battle zones, more overt and covert US operations in North Africa, more civilian deaths, more millions of refugees – on yet another "front in the war on terrorism."

What about Europe – the cradle of civilization? How would Malcolm X see Europe today? The blatantly racist policies of the EU, exacerbated by massive labor migrations into its aging population, and its unfailing support for (and hidden rivalries with and within) the US-led invasions of Afghanistan and Iraq have made it a solid accomplice in warmongering and thus in part explains the attraction of the disenfranchised, anomie-ridden youth of the immigrant communities to al-Qaeda-like cells. While Europe is going through what its philosophers and public intellectuals – from Julia Kristeva to Etienne Balibar to Jürgen Habermas – see as its identity crisis, waves of immigrant laborers have tested the thin veneer covering its endemic racism. Steadily falling birthrates, unsustainable welfare systems, major waves of labor migration, consistently resurfacing European racism (once against Jews and now against Muslims) and a contingency of Islamist militancy are now fast upon Europe. As if it did not have enough trouble with admitting Romania and Bulgaria into its civilizing bosoms, now even Turkey wants to be European too. Meanwhile even the European nation-states are themselves in danger of disintegration – from the Scots in the United Kingdom to the Flemish nationalists in Belgium. The racist attempts to keep Turkey out of the EU inevitably alienates European Muslims and makes evident the ludicrous attempts of people like Tariq Ramadan who are trying to define a place of dignity for "European Muslims" in that racist context. In these circumstances, the future of France is an index of what Europe holds in its days to come. That future was very much contingent on the presidential election 2007, when the outright fascist aspirations of Jean-Marie Le Pen and the neocon look-alike Nicolas Sarkozy defined the terms of the debate, where the centrist François Bayrou and the socialist Ségolène Royal needed to place themselves. The victory of Nicolas Sarkozy in the French presidential election of 2007 goes a long way to eradicate any delusion people might have about the constitutional racism that underlies French society and its anti-immigrant chauvinism. These immigrants, those from Africa in particular, did not fall from the sky, nor are they attracted to France because of its splendid weather. They are the children of French colonialism coming home to roost – as Malcolm X was wont of saying. In this context, the hypocrisy of Europeans (who actually perpetrated the Holocaust) in pointing the finger at the Islamic republic for denying it – as if that conference that Ahmadinejad convened to distract the world's attention from his faction's miserable failures at the municipal elections was anything but a subterfuge for a far more endemic disaster. But the stratagems of the clerical cliques in the Islamic republic can always rely on the hypocrisy, racism, and guilty conscience of Europeans – who will do anything to distract attention from the facts of their own history by shifting the attention somewhere else.

Inside the USA proper, Malcolm X would further add, the catastrophic consequences of the neoconservative project are yet to be mapped out and thoroughly assayed. What the neocons have done to the USA and its political culture would be something beyond Malcolm X's measures of expectation. So much flagrant thuggery around the globe might be identical with what the US did in Vietnam – but where is the antiwar and civil rights movement that it also engendered at the time? With what imperial audacity and self-righteous hubris did this band of militant fanatics take over the democratic institutions of a nation-state and allow themselves the mendacity of pre-emptive war, changing regimes, ending states, moral and intellectual parochialism running amuck, a global gangster mentality standing for international diplomacy, and promoting neoliberal thievery of the poor world for the benefit of the rich? Thus limited by terms domestic to their own moral and imaginative provincialism, Americans were getting ready for the presidential election of 2008 with their leading choices in ever more narrower and impoverished terms. The democratic victory in the 2007 midterm elections amounted to absolutely nothing when it came to the congressional allocation of yet another gargantuan military budget (US$100 billion) to President Bush to do as he pleases in/to the utterly annihilated Iraq.

The picture of the world at large framing this state of affairs befits its crocked timber. A desperate and disparate population almost the size of the USA's is now roaming the earth as migrant laborers. As many Indians live in desperate poverty in what advertises itself as "the greatest democracy in the world." The overwhelming majority of Indian Muslims living in rural areas are in fact landless laborers, while more than half of the urban Muslims in India lives under the poverty line. The influx of African and Asian migrant laborers into Europe has caused massive manifestations of European racism, while the flow of Asians and Latinos into the USA has already given rise to such racist vigilante groups as the Minutemen. That influx of migrant workers around the globe is the gateway of potential troubles on both sides of any border they cross, with catastrophic global consequences far beyond the ability or willingness of the World Bank or the IMF to address. Thus a mobile army of homeless laborers, war and terrorism in the Middle East, hunger and AIDS in Africa, imperialist hubris and religious fanaticism in the USA, belligerent military thuggery of Israel, rampant racism in Europe are the most compelling signs of the new century. Add to these the fact that according to the most recent scientific reports (February 2007), there is now incontrovertible evidence that the Arctic is irrevocably melting away and by the year 2040 global summers will be entirely ice-free. Instead of waiting for Doomsday, the logic of capitalism is already thinking of how to bank on this thing called climate change and turn it into a business proposition. These facts and the human cost of their consequences would be on Malcolm X's mind were his noble and defiant soul still with us, and were he to begin from the ground zero of our evident history and think through the otherwise than what we have now inherited on this earth.

In 1948, a young Egyptian intellectual named Sayyid Qutb (1906–1966) came to the USA for his higher education and went to Greeley, Colorado, where he enrolled at Colorado State Teachers College, now the University of Northern Colorado. By the time he received his degree in education and went back to Egypt in 1951, Sayyid Qutb was convinced that American society was fundamentally corrupt, decadent, and irredeemable. In part because of this American sojourn and his hasty conclusions, as soon as Sayyid Qutb arrived in his homeland he joined a thriving Islamist organization called Muslim Brotherhood. For the rest of his life, Sayyid Qutb had a lasting influence on the rise of militant Islamism in the Arab and the Muslim world.[3]

As historical fate would have it, and by way of a strange historical coincidence, precisely in the same year that Sayyid Qutb came to the USA, a young delinquent African American who would later be known as Malcolm X (1925–1965) was introduced to and converted to Islam while serving time at Concord Reformatory in Massachusetts on charges of grand larceny and breaking and entering. Almost exactly at the same time that Sayyid Qutb was a student in the USA (1948–1951), Malcolm X was in various US jails (1946–1952). And there is the paradox: Sayyid Qutb came to the USA and there in complete freedom became increasingly incarcerated inside a tunnel vision of his own faith, while imprisoned inside a jail at the very same time, Malcolm X discovered an emancipatory vision of Islam far more liberating and entirely outside the limits of the great Egyptian Islamist's horizon. A year after Sayyid Qutb returned to Egypt and joined the Muslim Brotherhood, Malcolm X was freed from prison and joined the Nation of Islam as a devout Muslim and began a valiant, however brutally short, career as a revolutionary vanguard of increasingly more global horizons. One can look forward to the future of Islam in the twenty-first century by a comparison and contrast between these two Muslim revolutionaries, one, Sayyid Qutb, an Egyptian militant Islamist who *came to* the USA and his encounter with America led him and the brand of Islamism he represented to an entrapment of his faith in a self-defeating ideology; and the other, Malcolm X, an African American Muslim who increasingly *left* the USA for the world and his liberating reading of Islam led to an emancipation of his faith in a progressively revolutionary direction.[4]

Revisiting the extraordinary life and the short career of Malcolm X as a Muslim revolutionary is important not despite his flaws and missteps, but in fact precisely because of them. From the heart of his and his people's entrapment in misery, Malcolm X resurrected hope and cultivated a vision of the world at once fully cognizant of its factual flaws and yet charged with a determination to set it right. Malcolm X was both a victim of racism and had to overcome his own reverse racism to reach the moment of liberation for Muslims at large. In many ways, Muslims around the world today are where Malcolm X was just before his historic Hajj pilgrimage, and as historical fate would have it, Muslims too, in their millions seem to be in need of not just a regular and habitual Hajj pilgrimage, but a pilgrimage that cleanses their own soul of much malady that has afflicted them, and if they are to face the abuse of power by warmongers outside and descending upon them they will have to first and foremost face their own innate enduring fallacies and endemic faults. In a long and arduous conversation with a barbaric European colonialism that ravaged the earth, Muslims effectively turned their own faith into the split image of the ideologies of their enemies – intolerant, abusive, fanatical, single-minded.

As Sayyid Qutb abandoned his earlier literary career and commenced his life as a Muslim revolutionary, he was instrumental in leading Islam of his time (with the best of intentions) into the cul-de-sac of a militant politics trapped inside a binary opposition with its arch nemesis, "the West." Exactly in the opposite direction, Malcolm X shed one revolutionary skin after another, reaching out for nothing but a consistently emancipatory project, seeing in Islam not a matter of identity politics but a manner of liberating promises. His was the zeal of a new convert and the vision of a world revolutionary in tune with the spirit of his time. The more Sayyid Qutb vilified the USA blindly (including some of his racist comments about African Americans and about jazz, from which he understood absolutely nothing – and from whose democratic spirit he could have learned much), the more he was trapped into a blindfold celebration of an intolerant, belligerent, and combative Islam. Islam for Malcolm X was an equally combative occasion, but as an infinitely more liberating, progressive, alive, and living organism. In more than 200 years of encounter with colonial modernity, and literary hundreds of radical Muslim thinkers, no Muslim revolutionary comes even close to Malcolm X in the liberating, global, and visionary grasp of his faith and its place in facing the barefaced barbarity of economic and military world domination. Perhaps because he emerged from the heart of that barbarity, perhaps because he was the direct target of its most racist ideas and practices – Malcolm X personified the life of a Muslim revolutionary for generations after "Islam and the West" had exhausted its historical calamities.

There is much need of soul-searching in and about Islam. If a religion at its current stage has managed at one and the same time to produce a Molla Omar and a Hirsi Ali, an Osama bin Laden and an Ibn Warraq, an Ayman al-Zawahiri and a Fouad Ajami, an Ayatollah Khomeini and an Azar Nafisi (identical fanaticism in different buckets), that religion then is indeed in dire need of soul-searching. Beginning with juridically stipulated gender apartheid constitutional to Islamic law, Muslims today face a range of moral and political dilemmas at the root of the systematic mutation of their collective faith into a singular site of political resistance to imperialism at the heavy and unacceptable price of leveling their own religion to the ground of the imperial assault against Muslims. The nomocentricity of Islamic law has historically been checked and balanced by the logocentricity of its philosophy and the anthropocentricity of its mysticism – and all of that by the literary humanism definitive to Arabic, Persian, Turkish, and Urdu languages. All the polyfocality of voices with which Islam has historically spoken has over the last 200 years been systematically muted and silenced by the aggressive formation of a singularly juridical fanaticism, hitherto justified by virtue of an all-out war against a predatory European colonialism and American imperialism – with the Jewish state of Israel linking the heritage of one to the calamities of the other. What Muslims need is not a *reformation* (for which neoliberal European and American journalism have created a few would-be "Muslim Martin Luthers") but in fact a *restoration* of the classical polyfocality of their worldly religion, before it was aggressively mutated into a singular site of contestation against colonialism. The unconditional equality of men and women in all matters of legal, social, economic, and political domains is not something that needs to await a "modernization" or "reformation" of Islamic societies, but a matter soundly at the root of the democratic polyfocality of Islamic intellectual history. The unconditional freedom of expression for all political positions and parties, entirely independent of their compatibility with Islamic legal precepts, is the only way in which Muslims can remain Muslims but within a larger normative polity that embraces them but is not embraced by them. Reaching for a complete acknowledgment of the ideological and normative variations at the root of contemporary societies is not inimical but in fact entirely normative to Islamic intellectual history. The moral autonomy of the creative soul, at the widest spectrum of its worldly presence, is constitutional to the lived experiences of Muslims the world over – lost all but entirely through the vapid ideologization of Islam by Muslim thinkers themselves. A historic return to their own worldly and cosmopolitan cultures (in liberating plurals) is the swiftest manner in which Muslims can remember and re-enact the polyfocality of their own faith. Muslims have always had this cosmopolitanism but never seen it *in toto* because they have seen it through the lenses of extreme close-ups of their own angle on reality. What they need today is a long take/long distance shot of their own cosmopolitan culture, a frame that remembers and embraces all their historical differences, without eradicating them – their philosophers, mystics, jurists, and literary humanists standing at large and in adjacent proximity of their enduring differences. At the threshold of that recognition is where Malcolm X has left us, and it is at the threshold of his unfinished project and that universal conception of Islam that we need to pick up our senses and come up with a mode of liberation theodicy that does not dismiss but in fact wholeheartedly embraces and lovingly welcomes all the shades and shadows of its differences. What Islam needs, in short, is a Levinasian phenomenology wedded to the unfinished revolutionary project of Malcolm X as a Muslim revolutionary.

Retrieving the legacy of Malcolm X as a Muslim revolutionary in the heart of the globalizing empire shows how in his character and culture he represents a radical epistemic shift in the manufactured opposition between "Islam and the West." No globally minded liberation movement will have any legitimacy without categorically including the disenfranchised communities within the USA (or within the so-called "West") – in the very heart of the globalizing empire. Contrary to what Sayyid Qutb perceived, and exactly as Malcolm X realized, the USA is a microcosm of the world at large – there is already a Third World in that part of the First World: they are the poor and the disinherited among the Native Americans, African Americans, Latino-Americans, Asian Americans, and then among a rainbow of new – legal and illegal – immigrants from around the globe. If Islam does not have anything to say or to offer to these disenfranchised communities – the legal and illegal immigrants at the mercy of Minutemen sharpshooters – without asking them to convert to Islam, then it is nothing but the fatuous faith of the Khaliji, Kuwaiti, and Saudi sheikhs having difficulty bending over their overfed bellies when pretending to prostrate to pray, or else the rambling gibberish of Osama bin Laden and Mulla Omar when replicating the American neocons in their advocacy of terror. There is another Islam unknown to those crooked bodies – the Islam of South Asian migrant laborers in the United Arab Emirates, the Islam of Malcolm X – the Islam that knows how to speak to those multitudes of misery without asking them first to believe in Allah (for they already do, in their own mind and manner). In his revolutionary character and iconoclastic legacy, Malcolm X links any global conception of an Islamic liberation movement to the heart of the most progressive uprising of the wretched of this earth. As such, Malcolm X is a singularly important rebellious character whose conversion to Islam and the massive epistemic shift that it occasioned in the course of his revolutionary career is yet to be properly understood and thoroughly theorized. In the revolutionary character of Malcolm X is gathered the most critical link necessary between the alienated colonial corners of capitalist modernity and the disenfranchised communities within its metropolitan center. The significance of Malcolm X is that he rises from the heart of the metropolitan disenfranchised poor and moves out to reach one of the most massively manufactured civilizational others of "the West" in the Islamic world. In his revolutionary legacy, as a result, we already have a radical bridge connecting the center and periphery of a globe that is no longer thus divided. Retrieving his critical character as a Muslim revolutionary is thus quintessential to any assessment of an Islamic liberation project.

The most pernicious achievement of Orientalism was not that it was a discourse of *domination* – but that it was a discourse of *alienation*. Through the generation of a false consciousness in the form of civilizational divides, Orientalism has been instrumental in alienating the colonial corners of capitalist modernity from their integral connection to the vicious cycle of capital. By summoning and dispatching the colonial world into a manufactured civilizational other – Islamic, African, Chinese, Indian, etc. – Orientalism was the most insidious ideological force at the service of colonial modernity, systematically alienating the living labor of the colonials from their accumulated labor coagulated in the heartlands of metropolitan capital. A false categorical distinction was thus generated and sustained between the working class in the heart of capitalism and those in its colonial periphery, because they were assigned to two colonially fabricated civilizations – "the West" versus "the Rest." It is not until the dawn of the so-called *globalization* that the sheer inanity of this fabricated distinction between metropolitan capital and colonial labor has been *ipso facto* bridged.

The significance of Malcolm X is that he rises from the heart of the metropolitan disenfranchised poor in the USA and moves out to reach one of the most massively manufactured civilizational other of "the West" in the Islamic world. In his revolutionary character, as a result, we already have a transgressive bridge connecting the wretched of the earth otherwise treacherously separated by the project of Orientalism (squarely at the service of European colonialism) into two false civilizational camps – a project initiated and sustained by European colonialism (and followed by American imperialism) to divide the world in order to rule it better. If Bernard Lewis has spent a long life manufacturing and perpetuating a division between "Islam and the West," Malcolm X spent a short but fruitful life linking that binary opposition and proving Bernard Lewis and his band of Orientalists wrong. Malcolm X successfully crossed the powerful psychological divide that Bernard Lewis and a whole herd of like-minded Orientalists spent manufacturing. There is no other revolutionary figure who like Malcolm X so gracefully and courageously climbs over that dilapidated wall that mercenary Orientalists have constructed between the Western part of their own perturbed imagination and the rest of the world to separate the poor and the working class into the colonially engineered cultures and civilizations – in order to be able to dispatch impoverished Americans to maim and murder their own brothers and sisters half way around the globe. Retrieving the critical character of Malcolm X as a Muslim revolutionary is quintessential to any Islamic liberation theodicy that must by definition include the ailing heart of this empire.

In any assessment of Malcolm X's life and revolutionary appeal, one must pay close attention to his episodic changes and epistemic shifts. In his own autobiographical account, Malcolm X divides his life into the period before his conversion to Islam and the period after that.[5] One might further extrapolate the periods after his historic Hajj pilgrimage that resulted in abandoning the racist assumption that only black people could be Muslim (a natural but fallacious reaction to the endemic racism he faced in the USA), and soon after that his break with the Nation of Islam and the establishment of his own mosque. This period is marked by an expansive contact with the most progressive revolutionary movements of his time. The closer we look at the episodic moves in Malcolm X's short but tumultuous life the more we notice the heroic shifts that he initiated in his thinking and activism. With each move, he expanded his horizons, widened his vision, and embraced a more global conception of what needed to be done. With every move, he became less authentic in any identity claim to his character – black, American, or even a Muslim – and more of a revolutionary in his commitments to a global uprising against the moral decadence that underlined the political domination of a few over the historic fate of the overwhelming majority of the inhabitants of the globe. With every move, he expanded what it meant to be a Muslim revolutionary, in terms tolerant of diversity and dissent, intolerant of dogmatism and essentialism. In his identitarian inauthenticities (for he ran away from many stereotypes) he was far more of an authentic revolutionary, his religious monotheism always seasoned by a political polytheism. For Islam in its widest and most global reach to become a relevant force in the age of rapid globalization, this expansive, tolerant, self-transformative, and auto-critical legacy of Malcolm X will have to become exemplary. Malcolm X had a reckoning with Islam. It is time Islam had a reckoning with Malcolm X.

In the biographical account now available through the monumental Malcolm X Project at Columbia University, we read a far more nuanced distribution of the varied phases of his life. Predicated on an early and brutal exposure to violent racism (1925–1940), Malcolm X witnessed the murder of his own father, Earl Little, in the hands of a gang of Ku Klux Klan in 1931 when he was only six years old. In his youthful years, Malcolm X moved to Boston and led the life of a small time hustler (1941–1946), was arrested, and jailed. It was during his prison years (1946–1952) that Malcolm X successfully broke through the cycle of racism and violence that had so far defined his young life. His conversion to Islam, membership in the Nation of Islam, and subsequent political activism took shape right here and far into future. After he was released from prison, Malcolm X spent the next five years (1952–1957) transforming the Nation of Islam from its limited, ghettoized, and parochial vision into a vastly popular and increasingly revolutionary movement among African Americans. The next four years of Malcolm X's life (1957–1961) marked two crucial encounters that amount to a major epistemic shift in his revolutionary thinking: one was his trip in July 1959 to the Arab and Muslim world – he traveled to Egypt on an invitation of Gamal Abd al-Nasser and from there he went to Saudi Arabia, Sudan, Nigeria, and Ghana; and the other was in September 1960, when he met with Fidel Castro at Harlem's Hotel Theresa. These two events, plus the July 1959 broadcasting of a five-part television report called "The Hate That Hate Produced" (by journalists Louis Lomax and Mike Wallace) effectively turned Malcolm X into a national figure with a global perspective to his revolutionary politics. He now defined the Nation of Islam, but the Nation of Islam did not define him.

The next two years of Malcolm X's life, (January 1961 to December 1963) marked the end of his involvement with the Nation of Islam, and his increasingly militant disposition against racist violence targeted towards blacks and Muslims. The assassination of President Kennedy on Friday November 22 1963, and Malcolm X's dismissal of the national tragedy as "chickens coming home to roost," resulted in his eventual banishment and his own subsequent official resignation from the Nation of Islam on March 8 1964. The period between March and June 1964 marked the most important emancipatory move of Malcolm X away from the limited provincialism of the Nation of Islam and toward the articulation of a more global revolutionary agenda – all occasioned by his historic Hajj pilgrimage.

His break from the Nation of Islam and his Hajj pilgrimage point to the expansion of a far wider circle of revolutionary commitments that certainly embrace but are not limited by the suffocating parochialism that forced him out of his debilitating entanglements with his American Muslim brothers. He was already, by the time he left the Nation of Islam, looking at a revolutionary prospect far wider and more radical than what the American version of "Muslim Brotherhood" could possibly sustain or even imagine or represent. This larger and more global vision, and certainly not merely his disillusion with Elijah Muhammad, was at stake when he finally broke away from the Nation of Islam.

After he performed his Hajj pilgrimage, Malcolm X's life yet again assumes an expansive horizon towards a larger frame of revolutionary references. He went on a whirlwind tour in April and May 1964, traveling all the way from New York to Beirut, and from there to Cairo, and then to Lagos, Nigeria and from there to Ghana, Liberia, Senegal, Morocco, Algeria, etc. Everywhere he went he was widely received by the most progressive forces in the Arab and Muslim world, as well as in Africa. It was after this trip and in the following summer, in June 1964, that Malcolm X announced the establishment of the Organization of Afro-American Unity (OAAU), an organization that was no longer limited to Muslims or Americans in the range of its ambitious projects, linking, in effect, the freedom of African Americans to those of Africans at large. He formulated a wide-ranging social and political agenda for OAAU, and established its branches in Asia, Africa, and Europe. When by January 1965, he was forced by the Nation of Islam to leave his home in East Elmhurst, he no longer needed a home. The world was his home.

What was he doing on these trips, navigating one political clime and country after another? Without abandoning his base as a Muslim revolutionary, he used these trips to expand the moral domain of his concern to even larger global perspectives. By the time that in December 1964 Malcolm X spoke before 500 people alongside the Tanzanian revolutionary Abdul Rahman Mohammad Babu and read a message to the audience from none other than Che Guevara (who had been invited but could not attend), his stature and message as a global revolutionary had reached a far more embracing horizon than any Muslim revolutionary of his (or any other) time. By the time that in February 1965 he took his revolutionary message to Europe, he spoke for the universality of a global uprising on par with anyone, ranging from Lenin and Trotsky to Frantz Fanon and Che Guevara. He was and he remained a Muslim, but the Islam of Sayyid Qutb and that of generations of other Muslim revolutionaries trapped inside a binary opposition between two false consciousness, "Islam and the West," no longer limited, defined, or confined him. He globalized the revolutionary quintessence of Islam long before *globalization* became a fashionable catchword.

When early in February 1965 Malcolm X turned his attention to domestic American issues and went to Alabama for a series of lectures, he was no longer a mere national figure. His global vision had already wedded domestic American issues to larger revolutionary projects. His trip later that month to London and Birmingham and his denial of entry into Paris were the further indices of his global stature. The more this revolutionary message becomes global, the less Malcolm X has a claim even to a home for his family in New York. Soon after his return from Europe, early in the morning of February 14 1965, his home, with his entire family in it, was firebombed. Soon after this bombing, the title of his talk at Colgate Rochester Divinity School on February 16 1965, "Not Just an American Problem, but a World Problem" pretty much sums up his state of mind at this point. When in the afternoon of February 18 1965 he delivered a lecture to about 1500 Barnard and Columbia students, he may have had no clue that this was the last speech he was to give, but he knew full well of his global significance. Is it then accidental, or merely symbolic, that he spent the last night of his life on February 19 1965 homeless and in a hotel room? On February 21 1965 Malcolm X's earthly life was abruptly ended and he became a legend.[6]

Paramount in my conception of Islam in its encounter with colonial modernity is a dialogical reading of any world religion in active conversation with its location in history. The Islam of the last 200 years was the result of a combative conversation between Muslims and their European colonial occupiers. At the threshold of the twenty-first century, when this particular Islam has ended by virtue of both its own internal contradictions (radically mutating its own multifaceted visions of reality into a singular site of absolutist ideological resistance to colonial modernity) and also because "the West," as its principal interlocutor that had teased out of Muslims a particularly combative reading of their own faith has ended. That Islam has come to an end because the "Western modernity," with which it was in a prolonged, combative, and collective conversation has self-imploded, ended under the pressure of its own contradictions – as outlined, argued, and demonstrated by European philosophers all the way from Nietzsche and Kierkegaard to Adorno and Horkheimer and down to Deleuze and Guattari.

The dialogical disposition of Islam, or any other world religion for that matter, is not manifested only in its encounter with colonial modernity. Throughout its long and languid history, Islam has always been the dialectical outcome of a creative encounter between the Qur'anic revelation and Hadith narratives on one side and the social, intellectual, moral, and political powers that have come to face, challenge, augment, or else to contradict it. From Greek philosophy to the Persian empire, from Jewish theology to Christian monasticism, from Chinese astronomy to Indian mathematics – historically a succession of intellectual and political forces have been formative in negotiating out of Muslims particular readings of their own collective faith. The same is true with the European colonial modernity over the last 200 years, both in terms of the brute colonial power that dispatched

Europeans around the world to plunder, maim, and murder people, and their Enlightenment project that commenced, coincided, and concurred with these globe-trotting adventures, putting an inordinate amount of pressure on Christianity to hurry up, revise its medieval doctrines, dogmas, and practices and prove more useful to European colonialism. Thus began the Muslim dialogical encounters with "Western modernity." This dialogical disposition extended from a combative conversation with "the West" – a figment of imagination that this particular Islam epistemically corroborated by being its mirror image – to an equally belligerent dialogue with rival ideologies, competing for the strategic alliances of classes and masses for political resistance to colonialism. Islamism thus joined nationalism and socialism and formed the three most dominant political ideologies of the nineteenth and twentieth century in Muslim lands. Islamism was as much influenced by anti-colonial socialism and nationalism, as these two ideologies in their Muslim mutations were by Islam. The result of this vertical (colonial) and horizontal (in competition with nationalist and socialist ideologies) is that Islamism itself freely and unconsciously partook not only in the nationalist rhetoric and socialist agenda, but *ipso facto* (albeit negationally) corroborated the globalizing project of "Western modernity."

The manufacturing of this "Western modernity" corresponded to a particular phase of European capitalism, and the advent of postmodernism, correlated to what Frederic Jameson calls, "the cultural logic of late capitalism," has radically changed the innate correspondence between Eurocentric capital, manufacturing of "the Western civilization," and the Orientalist engineering of pre-modern civilizations as "Islamic, Chinese, Indian," by way of corroborating "The West" as the Hegelian promise of history. In this schemata, while the Eurocentric operation of capital was culturally code-named "the West," all its colonial peripheries were delegated to "the East" or the Orient, which for the father of European Enlightenment Immanuel Kant extended from the East of Danube, all around the globe, to the west of the British Isles. The postmodern condition of the late capitalist dismantling of "the West," corresponding to the amorphous nature of a globalized capital that is no longer in need of civilizational divides will have to face alternative modes of dividing the world to conquer it – for the axis of East and West, or even North and South, have now melted down to a shapeless and amorphous world. In this context, Islam is no longer in combative conversation with "the West," for "the Western modernity" itself, as the logic of early capitalism, has been superceded by that very logic that once created it – and thus Islam has lost its principal colonial interlocutor of the last 200 years. In the aftermath of the current phase of iconic and spectacular violence – code-named Osama Bin Laden – the world will have to face an amorphous capital, a predatory empire with no hegemony, and thus necessarily pockets of regional, cross-cultural resistance to this empire; in this world, the future Islamic liberation theology will have to face not a concrete "West," for it no longer exists, but an amorphous capital and a shapeless, graceless, brute, and naked predatory empire (with no hegemony).

Under these circumstances and against a nebulous empire, global and always tenuous, there is only one way of resistance – regional and cross-cultural. Islamic liberation theology must learn from Christian liberation theology, and vice versa[7] – and they must account for the existence of what in the language of political tolerance will have to be named alternative ideologies of resistance, with which any liberation theology (Islamic or otherwise) must come into coalition and conversation, not combative rivalry. This is the singular lesson of Islamic revolution in Iran and if from the ashes of that failed revolution the fire of a new liberation theology is to emerge it is though a *theodicy*, a *liberation theodicy*, a mode of theology that embraces its own opposites and alternatives. Examples in our contemporary world abound. Hamas in Palestine cannot be a legitimate component of the Palestinian national liberation movement unless and until it learns the art of compromise with its Fatah rivals. The Hezbollah in Lebanon cannot be a *bona fide* force in the emergence of Lebanon as an enduring nation-state unless and until it accepts the legitimate presence of non-Shi'i and particularly non-Islamic and non-religious forces in the Lebanese polity. The same is true of the Shi'is in Iraq who will have to, when the occupiers of Iraq have collected their belonging and left, enter into negotiation with non-Shi'i, non-Islamic, and non-religious factions and forces in Iraq. In this respect, the increasing presence of Muslims in Europe is equally crucial for the rise of a mode of resistance to the predatory powers of empires – American or European in denomination – that is not reducible to one religious or ideological denomination or another. By way of correcting their own blind spots and becoming part of not just national but also regional and cross-cultural liberation movements, no liberation movement can any longer afford tribalism of the sort that the Islamic republic of Iran, the Jewish state of Israel, and the Christian empire of the USA now collectively espouse, despite their outward protestations.

Both the US empire and the emerging pockets of resistance to it will have to cross over presumed cultures and their corresponding countries. With the massive presence of Muslim migrant laborers throughout the globe, Islam is now irreversibly globalized as is its very sacred language spoken with a solidly American English intonation and with neologisms on al-Jazeera. The globalized empire has arisen from the same material forces that have occasioned the globalization of Muslim migrant laborers and thus the emerging Islam itself. The beneficiaries of globalized capital are no longer (if they ever were) some fictitious white Euro-Americans, nor indeed are those disenfranchised by it are all Muslims, Orientals, or colored. The Saudi and Khaliji Sheikhs are as much the beneficiaries of globalized capital as more than 35 million US citizens who live under the poverty line are disenfranchised by it. The color line is no longer the defining moment of the twenty-first century, even if it were in the twentieth. An Islamic liberation theology that still divides the world into an East–West, or Muslim–non-Muslim, believer–non-believer, practicing–non-practicing will mean nothing in the troubled years ahead. The inanity of Christopher Hitchens writing a book and calling it *God is not Great* (2007), mocking the Muslim creedal concept "The God is Great," may indeed entertain some in Washington DC but is of no consequence to the fate of millions of believing and non-believing Muslims and non-Muslims roaming the earth in search of sober decency. The only liberation movement against the terror of a globalizing empire that will be meaningful and mobilizing will have to be cross-cultural and global precisely in the same way that the empire it must oppose and the capital it must curtail are global. That liberation movement will have to account for the existence and accommodate the inclusion of the non-Islamic and as a result be more than a liberation theology but a liberation theodicy that at once recognizes and celebrates diversity. The only way that the innate paradox at the heart of Islam can be put to work for a permanent good is for Islam no longer to be triumphalist but tolerant, and in that tolerance not just to resist the abuse of power but also the temptation of power. The massive globalization of Islam by Muslim labor migrations throughout the world now provides for the former, its liberation theodicy for the latter.

No globally minded liberation movement will have a spec of legitimacy without categorically including the disenfranchised communities within the USA in the very heart of the empire. The fat beneficiaries of globalized capital in the USA cannot and must not be allowed to appropriate its revolutionary history. The anti-colonial history of the USA needs to be retrieved in the name and for the cause of its poor, sick, homeless, unemployed, uninsured, illegal immigrants, and other massively impoverished communities. The revolutionary disposition at those colonies that once fought the British Empire is not a distant and forgotten memory. It has a glorious paragon of hope, and his name is Malcolm X. In his defiant character and revolutionary legacy, Malcolm X can link any global Islamic liberation movement to the heart of the most progressive uprising of the wretched of this earth against their obscene oppressors. But that Islam is not the Islam of a pathological mass murderer like Osama bin Laden or Saddam Hussein. That Islam has the resolute history of an American Muslim revolutionary written all over its future countenance.

The campaign of shock and awe that announced the commencement of the US war against Iraq in Spring 2003, combined with the mind-numbing theft and destruction of world cultural heritage in Mesopotamia that it occasioned, have indeed frightened us all out of our wits. Artifacts that were testaments to the very alphabets of our humanity and had survived from Chengiz Khan to Attila the Hun, from Tamerlane to Hitler, finally collapsed at the foot of Donald Rumsfeld. The whole world is indeed in a state of shock and awe at the sheer enormity of this unforgivable crime against humanity – with hundreds of thousands of innocent Iraqi lives perished and millions more maimed for life or dispatched into the indignity of exile. Today more than ever, voices of reason and visions of sanity must prevail. We are no longer safe in the serenity of our professional careers. We must speak truth to power in a clear and concise language. Reading the history of our vanishing present is now more than ever the guiding light of our future. I have written this book as a sustained moment of pause to reflect against the grain of that speed with which our historical memory is being corroded. How and why did militant Islam begin to converse with colonial modernity? When and why did it run out of ideological energy? And ultimately what are the emerging forces of discontent that seek and must liberate Muslims from their own local tyranny in face of the predatory global empire in terms domestic to their hopes, loyal to the best in their character and culture? Posing these questions and seeking to answer them is no longer limited to Muslims or non-Muslims. We are all trapped. The cycle of violence benefits the worst among us and destroys the best. We must be put on reverse gear to maneuver out of this nasty spot and then move on.

Conclusion
Prolegomena to a future liberation theodicy

> The theology of liberation attempts to reflect on the experience and meaning of the faith based on the commitment to abolish injustice and to build a new society; this theology must be verified by the practice of that commitment, by active, effective participation in the struggle which the exploited social classes have undertaken against their oppressors. Liberation from every form of exploitation, the possibility of a more human and dignified life, the creation of a new humankind – all pass through this struggle.
>
> Gustavo Gutiérrez

Definitive to Islamic theology (*Kalam*) is the irreducible Otherness of God Almighty (*Allah*) that in turn and in theological self-projection becomes the irreducible ipseity of existence (*Wujud*). In various Islamic philosophical schools, there is a theocentric ontology (or a theo-ontology, to be more exact) that in its last theoretical articulations, say in the theocentric philosophy of Mulla Sadra Shirazi (1571–1640), aspires to an absolutist ontology that in effect comes as a prelude to his speculative theology – constituting the world in a condition of *Huduth* (or "Creative/Chaotic Createdness"), predicated upon the primacy of God as *Qidam* (or "Everlasting"). The absolute Otherness of God thus translates (in human terms) into the stated principiality of existence, its matter of factness, which in turn gives a moral immediacy to the most abstract dimension of Islamic speculative theology. At the thither end of Islamic intellectual history, at a moment when the dialogical synergy among various Islamic discourses has been overshadowed by the immediacy of bare political events, it would be good to remember that existential anxiety at the heart of Muslim theologians – when they put pen to paper to write about the Essence (*Dhat*) and Attributes (*Sifat*) of God, not knowing they were in fact writing out loud the intemperate temporality of their own historical whereabouts.

At the threshold of the twenty-first Christian century, Islam has only a dim scholastic memory of its long and illustrious intellectual history. All the major and minor Islamic theological, philosophical, and mystical discourses have long since categorically exhausted their epistemic synergy and have scarce anything left to say to each other, or, *a fortiori*, about and to the world. The same holds true for the fabricated opposition between "Islam and the West," a binary banality that effectively overshadowed all epistemic modes of knowledge production in and about Islam and quintessentially posited its polyfocal reality against the principal ipseity of an abstraction called "the West." Islam is thus (once again) up for its own metaphysical grabs. Who and what will yet again define it, and upon what grand epistemic synergy will that eventuality once again make it speak the worldly terms of an otherworldly religion – still remains to be seen.

Its modern and medieval modes and manners of knowledge production having been thoroughly exhausted, Islam now resumes its historic life within the bosom of its millions of inhabitants scattered around the globe at the most sacrosanct moments of their pieties, with Muslim masses' lives and livelihood at the mercy of a vastly changed world not completely at home with itself. What we are witnessing in much of the Muslim world today, as indeed in much of the world at large, is the rightful struggle of ordinary people for their pride of place, for social equanimity, economic justice, political participation, a legitimate and assertive place in the global redistribution of power. Muslim or non-Muslim, the world is at its normative and epistemic thither – waiting to deliver itself to a renewed significance, where its wars and its peaces will once again mean something – anything. "In the last instance," says the distinguished Peruvian liberation theologian Gustavo Gutiérrez, "we will have an authentic theology of liberation only when the oppressed themselves can freely raise their voice and express themselves directly and creatively in society and in the heart of the People of God, when they themselves 'account for the hope,' which they bear, when they are the protagonists of their own liberation."[1] For that to happen, that hope will have to transcend its particular (Jewish, Christian, Islamic, or any other) denominational divide and speak a metaphysics of liberation beyond the theology of one or another divisive claim on God. The particularity of that theology will have to speak a universal language, from the bosom of its particularity.

The condition of Muslims around the globe is now integral to that of non-Muslims and the world at large is at the mercy of a single superpower that rules the world at its own whims – sometimes even against its own stated interests (such as creating an effective Islamic Republic of Iraq right next to the Islamic Republic of Iran). The USA and its European allies had absolutely no business invading the two sovereign nation-states of Afghanistan and Iraq. The horrendous crimes of 9/11, committed by a band of angry and misguided Muslims, and the imperialist projects of a post-Soviet Union monopolar planet, perpetrated against humanity at large by the most brutal military machinery in history, are two entirely unrelated facts and phenomena. 9/11 is a misnomer. Nothing happened on September 11 2001 that was outside the fold of history. If what happened on 9/11 was a supreme sign of militant adventurism, vile violence, and unwonted fanaticism, the world at large has been at the receiving end and has endured much worse calamity caused by the US/Israel version of the selfsame maladies. That what passes for "progressive" politics in the USA, of *The Nation* variety, has miserably failed to understand the nature of American imperialism, and has thus linked the events of 9/11 to the US imperial adventurism, and in fact declared the US-led invasion of Afghanistan a "Just War,"[2] only goes to show the poverty of critical thinking in the entire spectrum of the North American scene, where neo-liberalism of the absurdist sort passes for critical thinking in the belly of the most vicious military machinery the world has seen. Both the events of 9/11 and the military adventurism that American neocons have theorized and unleashed and American liberals consider "the first truly just war since World War II" are the active signs of a world at a loss for political significance. A band of militant criminals (who happened to be Muslims) were the perpetrators of the 9/11 atrocities and millions of innocent people (who too happen to be Muslims) were the victims of militant imperialism that has been wildly unleashed in vengeful retaliation against it. 9/11, I have argued in this book, marks, if anything, *the end* of militant Islamism as we have known it over the last 200 years and the commencement of a mode of senseless iconic violence for immediate and spectacular result, while the renewal of American imperialism marks *the commencement* of a manner of globalized imperialism after the wild goose chase of bringing the wavering capital under American control. The two developments are entirely irrelevant, forcefully connected, and mutually the indices of a world at loss for the meaning of its purposeful indices of meaning and significance.

What American neoconservatives, conservatives, liberals and neo-liberals have collectively failed to understand is that global warmongering and aggressive militarism is not accidental but in fact definitive to the history of their country, from its very inception to this day. In the immediate context of the so-called post 9/11 world (which is entirely in line with the American crimes against humanity in all its previous military engagements in nineteenth and twentieth century), the USA and its European allies are the principal source of calamity around the globe. They are the ones that carved an apartheid colonial settlement on the broken back of Palestinians and called it Israel; they are the ones that have endorsed and supported every single corrupt and backward Arab potentate that has facilitated their domination in the region; they are the ones that have subverted and staged military coups to bring down every democratic movement in the world (from Muhammad Mosaddiq in Iran to Salvador Allende in Chile), and up to the present, they are the ones who created Mulla Omar, Osama bin Laden, and Saddam Hussein when it suited their regional interests and then went after them when doing so furthered their military domination of the region. One has to be either politically blind or else in total agreement with the hubris of American arrogance around the globe to have thought of the

US-led invasion of Afghanistan as "Just War." The factual evidence of the USA and its European allies, and not some innate calamity definitive to Islam, is responsible for the horrors of the world. Nothing is definitive to Islam – positive or negative, praiseworthy or blameworthy. Islam is the miasmatic metaphysics of millions of different people and nations around the world. No two Muslims are alike (what an unsurpassed calamity – caused by American conservatives and what passes for progressives there alike – that one has to even write this sentence). And yet all Muslims, like all human beings, are entitled to fight, demand, and exact their rightful place in this world. The Israeli apartheid state has been a historical calamity upon the legitimate inhabitants of Palestine – Jews, Christians, Muslims, or plain agnostics. An equally pestiferous plague on Iraq and Afghanistan has been the USA and its European allies that helped in these two illegal, immoral, and barbaric invasions (making people miss the time when they were ruled by a mass murderer like Saddam Hussein). The blood of millions of innocent Afghans and Iraqis is on the hands of the elected officials of both Americans and Europeans. Such simple and rudimentary facts have to be first and foremost understood before we move on to the next phase of our understanding of this current condition of Muslims and fully recognize their legitimate struggles for freedom, decency, and justice in this world.

Muslims' struggle for freedom, decency, and justice is perfectly legitimate and praiseworthy – and no amount of propaganda demonization of it can diminish its rightful objectives. This struggle has to be seen in a historical continuum, and not as a mere knee-jerk reaction to self-raising, other-lowering banalities of either European colonialism or American imperialism. Classical Islamism until recently was a phase of Islam in combative contestation with European colonialism, while engaged in conversation with its two major ideological rivals – nationalism and socialism. Whatever degree of violence was evident in militant Islamism, anti-colonial nationalism, or revolutionary socialism was perfectly legitimate and proportionate to their political, social, and economic projects. It is sheer historical illiteracy to equate the banalities of Osama bin Laden today with the struggle of Muslims as Muslims over the last 200 years to safeguard a modicum of freedom, decency, and justice for themselves. They had every right to pick up arms and shoot back at the criminal colonizers who set foot on their lands and robbed them of their natural resources and common humanity at one and the same time. Beyond that legitimate history, Muslims as Muslims now face an uncharted future in anticipation of which a liberation theology of an entirely different disposition is needed – a theology that is geared "to liberate humankind from everything that dehumanizes it."[3]

The absolute Otherness of God in Islamic theology amounts to the irreducible facticity of the world, the absolutism of its realities, if Hans Blumenberg were to theorize it. The epistemic exhaustion of Islamic intellectual discourses – from its diverging philosophies to the varieties of its mysticisms – faces a naked (and violent) world stripped of all its forms of sacred significations. The global exhaustion of the colonially fabricated binary between "Islam and the West" has further released Islam from its debilitating, self-defeating, and other-empowering trap in which it has exhausted all its creative politics for over 200 years. "The end of modernity" (Gianni Vattimo's apt term) and the rise of a shapeless, tasteless, gargantuan, and amorphous empire is also a sign of the world facing the abyss of its own meaningless demise. Pointless acts of violence, ranging from those perpetrated by a band of enraged militant Muslims (9/11) to those committed by the most sophisticated military machinery in human history (the USA) have lost all claims to any notion of legitimacy and sunk the world into the depth of diabolic anomie. In Islamic theological terms, the world is in its creative/chaotic moment of *huduth* (createdness), predicated on the pre-eternity (*qidam*) of its sacred assumption. If this renewed possibility of *huduth* is to be predicated on an assumption of *qidam* with any enduring legitimacy, it will have to posit a polytheist vision of the world at the root of its monotheist theology. This is what medieval theologians called *Vahdat dar Takassur* (Unity in Diversity). *Seh nagardad barisham ar ou ra parnian khanish ya harir-o-parand*, says the great Persian poet Hatif Isfahani (d. 1783), "Silk will not become three different things, if you were to call it *parnian, harir,* or *parand*" (three Persian words for "silk"). The new dispensation of *huduth* must be in terms of a theodicy that celebrates and embraces diversity rather than competing, condemning, or demonizing them – and only in such terms will the *qidam* it theologically (wishfully) promises will have a renewed pact with history.

The end of Islamic ideology, the implosion of "the West," the collapse of "Islam and the West" as the one of the most dangerous binary delusions of the last 200 years, the complete exhaustion of Islamic epistemics of significant and meaningful knowledge production, and the rise of senseless acts of spectacular violence for sheer visual and iconic impacts, have all coincided with what Giorgio Agamben has ingeniously diagnosed as the evident rise of "the state of exception," "the exposure of the naked life," "the spectre of the *homo sacer*," and the overwhelming fact of the metastasis of idea and practice of concentration camps into daily lives of immigrant communities swarming into the unwelcoming heart and perturbed imagination of Western Europe and North America.

Beginning with a simple but frightful distinction that he makes between the two oppositional Greek terms of *zoë* (the biological fact of living) and *bios* (the political form of living), Agamben began to trace a genealogy of what Michel Foucault had already identified as *biopolitics* as the defining moment of biological modernity, namely "a kind of bestialization of man achieved through the most sophisticated political techniques. For the first time in history, the possibilities of social sciences are made known, and at once it becomes possible both to protect life and to authorize a holocaust."[4]

From here, Agamben proceeds to argue that even before Foucault, Hannah Arendt, in her *Human Condition*, had already recognized "the transformation and decadence of the political realm in modern societies to this very primacy of natural life over political action."[5] That Foucault came to this conclusion with no reference to Arendt, or that Arendt did not make a connection between her own insight into *biopolitics* and her study of totalitarianism, or that Foucault did not connect his own notion of *biopolitics* to the fact and phenomenon of European concentration camps, Agamben all attributes to "the difficulties and resistances that thinking had to encounter in this area"[6] – namely the resistance of what he calls "Western politics" first and foremost to acknowledge and then to come to terms with its own hidden anxieties, or its inability to see its own blind spots. Agamben sees his own entire philosophical project as an attempt to identify and expose that blind spot.

Agamben believes that "the entry of *zoë* into the sphere of the *polis* – the politicization of bare life as such – constitutes the decisive event of modernity and signals a radical transformation of the political-philosophical categories of classical thought."[7] Agamben's ambition is to go beyond Foucault's proverbial truism that the final marker of European modernity is the paradoxical combination of subjective individualization of the social person and the simultaneous objective totalization of the society in which this subjection takes place. Agamben is not content with considering this a mere psychological explanation of "a parallelism between external and internal neurosis."[8] His frightful revelation, something that neither Foucault nor any other theorist of power in European legal and philosophical tradition has been able (or willing) to see, is the fact that "the inclusion of bare life in the political realm constitutes the original – if concealed – nucleus of sovereign power. *It can even be said that the production of a biopolitical body is the original activity of sovereign exception.* Placing biological life at the center of its calculations, the modern State therefore does nothing other than bring to light the secret tie uniting power and bare life. ... "[9] Biopolitics, as a result, is not a marker of biological/political modernity, as Foucault had suspected, but at the very roots of "the Western politics" in general, as Agamben sees it. He thus speaks in a manner that shows his discovery of this very blind spot of Aristotelian politics, the exception that has made every rule possible, as something already present and yet powerfully repressed: "In Western politics," he says (by which he means post-Aristotelian politics), "bare life has the peculiar privilege of being that whose exclusion founds the city of men."[10] Bring back and place "the bare life" where it belongs, in other words, the very center (blind spot) of Aristotelian politics, and that politics collapses on precisely what it has termed (nervously) "the state of exception".[11]

Agamben's argument, surpassing Foucault's definition of modern politics as the inclusion of *zoë* into *polis*, is that "what characterizes modern politics ... is that ... the realm of bare life ... gradually begins to coincide with the political realm, and exclusion and inclusion, outside and inside, *bios* and *zoë*, right and fact, enter into a zone of irreducible indistinction."[12] On this realm, which is the realm of our contemporary politics, the realm of the society of the spectacle, a society of camps, where Guantanamo Bay is no longer the exception but the rule that beginning from the periphery starts to eat into the center and thus re/define it, humanity at large (or more precisely the subject of the "Western" jurisprudence) have become the exact replica of its othered enemy, "the terrorist."

Agamben sees and argues his point through the internal dynamics of the "Western politics": "At once excluding bare life from and capturing it within the political order, the state of exception actually constituted, in its very separateness, the hidden foundation on which the entire political system rested."[13] The face of that enemy, however, today looks peculiarly Muslim. He is an Afghan "enemy combatant" that does not and will not, following Agamben's argument, receive the status of POW (prisoner of war). He is (not) a POW, for if he were to be a POW, then he would not be an exception. So he is the exception that makes the rule of "Western politics" possible. But (and here is the frightful insight of Agamben) the Afghan "enemy combatant" or the Iraqi "insurgent" is also the exception that is eating into the rule, that becomes the rule, just like a cancerous cell eating into a healthy body (Agamben's otherwise "Western politics"). But, and there is Agamben's bone of contention, the presumed health of that ("Western") body was always contingent on the public secret of the fact of that exception. There was always an Afghan "enemy combatant" at the heart of "Western politics," if we were to follow Agamben's argument. But he was a Jew in a concentration camp in one reading of it and now a Muslim in Abu Ghraib in another.

The Afghan "enemy combatant" in Bagram Air Base or the Iraqi "inmates" in Abu Ghraib torture chambers is the figure and phenomenon of Agamben's *homo sacer*. He cannot be sacrificed because he is outside the fold of humanity, and he can be killed without any legal recourse because he is outside the domain of law. Embedded in the modern democratic state is this inherent contradiction, the active politicization of *zoë*, down and out against the assumption of *bios*. There is no more *bios*, no political person with inherent rights to citizenship. *Zoë*, the animal life embedded in the political formalism of *bios*, today has a manifest body, the living dead, the dead man walking, just like the figure of "musulman" (Muslim) in Nazi concentration camps. But that figurative "musulman" has now become the real Musulman, the Muslim, the Muslims incarcerated in Bagram Air Base, in Guantanamo Bay, in the Abu Ghraib torture chambers. In a frightful way, the figure of "the enemy combatant" in Bagram Air Base, Guantanamo Bay, or Abu Ghraib is *figurative*, the symbol of itself, the sign of its own foreclosure, and thus the signature at the concluding moment of Agamben's "Western politics." But, and there is the rub, the point of Agamben's insights, Lynndie England has brought back the virus of the terrorist with herself back to America, back to "the West," back to "Western politics."

When he dismissed Muslim "enemy combatants" from inclusion in the articles of the Geneva Convention, the US Attorney General Alberto R. Gonzales may have thought he was doing Americans a favor. He was not. He was writing the death sentence of every single citizen of every single "liberal democracy" in "Western politics. If what Agamben has discovered is true, and is frightfully true, then with Lynndie England all Americans, all "Westerners," have become terrorists in and of themselves – for *zoë* is the implosion of *bios*, the melt down of its formal claim to citizenship. This insight, Agamben traces as far back as when Alexis de Tocqueville wrote on democracy in America, back to when *zoë* began to take over *bios* – and by taking it back to the origin of the Roman Law, Agamben is having a much larger claim on the longevity and endurance of *homo sacer*, the public secret of "Western politics."

Agamben's frightful proposition is at once uncanny and liberating: "The idea of an inner solidarity between democracy and totalitarianism (which we must, with every caution, advance) ... must nevertheless be strongly maintained on a historico-philosophical level, since it will allow us to orient ourselves in relation to the new realities and unforeseen convergences of the end of the millennium."[14] The world at large, however, as always at the receiving end of Euro-American democracies going on their colonial conquests, did not have to wait for "the new realities and unforeseen convergences of the end of millennium." These may indeed be new realities to Agamben and from his vantage point in "the Western politics." They certainly are not from any place in Asia, Africa, or Latin America, where no one was ever granted the status of a *bios* and taken *ipso facto* for the *zoë*. Beginning with Aristotle himself and his racial theories, down to Immanuel Kant and his unsurpassed racism, and down to the status of "the enemy combatant" give to Afghans, Iraqis, and other Muslims, *zoë* was the order of the day. When Alan Dershowitz theorizes legalized torture of Muslims from the heart of "Western" jurisprudence (recommended to Americans on the Israeli model), or when the US attorney General Alberto R. Gonzales categorically places (Muslim) "enemy combatants" outside the realm of law, or when Michael Ignatieff theorizes torturing of (Muslim) people form the heart of the human rights discourse, they are all doing so in the grand "Western" tradition that Agamben has now laid bare. We, and this "we" speaks that language of the world at large that is outside the domain of "Western politics" have always had our lives naked; our *bios* degenerated into *zoë*, entirely unbeknown to ourselves. We were theorized/terrorized unbeknown to ourselves. We were/are "the state of exception" that has made the rule of "Western politics" possible. We are the bare life, our lives the *zoë* of their *polis*.

The "new politics," Agamben contends in his *Homo Sacer*, "remains largely to be invented."[15] My hope and purpose in this book has been to argue and pave the way towards a recognition of that new politics in terms at once domestic to the current condition of Islam as a world religion and yet conversant with the larger world it faces. Agamben's "state of exception" corresponds to the theological moment of *huduth* in Islamic cosmogonic metaphysics – we are today (perhaps as always) at the key moment of chaos. The "state of exception" for Agamben is the moment of the meltdown when "the Western politics" is no more, when its alien enemy has been internalized, its blind spot exposed, and its most pubic secret metastasized. The face of the enemy hitherto hidden to that politics is today the face of a Muslim – the iconic features of Osama bin Laden, Mulla Omar, Saddam Hussein as he was being hanged, Abu Musab Zarqawi's head beheaded in "Western" media – but above all the anonymity of "the enemy combatant." The face of the Muslim (enemy) today is the face of "the Western other" – its bare life, the *zoë*, and the *musulman* of the German concentration camps running amuck, the living dead. Precisely for that reason, and since the face of the Muslim has now completely taken over the face of the Jew (the Danish cartoons of Muslims recycled the anti-Semitic features of the European Jew for Muhammad), there is no other post-metaphysician better than Emmanuel Levinas to diagnose the face of that other, the Muslim other – and precisely for the same reason the memory of no better revolutionary figure than Malcolm X can resurrect the fighting spirit of a just cause. With the inverted metaphysics of the face of the enemy at the center of its future emancipation, the (Islamic) theodicy of a liberation that is to come will have to embrace the body of all its enemies for the corporeality of its claim upon the world.

To mark my way towards that theodicy, I have in this book first and foremost argued that the very notion of "the West" has ended. The epistemic collapse of the sustained and lopsided dialogue between "Islam and the West" is no longer a viable proposition first and foremost because "the West," as the iconic referent of the European Enlightenment modernity, has self-destructed in what is now code-named postmodernity, and second because the emerging geopolitics of the capital has generated a new and unprecedented *miasmatics* of power. Precisely for the same reason, the assumption of "Islam and the West" can no longer command meaningful referents. As a set of binary opposition that in its cross-essentializing force gave both its components an aura of ontological authenticity, "Islam and the West" can no longer hold because "the West" having imploded Islam does not know to whom it is talking. The entire oeuvre of Abdolkarim Soroush, as one of the most prolific Muslim thinkers, is an eloquent, persuasive, at times exceptionally erudite set of conversations with a dead interlocutor. With the end of "Islam and the West" the Islamic ideology has ended, and the chaotic moment of a rebirth is now fast upon Islam. "Islam and the West," I have sought to argue in this book, were created under specific colonial conditions of the capital, with a presumed center for the capital and a designated periphery to its colonial operations. That center and periphery have now disappeared, for the rapidly and blatantly globalized capital no longer allows for such illusions. The chaotic moment of *huduth*, the terms of a new politics about to emerge – now at the roots of volcanic eruptions of violence with no end, no purpose, no result – at once exposes the bare life of the Muslim and yet readies it for its meaningful reconstitution – a body at once sacred, exposed, naked, *zoë*, and yet explosive.

As a mode of resistance to "the West" that the colonial condition had dialectically generated and sustained, Islamic ideology was once essentialized, categorical, and monolithic. It allowed for no diversity; it in fact eliminated and destroyed its own diverse intellectual traditions under the pressure and in correspondence with the European Enlightenment modernity to which it was beholden, whether it resisted it in its radical versions or else embraced it in its more liberal takes. That "West" has now withered in correspondences with the amorphous capital. The amorphous capital has in turn generated a globalized empire that operates without a hegemony and with brute force. Neither evangelical fundamentalism (the Christianity of American imperialism, as opposed to the Christianity of the poor people as liberation theology in Latin America), nor the belligerent Zionism can lend that brute force legitimacy. Betraying even its own Zionist aspirations, Israel is now (just like the United Arab Emirates) a shopping mall extension of the US global capitalism. None of these bankruptcies constitutes a *bona fide* hegemony. They not only do not generate consensus, acceptance, and compliance among those they seeks to dominate; they in fact generate hatred and revulsion against them. So what we are dealing with is a globalized empire, seeking to protect and promote (on a neoliberal economy) the operation of an amorphous capital so fragile in its fictive constitution that the breaking of a hurricane can send jitters through its spines, with a mercenary army, a phantasmagoric military machinery extended into the outer space, and an al-Qaeda blueprint for its own guerrilla operations. Even the bare life and the state of exception have found a metaphysics of authenticity.

Resisting the US-inspired globalized empire (which should never be equated with Americans at large, the overwhelming majority of which have a healthy dose of either active resistance to or else nagging suspicion about its efficacy) can no longer be in terms of a singular ideology embedded in a medieval theology, or an ideologically updated version of it to resist a center-based "Western" empire, or else contingent on spectacular acts of senseless and iconic violence. Resisting that empire requires regional alliances based on crosscurrents of ideas, sentiments, ideologies, and cultures. The worst aspect of Islamic ideology was its persistent reliance on Islamic Law (Shar-i'ah), the consequences of which for a free and democratic society is simply catastrophic, for it mutates the free and autonomous citizens of a potential republic into the legal subjects of a medieval jurisprudence that no matter how liberally it is interpreted it remains deadly contrary to creation of free and autonomous citizens of a republic. The only way that an (Islamic) liberation theology can be part of a global resistance to the US (or any other) empire is to be party to an equally liberating and global conversation, safeguard its theological monotheism by embracing it within a multifaceted theodicy that instead of trying to account for the existence of evil in the world in fact embraces its own alternatives and oppositions.

The events of 9/11 have camouflaged the contours of our most recent history. History has in fact been declared dead and done for. History more than ever needs to be revived, restored, and renarrated in an emancipatory and enabling way. I have argued in this book that the events of 9/11 were not the indication of Islamism triumphant. Quite to the contrary: they were the very final and lasting flame of a dying candle, Islamism at its thither. Precisely for that very reason, we need to rehistoricize Islamism in its nineteenth and twentieth century origin and disposition. Islam has now entered a globalized condition that demands an entirely different manner of reading the present history of Muslims and their political whereabouts.

My principal argument in this book has been the absolute necessity of resisting this predatory (US or any other) empire. Before any other move, the senseless, horrid, and barbaric acts of indiscriminate violence perpetrated in 9/11 must be unconditionally and categorically condemned and dismissed. This dismissal must first and foremost distinguish between such acts of senseless violence, and all other acts of (what Weber always parenthetically considered "legitimate") violence that from Karl Marx and Max Weber to Frantz Fanon and Malcolm X have been theorized and understood within revolutionary projects evident in all acts of national liberation movements. What we have witnessed in 9/11 was the sign of a new mode of iconic violence meant and launched for immediate spectacular purposes, without any integral link to larger national liberation movements. In this sense, the events of 9/11 represent an iconic mode of violence that correspond to the miasmatic disposition of the globalized capital, which an equally chaotic empire in turn seeks to control and ride. Thus there is a direct link between the disposition of the Milton Friedman kind of predatory capitalism going global and berserk, the predatory empire that seeks to control and ride it and the sorts of miasmatic and iconic violence that in turn generates and sustains and that has now been code-named Taliban, al-Qaeda, or Osama bin Laden. There is a direct link between Milton Friedman mutating into neoliberal economics and Islam degenerating into Osama bin Laden.

Upon that preliminary premise, I have then sought to provide a brief history of the success and failures of political Islamism over the last 200 years, in direct response to European colonialism and American imperialism. I have also argued that we must make a categorical distinction between this sustained history of anti-colonial Islamism during the nineteenth and twentieth centuries, and the sort of Islamism that Osama bin Laden represents at the threshold of the twenty-first century. The classical Islamism of the last 200 years was in direct response to European colonialism and had "the West" as its principal interlocutor. That interlocutor having now effectively imploded, Islam will negotiate its historical whereabouts in dialogical disputation with an entirely different creature we have now codenamed *globalization*.

At this particular juncture in Islamic history, Islam in the age of globalization, what seems to be needed and thus emerging is a mode of liberation theology (theodicy) that will in fact first and foremost liberate Islam itself from any number of endemic afflictions currently associated with it: first and foremost its identification with succession of senseless violence *à la* 9/11 in the US or 7/7 in the UK, acts of violence (categorically identified with al-Qaeda) that may correspond to any number of legitimate grievances that the world may have with both the USA and the UK and yet are manifested in utterly useless, senseless, and criminal modes of indiscriminate violence. This liberation will equally include the institutionalized fanaticism and anti-democratic disposition of the Islamic Republic of Iran as a particularly violent theocracy. The domains of the liberation will also in turn extend to the systematic and endemic abuse of Islamic sentiments by retrograde and corrupt Arab and Muslim states such as those now in power anywhere between Jordan and Morocco.

To reach for the enduring foundations of this liberation theology, the current condition of Islam as a moral and intellectual heritage must be linked to its premodern cosmopolitan disposition, which from the rise of the Abbasids in the middle of the eighth century to the demise of the Ottomans early in the twentieth has been the single most abiding characteristics of Muslim societies. Definitive to that polyvocal cosmopolitanism is a catholicity of learning, a multiplicity of legitimate discourses of authority that precisely in their multifaceted and contradictory dispositions has constituted the syncretic disposition of Islamic polyfocal culture. Rooted in that cosmopolitanism, Islam in its globalized disposition will have no discursive or institutional fears to be creatively conversant with a variety of (so-called sacred or secular, modern or premodern) cultures and disposition.

The collective impact of all these developments will ultimately result in the active and creative integration of Islam and Muslim communities into global, transnational, liberation movements that will collectively resist the predatory US (or any other) empire. Beyond the classical mode of Islamism as experienced in the nineteenth and twentieth centuries, and beyond spectacular acts of senseless violence, there must be a mode of liberation theology that closer to the roots of its metaphysics of salvation is a theodicy that will have to embrace the extended shadows of the faith and thus engendering a mode of cultural cosmopolitanism that is the only way to combat the Christian empire and the Jewish state by a mode of theology that reestablishes its roots in the moral authority of Judaism, Christianity and Islam alike. The four modes of religious tribalism now rampant in the world – Christian imperialism, accentuated by a Jewish state, an Islamic Republic, and a pervasive Hindu fundamentalism – will have to be resisted and overcome by varied modes of liberation theologies that partake in the moral authority of all world religions but are irreducible to any tribal reading of any one of them.

Because the terrorizing binary of East versus West is no longer operative, humanity at large faces a new geography of liberation by virtue of the syncretic disposition of societies hitherto pigeonholed in such false and falsifying categories. From the ashes and rubble of societies such as Lebanon, Iraq, or Palestine, from the ethnically mixed and historically multifaceted European sites of Muslim communities, medieval or modern, from the empowered communities of hardworking Muslim communities in the USA, and ultimately by invoking and re-appropriating the historically cosmopolitan disposition of Islam throughout its history, the ingredients of a liberation theology is evident and paramount the world over.

By re-reading Emanuel Levinas in a manner that posits the prophetic Jewish visionary of the Other as a "Muslim" metaphysician, by looking at Christian liberation theology of Latin America, by remembering Gandhi as the last and lasting Hindu of non-violence, and then by claiming the fact and figure of Malcolm X as a Muslim revolutionary who emerged from the most dilapidated corners of American ghettos to become a beacon of revolutionary hope the world over, and then by placing them all at the heart of a liberation theology that will have no denomination, the movement becomes universal in the very fabric of its globalized disposition. By claiming the figure of Malcolm X in particular, I am in effect bringing his homeland, the USA, into the fold of a renewed vision of global history, and thus dismantle and transgress the colonial divide of Orientalism, separating me and my Black Muslim brother across two civilizational divides. In the color and character of our brother Malcolm we – Muslims and otherwise – come together the rainbow coalition of a whole new promise in this world.

Notes

1 Resisting the empire

1 The city of Bam in Iran was devastated in a major earthquake in December 2003.
2 This poem by the expatriate Iranian satirist Hadi Khorsandi was released all over the Internet soon after Hurricane Katrina. I read it on Hadi Khorsandi's own website at http://www.asgharagha.com. The translation from original Persian into English is mine.
3 As David Brook put it on PBS, *NewsHour* program, on 2 September 2005. See also his op-ed (opposite editorial), "The Storm After the Storm" (*The New York Times*, 1 September 2005).
4 Cornel West, "Exiles from a city and from a nation" (*The Observer*, 11 September, 2005).
5 Ibid.
6 Ibid.
7 A major component of this propaganda machinery is fed by American Zionists who, in defending the illegitimate cause of the initially European and now American colonial settlement they call "Israel," they spare not a single moment in defaming Islam and demonizing Muslims. For further details of the power that the pro-Israeli Zionists exercise over US foreign policy, and particularly in casting Arabs and Muslims as terrorists and barbarians, see the groundbreaking work of John Mearsheimer and Stephen Walt, "The Israel Lobby" (*London Review of Books*, March 23 2005).
8 For a cogent reading of these conspiracy theories see Christopher Hayes, "9/11: The Roots of Paranoia," (*The Nation*, December 25 2006): 11–14. As Hayes rightly observes, such conspiracy theories as "9/11 Truth Movement" point to the resurgence of a "paranoid style" in American politics in large part because of "the lack of skepticism by the establishment press." In other words, the major mass media is so thoroughly integral to the Bush administration's propaganda machinery that there is no room for a healthy dose of legitimate skepticism about what Wolf Blitzer and CNN are feeding the American public, and thus the rise of illegitimate and self-discrediting conspiracy theories, which, in turn, again as Hayes rightly points out, "discredit and deform the salutary skepticism Americans increasingly show toward their leaders." For a thorough indictment of *The New York Times* as a major component of the US propaganda machinery see Howard Friel and Richard A. Falk's *The Record of the Paper: How The New York Times Misreports US Foreign Policy*. New York and London: Verso, 2004.
9 A case in point is Marisa Berenson, the sister of Bary Berenson, an innocent victim of 9/11 aboard a US flight that crashed into the World Trade Center.

In memory of her sister, Ms. Berenson has become an ambassador of peace for UNESCO. Soon after 9/11 I invited Ms. Berenson to Columbia University in New York to be part of a panel discussion after the screening of Mohsen Makhmalbaf's film "Kandahar" (2001), the only visual encounter with Afghanistan at the time of the US-led invasion contrary to the propaganda machinery of CNN and Co. For more detail on this event see my chapter on "Kandahar" in my forthcoming book on Mohsen Makhmalbaf, *Makhmalbaf at Large: The Making of a Rebel Filmmaker*. London: I. B. Tauris, 2007.

10 As a chief propaganda officer, Thomas Friedman of *The New York Times* never misses an opportunity to abuse the occasion of a senseless act of violence perpetrated against American or European targets to ridicule and dismiss the very uses of the terms imperialism, Zionism, and colonialism. "After every major terrorist incident," believes Friedman, "the excuse makers come out to tell us why imperialism, Zionism, colonialism or Iraq explains why the terrorists acted. These excuse makers are just one notch less despicable than the terrorists and also deserve to be exposed" (*The New York Times*, 22 July 2005). Thus with the stroke of one sentence, the ingenious columnist dismisses an entire history of the barbaric terror that these three horrendous terms and the facts they represent have perpetrated on humanity at large. That one might categorically denounce senseless acts of violence (perpetrated by the genocidal policies of Israelis or suicidal operations of Palestinians – or else by Jewish, Christian, or Muslim terrorists), while at the same time holding Thomas Friedman and other pestiferous propaganda officers defending "imperialism, Zionism, and colonialism" responsible for the plague they have unleashed on earth is beyond the scope of this columnists' critical faculties. Contrary to Thomas Friedman, I am not quite sure if propaganda officers like him are "just one notch" less or more despicable than the imperialism, Zionism, and colonialism they categorically defend and propagate.

11 The manufacturing of this Islamic threat is not limited to such grand ideologues as Bernard Lewis and Samuel Huntington, who are now the master narrators of a global confrontation between "Islam and the West." Even such observers as John L. Esposito, who project a more pro-Muslim disposition in their work, in effect corroborate this opposition by seeking to fine-tune or alleviate it. See John Esposito's *The Islamic Threat: Myth or Reality?* Oxford: Oxford University Press, 1999, in juxtaposition to Bernard Lewis's *Islam and The West*. Oxford: Oxford University Press, 1994, and Samuel Huntington's *The Clash of Civilizations and the Remaking of World Order*. New York: Simon & Schuster, 1998. The common thread of their narrative, from parallel or opposing perspectives, is the categorical opposition they presume and project between "Islam and the West." An earlier version of the same idea is provided by Norman Daniel in his *Islam and the West*. Oxford: Oneworld Publications, 1960/2000.

12 I have made this argument in some detail in my "For the Last Time: Civilization," *International Sociology*. September 2001. Volume 16 (3): 361–368.

13 The initial signs of the end of "the West" have already begun to be noted and read in various ways. Consider for example T. R. Reid's *The United States of Europe: The New Superpower and the End of American Supremacy*. London and New York: Penguin Press, 2004) in which the author warns Americans of the emerging superpower from the very belly of a presumed North-American–Western-European natural cultural alliance. See also Laurent Cohen-Tanugi and George A., Jr. Holoch, *An Alliance at Risk: The United States and Europe since September 11*. Baltimore, MD: The Johns Hopkins University Press, 2003, for a similar diagnosis. Equally compelling is the argument of Timothy Garton Ash in his *Free World: America, Europe, and the Surprising*

Future of the West. New York: Random House, 2004. These observers, however, still see the rift between the USA and EU in strategic and political terms and as such are entirely oblivious to the more seismic and enduring changes in the global operation of capital and the cultures that it habitually generates and authenticates. For these people "the West" is a quintessential and natural category, whereas "the West" itself is of a very recent vintage in the course of the global operation of capital and long since exhausted itself usefulness. For more details of this argument see my essay, "For the Last Time: Civilization" (op. cit.). There has never been any "natural" alliance or cultural cohesion between North America and Western Europe, a specifically historical correspondence manufactured in a specific phase of the global operation of capital. Retrograde observes ranging from Allan Bloom (*The Closing of the American Mind*. New York: Simon & Schuster, 1988) to Patrick J. Buchanan (*State of Emergency: The Third World Invasion and Conquest of America*. New York: Thomas Dunne Books, 2006) have been up in arms for decades now because they think their "Western" country has been invaded by barbaric colored people from the Third World. Well in a way they are right – for their delusions have indeed been shattered. The racialized "Third World" has indeed moved into the belly of "The First World" (they are usually looking for a job), made a historic alliance of a different sort with the racialized minorities within the USA, and thus exposed the delusional assumption that "The West" had any cultural cohesion other than a racist-supremacist appropriation of Christianity.

14 For a more global account of the catastrophic consequences of US imperialism see the excellent book of Chalmers Johnson, *Blowback: The Costs and Consequences of American Empire*. New York: Metropolitan Books, 2000.

15 As argued by Olivier Roy in *The Failure of Political Islam*. Cambridge, MA: Harvard University Press, 1996.

16 I have developed this argument in some detail in a new introduction to a new edition of my *Theology of Discontent: The Ideological Foundation of Islamic revolution in Iran*. New Brunswick, NJ: Transactions, 2005.

17 On Wahabism see Hamid Algar, *Wahhabism: A Critical Essay*. North Haledon, NJ: Islamic Publications International, 2002. On Babism see Abbas Amanat, *Resurrection and Renewal: The Making of the Babi Movement in Iran, 1844–1850*. Ithaca, NY: Cornell University Press, 1989.

18 For a more detailed reflection on the nature of this colonial modernity see the Postscript to my *Iran: A People Interrupted*. New York: The New Press, 2007.

19 Juan Cole has made quite a compelling argument that the rise of Baha'ism, a religious offshoot of Babism, can be considered in favorable lights as a form of indigenous modernity. See his *Modernity and the Millennium: The Genesis of the Baha'i Faith in the Nineteenth-Century Middle East*. New York: Columbia University Press, 1998. Though cogent and worthy of critical attention, Juan Cole's argument is untenable. From its very inception, the pacifist universalism of Baha'ism has played squarely into the hands of British colonialism, and as such has been a hindrance rather than a help in the course of Muslim and Arab encounters with their colonial conquerors.

20 For an excellent introduction to the ideas of al-Afghani see Nikki R. Keddie's *An Islamic response to Imperialism: Political and Religious Writings of Sayyid Jamal al-Din al-Afghani*. Berkeley, CA: The University of California Press, 1968. See also Albert Hourani, *Arabic Thought in the Liberal Age, 1798–1939*. Cambridge: Cambridge University Press, 1962: 103–129.

21 For more on Abduh and Rida see Hourani, *Arabic Thought in the Liberal Age*: 130–192 and 222–244; and Hamid Enayat, *Modern Islamic Political Thought*. Austin, TX: Texas University Press, 1982: 69–82.

22 For more on al-Afghani's philosophical and theological disposition see Keddie, *An Islamic response to Imperialism*: 45–52.
23 For an apt critic of al-Afghani's proclivity to a rhetoric of authenticity see Aziz al-Azmeh's *Islam and Modernities*. New York: Verso, 1993: 80–100. Al-Azmeh's critic of "authenticity," however, is seriously marred by his being totally enamored by European Enlightenment modernity, which is not quite clear by what authority he calls "Enlightenment Universalism." Nothing has universalized that European Enlightenment except brute and entirely un-enlightened European barbarism, aka colonialism. Al-Azmeh's argument is equally flawed when at the height of his critic he remains steadfast to the cliché-ridden distinction between "the East" (which he says he uses "only for convenience" – whatever that means) and "the West" which apparently does not inconvenience him either (see ibid: 80). Al-Azmeh declares that he takes it "as an accomplished fact that the modern history is characterized by the globalization of the Western order" (ibid: 80) – and nothing in that fact – which *ipso facto* authenticates a fictive figment of imagination called "the West" – bothers or agitates his analytics. Despite some apt and appropriate critics of Islamism, Al-Azmeh's *Islam and Modernities* is a prototypical example of a mesmerized obsequiousness to the very notion of "the West," which he (in his own blind spot) radically authenticates while criticizing the rhetoric of authenticity by Muslim ideologues. In this respect Al-Azmeh is typical of a counter-authentic authentication rhetoric that can only criticize the failures of Islamism from the vantage point of European Enlightenment, which perforce they must fiat to have become "universal." It has not. Daryush Shayegan, Bassam Tibi, Fatima Mernissi, and Fouad Ajami are Aziz Al-Azmeh's cohorts in this confusion.
24 For an excellent essay on anti-colonial uprisings by Muslims in this period see S. V. R. Nasr, "European Colonialism and the Emergence of Modern Muslim States," in John L. Esposito (ed.), *The Oxford History of Islam*. Oxford: Oxford University Press, 1999: 549–599.
25 For a good example of Sayyid Qutb's ideas see his *Social Justice in Islam*. Translated by John B. Hardie. Translation Revised and Introduction by Hamid Algar. North Haledon, NJ: Islamic Publications International, 2000. For a cogent study of Sayyid Qutb's ideas see Yvonne Y. Haddad, "Sayyid Qutb: Ideologue of Islamic Revival," in John L. Esposito (ed.), *Voices of Resurgent Islam*. Oxford: Oxford University Press, 1983: 67–98. For a comparative study of Qutb and Mawdudi see Leonard Binder, *Islamic Liberalism: A Critique of Development Ideologies*. Chicago: University of Chicago Press, 1988: 170–205. Much nonsense was written on Sayyid Qutb in the aftermath of 9/11 connecting his ideas to the actions attributed to Osama bin Laden. All such impressionistic suggestions by dilettantes are entirely false and devoid of any scholarly merit.
26 These assessments are suggested by such observers as Emmanuel Sivan and R. J. Zwi Werblowsky, both of the Hebrew University of Jerusalem. See Sivan's *Radical Islam: Medieval Theology and Modern Politics*. New Haven, CT: Yale University Press, 1985: 16–49; and Werblowsky's *Beyond Tradition and Modernity*. London: The University of London, The Athlone Press, 1976: 61–82. Direct beneficiaries of a European (and now American) colonial settlement in Palestine, Emmanuel Sivan and R. J. Zwi Werblowsky have completely repressed the entire history of European colonialism, in response to which anti-colonial Islamic ideologies and movements have taken form.
27 That there are alternative modes of anti-colonial modernities is a subject of extensive literature. See the Postscript to my *Iran: A People Interrupted* (op. cit.) for more details.
28 See Frantz Fanon, "Algeria Unveiled," in *A Dying Colonialism*. New York: Grove Press, 1959/1965: 35–67.

29 See Gianni Vattimo, *The End of Modernity: Nihilism and Hermeneutics in Postmodern Culture.* Baltimore, MD: The Johns Hopkins University Press, 1991.
30 For an account of Mawlana Mawdudi's life and thoughts see Seyyed Vali Reza Nasr, *Mawdudi and the Making of Islamic Revivalism.* Oxford: Oxford University Press, 1996. In a previous book, *The Vanguard of the Islamic revolution: The Jama'at-i Islami of Pakistan.* Berkeley, CA: University of California Press, 1994, Nasr paid exhaustive attention to the political legacy of Mawlana Mawdudi in the political apparatus of his party. In *Mawdudi and the Making of Islamic Revivalism,* he traces the origin of his ideas in the formative forces of Muslim–Hindu sectarianism, Indian nationalism and socialism, and the communal politics of a premodern society being dragged into modernity under the bayonets of British colonial officers. The strength of these two significant contributions is modified by two principal problems with Nasr's reading of Mawlana Mawdudi. First, he almost completely disregards the colonial context in which Mawlana Mawdudi's Islam is produced; and second, having lost sight of the colonial presence, he bounces the active formation of this politically mandated Islam against an utterly empty abstraction he calls, after his father Seyyed Hossein Nasr, "traditional Islam." Had Vali Reza Nasr been more cognizant of the larger project of colonial modernity in active response to which Mawdudi formulated his Islam, or, to look at the same reality through another angle, had he recognized that there is no "traditional Islam" in isolation from the moral and political imperatives of actively imagining it, he would have produced a much richer book. Vali Reza Nasr, however, has written a quite comprehensive essay on the impact of European colonialism on the formation of modern nation-states. See his "European Colonialism and the Emergence of Modern Muslim States," op. cit. This time around, however, he almost entirely disregards the function of ideological formations in the making of these Muslim states.
31 For more on the details of Mullah Ahmad Naraqi's notion of the "authority of the Jurisconsult" see my "Early Propagation of *Wilayat-i Faqih* and Mull Ahmad Naraqi," in S. H. Nasr, H. Dabashi, and S. V. R. Nasr (eds.), *Expectations of the Millennium: Shi'ism in History.* New York: State University of New York Press, 1988. For Khomeini's appropriation of this idea see the chapter on Khomeini in my *Theology of Discontent.* Op. cit.
32 See for example Mirza Muhammad Tunikabuni, *Qissas al-Ulama.* Tehran: Entesharat-i Islamiyyah, 1985: 129–132; and Mir Seyyed Muhammad Baqer Khwansari's *Rudat al-Jannat.* Tehran: Islamiyyah Publications, 1977, Volume I: 140–147.
33 Tunikabuni, *Qissas al-Ulama*: 130; Khwansari's *Rudat al-Jannat,* Volume I: 141.
34 On the revolutionary ideas of all these figures see my *Theology of Discontent.* Op. cit.
35 This according to Phillip Berryman, who was a priest in a barrio in Panama in 1965–1973, and who had attended the famous mass on Sunday March 23 1980 in which Archbishop Romero had openly called for the army to mutiny. See Phillip Berryman, *Liberation Theology: Essential Facts about the Revolutionary Movement in Latin America and Beyond.* New York: Pantheon Books, 1987: 3.
36 See Daniel Bell, *The End of Ideology: On the Exhaustion of Political Ideas in the Fifties, with "The Resumption of History in the New Century."* Cambridge, MA: Harvard University Press, 2000.
37 For more details on the history and propositions of Latin American liberation theology see Gustavo Gutiérrez, *A Theology of Liberation: History, Politics and Salvation.* New York: Orbis Books, 1988.

38 See Heinrich Meier, *Carl Schmitt and Leo Strauss: The Hidden Dialogue*. Translated by J. Harvey Lomax. Foreword by Joseph Cropsey. Chicago: The University of Chicago Press, 1995.
39 Ibid: xvi.
40 For an account of the American students of Leo Strauss and their role in the rise of American neoconservative imperialism see Anne Norton's astonishing revelations in her *Leo Strauss and the Politics of American Empire*. New Haven, CT: Yale University Press, 2004. For a shorter but equally compelling account see Earl Shorris, "Ignoble Liars: Leo Straus, George Bush, and the Philosophy of Mass Deception" (*Harper's*, June 2004).
41 Ibid: xvii.
42 "The dominant intellectual figures among East Coast Straussians," Ann Norton reports, "are Joseph Cropsey of Chicago and Harvey Mansfield of Harvard. Both are respected political philosophers. Both are conservative. Harvey Mansfield taught Francis Fukuyama, author of *The End of History*, and William Kristol, editor of *Weekly Standard*. Joseph Cropsey taught Paul Wolfowitz and Abram Shulsky, both prominent members of the defense establishment." (Anne Norton, *Leo Strauss and The Politics of American Empire* (op. cit: 7).
43 Ibid: 131.
44 See Heinrich Meier, *Carl Schmitt and Leo Strauss* (op. cit: 123–131).
45 For a pioneering study of liberation theology in an African American context see James H. Cone, *A Black Theology of Liberation*. New York: Orbis Books, 1990. The link between liberation theologies around the globe and those domestic in the USA and identified principally with Martin Luther King Jr. for Christianity and Malcolm X for Islam has far-reaching resonances that are written well into the future of the USA itself. The anti-Muslim markers of this future are already evident. Early in January 2007, the complacency of the CNN in aiding and abetting the Bush administration's global warmongering in a manner directly influencing domestic policies hit a new and rather scandalous low when an announcement for a program about the location of Osama bin Laden carried the caption "Where's Obama?" over the images of Bin Laden – thus identifying the notorious terrorist with the first African American ever to have a serious hope for the White House. CNN subsequently apologized for what it called "a very bad typographical error." In response to CNN apology, a spokesman for Mr. Obama said, "Though I'd note that the 's' and 'b' keys aren't all that close to each other, I assume it was just an unfortunate mistake." A presidential hopeful of Kenyan Muslim descent, Mr. Obama is reported to be quite conscious of his (particularly middle) name. According to the BBC he has said, "When I first started to work in public life ... people would ask: 'Hey brother, what's with your name? You called Alabama or Yo' Mama?'" The BBC also adds, "he has also acknowledged that his full name, Barack Hussein Obama, is not ideal for someone involved in politics." (For more details of the incident see BBC NEWS "CNN apology over Obama name slip" (January 4 2007)).
46 A misguided mode of scholarship now best represented by the work of Gilles Kepel (*The War for Muslim Minds: Islam and the West*. Cambridge: Belknap, 2004) and Olivier Roy (*Globalized Islam: The Search for a New Ummah*. New York: Columbia University Press, 2004) at best and Bernard Lewis (*What Went Wrong? The Clash Between Islam and Modernity in the Middle East*. New York: Perennial, 2003) at worst.
47 For more moral voices raised against the criminal atrocities of the state of Israel see Seth Farber's *Radicals, Rabbis and Peacemakers: Conversations with Jewish Critics of Israel*. Monroe, Maine: Common Courage Press, 2005. In this single

volume, and against the overwhelming propaganda machinery at the disposal of the American Zionists (not all of whom are Jews and in fact the most powerful segments of it are Christian Fundamentalists), is already evident the shape of an emerging Jewish liberation theology. In his Introduction to this volume, "The Return of the Jewish Prophetic: The support of the Palestinian Resistance," Seth Farber writes, "This book ... is intended to be an affirmation of the moral and spiritual tradition of Judaism. ... It is based on my conviction, shared by most of the individuals interviewed in this book, that this legacy ... was betrayed, and is currently threatened with extinction, by the policies of the state of Israel, and in particular its violation of the human rights of the Palestinian people" (ibid: 11).

48 See for example the report in BBC NEWS, "US 'biggest global peace threat'" (14 June 2006): "People in European and Muslim countries," the report says, "see US policy in Iraq as a bigger threat to world peace than Iran's nuclear program. ... The survey by the Pew Research Group also found support for US President George W Bush and his 'war on terror' had dropped dramatically worldwide." In another survey, this one for the BBC, nearly two-thirds of respondents, "say they have an unfavorable opinion of George W Bush." The poll further revealed that "The survey of 11 countries ... revealed that 57 percent of the sample had a very unfavorable, or fairly unfavorable attitude towards the American President. The figure rose to 60 percent when discounting the views of the American respondents. ... Over half the sample felt that the US was wrong to invade Iraq – this included 81 percent of Russian respondents, and 63 percent of the French response. Thirty-seven per cent thought it right to invade – including 54 percent of the UK response, 74 percent of the US response and 79 percent of the Israeli sample. Asked who is the more dangerous to world peace and stability, the USA was rated higher than al-Qaeda by respondents in both Jordan (71 percent) and Indonesia (66 percent). America was also rated more dangerous than two countries considered as 'rogue states' by Washington. It was rated more dangerous than Iran, by people in Jordan, Indonesia, Russia, South Korea and Brazil, and more dangerous than Syria by respondents all the countries, except for Australia, Israel and the United States." (BBC NEWS, "Poll suggests world hostile to US," June 16 2003). In yet another EU survey, "nearly 60 percent of Europeans regard Israel as the greatest threat to world peace." (BBC NEWS, November 5 2003).

49 The hypocrisy of European partners of the USA in their reaction to the execution of Saddam Hussein on December 30 2006 outshined the mere matter of factness with which the USA reacted to the same spectacle, captured on a mobile phone. The reaction of the White House was a typical flaunting of a non-existent autonomy for the "Iraqi court," adding that the sentence "marks an important milestone in the Iraqi people's efforts to replace the rule of a tyrant with the rule of law." The same Iraqi people who have been under military occupation for more than three years, their country disintegrated into chaos and anarchy, were praised, "for continuing to utilize the institutions of democracy to pursue justice." But the hypocrisy of the British topped it all. "As the prime minister has made clear," read a UK Foreign Office statement, "it [Saddam's execution] is entirely a matter for the independent Iraqi tribunal." What "independent Iraqi tribunal?" As reported by BBC NEWS, "In quotes: Reaction to Saddam sentence," December 27 2006).

50 See Jonah Goldberg, "Baghdad Delenda Est, Part Two" (NRO, April 23 2003).

51 See Michael A. Ledeen, *Machiavelli on Modern Leadership: Why Machiavelli's Iron Rules are as Timely and Important Today as Five Centuries Ago*. New York: St. Martin's Griffin, 2000.

2 The end of Islamic ideology

1. An earlier and much shorter version of this chapter appeared as "The End of Islamic Ideology" in *Social Research*. 2000. Volume 67 (2): 475–518). I am grateful to professor Arien Mack for having commissioned that essay and for her kind permission to use it in this chapter.
2. "Islamic Ideology" *(Ideology-ye Islami)* is a term that Ali Shari'ati used most effectively. Following him, I use it though in a far more generic sense of any political project predicated on an anti-colonial reading of Islam over the last 200 years.
3. The subject of the systematic mutation of Islam into Islamic ideologies is usually treated in the context of the Islamic encounter with "modernity," in a very general and uncritical reading. An excellent example of this reading would be Fazlur Rahman's *Islam and Modernity: Transformation of an Intellectual Tradition*. Chicago: The University of Chicago Press, 1984.
4. The classical account of this colonially mitigated encounter with the European Enlightenment is still Albert Hourani's *Arabic Thought in the Liberal Age, 1798–1939*. Cambridge: Cambridge University Press, 1962. A good updating of that account is Hamid Enayat's *Modern Islamic Political Thought*. Austin: Texas University Press, 1982. For an extension of this account into the specific ideological disposition prior to the Islamic revolution in Iran see my *Theology of Discontent: The Ideological Foundations of the Islamic revolution in Iran*. New York: New York University Press, 1993/New Brunswick, NJ: Transactions Publishers, 2006. A representative collection of primary sources is to be found in John J. Donohue and John L. Esposito (eds.), *Islam in transition: Muslim Perspectives*. Oxford: Oxford University Press, 1982.
5. While many contemporary scholars have added fuel to the fire of this presumed confrontation between "Islam and the West," others have persuasively argued against its validity. Among the latter is Fred Halliday's *Islam & The Myth of Confrontation: Religion and Politics in the Middle East*. London: I. B. Tauris, 1995.
6. On the ideas of Mulla Ahmad Naraqi see my "Early Propagation of *Wilayat-i Faqih* and Mulla Ahmad Naraqi," in S. H. Nasr, H. Dabashi, and S. V. R. Nasr (eds.), *Expectation of Millennium*. New York: State University of New York Press, 1989: 287–300. On Shari'ati see *Theology of Discontent* (op. cit.: 102–146).
7. The most recent account of this critical phase in Shi'i doctrinal history is Said Amir Arjomand's "The Consolation of Theology: Absence of the Imam and Transition from Chiliasm to Law in Shi'ism," *The Journal of Religion*. 1996: 548–571. For further elaboration see Arjomand's "Crisis of the Imamate and the Institution of Occultation in Twelver Shi'ism: A Sociological Perspective," *International Journal of Middle East Studies*. 1996. Volume 28 (4). For the most comprehensive study of Shi'ism in history see Said Amir Arjomand, *The Shadow of God and the Hidden Imam: Religion, Political Order, and Societal Change in Shi'i Iran from the Beginning to 1890*. Chicago: Chicago University Press, 1984. Specifically on the doctrine of *ghaybah* see also Abdulaziz Abdulhussein Sachedina, *Islamic Messianism: The Idea of the Mahdi in Twelver Shi'ism*. Albany: State University of New York Press, 1981. Equally crucial and groundbreaking in its critical re-evaluation of the historical roots of the doctrine is Hossein Modarressi's *Crisis and Consolidation in the Formative Period of Shi'ite Islam*. Princeton: The Darwin Press, 1993.
8. For an account of Shi'ism as the attempted institutionalization of the charismatic authority of Prophet Muhammad see my *Authority in Islam: From the Rise of Muhammad to the Establishment of the Umayyads*. New Brunswick: Transaction Publishers, 1989: 95–120.

9 For the most comprehensive account of the Isma'ilis see Farhad Daftary, *The Isma'ilis: Their History and Doctrines*. Cambridge: Cambridge University Press, 1990. For an excellent account of the philosophical disposition of Shi'ism underlying the proto-Isma'ili movements see Paul Walker, *Early Philosophical Shi'ism: The Isma'ili Neoplatonism of Abu Ya'qub al-Sijistani*. Cambridge: Cambridge University Press, 1993. Matti Moosa's *Extremist Shi'ites: The Ghulat Sects.* Syracuse: Syracuse University Press, 1988, gives a full historical account of Shi'ism being carried to its rhetorical charismatic conclusions.
10 For an account of Shari'ati's thoughts see Ervand Abrahamian, "Ali Shari'ati: Ideologue of the Iranian Revolution," in Edmund Burke, III and Ira M. Lapidus (eds.), *Islam, Politics, and Social Movements*. Berkeley: University of California Press, 1988: 289–297; and Dabashi 1993: 102–146.
11 See "Review with M. Mauss, 'Frazer – *Totemism and Exogamy,* Volume IV' and 'Durkheim – *Les Formes élémentaires de la vie religieuse. Le système totémique en Australie*' in *Durkheim on Religion: A Selection of Readings with Bibliographies and Introductory Remarks.* Edited by W. S. F. Pickering. London: Routledge and Kegan Paul, 1975: 180. See also Emile Durkheim, *The Elementary Forms of the Religious Life.* New York: The Free Press, 1915: 462–496.
12 See Max Weber, *On Charisma and Institution Building.* Selected Papers, Edited and with an Introduction by S. N. Eisenstadt. Chicago: the University of Chicago press, 1968: 49.
13 On Muhammad's charismatic authority see Dabashi 1989: 33–46.
14 I have already elaborated this aspect of Shi'ism as a charismatic movement in more detail. See Dabashi 1989: 95–120.
15 As for example evidenced in the following qualification: "But collective consciousness is something more than a mere epiphenomenon of its morphological basis, just as individual consciousness is something more than a simple efflorescence of the nervous system" when read after the superfluous warning that: "Therefore it is necessary to avoid seeing in this theory of religion a simple restatement of historical materialism: that would be misunderstanding our thought to an extreme degree." (Durkheim 1915: 471).
16 As evidenced throughout Weber's repeated oscillations among the "berserker," the "shaman," the "epileptoid," or the "swindler" in order to locate the ideal type of the charismatic figure (see Weber 1968: 48–49).
17 On state as the monopoly of violence see Max Weber, "Politics as a Vocation," in Hans Gerth and C. Wright Mills (eds.), *From Max Weber: Essays in Sociology.* Oxford: Oxford University Press, 1946: 78.
18 For a good introductory account of Mulla Sadra's philosophy see Mulla Sadra, *The Wisdom of the Throne: An Introduction to the Philosophy of Mulla Sadra.* Translated by James Winston Morris. Princeton: Princeton University Press, 1981.
19 Emmanuel Levinas, *Totality and Infinity.* Translated by Alphonso Lingis. Pittsburgh: Duquesne University Press, 1961: 43.
20 For a biographical sketch of Hajji Seyyed Mohammad Baqer Shafti see my translation, "Lives of Prominent Nineteenth-Century 'Ulama' from Tunikabuni's *Qisas al-'Ulama',*" in Said Amir Arjomand (ed.), *Authority and Political Culture in Shi'ism.* Albany: State University of New York Press, 1988: 305–318.
21 See Moojan Momen, *An Introduction to Shi'i Islam.* New Haven: Yale University Press, 1985: 135, for more details. By this time the victory of the Usulis over the Akhabaris was so emphatic that in fact Fath Ali Shah could not have possibly delivered on his promise. Mirza Mohammad was subsequently brutally murdered by the Usulis.

22 For more on Mulla Ahmad Naraqi and his historical significance see Hamid Algar, *Religion and State in Iran, 1785–1906: The Role of the Ulama in the Qajar Period.* Berkeley: University of California Press, 1969: 57, 63, 79, 89, and 101.
23 As suggested by Algar (1969: 87).
24 See Algar 1969: 92–93.
25 Momen 1985: 138.
26 Algar 1969: 93. Algar is of course very cavalier here in identifying the nobility of a people's collective anger against colonial aggression and territorial conquest of their homeland as "arousing [their] religious emotions," as if he is speaking of an infantile band of indigents. This generic characterization also misreads the diversity and complexity of the Shi'i clerical establishment and their relationship with their constituency.
27 On the early evolution of the office of clerical authority see Said Amir Arjomand's "The Mujtahid of the Age and the Mulla-bashi: An Intermediate Stage in the institutionalization of Religious Authority in Shi'ite Iran," in Arjomand 1988: 80–97.
28 See Algar 1969: 170.
29 Algar 1969: 172.
30 For an account of the revolutionary significance of the Tobacco Revolt see Ann K. S. Lambton, "The Tobacco Régie: a prelude to revolution," in her *Qajar Iran.* London: I. B. Tauris, 1987: 223–276.
31 See Algar 1969: 207.
32 Hamid Algar does a fairly conscientious job in intimating the uncertainty of whether or not Shirazi actually wrote this edict or not. See Algar 1969: 211–212.
33 Like Hamid Algar in Algar 1969: 214–215.
34 For a more sympathetic reading of Baha'ism, see Juan R. I. Cole, *Modernity and the Millennium: The Genesis of the Baha'i Faith in the Nineteenth Century Middle East.* New York: Columbia University Press, 1998. For an equally panegyric account of Baha'ism by a practicing Baha'i see Peter Smith, *The Babi and Baha'i Religions: From Messianic Shi'ism to World Religion.* Cambridge: Cambridge University Press, 1987. These two statements, quite erudite and scholarly, are uttered from a position of faith and lack any critical stand in their analytical disposition.
35 For more on the school of Isfahan see my "Mir Damad and the School of Isfahan," in Oliver Leaman (ed.), *A History of Islamic Philosophy.* London: Routledge, 1994.
36 For more on Mulla Sadra see Morris 1981.
37 On the Shaykhi School and the Babi Movement in general see the exemplary scholarship of Abbas Amanat, *Resurrection and Renewal: The Making of the Babi Movement in Iran, 1844–1850.* Ithaca: Cornell University Press, 1989. But by far the most brilliant study of the Babi Movement is in Persian and richly deserves a translation: Mohammad Reza Fashahi, *Vapasin Jonbesh-e Qurun-e Vusta'i dar Duran-e Feudal* ("The Last Medieval Movement in the Feudal Period"). Tehran: Entesharat-e Javidan, 2536/1977.
38 As rightly suggested by Fashahi in Fashahi 1977: 66–73.
39 For a systematic examination of the rise of Iranian civil society see Said Amir Arjomand, *The Turban for the Crown: The Islamic Revolution in Iran.* Oxford: Oxford University Press, 1988: 11–90. The most perceptive study of the infiltration of ideas of modernity into religious sentiments is by H. E. Chehabi in *Iranian Politics and Religious Modernism: The Liberation Movement of Iran under the Shah and Khomeini.* Ithaca: Cornell University Press, 1990. For a similarly perceptive reading of modernity in the course of the Constitutional Revolution see Vanessa Martin, *Islam and Modernism: The Iranian Revolution of 1906.* London: I. B. Tauris, 1989.

40 The territorial constitution of Iran as a nation is now the subject of a brilliant study by Firoozeh Kashani-Sabet in her *Frontier Fictions: Shaping the Iranian Nation, 1804–1946*. Princeton: Princeton University Press, 1999.
41 Arjomand 1988: 35.
42 Arjomand 1988: 35.
43 As exemplified by phrases such as " ... the ulama embodied the aspirations of the people. The adulation accorded their persons proves this more even than their voicing of demands popularly felt, demands that were in any event seldom conscious and frequently stimulated" (Algar 1969: 90) or that "Pretexts were sought and found for the excitement of popular emotions against the state ... " (Algar 1969: 240); for similar sentiments see pp. 245–246 about the site of the Russian Bank in Tehran, or p. 249 about the incident in the Shrine of Imam Reza in Mashhad. The "exploitation" or alternatively "arousal" of "popular sentiments" and "emotions" is the key conceptual category of Algar's historiography of the "The Role of the Ulama in the Qajar Period." Throughout this book he treats the Shi'i clergy as shepherds in charge of a flock of sheep, shepherds who can use the raw energy of their flock for effective assertion of power. It is a peculiar combination of inanity and hubris to assume that the material misery of a people is not sufficient reason to generate moral outrage, and that people are to be "stimulated" and "aroused" to put their lives on the line for demands of which they are not even fully conscious.
44 See Algar 1969: 240–241.
45 Algar 1969: 240.
46 Still the most insightful study of the relationship between Islam and Socialism is Maxime Rodinson's *Marxism and the Muslim World.* New York: Monthly Review Press, 1981. Although Rodinson's attention to Shi'ism in this study is quite limited, his general observations remain quite critical.
47 See Ervand Abrahamian, "Ali Shari'ati: Ideologue of the Iranian Revolution." in Burke, III and Lapidus 1988: 292.
48 For an introductory essay to the ideas of Abdolkarim Soroush see John Cooper, "The Limits of the Sacred: The Epistemology of Abd al-Karim Soroush," in John Cooper, Ronald Nettler and Mohamed Mahmoud (eds.), *Islam and Modernity: Muslim Intellectuals Respond*. London: I. B. Tauris, 1998: 38–56.
49 As suggested and celebrated by now the chief ideologue of the American right Francis Fukuyama in *The End of ideology and the Last Man*. New York: The Free Press, 1992.
50 As suggested by Oliver Roy in *The Failure of Political Islam*. Translated by Carol Volk. Cambridge, MA: Harvard University Press, 1994. Oliver Roy's specifics on Shi'ism and Iran in his general assessment of the failure of political Islam is simply too random to be taken seriously. Identifying Shi'ism as "a history" and "not as a corpus" (p. 168) and then reaching for the outlandish conclusion that "nothing in Shi'i thought ... predisposes the clergy to play a contestant political role" not only suffers from the inner contradiction that how could Shi'ism, not conceived as corpus but as history, have a *thought* but far more seriously lacks a rudimentary grasp of this religion as a metaphysical corpus with a very long history and with a constitutional claim on political life matched only by the 22 years of the Prophet's own career. What boggles the mind is the hubris with which Roy dismisses an entire faith and its monumental architectonic achievement of a metaphysical corpus, in its full scholastic panorama of jurisprudence and theology, philosophy and mysticism.
51 As diagnosed by a wide array of observers ranging from Oliver Roy and Bernard Lewis to Fatima Mernissi, Daryush Shayegan, Bassam Tibi, and Fouad Ajami.
52 See Gustavo Gutiérrez, *A Theology of Liberation*. New York: Obis, 1971/1988: 33.
53 Ibid: 31–32.
54 Ibid: 32.

3 Blindness and insight

1. Habermas, as we will soon see, never calls modernity *European* modernity. This is not because he has a global conception of modernity. That is because he has a global (one might even say imperial) conception of Europe. For him Europe is global – Europe *is* the whole world. It is not.
2. Habermas considers this a principal contradiction in Foucault's thinking about Kant. See Jürgen Habermas, *The New Conservatism: Cultural Criticism and Historians' Debate.* Edited and Translated by Shierry Weber Nicholsen. Cambridge, MA: The MIT Press, 1989: 173–179.
3. See Immanuel Kant, *Observations on the Feeling of the Beautiful and Sublime.* Translated by John T. Goldthwait. Berkeley, CA: University of California Press, 1960: 111.
4. Ibid: 113.
5. As quoted by Habermas in Habermas 1989: 175.
6. Habermas 1989: 175–176.
7. Habermas 1989: 176.
8. Habermas 1989: 176.
9. Kant 1960: 112.
10. This according to Jürgen Habermas in "The Entwinement of Myth and Enlightenment: Re-reading *Dialectic of Enlightenment,"* *New German Critique* 26 (1982), as quoted by Richard Rorty in his "Habermas and Lyotard on Postmodernity," in Richard Rorty's *Essays on Heidegger and Others.* Cambridge: Cambridge University Press, 1991: 164.
11. Rorty 1991: 165.
12. Rorty 1991: 165.
13. Immanuel Kant, *Observations on the Feeling of the Beautiful and Sublime.* 1960: 111.
14. Ibid: 111.
15. John Stuart Mill *Disquisitions and Discussions*, Volume 3: 167–168; as quoted in Edward W. Said, *Culture and Imperialism.* New York: Vintage Books, 1993: 80.
16. Habermas 1989: 177.
17. Jean-François Lyotard, *The Postmodern Condition: A Report on Knowledge.* Translated from the French by Feoff Bennington and Brian Massumi. Foreword by Fredric Jameson. Minneapolis, MN: University of Minnesota Press, 1984: xxiii.
18. Lyotard 1984: xxiii.
19. Rorty "Habermas and Lyotard on Postmodernity," (op. cit.: 168).
20. Frantz Fanon, *The Wretched of the Earth.* Translated by Constance Farrington. New York: Grove, 1968: 77.
21. See Jürgen Habermas, *The Philosophical Discourse of Modernity: Twelve Lectures.* Translated by Frederick G. Lawrence. Cambridge, MA: The MIT Press, 1990: 184.
22. Tracy B. Strong and Frank Andreas Sposito, "Habermas's significant other," in Stephen K. White (ed.), The Cambridge Companion to Habermas. Cambridge: Cambridge University press, 1995: 267.
23. White 1995: 267.
24. For more on the influence of Ernst Jünger on Al-e Ahmad see my *Theology of Discontent* (op. cit.: 76). For more on the influence of Ernst Jünger on Heidegger see Pierre Bourdieu, *The Political Ontology of Martin Heidegger.* Translated by Peter Collier. Stanford, CA: Stanford University Press, 1991: 29–40.
25. See Luc Ferry and Alain Renaut, *Heidegger and Modernity.* Translated by Franklin Philip. Chicago: The University of Chicago Press, 1990: 62–71.
26. Ibid: 66.

27 See for example the extraordinary work of Jeffry A. Frieden, *Global Capitalism: Its Fall and Rise in the Twentieth Century*. New York: W. W. Norton, 2006, particularly Chapters 6–10, under the section heading, "Things Fall Apart, 1914–1939: 127–250.
28 Janet Afary and Kevin Anderson have collected and translated Foucault's writings on the Islamic revolution, *Foucault and the Iranian Revolution: Gender and Seduction of Islamism*. Chicago: University of Chicago Press, 2005. Despite all its good intensions, the book is unfortunately constitutionally flawed in its reading of Foucault's attraction to the Islamic revolution in Iran and thus it categorically fails to mark Foucault's misreading of the ideological complexity of the Iranian revolution of 1979. For a cogent review of this book see Jonathan Rée's "The Treason of the Clerics," *The Nation*, August 15–22, 2005.
29 For more on this point see my Iran: A People Interrupted (op. cit.: 294–95).
30 This distinction I feel obligated to make because every time someone mentions the colonial fabrication of terms such as "Iran" or "Islamic civilization," etc., Iranian jingoist nationalists (in particular) are up in arms and digging out a million references in the *Shahnameh* and other sources arguing that the term "Iran" or the identity "Iranian," etc., have long been in use. (For a good example of this sort of argument see Jalal Matini, "Iran dar Gozar-e Ruzegaran: Dowran-e Eslami," *Iranshenasi*, 4/2, 1992: 243–68.) The point is not to question the perfectly evident fact that the term Iran and the identity Iranian have long since existed and even more fundamentally Iranians have had a historical sense of who they are (for a cogent treatment of the question of Iranian identity see the excellent articles by Ahmad Ashraf and Gherardo Gnoli in *Encyclopedia Iranica*, under "Iranian identity".) This indubitable fact, however, is not limited to Iranians. Other people have had it too – Arabs, Africans, Egyptians, Indians, Japanese, and most recently the British, Germans, French, Americans, Mexicans, Canadians, etc. The question thus is not the presence of a collective sense of identity but that there is no aggregation of creatures (let alone humans) on earth that could possible lack. This is what Emile Durkheim called "conscience collective" and all human gatherings have it in one way or another. The question is when it comes to the history of European colonialism and its extended arm of Orientalism then the *colonial* fabrication of civilizational others such as "Islam," "Persia," "India," or "Africa" was integral to the manufacturing of "the West" as the civilizational master term, the arbiter of truth, and the measure of moral and normative historicity. State-sponsored Iranian nationalism of the Reza Shah variety in particular has been a singular cornerstone of assimilating Iran into European colonialism and such examples as Mosaddeq's anti-colonial nationalism only goes so far in balancing the notoriously more powerful colonial nationalism of Reza Shah.
31 In Ahmad Ashraf's careful periodization, these identities fall into the following categories: "The main development of Iranian identity, from its literary foundation during the Sasanid era to the present time, may be divided into the following phases: the foundation phase of arranging a pre-modern ethno-national identity with a sense of ancient ethno-nationalism during the late Sasanid era; the dormant phase following the Arab conquest of Persia; the revival phase of Iranian cultural identity under the Iranian regional dynasties during the ninth–eleventh centuries; a complex phase of Iranian identity during the Saljuq era; the resurgence phase during the Mongol and Timurid periods; the formation of a hybrid Iranian–Shi'ite identity during the Safavid era; and, finally, the national phase of the formation of a modern Iranian "national identity" during the last two centuries." (Ahmad Ashraf, "Iranian Identity" in *Encyclopedia Iranica*, op. cit.) It is in this very last phase of Iranian identity in which colonial and anti-colonial modes of narrating the nation come into conflict. While in all these phases

political and cultural forces have been instrumental in the social construction of identity.
32 See Anthony D. Smith, *The Ethnic Origins of Nations*. Oxford: Blackwell, 1986, for the most thorough presentation of this view.
33 See Smith 1986: 209–226.
34 E. J. Hobsbawm, *Nations and Nationalism Since 1780: Programme, Myth, Reality*. Cambridge: Cambridge University Press 1990.
35 Hobsbawm 1990: 14.
36 See Ernest Gellner, *Nations and Nationalism*. Ithaca: Cornell University Press, 1983: 53–62.
37 See Benedict Anderson, *Imagined Communities: Reflections on the Origin and Spread of Nationalism*. New Edition. London: Verso, 2006.
38 See Partha Chatterjee, *Nationalist Thought and the Colonial World: A Derivative Discourse*. Princeton: Princeton University Press, 1994.
39 An earlier version of this segment of the chapter was published as "Blindness and Insight: The Predicament of a Muslim Intellectual" in Ramin Jahanbegloo (ed.), *Iran Between Tradition and Modernity*. Lanham, MD: Lexington Books, 2004: 95–116.
40 There is an excellent essay on the paradigmatic shifts in the ideas and practices of religious intellectuals by Sohrab Razaqi, "Paradigm-ha-ye Roshanfekri-ye Dini dar Iran-e Mo'asser" (Paradigms of Religious Intellectualism in Contemporary Iran), in *Majmu'eh Maqalat-e Motale'at-e Irani* 2 (1378): 160–89.
41 For a brief account of Soroush's ideas in English, see John Cooper, "The Limits of the Sacred: The Epistemology of 'Abd al-Karim Soroush," in John Cooper, Ronald Nettler, and Mohamed Mahmoud (eds.), *Islam and Modernity: Muslim Intellectuals Respond*. London: I. B. Tauris, 1998: 38–56. For a more thorough reading of Soroush, see Afshin Matin-Asgari, "Abdolkarim Soroush and the Secularization of Islamic Thought in Iran," *Iranian Studies*. 1997. Volume 30 (1–2): 97. Valla Vakili's "Abdolkarim Soroush and Critical Discourse in Iran," in John L. Esposito and John O. Voll's *Makers of Contemporary Islam*. Oxford: Oxford University Press, 2001: 150–76 is a thorough and sympathetic account. Thanks to Mahmoud Sadri and Ahmad Sadri we now have a sound and sympathetic introduction to Soroush's thoughts in English. See their edited volume, *Reason, Freedom, and Democracy in Islam: Essential Writings of Abdolkarim Soroush*. Oxford: Oxford University Press, 2000. All of these introductory essays benefit from a close and careful reading of Soroush and yet suffer from a categorical absence of any critical stance.
42 I have developed this idea more extensively in my essay "For the Last Time: Civilization," *International Sociology*. September 2001. Volume 16 (3): 361–368; as well as in my book, *Iran: A People Interrupted* (op. cit.: Postscript).
43 There are other claimants to that dubious distinction. In addition to Abdolkarim Soroush, Tariq Ramadan and even a precocious graduate student named Reza Aslan, the author of *No god but God: The Origins, Evolution, and Future of Islam*. New York: Random House, 2006, are the other nominees for this political manufacturing of an Islamic Reformation.
44 Abdolkarim Soroush, *Qabz-o-Bast-e Teoric-e Shari'at* ("The Theoretical Contraction and Expansion of Religious Knowledge") Tehran: Mo'assesseh-ye Farhangi-ye Serat, 1991: 31.
45 Ibid: 31.
46 Ibid: 32.
47 Ibid: 32–33.
48 Ibid: 33.
49 Ibid: 34.
50 Ibid: 34.

51 Ibid: 165.
52 Ibid: 170.
53 Ibid: 173–74.
54 Ibid: 180.
55 Ibid: 181.
56 Ibid: 190.
57 Ibid: 192.
58 Ibid: 201.
59 Ibid: 205.
60 Ibid: 206.
61 Ibid: 214–15.
62 Ibid: 220–24.
63 Ibid: 231–32.
64 Ibid: 234–35.
65 Ibid: 239–44.
66 Ibid: 245–46.
67 Ibid: 247.
68 Ibid: 252–59.
69 Ibid: 264.
70 Ibid: 276.
71 Ibid: 280.
72 Ibid: 285.
73 Ibid: 287.
74 Ibid: 289–98.
75 See Abdolkarim Soroush, "The Theoretical Contraction and Expansion of Religious Knowledge" (op. cit.: 34). The quotation is from a Qur'anic phrase.
76 Michael Hardt and Antonio Negri's *Empire*. Cambridge, MA: Harvard University Press, 2000, though still very much Eurocentric in its narrative, remains the best assessment of the emergence of this nascent globalized empire. I have addressed the causes and conditions of the end of civilizational thinking and its last gasp for air in the works of Samuel Huntington *et al.* in my "For the Last Time: Civilization" (op. cit.).
77 For a sample of the astounding output of Nasr Hamid Abu Zayd and his groundbreaking work in Qur'anic hermeneutics, which caused him great political problems in Egypt and forced him into exile from his homeland, see *Al-Ittijâh Al-'Aqlî fi al-Tafsir: Dirasa fi Qadiyat al-Majaz fi 'l-Qur'an ind al-Mu'tazila* ("Rational Argument in Qur'anic Exegesis: A Study of the Question of Metaphor in the Qur'an among the Mutazilites") (Beirut, 1982); *Falsafat al-Ta'wil: Dirasa fi Ta'wil al-Qur'an 'ind Muhiy al-Din ibn 'Arabi* ("The Philosophy of Hermeneutics: A Study of Ibn 'Arabi's Hermeneutics of the Qur'an") (Beirut, 1983); *Mafhum al-Nass: Dirasa fi 'Ulum al-Qur'an* ("The Concept of the Text: A Study of the Qur'anic Sciences") (Beirut, 1991); *Ishkaliyat al-Qira'a wa Aliyyat al-Ta'wil* ("The Problematic of Reading and the Method of Interpretation") (Beirut, 1995); *Naqd al-Khitab al-Dini* ("Critique of religious Discourse") (Cairo, 1998); *Al-Tafkir fi Zaman al-Takfir* ("Thinking in the Time of Excommunication") (Cairo, 1998); *Al-Khitab wa al-Ta'wil* ("Discourse and Hermeneutics"), (Beirut, 2000); and in English, *Reformation of Islamic Thought: A Critical Historical Analysis* (Amsterdam: Amsterdam University Press, 2006); *Rethinking the Qur'an: Towards a Humanistic Hermeneutics*. Utrecht: Humanistics University Press, 2004. None of these extraordinary books and learned essays are known outside a very limited circle of Abu Zayd's readership, certainly compared with the media hoopla created around Tariq Ramadan.
78 For a sample of her work see her *Woman at Point Zero*. London: Zed Books, 1983; *The Hidden Face of Eve: Women in the Arab World*. London: Zed Books, 1980; or

The Nawal El Saadawi Reader. London: Zed Books, 2005. Nawal El Saadawi's work is known to a wider circle of readership. But she is never called "the Martin Luther of Islam," despite her groundbreaking work as both a theorist and an activist, which fact points to yet another bizarre disposition of this search for the "Muslim Martin Luther." He not only has to be modeled on the Christian exemplar of Martin Luther but he has to be a man. Here is where the Christian/European sexism meets Muslim/Arab misogyny and confounds one's bafflement at the spectacle.

79 The titles of his books in French bespeak his preoccupation with the centrality of "the West" in his captured imagination: *Les musulmans dans Laïcité, responsibilities et droit des musulmans dans les sociétés occidentals*. Lyon: Tawhid, 1994/1998; *Islam, le face á face des civilisations, Quel project pour quelle modernité?*. Lyon: Les deux Rives, 1995/1998; *Aux sources du renouveau musulman, Un siécle de réformisme islamique*. Paris: Bayard-centurion, 1998; *Peut-on vivre avec l'Islam?* Lausanne: Favre, 1999.

80 See for example, Tariq Ramadan's *In The Footsteps of the Prophet: Lessons from the Life of Muhammad*. Oxford: Oxford University Press, 2007. Notice that there is no indication of the name of Claude Dabbak as the translator on the cover or the title page of this book, but nevertheless the book is in part dedicated to her (as translator) (ibid: vi), and then again acknowledged as such in the Acknowledgement: "Claude Dabbak has translated this book and has, with great humility, never failed to put her learning at the service of the necessary corrections" (ibid: viii). The same is true about another book by Tariq Ramadan, *Western Muslims and the Future of Islam*. Oxford: Oxford University Press, 2004), where he writes, "I want to thank with all my heart Carol Bebawi for her excellent work on the translation and for her discreet and modest generosity – a real gift" (ibid: ix). Again, the name of Carol Bebawi does not appear as the translator on the title page.

81 See Tariq Ramadan, *To Be a European Muslim*. Leicester: The Islamic Foundation, 1999: the table on page 40.

82 Ibid: 179–197.

83 Ibid: 123–131.

84 Tariq Ramadan repeats the precise same dichotomy, and the identical graphs to illustrate it, both in his *To be a European Muslim*. 1999: 123–150, and his *Western Muslims and the Future of Islam*. Oxford: Oxford university Press, 2004: 62–101. Almost identical ideas and suggestions are expanded in varied forms and made in his *Islam, the West and the Challenges of Modernity*. Translated by Saïd Amghar. Leicester: The Islamic Foundation, 2001. The tone of Tariq Ramadan is invariably pious, ponderous, meditative, and aloof, with a pronounced sense of his faith and heritage informing a belatedly prophetic disposition to his language and diction. He thinks, feels, and writes as if from the edge of a revelatory moment – Qur'anic Verses, Prophetic Traditions, and other sacred signs of piety and belief interwoven and indistinguishable from his own utterances – lending legitimacy and investing authority in his prose. Thus the idiomaticity of his diction mirrors and reflects a sacred supposition identical to those of Abdolkarim Soroush and before them people like Seyyed Hossein Nasr, Fritjof Schuon, and Deepak Chopra.

85 Ibid: 126.

86 Ibid: 127.

87 Ibid: 148.

88 Ibid: 148. All the emphasis are in the original.

89 Ibid: 149.

4 Islam and globalization

1 See Arundhati Roy, "Confronting Empire," in her *War Talk*. Cambridge, MA: South End Press, 2003. 103.

2 Ibid: 105.
3 Ibid: 106.
4 See Judith Butler, *Precarious Life: The Power of Mourning and Violence*. London and New York: Verso, 2004. 46.
5 Ibid: 47–78. See also ibid: 141–142 for further reflections of Judith Butler on *burka*, this time predicated on Lila Abu-Lughod's paper "Do Muslim Women Really Need Saving?" *American Anthropologist*. September 2002. 104 (3): 783–790.
6 See Judith Butler, *Precarious Life* (ibid: 131–5 and 144–5).
7 See Susan Willis, *Portents of the Real: A Primer for Post-9/11 America*. London: Verso, 2005. 15.
8 Ibid: 17.
9 Ibid: 17.
10 Ibid: 18.
11 Ibid: 21.
12 Julia Kristeva, "Europe Divided: Politics, Ethics, Religion" in *Crisis of the European Subject*. New York: Other Press, 2000. 114.
13 See Dipesh Chakrabarty, *Provincializing Europe: Postcolonial Thought and Historical Difference*. Princeton: Princeton University Press, 2000.
14 Ibid: 117. Emphasis added.
15 Ibid: 117. Particularly noteworthy to Tariq Ramadan should be this triumvirate of "Greek, Jewish, and Christian" on Kristeva's mind. Between Kristeva and Ramadan, these "Europeans" ought to decide where exactly is the place of Islam and where precisely should stand this "Muslim Martin Luther," where he cannot do otherwise.
16 See Susan Sontag, "Literature is Freedom" in Daniel Levy *et al.* (eds.), *Old Europe, New Europe, Core Europe: Transatlantic Relations after the Iraq War*. London: Verso, 2005: 212.
17 Ibid: 214. Emphasis added.
18 What Susan Sontag inadvertently exposes here, and we have also seen in the most progressive pages of the organ of the left-liberal Americans *The Nation*, leads, in another variation of it, to arguing effectively for the idea of a "just war." "I have never since my childhood," declared Richard Falk in *The Nation* soon after the commencement of the US-led invasion of Afghanistan, "supported a shooting war in which the United States was involved, although in retrospect I think the NATO war in Kosovo achieved beneficial results. The war in Afghanistan against apocalyptic terrorism qualifies in my understanding as the first truly just war since World War II." (Richard Falk, "Defining a Just War," *The Nation*, 11 October 2001). Richard Falk of course went on to qualify his assertion and stipulate, "but the justice of the cause and of the limited ends is in danger of being negated by the injustice of improper means and excessive ends." That stipulation notwithstanding, to this day Richard Falk's justification of the US invasion of Afghanistan (later exacerbated by the US-led invasion of Iraq in March 2003, the Israeli invasion of Lebanon in July 2006, and the unprecedented rise of violence in the region, all inaugurated by what Falk thought was a just war) is no mere indication of historical fallacy but, far worse, of political blindness. Afghanistan as a country had no reason to be the target of the US invasion for the events of 9/11, which Falk identifies as "apocalyptic terrorism." If the Taliban had anything to do with Osama bin Laden, and if Osama bin Laden had anything to do with 9/11 (all to this day conjectural and circumstantial), then by October 2001 Richard Falk should have known, as everyone else, that both the Taliban and Osama bin Laden were the creation of his own elected government, serving the American anti-Soviet imperial designs when it best suited it. Falk's record of identifying the US invasion of Afghanistan as a prime example of a "just war" also shows how myopic he was at a time when the US invasion of Afghanistan

was the clear prelude to a much more pervasive globalization of its military might. The fault with Richard Falk's position, however, is a noble fault, the fault of a progressive multitude of Americans who refuse to see the systematic degeneration of their republic, from its very inception, into a predatory empire. They refuse to see imperialism as definitive to the historical character and economic foregrounding of the USA. They think these are mere follies of a bad "foreign policy," so that if the left-liberal wing of the Democratic Party, which *The Nation* seems to think it represents, were to come to power all will be good and dandy about America and the world. It won't. For a rebuttal to Richard Falk's argument for "just war," endorsed by a *Nation* editorial as well, see Alexander Cockburn, "The Left and the Just War" (*The Nation*, 25 October, 2001). This idea of "just war" is by no means the only time that the so-called American left-liberals have exposed their otherwise guarded secrets. *The Nation* has been systematically integral in the mutation of Islam and Muslims into active metaphors of fanaticism, bigotry, and backwardness. Consider, as one example among many, the title of Katha Pollitt's review of Dinesh D'Souza's book *The Enemy at Home: The Cultural Left and Its Responsibility for 9/11* (2007) ("Ayatollah D'Souza" *The Nation*, February 5, 2007). Why "Ayatollah" D'Souza? Would *The Nation* publish something under the title of "Rabbi D'Souza"? Systematic abusing of such Arabic and Islamic terms as "Ayatollah," for example, is now endemic to *The Nation*. No one ever bothered to teach these "left-liberals" that the term "Ayatollah" (literally, "the sign, proof, or indication, of God") is an honorific title for religiously learned people, very similar to "Rabbi" or "Archbishop." There are certainly Ayatollahs in Qom, as there are plenty of Rabbis in Tel Aviv and New York, and Archbishops in Rome and Boston, who may indeed share a common denominator with the Neocon D'Souza. But with the same logic that "Rabbi D'Souza" or "Archbishop D'Souza" are not appropriate terms and speak of bigotry, then *The Nation*, of all places, might have reconsidered partaking in this epidemic mutation of a world religion and all its honorific insignia into terms of fanaticism, warmongering, and abuse.
19 See Zillah Eisenstein, *Against Empire: Feminisms, Racism and 'the' West*. London: Zed Books, 2004. 2.
20 Ibid: 2–3.
21 Amy Kaplan, *The Anarchy of Empire in the Making of US Culture*. Cambridge, MA: Harvard University Press, 2002: 212.
22 Ibid: 22.
23 Ibid: 22.
24 Ibid: 22.
25 Ibid: 171.
26 Ibid: 173.
27 Ibid: 174. Corroborating Amy Kaplan's point about Du Bois' reading of domestic racism along with global imperialism is the identification of Barack Hussein Obama, precisely at the moment that he was about to announce his candidacy for the US presidency, with Osama bin Laden by CNN early in January 2007 – a perfect example of the fusion of domestic racism and global imperialism that Du Bois had in mind, almost a century after his groundbreaking observations. For more details see Note 45 in Chapter 1. The CNN inadvertent revelation of its racism, in a program run by Wolf Blitzer, was repeated shortly after by Senator Joseph R. Biden Jr. of Delaware, who while announcing his own candidacy for presidency in 2008 said of Senator Barack Obama that he "is the first mainstream African American who is articulate and bright and clean and a nice-looking guy." (As reported by *The New York Times*, 1 February 2007).
28 Ibid: 175.
29 For the original formulation of their idea, see Michael Hardt and Antonio Negri, *Empire*. Cambridge, MA: Harvard University Press, 2000.

30 See Michael Hardt, "From Imperialism to Empire" (*The Nation*, 31 July 2006).
31 Ibid.
32 According to Chalmers Johnson, "our country deploys well over half a million soldiers, spies, technicians, teachers, dependents, and civilian contractors in other nations and just under a dozen carrier task forces in all the oceans and seas of the world. We operate numerous secret bases outside our territory to monitor what the people of the world, including our own citizens, are saying, faxing or e-mailing to one another. ... As of September 2001, the Department of Defense acknowledged at least 725 American military bases existed outside the United States. Actually there are many more, since some bases exist under leaseholds, informal agreements, or disguises of various kinds. And more have been created since the announcement was made. The landscape of this military empire is as unfamiliar and fantastic to most Americans today as Tibet or Timbuktu were to nineteenth-century Europeans." (See Chalmers Johnson, *The Sorrows of Empire: Militarism, Secrecy, and the End of the Republic.* New York: Henry Holt and Company, 2004: 1–4.) As they say, "if it walks like a duck, quacks like a duck, and looks like a duck, it must be a duck." In his astonishing analysis of the global visual culture in the aftermath of 9/11, Nicholas Mirzoeff also speaks of what he calls "the empire of camps," by which he means a radical revision of Michel Foucault's notion of the substitution of discipline for physical incarceration. Particularly noting the case of an increasing number of camps for refugees, asylum seekers, etc., in Western Europe and North America, Mirzoeff uses the notions of "detention and deportation" as the *modus operandi* of this "empire of camps." (See Nicholas Mirzoeff, *Watching Babylon: The War in Iraq and the Global Visual Culture.* London and New York: Routledge, 2005: 117–171.)
33 For the American media's reaction to this visit between Kharrazi and Nasrallah see *The New York Times*, 15 October 2000, "Guerrilla Sect Emerges as Force in Palestinian Uprising."
34 See Partha Chatterjee, *The Nation and its Fragments: Colonial and Postcolonial Histories.* Princeton: Princeton University Press, 1993.
35 The creative and critical task of doing such defiant remapping of the imperial imaginary does not preclude viciously racist policies in the opposing direction, such as those implemented by the barefaced racism of the Australian Prime Minister John Howard in his so-called "Pacific Solution" to "the problem of refugees." As Nicholas Mirzoeff reports in his *Watching Babylon* (Ibid: 143–144), John Howard bribed the officials of the small pacific island of Nauru in encamping Afghan and Iraqi asylum seekers so they would not come to Australia and pollute the all-white disposition of his country. In other words, and Mirzoeff brilliantly demonstrates, the empire of camps is itself remapping itself in resistance to the critical remapping of the imperial imaginary. Meanwhile, "Muslim Martin Luthers" like Tariq Ramadan seek to whitewash the immigrant Muslim communities into believing that they are "European Muslims." Either incarcerated into remote pacific islands or else accepted into whites-only European country clubs, the massive Muslim immigrant communities around the globe are prevented from populating an alternative, more emancipatory, mapping of the world.
36 See for example Saskia Sassen, *Losing Control? Sovereignty in an Age of Globalization.* New York: Columbia University Press, 1996, and Saskia Sassen, *Globalization and Its Discontent: Essays on the New Mobility of People and Money.* With a Foreword by K. Anthony Appiah. New York: The New Press, 1998.
37 Sassen 1998: xix-xx.
38 Sassen 1998: 177. It is crucial to note here that Nicholas Mirzoeff's notion of "the empire of camps" has the potential of gradually overcoming what Sassen calls "the global city." "Their location," referring to these camps in Australia for

example, Mirzoeff points out, "is meant to emphasize that they are not part of the nation state and that their inmates will not achieve asylum, let alone citizenship" (ibid: 144). This means that Mirzoeff's "empire of camps" has the better likelihood of replacing, by a cruel act of supplementarity, the notion of the nation-state than does Sassen's "global city." By "the nation state," Mirzoeff of course means the national polity, which in a peculiar way makes human refugees camps the functional equivalent of "offshore bank accounts" for billionaires in economic terms escaping taxation on their accumulated capital. Offshore bank accounts of billionaires and the equally invisible "offshore," refugee camps of aliens in economic and political terms replicate and reflect each other. For a groundbreaking cinematic vision of what Nicholas Mirzoeff calls "the empire of camps" see the futuristic masterpiece of Alfonso Cuarón, "Children of Men" (2006).
39 Stanley Rosen, *Hermeneutics as Politics*. New York: Oxford University Press, 1987: 3.
40 Rosen 1987: 5.
41 Rosen 1987: 5.
42 Rosen 1987: 5–6.
43 Rosen 1987: 6.
44 As quoted by AP (Associated Press) in "Iran: Oil Prices Should Rise Slowly" on the Yahoo.com site for Iran News, Tuesday February 15, 2000, 9.05 am ET.
45 Ibid.
46 As quoted by AFP (Agence France-Presse) in "Khatami submits balanced budget to Iranian parliament," on the Yahoo.com site for Iran News, Wednesday December 15 1999, 6.10 pm SGT.
47 Ibid.
48 As quoted by BBC News, "Iran set for election fight," on the Yahoo.com site for Iran News, Thursday February 17 2000, 14.06 GMT.

5 The Shi'i passion play

1 "US journalist shot dead in Iraq" (BBC News, August 3, 2005).
2 Edward Wong, "American Journalist is Shot to Death in Iraq" (*The New York Times*, August 3, 2005).
3 Steven Vincent, "Switched Off in Basra" (*The New York Times*, July 31 2005).
4 See Steven Vincent, *In The Red Zone: A Journey Into The Soul Of Iraq*. Dallas, Texas: Spence Publishing Company, 2004.
5 This according to a piece I read, "Steven Vincent, RIP," quoting from his blog, at http://occhronicle.blogspot.com/2005/08/steven-vincent-rip.html. (Retrieved February 19 2007.)
6 Ibid. Emphasis added.
7 Ibid.
8 To err on the side of the conquerors' take on the ghastly event, I take this account of the Haditha Massacre from the BBC News, in the report by Martin Asser, "What happened at Haditha?" (BBC News, December 21 2006). http://news.bbc.co.uk/2/hi/middle_east/5033648.stm. Retrieved on 22 February 2007.
9 See Martin Asser, "What happened at Haditha?" (Ibid).
10 Ibid.
11 Ibid.
12 Ibid.
13 Ibid.
14 Ibid.
15 The best introductory text in English to the history of Shi'ism and the origin of the conflict between the Sunnis and the Shi'is is Moojan Momen's *An Introduction to Shi'i Islam*. New Haven: Yale University Press, 1985.

16 See Seyyed Vali Reza Nasr, *The Shia Revival: How Conflicts within Islam Will Shape the Future*. New York: W. W. Norton, 2006. For my reflection on the role of this book in seeking to shift the responsibility of the carnage in Iraq from the US-led invasion of a sovereign nation-state to Muslims in general and the Iraqis in particular see my "State of War: Thinking beyond the US invasion of Iran" (*Al-Ahram Weekly*, 8 – February 14 2007).
17 I take all these dates and statistics from BBC NEWS, "Timeline: Iraq" at http://news.bbc.co.uk/2/hi/middle_east/737483.stm (Retrieved February 20 2007). When in February 2007, almost four years into his aping of President George W. Bush, the British Prime Minister Tony Blair finally announced the withdrawal of some 1600 British soldiers from the total force of 7100 stationed in Iraq, even the US-UK-installed Iraqi President Jalal Talebani welcomed the news. From their most radical Shi'is to their most complicit Kurds, the Iraqis have declared, in one way or another, their collective will that they are against the colonial occupation of their homeland. From polite protest to violent rebellion, in how many languages did the Iraqis need to tell their military occupiers they wished to be left alone to decide their own national fate?
18 See David Brown, "Study Claims Iraq's 'Excess' Death Toll Has Reached 655,000" *The Washington Post*, October 11 2006.
19 Here I am not talking about the Ron Kovic (Tom Cruise) of Oliver Stone's "Born on the Fourth of July" (1989) who after his tour of duty in Vietnam joins the antiwar movement. Here I am referring to the far more powerful and poignant gang in Albert and Allen Hughes' revelatory "Dead Presidents" (1995). Watch this absolute masterpiece of the Vietnam syndrome and anticipate the next generation of Anthony (Larenz Tate), Skip (Chris Tucker), and Jose (Freddy Rodriguez) coming to haunt the veterans of the Afghan, Iraq (and perhaps Iran) wars.
20 For a preliminary reflection on Ta'ziyeh in Iraq before the US-led invasion, see Elizabeth Fernea. "Remembering Ta'ziyeh in Iraq" in *TDR: The Drama Review* (Volume 49, Number 4 [T 188], Winter 2005): Special Issue: From Karbala to New York: Ta'ziyeh on the Move, Guest Editor: Peter J. Chelkowski: 130–139. For a more general discussion of the relation between Ta'ziyeh and politics see Gustav Thaiss, "Religious Symbolism and Social Change: The Drama of Hussain," in Nikki Keddie (ed.), *Scholars, Saints and Sufis: Muslim Religious Institutions in the Middle East since 1500*. Berkley, CA: University of California Press, 1972: 349–366.
21 An earlier draft of this part of this chapter appeared as an essay. See Hamid Dabashi, "Ta'ziyeh as Theatre of Protest," in *TDR: The Drama Review* (op. cit.): 91–99.
22 That this was not an initially "Islamic" revolution and was made into one is the subject of my detailed reflection in Iran: A People Interrupted. New York: The New Press, 2007: Chapter Five and the Postscript.
23 Michel Foucault's reflections on the Iranian Revolution of 1979 were later the subject of a book by Janet Afary and Kevin B. Anderson, *Foucault and the Iranian Revolution: Gender and the Seductions of Islamism*. Chicago: The University of Chicago Press, 2005). For a critical consideration of Foucault's reading of the Iranian Revolution and Afary and Anderson's response to it see my *Iran: A People Interrupted* (op. cit.: 294–295).
24 For a pioneering volume of critical reflections on Ta'ziyeh see Peter J. Chelkowski (ed.), *Ta'ziyeh: Ritual and Drama in Iran*. New York: New York University Press, 1979. For the most recent body of scholarship on Ta'ziyeh see *TDR: The Drama Review* (op. cit.).
25 Peter Chelkowski has traced the journey of Ta'ziyeh from Iran to the Caribbean in his wonderful essay, "From Iran to Trinidad" in *TDR: The Drama Review* (op. cit.: 156–169).

26 For the pioneering studies of Ta'ziyeh as a form of theater see A. Chodzko, *Le Théâre persan*. Paris: Choix de Tazie, 1878); Sir Lewis Pelley's *The Miracle Play of Hasan and Husain*. Two Volumes.. London: H. Allen Co. 1879); A. Bausani, "Drammi popolari inediti persiani," in *Atti del Convegno Internazionale di Studi Etiopici*. Rome, 1960); and E. Bertels, "Persidskiy Teatr" in *Vostochniy Teatr*. Leningrad, 4: 1924).

27 For a comprehensive study of Ta'ziyeh and its performative immediacy see Sadeq Homayouni, *Ta'ziyeh dar Iran*. Shiraz: Navid Publications, 1368/1989.

28 As quoted by Augustus Richard Norton in his "Ritual, Blood, and Shiite Identity: Ashura in Nabatiyya, Lebanon," in *TDR: The Drama Review* (op. cit.: 140–155).

29 The historical unfolding of this routinization is the subject of my *Authority in Islam: From the Rise of Muhammad to the Establishment of the Umayyads*. New Brunswick, NJ: Transactions, 1989.

30 Directed by the distinguished Iranian director Mohammad Ghaffari, a series of Ta'ziyeh performances was staged at the Damrosch Park, Lincoln Center in New York on 12–21 July 2002. For Ghaffari's reflections on Ta'ziyeh see the article that he and William O. Beeman wrote on those occasion, "Acting Style and Actor Training in Ta'ziyeh" in *TDR: The Drama Review* (op. cit.: 48–60).

31 At the writing of this chapter, the Museum of Modern Art (MoMA) in New York is about to host a major retrospective on the work of the prominent Iranian filmmaker Abbas Kiarostami, "Abbas Kiarostami: Image Maker" (March 1–19, 2007). Included in the program is Kiarostami's Ta'ziyeh video installation. In this installation, Kiarostami does not just screen a particular performance of Ta'ziyeh. He also projects the close-up of the faces of Iranian audiences watching that performance. In other words, he is exporting for a New York, and before that a London, Paris, etc, audience not just the play but the Iranian audience that is watching it. So in effect the Iranian spectators have become the spectacle for the non-Iranian spectators. The Question here is who is watching these latter spectators? *Quis custodiet ipsos custodes?*

32 For an account of this event see Milla Cozart Riggio, "Moses and the Wandering Dervish: Ta'ziyeh at Trinity College," in *TDR: The Drama Review* (op. cit.: 100–112).

33 Eric Foner, *Forever Free: The Story of Emancipation and Reconstruction*. Illustrated, Edited, and with Commentary by Joshua Brown. New York: Alfred Knopf, 2005: 209.

6 Liberation theodicy

1 See the chapter on "Concerning Violence" in Frantz Fanon, *The Wretched of the Earth*. Preface by Jean-Paul Sartre. New York: Grove Press, 1963: 35–106. "Decolonization," Fanon declared at the very outset, "is always a violent phenomenon" (p. 35).

2 See Max Weber, "Politics as a Vocation" in Hans Gerth and C. Wright Mills (eds.), *From Max Weber: Essays in Sociology*. Oxford: Oxford University Press, 1946: 78.

3 For George Sorel's scathing critique of passivity and praise for violence see in particular his chapter on "The Ethics of Violence" in his *Reflection on Violence*. Translated by T. E. Hulme. Introduction by Edward A. Shils. New York: Collier Books, 1950: 180–215.

4 Karl Marx, *Critique of the Gotha Program*. With Appendices by Marx, Engels and Lenin. New York: International Publishers1938: 18.

5 The assumption of a pre-eternal conflict between "Islam and the West" is not merely a matter of Samuel Huntington's thesis in his book on clash of civilization. As late as February 2007, the BBC World Service conducted a global survey

of the relationship between this very binary opposition. It did not matter that in fact according to this very poll, "most people believe common ground exists between the West and the Islamic world despite current global tensions." (See "Poll sees hope in West–Islam ties," BBC News, February 19 2007.) What matters is that the very question put to the people thus polled, "Can [Muslims and the West] find common ground, [or is] violent conflict inevitable [between them]" is itself a pointed and leading question that will not be allowed in any court of law and as a result is a self-fulfilling prophecy. Blaming "radical groups on both sides," as the BBC puts it, in fact creates and sustains these two presumably hostile sides. The fact that the survey chooses 27 countries and divides them into Western and Muslim countries itself corroborates and prejudices that presumed opposition. It does not matter that according to this very poll "an average of 56 percent said they saw positive links between the cultures," and that only "28 percent of respondents told questioners that violent conflict was inevitable." It did not matter that "Doug Miller, president of polling company Globescan, said the results suggested that the world was not heading towards an inevitable and wide-ranging "clash of civilisations." What matters was this very clash was assumed to be present, and thus the two sides of the proposition were thus corroborated. According to Doug Miller, "most people feel this is about political power and interests, not religion and culture." But nevertheless he and the BBC stack the deck when they even put the question to people they have already divided between Muslims and the inanity they keep calling "the West." Congratulating "the West" on the fabricated dichotomy, the BBC reports that "the most positive respondents came from Western nations, with 78 percent of Italians, 77 percent of Britons and 73 percent of Canadians saying it is possible to find common ground." The function of these sorts of polls is not to gauge the measure of opposition between "Islam and the West" but in fact to regenerate and sustain it. In his Monday February 19 2007 piece, Roger Hardy, the BBC Islamic affairs analyst, reports that "a new BBC poll shines light on ofne of the most pressing and contentious issues of our time. What drives tension and conflict between Islam and the West? Is there an inherent incompatibility between the two, making a clash of civilisations inevitable?" By the time the question is thus posed, it no longer matters what the response is. The question itself, Roger Hardy of the BBC himself, has already posited and fabricated the hostility by merely posing the question. Any reference to what Osama bin Laden has said, or what Samuel Huntington has theorized simply re-authenticates the binary. To corroborate the question, Roger Hardy has no choice but to refer to Ms. Ayaan Hirsi Ali and her considered opinion that "Islam and the West" are not compatible.

6 See Nicholas Dirks, *Castes of Mind: Colonialism and the Making of Modern India.* Princeton: Princeton University Press, 2001. "Caste," Nicholas Dirks proposes, "as we know it today, is not in fact some unchanged survival of ancient India, not some single system that reflects a core civilizational value, not a basic expression of Indian tradition. Rather, I will argue that caste ... is a modern phenomenon, that it is, specifically, the product of an historical encounter between India and Western colonial rule. By this I do not mean to imply that it was simply invented by the too clever British, now credited with so many imperial patents that what began as colonial critique has turned into another form of imperial adulation. But I *am* suggesting that it was under the British that "caste" became a single term capable of expressing, organizing, and above all "systematizing" India's diverse forms of social identity, community, and organization" (ibid: 5). It is precisely in the spirit of the same argument that I propose that the sectarian bifurcation between the Sunnis and the Shi'is emerged anew as a *modus operandi* of imperial domination in Iraq in the aftermath of the

US-led invasion of 2003. Seyyed Vali Reza Nasr's function at the US Naval academy was to be the native informer for this insidious argument and colonial practice.
7 I have dealt with this aspect of Seyyed Vali Reza Nasr's contribution to sustaining the state of war at the service of the US army in my "Thinking beyond the US invasion of Iran" (*al-Ahram Weekly*, 8–14 February 2007, Issue No. 831). For a more extensive discussion of the evolving modes of knowledge production from the period of classical Orientalism to the age of think thanks see my introductory essay, "Ignaz Goldziher and the Question concerning Orientalism" to a new edition of Ignaz Goldziher's *Muslim Studies*. New Brunswick: Transactions, 2006.
8 At the writing of this chapter, the Iranian President Mahmoud Ahmadinejad has just paid an official visit to Saudi Arabia, jointly declaring their determination to oppose sectarian violence in the region. "Iran's President Mahmoud Ahmadinejad," BBC reports, "and Saudi Arabia's King Abdullah have agreed to work together to fight sectarian strife in the Middle East. The announcement followed a visit by Mr. Ahmadinejad to Riyadh for rare talks. Speaking on his return to Tehran, he said the two countries would stand together against "enemy plots" seeking to divide the Muslim world." (BBC News, March 4 2007). Whatever the merits of this visit, and however real or fictitious this determination to oppose sectarian violence in the region might be, the visit itself shows the astounding shallowness of the US military intelligence as produced by such employers as Seyyed Vali Reza Nasr. A single official visit by the Iranian president to Saudi Arabia, however inconsequential it might be, throws the whole spectrum of Sunni–Shi'i divide, as manufactured by the US military intelligence (e.g. Seyyed Vali Reza Nasr), off balance. As sharp and diligent an observer of US military operations as Seymour Hersh has also fallen into the trap of this presumed hostility. See his "Redirection" (*The New Yorker*, March 5 2007), in which he relies on Seyyed Vali Reza Nasr and his kindred soul at the Washington Institute for Near Eastern policy Patrick Clawson for corroborating this presumed binary.
9 Seyyed Vali Reza Nasr, *The Shia Revival: How Conflicts within Islam Will Shape the Future*. New York: W. W. Norton, 2006: 241.
10 Ibid: 241.
11 What Seyyed Vali Reza Nasr is arguing in his *Shia Revival* in a seemingly scholarly language is almost identical with what the former mayor of New York City, Mr. Ed Koch, has also suggested to his readers in *The Jewish Press*: "President George W. Bush, vilified by many, supported by some," Mr. Koch put forward, "is a hero to me. Why do I say that? It's not because I agree with the president's domestic agenda. It's not because I think he's done a perfect job in the White House. George Bush is a hero to me because he has courage. The president does what he believes to be in the best interest of the United States. He sticks with his beliefs, no matter how intense the criticism and invective that are directed against him every day. The enormous defeat President Bush suffered with the loss of both Houses of Congress has not caused him to retreat from his position that the U.S. alone now stands between a radical Islamic takeover of many of the world's governments in the next 30 or more years. If that takeover occurs, we will suffer an enslavement that will threaten our personal freedoms and take much of the world back into the Dark Ages. Our major ally in this war against the forces of darkness, Great Britain, is still being led by an outstanding prime minister, Tony Blair. But Blair will soon be set out to pasture, which means Great Britain will leave our side and join France, Germany, Spain and other countries that foolishly believe they can tame the wolf at the door and convert it into a domestic pet that will live in peace with them. These dreamers naively believe that if we feed the wolves what they demand, they will go away. That won't happen. Appeasement never works. The wolves always come back for more and more, and when we

have nothing left to give, they come for us." As to who exactly are these hungry wolves, the former mayor of New York is quite clear: "The countries surrounding Iraq – Saudi Arabia, Egypt, Jordan – made up of Sunni Arabs, know that for them, the wolves who are the radical Shia are already at their door." (Ed Koch, "We Need Bush's Courage Now More Than Ever," *The Jewish Press*, 3 January 2007). Professor Seyyed Vali Reza Nasr could not have put it more eloquently.
12 Seyyed Vali Reza Nasr now regularly gives strategic advice to the US foreign policy, mostly warning of the increasing power of the Islamic Republic in the region and how the USA ought to confront of it. For a vintage example see Seyyed Vali Reza Nasr's "Who Wins in Iraq? 1. Iran" (Foreign Policy, March/April 2007), http://www.foreignpolicy.com/story/cms.php?story_id = 3705&fpsrc = ealert070226 (retrieved on 6 March 2007).
13 See Walter Benjamin, "Critique of Violence," in Marcus Bullock and Michael W. Jennings, *Walter Benjamin: Selected Writings: Volume 1–1913-1926*. Cambridge: The Belknap Press of Harvard University, 1996: 236–252.
14 See Giorgio Agamben, "The State of Exception," in Andrew Norris (ed.), *Politics, Metaphysics, and Death: Essays on Giorgio Agamben's* Homo Sacer. Durham, NC: Duke University Press, 2005: 284–297.
15 Ibid: 289–290.
16 Walter Benjamin, "Critique of Violence" (ibid): 241.
17 Ibid: 243.
18 Ibid: 252.
19 Agamben, "The State of Exception," (ibid): 290.
20 For the intimate link (both theoretical and personal) between the Nazi political theorist Karl Schmitt and the neocon guru Leo Strauss see Heinrich Meier, *Karl Schmitt and Leo Strauss: The Hidden Dialogue*. Translated by Harvey Lomax. Foreword by Joseph Cropsey. Chicago: The University of Chicago Press, 1995. For the link between Leo Straus and the US neocons see the extensive documentation of Anne Norton in her *Leo Strauss and the Politics of American Empire*. New Haven: Yale University Press, 2004.
21 See Agamben, "The State of Exception" (ibid): 291.
22 Ibid: 294.
23 Ibid: 294.
24 Ibid: 296. Emphasis added.
25 For a critique of civilizational thinking see my "For the Last Time Civilization" (op. cit.).
26 For the most recent spiritual revelations of Seyyed Hossein Nasr, spoken from the high altitude of a mystic guru talking to mere mortals see his *Heart of Islam: Enduring Values for Humanity*. New York: Harper's, 2002.
27 What I am mapping out here as the site of the re-emergence of a cosmopolitan Islam, Bernard Lewis laments as the sign of yet another attempt by Muslim to conquer the world. In his "2007 Irving Kristol Lecture," Bernard Lewis warns his American audience that the "cosmic struggle for world domination" has long since stopped in Christianity but is still paramount in Islam. In his manner of counting the historic Muslim designs for world domination and the conquest of "the West," "the third wave of attack on Europe has clearly begun. We should not delude ourselves as to what it is and what it means. This time it is taking different forms and two in particular: terror and migration." It is quite satisfying to know that at the age of 90 and ready to meet his creator, Bernard Lewis is leaving this world convinced that Muslims will soon conquer the world. The rest of the world may laugh or at least chuckle at the idea, but what an apt ending for an Orientalist who spent a lifetime warning of Muslims coming to conquer the world. For the full text, see "The 2007 Irving Kristol Lecture by Bernard Lewis"

at the American Enterprise Institute website, http://aei.org/publications/filter.all, pubID.25815/pub_detail.asp.
28 I have developed in some detail the particulars of this paramount mode of realism in my *Masters and Masterpieces of Iranian Cinema*. Washington DC: Mage Publishers, 2007.
29 An earlier and shorter version of this part of this chapter appeared as "Lessons from Lebanon: Rethinking national liberation movements" in *al-Ahram Weekly* (7–13 September 2006). Its Arabic translation by Samah Idriss appeared in *al-Adab* (Beirut: October 2006).
30 For the most recent study of Lebanese history see the groundbreaking work of Fawwaz Traboulsi, *A History of Modern Lebanon*. London: Pluto Press, 2007.
31 This according to a report in *Financial Times*, August 23 2006.
32 *Financial Times*, August 23 2006.
33 See William Wallis, "Industrialists Count Cost of Bombing," *Financial Times*, August 5–6 2006.
34 See *Financial Times* August 23 2006.
35 See for example *Independent*, August 11 2006.
36 *Independent*, August 5 2006.

7 Malcolm X as a Muslim revolutionary

1 For example read the following pieces on BBC World Website, as a minor sample of much more civilian casualties in Afghanistan: "Nato laments Afghan civilian dead" (3 January 2007), "US troops kill Afghan civilians" (March 4 2007), "Civilians 'main Afghan victims'" (April 16 2007), "Air raid 'kills Afghan civilians'" (9 May 2007) and "US admits Afghan civilians killed" (May 11 2007).
2 Statistically, a far greater proportion of the leading ideologues of the American neoconservative movement are militant Jews than the percentage of Muslims identifying with the militant adventurism of Osama bin Laden or Mulla Omar – and yet no one would, or should, talk about "Judeofascism," while the very same band of neocons have invented and widely disseminated the term "Islamofascism." Identifying American or even Israeli neo-conservatism with Judaism is as fallacious and as singular a sign of anti-Semitism as extrapolating from the ideas and practices of their Muslim counterparts Mulla Omar and Osama bin Laden an Islamic proclivity towards Fascism. What Paul Wolfowitz did in the US Pentagon, or Baruch Goldstein in Hebron, has as much to do with Judaism as what their Muslim counterparts Osama bin Laden and Molla Omar have done in Afghanistan or elsewhere with Islam. The term "Islamofascism" is thus as much malicious as would be "Judeofascism."
3 For an introduction to Sayyid Qutb's ideas see Adnan A. Musllam, *From Secularism to Jihad: Sayyid Qutb and the Foundations of Radical Islamism*. New York: Praeger Publishers, 2005. For a sample of Sayyid Qutb's own writings see his *Basic Principles of Islamic Worldview*. New York: Islamic publications, 2005.
4 In addition to a massive body of scholarship on Malcolm X, The Malcolm X Project at Columbia University, under the leadership of my distinguished colleague Manning Marable, is now a groundbreaking scholarly output entirely dedicated to the study of the legendary Muslim revolutionary. For details visit: www.columbia.edu/ccbh/mxp.
5 See *Malcolm X, The Autobiography of Malcolm X: As Told to Alex Haley*. New York: Ballantine Books, 1987.
6 I take this sequence of Malcolm X's life from The Malcolm X Project at Columbia University, www.columbia.edu/ccbh/mxp.
7 A good point of departure for this purpose would be the work of Frantz Fanon, to which both Islamic and Christian liberation theologies are indebted and

attentive. See for example Gustavo Gutierrez's, *A Theology of Liberation*. New York: Orbis Books, 1988: p. 20 and p. 186 for his appreciation of Fanon's attention to the personal and psychological aspects of colonial domination.

Conclusion: Prolegomena to a future liberation theodicy

1 Gustavo Gutiérrez, *A Theology of Liberation* (op. cit.: 174).
2 See Richard Falk, "Defining a Just War" (*The Nation*, October 29 2001); see also Adam Shatz, "The Left and 9/11" (*The Nation*, September 23 2002). Richard Falk went so far as to say that "the war in Afghanistan against apocalyptic terrorism qualifies in my understanding as the first truly just war since world war II;" while Adam Shatz's memory of watching the World Trade Center burn from his apartment in Flatbush convinced him that al-Qaeda was the devil incarnate and that he was not going to be part of any anti-war demonstrations. These are not simple political misreadings of a terrorizing state apparatus commanding the army of Attila the Hun and pouring death and destruction over Muslim nations. These are historic signs of the bankruptcy of the public intellectuals in a violent country that has just dismantled two sovereign nation-states, its soldiers tortured and raped innocent civilians, maimed and murdered over a million Afghans and Iraqis, and made millions more refugees around the globe.
3 Gustavo Gutiérrez, *A Theology of Liberation* (op. cit.: 174).
4 Michel Foucault, as quoted by Giorgio Agamben in *Homo Sacer: Sovereign power and bare Life*. Translated by Daniel Heller-Roazen. Stanford, CA: Stanford University Press, 1995: 3.
5 Agamben, *Homo Sacer* (op. cit.: 4).
6 Agamben, *Homo Sacer* (op. cit.: 4).
7 Agamben, *Homo Sacer* (op. cit.: 4).
8 Agamben, *Homo Sacer* (op. cit.: 5–6).
9 Agamben, *Homo Sacer* (op. cit.: 6). Italics in the original.
10 Agamben, *Homo Sacer* (op. cit.: 6).
11 At this point of his argument, Agamben refers to the function of language in the making of the *polis*. "The link between bare life and politics," he points out, "is the same link that the metaphysical definition of man as 'the living being who has language' seeks in the relation between *phone* and *logos*" (Agamben, *Homo Sacer*: 7). From this point Agamben then concludes, in an obvious retort against Karl Schmitt, that "the fundamental categorical pair of Western politics is not that of friend/enemy but that of bare life/political existence, *zoë/bios*, exclusion/ inclusion. There is politics because man is the living being who, in language, separates and opposes himself to his own bare life and, at the same time, maintains himself in relation to that bare life in an inclusive exclusion" (ibid: 8). That last bit of internal dialectic would become entirely superfluous if we were to consider the structure and function of "foreign languages" in the making of the very same "Western" politics. The entire function of Orientalism, and by extension Islamic Studies, or Chinese Studies, Indian Studies, Iranian Studies, etc, is nothing but "to explain" the foreignness of these languages and cultures to their "Western" readers. To explain something is ipso facto to constitute its foreignness, and thus by definition point to the quintessential inexplicability of the phenomenon in its own terms – and thus to constitute the foreign as the enemy and the enemy as the foreigner, as he who does not speak one's language (literally, "the barbarian"), the enemy who speaks a foreign, estrange, and thus dangerous language, and thus acts in a strange and inexplicable manner, and is thus in need of a native informer (Fouad Ajami) or an Orientalist (Bernard Lewis) to explain him/her, and is thus outside *the form of the political* and

squarely in the realm of *zoë* or bare life. The singular function of Orientalism over the last 200 years has been nothing but to constitute the "Orient" as the enemy of "the West" by trying to understand and explain it – the same holds true for all Area Studies fields. They make strange and thus constitute as the enemy that which they seek to explain and made understood. In short, when Seyyed Vali Reza Nasr or Azar Nafisi write a book on Shi'ism or reading "Western classics" in Iran, and thus to explain Muslims, they are *ipso facto* constituting Muslims (Iranians, Arabs, Afghans, South Asians, etc.) as the enemy of "the West."

12 Agamben, *Homo Sacer* (op. cit.: 9).
13 Agamben, *Homo Sacer* (op. cit.: 9).
14 Agamben, *Homo Sacer* (op. cit.: 10).
15 Agamben, *Homo Sacer* (op. cit.: 10–11).

Index

7/7 265
9/11: blindness and insight 133, 141; future liberation theodicy 255, 256, 258, 264, 265; Islam and globalization 147, 149, 154, 159; liberation theodicy 198, 199, 200, 208; Malcolm X as Muslim revolutionary 236; overview 1–5, 8, 9, 11–13, 17; resisting the empire 28–32, 34, 53
Abdi, Ali 63
Abduh, Muhammad 38, 41, 42, 210
Abdullah, King 177, 201
Abrahamian, Ervand 92
Abu Ghraib prison 6, 32, 179–81, 206, 260
Adorno, Theodor 43, 101, 103, 162, 249
al-Afghani, Jamal al-Din 19, 38, 40, 41, 42, 210
Afghanistan: future liberation theodicy 255, 256, 257, 260; Islam and globalization 145, 154, 160; liberation theodicy 229, 230; Malcolm X as Muslim revolutionary 235, 236, 237, 238; overview 3–6, 8, 9, 11; resisting the empire 32, 33, 38, 39, 57
Afshar, Nader Shah 86
Agamben, Georgio 183, 205–8, 258–62
Ahmadinejad, Mahmoud 66, 236, 240
Al-e Ahmad, Jalal 47, 109
Ahsa'i, Shaykh Ahmad 80, 81, 82, 96
al-Ahsa'i, Sheykh Zeyn al-Din 40
Ajami, Fouad 199, 243
Alavid Shi'ism 70
Algar, Hamid 75
Ali, Chiragh 116
Ali, Hirsi 57, 199, 234, 243
Ali, Hussein ibn 176, 186

Ali, Mirza Hossein (Baha'ullah) 82, 83
Ali, Muhammad 25, 41
Ali, Zayd ibn 68
Allende, Salvador 256
Alves, Rubem 49, 50
Amal 203
American flag 147
Amnesty International 224, 225
Anderson, Benedict 112, 113
anti-9/11 28, 29, 30, 32
Arendt, Hannah 259
Arif, Colonel Abd-al-Salam Muhammad 177
Aristotle 96, 261
Arjomand, Said Amir 84, 85
Ashtiyani, Mirza Hasan 78, 79
Aslan, Reza 133
asylum seekers 217
"Axis of Evil" 4, 66, 186
Azal, Mirza Yahya Sobh 82
Bab, Ali Mohammad 40, 80, 81, 82
Babi movement 40, 79, 80, 82, 83
Babu, Abdul 248
Bagram Air Base 6, 181, 206, 260
Baha'ism 83
Baha'ullah (Mirza Hossein Ali) 82, 83
Bahonar, Mohammad Reza 64
Baker–Hamilton report 236
al-Bakr, General Ahmad Hasan 177
Balibar, Etienne 240
Bam 66
al-Banna, Hasan 42
Barghouti, Marwan 230

Bark, Coleman 213
Bartolomé de Las Casas, Father 43, 49, 50, 51, 55, 148
Battle of Karbala *see* Karbala

Bayrou, François 240
Begin, Menachim 192
Behbahani, Seyyed Abdullah 47, 78
Bell, Daniel 48
Benedict XVI, Pope 16, 19, 50, 55
Benjamin, Walter 206, 207, 208
Berlusconi, Silvio 32, 148, 234
bin Laden, Osama: blindness and insight 140, 141; end of Islamic ideology 60, 97; future liberation theodicy 256, 257, 262, 264; liberation theodicy 197, 199, 208, 211, 212, 213; Malcolm X as Muslim revolutionary 234–36, 238, 243, 245, 250, 252; overview 3–5, 9–12, 16–20; resisting the empire 28, 29, 31, 32, 37–39
biopolitics 259
Blair, Tony 16, 18, 19, 32, 232, 234
Blitzer, Wolf 7, 30
Blumenberg, Hans 257
Boston Tea Party 11
Bremer, Paul 180
burka 145, 146
Bush, George H. W. 178
Bush, George W.: blindness and insight 140; end of Islamic ideology 66; Islam and globalization 146, 161; liberation theodicy 199, 200, 202, 208, 225; Malcolm X as Muslim revolutionary 234–38, 241; overview 1, 4–6, 8, 16, 18, 19, 21; resisting the empire 25–28, 31–32, 36, 38, 53, 57–58; *Ta'ziyeh* as theater of protest 180, 184
Butler, Judith 145, 146, 147, 149, 152, 168

Cambodia 228
Camus, Albert 97
Carter, Jimmy 192
caste system 200
Castro, Fidel 247
Catholicism 50
Césaire, Aimé 43
Chakrabarty, Dipesh 147–48
Chalabi, Ahmad 6
Chatterjee, Partha 112, 113, 114, 156
Chelkowski, Peter 185, 194
Cheney, Dick 21, 58, 184
Cheney, Lynne 145
Chomsky, Noam 55
Chopra, Deepak 213
Christianity 9, 50, 96, 97, 207–8, 263

cinema 143, 180, 218
civilizational thinking 1, 34, 35, 141
civil rights 44, 53, 57, 240
clash of civilizations 1, 19, 34, 205
climate change 241
Clinton, Hillary 145, 146
CNN: Islam and globalization 145, 146; overview 5, 6, 7, 8, 10, 12; resisting the empire 25, 26, 30, 35, 57
colonialism: blindness and insight 107–10, 112, 114, 117, 141; end of Islamic ideology 59, 60, 66–67, 73–77, 83, 87–88, 94, 96, 98; future liberation theodicy 257, 264; Islam and globalization 152, 153, 156–58, 160, 161; liberation theodicy 209, 213, 214; Malcolm X as Muslim revolutionary 240, 249; overview 3, 17; resisting the empire 25, 35, 37–43, 44–48, 49–52, 54
concentration camps 258, 259, 260, 262
conscience collective 67, 70–71, 74, 77–79, 85, 91, 93
Constitutional Revolution (1906–11) 79, 80, 83, 86–90
Cropsey, Joseph 53

Dabbak, Claude 134
Damad, Mir 80
Danish cartoons 262
Dar al-Islam 20, 134–36, 139, 215, 216
Deleuze, Gilles 43, 249
Department of Homeland Security 4
Derrida, Jacques 105, 108
Dershowitz, Alan 7, 56, 261
al-Din, Aqa Munir 78
Dirks, Nicholas 200
Donnelly, Paul 133
al-Dowleh, Ayn 86
Du Bois, W. E. B. 138, 151–53, 157, 161, 168, 234
Duff, Grant 86
Durkheim, Emile 70, 71
al-Durrah, Muhammad 145
Dynamic Ijtihad 95

Ebadi, Shirin 66
Egypt 42
Eisenstein, Zillah 150, 151, 168
empire 154
England, Lynndie 260, 261
Enlightenment: blindness and insight 105, 106, 107, 108, 109; future liberation theodicy 263; Islam and

globalization 161, 162, 163; Malcolm X as Muslim revolutionary 250
Eshkevari, Hasan Yousefi 116
Ethiopia 239
Europe 18, 39, 163, 217, 239, 241
European colonialism *see* colonialism

Falasiri, Seyyed Ali Akbar 78
Falk, Richard 10
Fallaci, Oriana 148, 149
Falluja massacre 7, 180, 181
Fanon, Frantz: blindness and insight 99, 107, 114, 138; end of Islamic ideology 92; future liberation theodicy 264; liberation theodicy 198, 199, 206; Malcolm X as Muslim revolutionary 248; resisting the empire 43; US imperialism 11
al Farabi, Abu Nasr 134
fatwa 75
Faysal, King 177
Fazlollah, Shaykh 155
feminism 145, 146
Fendereski, Mir 80
Ferdowsi 88, 192
Ferguson, Niall 10
Ferry, Luc 109
Fisk, Robert 227
Foner, Eric 171
Foucault, Michel: blindness and insight 101, 102, 104, 110, 129; future liberation theodicy 258, 259; Islam and globalization 162; *Ta'ziyeh* as theater of protest 185
Fox News 5, 6, 8, 10, 145
France 240
French Revolution 102
Freud, Sigmund 105
Friedman, Milton 10, 264
Friedman, Thomas 184
Friel, Howard 10
Fukuyama, Francis 31, 52, 53, 60, 112

Gandhi, Mahatma 266
Ganji, Akbar 63, 115
Gellner, Ernest 112, 113
Geneva Convention 261
Ghaffari, Mohammad 194
ghaybah 67
globalization: blindness and insight 114, 140, 141; end of Islamic ideology 60; future liberation theodicy 265; Islam and globalization 143–70; liberation theodicy 209, 210; Malcolm X as Muslim revolutionary 23, 235, 245, 248, 252; overview 20, 21, 22; resisting the empire 34, 35
Goldstein, Baruch 31
Golestan Treaty 46, 74, 76
Gonzales, Alberto R. 261
Gramsci, Antonio 97
Green, Steven D. 145, 181, 183
Guantanamo Bay 7, 181, 260
Guattari, Félix 43, 249
Gucci revolutionaries 221, 222, 223, 231, 232
Guevara, Che 11, 50, 92, 138, 248
Gulf War 3, 39
Gutiérrez, Gustavo vii, 43, 49–50, 96–97, 254–55

al-Habashi, Bilal 140
Habermas, Jürgen 100–108, 110, 113, 213, 240
Haditha massacre 174, 175, 180, 181, 182
Hajjarian, Saeed 96, 116
al-Hakim, Abd al-Aziz 236
al-Hakim, Ayatollah Mohammed Baqer 179
Hamas: liberation theodicy 197, 214–15, 223–27, 228–32; Malcolm X as Muslim revolutionary 251; overview 15, 21
Hammurabi 174, 175
Hardt, Michael 153, 154
Hariri, Rafik 220, 221, 222, 231, 232
al-Hariri, Saad 221
Harper's Magazine 171, 172, 173, 176
Hashemi, Faezeh 166
Hawi, George 221
Hegel, G. W. F. 101, 113, 120
Heidegger, Martin 105, 107, 108, 109, 110
Heinrich Böll Foundation 208, 217
Hersh, Seymour 10
Herzl, Theodor 51
Hezbollah: Islam and globalization 155; liberation theodicy 197, 202–3, 214–15, 220, 223–27, 228–32; Malcolm X as Muslim revolutionary 251; overview 15, 21
historiography 123, 124
Hitchens, Christopher 252
Hobeika, Elie 220
Hobsbawm, E. J. 112
Hobson, J. A. 154

Index

Ho Chi Minh 228
Hölderlin, Friedrich 102
Holocaust: blindness and insight 102, 109, 111; Islam and globalization 148, 162; Malcolm X as Muslim revolutionary 240; resisting the empire 43, 51, 54
homo sacer 183, 258, 260
Horkheimer, Max 43, 101, 103, 249
Hughes, Langston 59
Huntington, Samuel: blindness and insight 141; colonialism 19; end of Islamic ideology 60; liberation theodicy 205; resisting the empire 31, 34, 36, 56
Hurricane Katrina 1, 8, 22, 25–30, 36, 236
al-Husayn 67, 69
Hussein, Saddam: future liberation theodicy 256, 257, 262; liberation theodicy 229; Malcolm X as Muslim revolutionary 236, 252; overview 3, 4, 5, 6, 20; resisting the empire 38, 39, 56; *Ta'ziyeh* as theater of protest 177, 178, 192, 193
Hyde, Emily 172

IDF (Israeli Defense Force) 33
Idriss, Samah 219
Ignatieff, Michael 7, 56, 261
imagined communities 113
Imamah 67, 68
Imamate 40, 71
IMF *see* International Monetary Fund
Imperial Tobacco Corporation 77
India 144, 200, 241
International Monetary Fund (IMF) 138, 144, 168, 241
Iqbal, Allamah Muhammad 19, 45
Iran: blindness and insight 110–13, 115, 125; end of Islamic ideology 61–66, 68–69, 75, 77–79, 83–88, 90–92, 94; future liberation theodicy 255; Islam and globalization 154, 155, 159, 160, 164–67; liberation theodicy 196, 201–2, 204–5, 208–12, 218, 226–31; Malcolm X as Muslim revolutionary 235, 236, 237, 238, 251; overview 3, 4, 15, 17, 21; resisting the empire 38, 44, 46; *Ta'ziyeh* as theater of protest 177, 185, 191, 192, 193
Iraq: future liberation theodicy 255, 257, 260, 266; Islam and globalization 145, 154; liberation theodicy 197–98, 200–203, 205, 214, 215, 226, 228–31; Malcolm X as Muslim revolutionary 235–37, 239, 241, 251, 252; overview 3, 5–11, 21, 23; resisting the empire 32, 33, 39, 56, 57; *Ta'ziyeh* as theater of protest 171–75, 177–84, 192, 193
Isfahani, Hatif 258
Islam: blindness and insight 111, 127, 128; future liberation theodicy 254; Islam and globalization 156, 157; liberation theodicy 209, 214; Malcolm X as Muslim revolutionary 243, 245, 249; overview 1, 2, 12, 13; resisting the empire 36
"Islam and the West": blindness and insight 128, 136, 141, 142; end of Islamic ideology 67; future liberation theodicy 255, 258, 262; Islam and globalization 156, 159, 167; liberation theodicy 197, 199, 200, 216, 217; Malcolm X as Muslim revolutionary 235; resisting the empire 33–37, 39, 54, 56
Islamic ideology: end of Islamic ideology 59–98; future liberation theodicy 258, 262, 263; Islam and globalization 156, 157, 159, 160, 166, 168; liberation theodicy 208, 209, 215, 216; overview 14, 15; resisting the empire 38, 39, 41, 43, 44, 48
"Islamism": liberation theodicy 209, 210, 264, 265; Malcolm X as Muslim revolutionary 250; overview 9, 11, 16
Israel: future liberation theodicy 256, 257, 263; Islam and globalization 155; liberation theodicy 197–98, 202–4, 221–27, 228–32; Malcolm X as Muslim revolutionary 236, 237, 239, 241, 243; overview 5, 9, 11, 14, 15; resisting the empire 51, 54, 55, 56, 57; *Ta'ziyeh* as theater of protest 178, 184

Jam'at-i Islami 45
Jameson, Frederic 250
al-Janabi, Abeer Qassim Hamza 145, 146, 149, 181, 183
al-Jaza'iri, Abdel Qadir 42
al-Jazeera 11, 21, 35
jihad 21, 75
John Paul II, Pope 50
Johnson, Chalmers 8, 10
Jones, Jim 31
Judaism 50–51, 54, 55

Jünger, Ernst 109

Kadivar, Jamileh 166
Kadivar, Mohsen 63, 166–67
Kalbasi, Hajji Muhammad 76
Kani, Hajji Mulla Ali 76, 77, 86
Kant, Immanuel: blindness and insight 101–4, 106, 107, 113; future liberation theodicy 261; Islam and globalization 148, 149, 161, 162; Malcolm X as Muslim revolutionary 250; resisting the empire 51
Kaplan, Amy 151, 152, 153, 157, 168
Karami, Omar 221
Karbala: end of Islamic ideology 68, 69; liberation theodicy 214; *Ta'ziyeh* as theater of protest 171, 176, 178, 182–84, 190–93
Karzai, Hamid 6, 238
Kashani, Ayatollah 90, 91
Kaveh 218
Kennedy, John F. 247
Kepel, Gilles 48
Khamenei, Ayatollah Ali 64, 65, 155, 223
Khan, Sir Seyyed Ahmad 45
Kharrazi, Kamal 155
Khatami, Mohammad: end of Islamic ideology 62, 63, 65, 94, 96; Islam and globalization 159, 164, 165; liberation theodicy 208, 211
Khomeini, Ayatollah: blindness and insight 110, 116, 129; end of Islamic ideology 65, 91, 92, 93, 98; Islam and globalization 159; liberation theodicy 201, 204, 210, 223, 230; Malcolm X as Muslim revolutionary 243; resisting the empire 38, 46, 47, 48; *Ta'ziyeh* as theater of protest 185, 191, 192, 193
Khorsandi, Hadi 27
Kierkegaard, Søren 249
Kiernan, V. G. 10
King Jr., Martin Luther 53
Kipling, Rudyard 146
Krauthammer, Charles 184
Kristeva, Julia 147–50, 152, 168, 240
Kuhn, Thomas 119, 122
Ku Klux Klan 247
Kurosawa, Akira 180
Kuwait 3, 39, 178

labor migration: blindness and insight 137–39; Islam and globalization 154, 158, 160; liberation theodicy 213, 215–17; Malcolm X as Muslim revolutionary 239, 240, 241, 252; overview 22
Latin American liberation theology 48, 49, 50
Lawrence, Bruce 11
Lebanon: future liberation theodicy 266; Islam and globalization 155, 160; liberation theodicy 197–98, 202–3, 205, 214, 219–25, 226–32; Malcolm X as Muslim revolutionary 235, 236, 237, 251; overview 21; *Ta'ziyeh* as theater of protest 193
Ledeen, Michael 57, 58
Lenin, Vladimir 154, 198, 248
Levinas, Emmanuel 14, 72, 146, 235, 244, 262, 266
Lewis, Bernard: blindness and insight 111, 141; end of Islamic ideology 60; Malcolm X as Muslim revolutionary 234, 239, 246; overview 19, 23; resisting the empire 31, 36, 48, 56, 57, 58
liberation theodicy 196–233; definition 20, 22, 61, 216; end of Islamic ideology 61; future liberation theodicy 254–66; Malcolm X as Muslim revolutionary 251; overview 20, 22
Little, Earl 247
Lomax, Louis 247
Luther, Martin 131, 133, 136, 137, 140, 212
Lyotard, Jean-François 103, 105, 161

Mahdi's army 227, 228, 230
Maher, Bill 1
Malcolm X: blindness and insight 99, 100, 111, 113–15, 137, 138, 140; end of Islamic ideology 98; future liberation theodicy 262, 264, 266; Islam and globalization 143, 152, 153; liberation theodicy 196, 197; as Muslim revolutionary 234–53; overview vii, 11, 15, 22–23; resisting the empire 53
al-Maliki, Nouri 179
Manji, Irshad 57, 199, 234
Mann, Michael 10
Mansfield, Harvey 53
Martí, Jose 50, 138
Martin, Henry 46
martyrdom 67, 68

Marx, Karl 11, 105, 167, 198, 199, 206, 264
Mashaal, Khaled 227
al-Mawdudi, Abu al-Ala 42, 43, 45, 116
mazlumiyyat 187, 214
Meier, Heinrich 51, 52, 53
Memmi, Albert 43
Mernissi, Fatima 137, 213
"Middle East" 111
Mikati, Najib 221
militant Islamism: end of Islamic ideology 61; future liberation theodicy 256; Islam and globalization 154; liberation theodicy 196, 197, 199, 211, 212; overview 2, 3, 9, 10, 17, 19, 20; resisting the empire 37, 38, 54, 55; *Ta'ziyeh* as theater of protest 184
Mill, John Stuart 104
Miller, Judith 6, 145
Minutemen 241, 245
Mirza, Abbas 74
Modarres, Seyyed Hassan 89, 90
modernity: blindness and insight 103–7, 108–12, 125–27, 129, 130, 132; future liberation theodicy 258, 259; Islam and globalization 163, 164, 168; Malcolm X as Muslim revolutionary 249, 250
Modi, Narendra 144
Mohanty, Chandra 145
Molla Omar *see* Mulla Omar
moral universalism 108
Mosaddeq, Muhammad 90, 91, 256
Motahhari, Morteza 47, 159, 210, 212
Mubarak, Husni 55
Muhammad, Elijah 248
Mujahedin *see* Taliban
Mulla Omar 140, 141, 243, 245, 256, 262
Mulla Sadra: blindness and insight 119, 131; end of Islamic ideology 71, 72, 80, 81, 96; future liberation theodicy 254; resisting the empire 40
Musharraf, General Pervez 6
Muslim Brotherhood 42, 45, 242, 248
Mu'tazalite 41
My Lai massacre 174

Nafisi, Azar 57, 199, 234, 243
Na'ini, Sheykh Muhammad Hossein 47
Najaf massacre 7, 180, 181, 193
Naraqi, Mulla Ahmad 46, 67, 75, 115
Nasrallah, Hassan 155, 227

Nasr, Seyyed Hossein 201, 212, 213
Nasr, Seyyed Vali Reza 177, 179, 200–205, 208, 238
al-Nasser, Gamal Abd 247
Nation of Islam 98, 152, 242, 246, 247, 248
nation-states 112, 114, 161, 217
al-Natshe, Sheik Abd-al-Khaliq 230
Nazism: blindness and insight 102, 107, 109, 110, 111; liberation theodicy 206, 260; resisting the empire 51, 52, 53
Negri, Antonio 153, 154
Negroponte, John 180
New Orleans 8, 16, 26, 27, 28
The New York Times: Islam and globalization 145; overview 5, 6, 8, 10; resisting the empire 26, 57; *Ta'ziyeh* as theater of protest 172
Nietzsche, Friedrich 43, 101, 105, 249
Nishapuri, Mirza Mohammad 74
North Korea 4
Norton, Augustus Richard 188
nuclear issue 66
Nuri, Abdollah 63, 64, 167
Nuri, Sheykh Fazlollah 47

OAAU *see* Organization of Afro-American Unity
oil 165
Omar, Mulla *see* Mulla Omar
Operation Enduring Freedom 4, 6
Operation Iraqi Freedom 5, 6, 33, 182
Organization of Afro-American Unity (OAAU) 248
Orientalism: blindness and insight 111, 117; future liberation theodicy 266; Islam and globalization 156; Malcolm X as Muslim revolutionary 23, 245, 246; resisting the empire 34, 35, 36; *Ta'ziyeh* as theater of protest 187
Ostadi, Ayatollah Reza 165

Pahlavi monarchy 38, 47–48, 62, 92, 115, 193
Pakistan 5, 6, 237, 238
Palestine: future liberation theodicy 256, 257, 266; Islam and globalization 160; liberation theodicy 197–98, 203, 214–15, 223–27, 228–32; Malcolm X as Muslim revolutionary 235, 236, 237, 239, 251; overview 21; resisting the empire 31, 32, 43, 51,

57; *Ta'ziyeh* as theater of protest 180, 193
Patriot Act 4
Phillips, Kevin 9, 205
Pol Pot 228
postmodernism: blindness and insight 105, 106, 107, 108, 110; Islam and globalization 162, 168; liberation theodicy 213, 262; Malcolm X as Muslim revolutionary 250
Powell, Colin 5, 21
"The Project for a New American Century" 4
propaganda 5, 6, 8, 12, 29–31, 145
"pure violence" 206, 207, 208

al-Qadesiyyah 192
al-Qaeda: blindness and insight 140; end of Islamic ideology 60; future liberation theodicy 263, 264, 265; Islam and globalization 154; liberation theodicy 197, 211, 212, 226–29, 232; Malcolm X as Muslim revolutionary – Iraq 238; overview 3, 9, 10, 12, 14, 17; resisting the empire 55
Qajar dynasty 73–77, 80, 83, 86
Qasim, Brigadier Abd-al-Karim 177
Qasir, Samir 221, 231, 232
Qu'ran 7, 187–88, 190, 214, 249
Qutb, Sayyid 19, 42, 43, 45, 241–44, 248

Rafsanjani, Ali Akbar Hashemi 64, 65, 166
Ramadan, Tariq: blindness and insight 100, 111, 132–38, 140; Islam and globalization 148, 149; Malcolm X as Muslim revolutionary 240; overview 12, 19
Rashti, Seyyed Kazem 81
Ratzinger, Joseph *see* Benedict XVI, Pope
refugees 217
religious intellectuals 115, 116
religious knowledge 117–20, 123, 124, 126, 160
Renaut, Alain 109
Reuter, Baron Julius 77
Rice, Condoleezza 21, 29, 237
Rida, Rashid 41, 42, 116, 210
Riggio, Milla Cozart 194, 195
Romero, Óscar 48
Rorty, Richard 103, 106

Royal, Ségolène 240
Roy, Arundhati 143–47, 150, 152, 168
Roy, Olivier 47, 48
Rumi 131, 213
Rumsfeld, Donald: liberation theodicy 206, 208; Malcolm X as Muslim revolutionary 252; overview 5, 7, 19, 23, 24; resisting the empire 32, 36, 58; *Ta'ziyeh* as theater of protest 178–84
Rushdie, Salman 210
Russia 74, 75

Saadawi, Nawal El 133, 135, 137
Sadr, Muqtada 179, 227–28, 227–28, 236
Safavid Shi'ism 70, 71, 72, 73, 74, 86
Samara 193
Sarkozy, Nicolas 240
Sartre, Jean-Paul 92
Sassen, Saskia 158
Schmitt, Karl 51, 52, 53, 206, 207, 208
Schumpeter, Joseph 154
Second Gulf War 3, 39
Sepahsalar, Mirza Hossein Khan 76, 77, 79, 86
Sepúlveda, Juan Ginés de 50, 51, 55
Seyavashan 186, 187
Shafti, Hojjat al-Islam 76
Shafti, Seyyed Mohammad Baqer 74
Shahada (martyrdom) 67
Shah, Fath Ali 46, 73, 74, 75
Shah, Mozaffar al-Din 86
Shah, Muhammad Ali 83
Shah, Naser al-Din 46, 77, 78, 79, 82, 86
Shah, Reza 89, 90, 193
Shamlu, Ahmad 115
Shamyl, Shaykh 42
Sharansky, Natan 10
Shari'ah law 15, 44, 263
Shari'ati, Ali: blindness and insight 99–100, 111, 114–15, 126, 137; colonialism 19; end of Islamic ideology 67, 70, 91, 92, 93, 98; Islam and globalization 160; liberation theodicy 210; resisting the empire 47, 49
Shari'atmadari, Mohammad 164
Shaykism 80, 82
Shi'i Passion Play *see Ta'ziyeh*
Shi'ism: blindness and insight 125, 126, 127, 142; end of Islamic ideology 66–72, 73–79, 80–83, 85, 87–92, 93–97;

Islam and globalization 155, 156, 160, 161, 164, 168; liberation theodicy 197, 200–205, 214, 231; Malcolm X as Muslim revolutionary 251; overview 15, 20, 21; resisting the empire 40, 41; *Ta'ziyeh* as theater of protest 177, 179, 180, 184–90, 192, 193

Shirazi, Mirza Hasan 46, 78, 79

Shirazi, Mulla Sadra *see* Mulla Sadra

Siniora, Fouad 221, 228

Sivan, Emmanuel 43

Snow, Jon 228

Snyder, Zach 239

Socrates 72

Somalia 239

Sontag, Susan 149, 150, 152, 168

Sorel, Georges 11, 198, 199, 206

Soroush, Abdolkarim: blindness and insight 100, 111, 115–21, 122–28, 129–33, 137; end of Islamic ideology 63, 94, 95, 96; future liberation theodicy 262; Islam and globalization 159, 160, 166; liberation theodicy 212; overview 12, 13, 18, 19

South Lebanon Army (SLA) 220

Soviet Union 3, 38, 39

space program 4

Spivak, Gayatri 109

Sposito, Frank 108

Strauss, Leo 51, 52, 53, 207

Strong, Tracy B. 108

Sunnis: liberation theodicy 200–204, 231; Malcolm X as Muslim revolutionary 237; resisting the empire 40, 41; *Ta'ziyeh* as theater of protest 177, 178, 188

surahs 188

Syria 223, 226, 229, 230, 232, 236

Tabataba'i, 'Allamah 122, 123

Tabataba'i, Seyyed Muhammad 47, 75

Tabrizi, Mulla Rajab Ali 80

Talafar massacre 7

Taleqani, Ayatollah Mahmud 47, 122, 210

Taliban: future liberation theodicy 264; Islam and globalization 160; liberation theodicy 211, 229; Malcolm X as Muslim revolutionary 236, 238; overview 3, 4, 6; resisting the empire 38, 39

Taqizadeh, Seyyed Hasan 218

Taylor, James 143, 169–70

Ta'ziyeh (Shi'i Passion Play) 20, 176–78, 180–84, 186–91, 192–95

terrorism: blindness and insight 140; future liberation theodicy 261; Islam and globalization 144, 147, 149; liberation theodicy 227; Malcolm X as Muslim revolutionary 238; overview 4, 6, 10, 14, 16; resisting the empire 33, 34, 36, 56, 58

Thabet, Taher 174, 175

theodicy 20, 22, 61, 216 *see also* liberation theodicy

theology 20, 22

Time Magazine 174, 175

Tobacco Revolt 77, 78, 79

Tocqueville, Alexis de 261

torture: future liberation theodicy 261; liberation theodicy 206, 211; overview 6, 7, 8, 10; resisting the empire 32, 56; *Ta'ziyeh* as theater of protest 179, 180, 181

Transcendental Theosophy 71, 72, 80

Tudeh Party 90, 91

Tueni, Gibran 221

Turkamanchai Treaty 75, 76

Turkey 215, 237, 240

al-Ulam, Bahr 76

USA (United States of America): future liberation theodicy 255, 256, 258, 266; Islam and globalization 151, 154; liberation theodicy 198, 203, 204, 217, 229–31; Malcolm X as Muslim revolutionary 236–40, 243, 244, 252; overview 3–5, 9–11, 14, 17, 18, 22; resisting the empire 34, 39, 56; US imperialism 59, 154, 198, 203, 231, 256

US Patriot Act 4

Vattimo, Gianni 14, 43, 44, 258

Vietnam 228, 240

Vincent, Steven 171–76, 179–82, 184, 185

violence 11, 206, 207, 264, 265

al-Wahab, Muhammad ibn Abd 40

Wallace, Mike 247

war on terrorism: Islam and globalization 147, 159, 161; Malcolm X as Muslim revolutionary 237, 239; overview 4, 10, 16; resisting the empire 27, 53

Warraq, Ibn 199, 234, 243

weapons of mass destruction (WMD) 5, 6
Weber, Max: blindness and insight 101; end of Islamic ideology 70, 71; Islam and globalization 154, 159; liberation theodicy 198, 199, 206, 264; overview 11
Werblowsky, R. J. Zwi 43
"the West": blindness and insight 99, 100, 117, 127–29, 136–40; end of Islamic ideology 59, 60, 97; future liberation theodicy 258, 262, 263, 264; Islam and globalization 156, 157, 161; liberation theodicy 209, 216; Malcolm X as Muslim revolutionary 235, 250; overview 1–3, 12, 13, 15, 16, 18; resisting the empire 34–37, 39, 54, 56
West, Cornel 28, 29
Willis, Susan 147, 151, 152, 168
WMD *see* weapons of mass destruction

Wolfowitz, Paul 7, 53, 57, 66, 207
women: Islam and globalization 145, 150, 166; liberation theodicy 199, 208; resisting the empire 44, 57
World Bank 138, 144, 168, 241
World Trade Center 2, 3, 13
World Trade Organization (WTO) 144

X, Malcolm *see* Malcolm X

Yazdi, Ayatollah Mesbah 234
Yugoslavia 215

al-Zarqawi, Abu Musab 18, 19, 31, 262
al-Zawahiri, Ayman 18, 19, 31, 243
Zayd, Nasr Hamid Abu 133, 137
Zionism: blindness and insight 111; future liberation theodicy 263; liberation theodicy 198, 225, 228; resisting the empire 31, 32, 51, 54, 55

CPSIA information can be obtained
at www.ICGtesting.com
Printed in the USA
JSHW020351070120
3405JS00001B/5